THE TROUBLE WITH PRINCIPLE

THE TROUBLE WITH PRINCIPLE

Stanley Fish

Harvard University Press

Cambridge, Massachusetts

London, England

1999

Library of Congress Cataloging-in-Publication Data

Fish, Stanley Eugene.

The trouble with principle / Stanley Fish.

p.   cm.

Includes bibliographical references and index.

ISBN 0–674–91012–5 (alk. paper)

1. Principle (Philosophy).   2. Political science—Philosophy.

3. Law and politics.   I. Title.

B105.P7F57   1999

323'.01—dc21   99–35759

CONTENTS

IV   *Credo*

To Barbara Herrnstein Smith

"keener sounds"

Theory

I am what is around me.

Women understand this.
One is not duchess
A hundred yards from a carriage.

These, then are portraits:
A black vestibule;
A high bed sheltered by curtains.

These are merely instances.

—*Wallace Stevens*

And freedom, oh freedom, well, that's just some people talkin'

—*The Eagles*

TAKING SIDES

While I was writing the chapters of this book, a scene from Sam Peckinpah's classic western *The Wild Bunch* was never far from my mind. The wild bunch is an outlaw gang led by two grizzled veterans played to a career-performance turn by William Holden and Ernest Borgnine. One evening the two are sitting around discussing an old comrade who has gone over to the other side and now rides at the head of the band of railroad detectives pursuing them. The Borgnine character is incensed and can't understand why their old friend doesn't abandon the pursuit and come home to where he really belongs. You have to remember, the Holden character says, he gave his word to the railroad. So what? is the response; it's not giving your word that's important, it's who you give your word to.

I read the scene as a profound and concise analysis of the great divide in political theory. On the one side is the man of principle for whom a formal contract must be kept irrespective of the moral status of the other party; when you give your word, you give your word and that's it. On the other side is the man who varies his obligations according to the moral worth of the persons he encounters; some people have a call on your integrity, others don't, and the important thing is to determine at every moment which is which.

There is, I think, no doubt about which of these two visions is today the more generally approved. The Holden character speaks in the accents of Enlightenment liberalism; what he says is in accord with maxims many of us have long since internalized: "A man's word is his bond." "Ours is a government of laws, not men." "You can't justify the means by the end." "Respect for your fellow man must be extended to all and not selectively." Each of these maxims urges us to enter a perspective wider than that formed by our local affiliations and partisan goals; each gestures toward a morality more capacious than the morality of our tribe, or association, or profession, or religion; each invites us to inhabit what the legal philosopher Ronald Dworkin calls "the forum of principle," the forum in which our allegiances are not to persons or to wished-for outcomes but to abstract norms that neither respect nor disrespect particular persons and are indifferent to outcomes.

Not that there has never been a strong argument on the other side. The Borgnine character is not alone in his sentiments, and among those who would support him in the exchange (although they would be an odd couple) is John Milton. Milton and his characters are always saying things like "You are not worthy to be convinced" (the Lady to Comus in the mask of that name), or "You don't owe any loyalty to a king who is not acting like one" (Milton to his countrymen in *The Tenure of Kings and Magistrates*), or "Everyone should be allowed to speak and publish, except of course Catholics" (Milton to the Parliament in the *Areopagitica*). When Satan describes himself to the angel Gabriel as a "faithful leader" (*Paradise Lost*, IV, 933), the angel immediately replies, "Faithful to whom? To thy rebellious crew?/ Army of fiends?" (953–954). Like the Borgnine character, Gabriel refuses a notion of fidelity that is indifferent as to its object; some are deserving of your faith, some others are not, and to maintain loyalty merely because you have once pledged it is to mistake an abstraction for an object of worship and to default on your responsibility first to determine what (or who) is good and true and then to follow it.

Let me say at the outset that I am with Borgnine and Milton and against an adherence to principle. The trouble with principle is, first, that it does not exist, and, second, that nowadays many bad things are done in its name. On the surface, this is a paradox: how can something that doesn't exist have consequences? The answer is to be found in the claim made for principle, or at least for the kind of principle—usually called neutral principle—favored by liberal theorists. The claim is that abstractions like fairness, impartiality, mutual respect, and reasonableness can be defined in ways not hostage to any partisan agenda. The importance of the claim is that if it can be made good, these and other abstractions can serve as norms or benchmarks in relation to which policies favoring no one and respecting everyone can be identified and implemented. The problem is that any attempt to define one of these abstractions—to give it content—will always and necessarily proceed from the vantage point of some currently unexamined assumptions about the way life is or should be, and it is those assumptions, contestable in fact but at the moment not contested or even acknowledged, that will really be generating the conclusions that are supposedly being generated by the logic of principle.

If, for example, I say "Let's be fair," you won't know what I mean unless I've specified the background conditions in relation to which fairness has an operational sense. Would it be fair to distribute goods equally irrespective of the accomplishments of those who receive them, or would it be fair to reward each according to his efforts? Is it fair to admit persons to college solely on the basis of test scores and grades, or is it fair to take into account an applicant's history, including whatever history he or she may have of poverty and disadvantage? Such questions sit at the center of long-standing political, economic, and social debates, and these debates will not be furthered by the simple invocation of fairness, because at some level the debate is about what fairness (or neutrality or impartiality) really is.

Moreover, even if the concept of fairness is filled in, you are by no means out of the woods. Perhaps I think it's fair when everyone has a chance to have his say, but you think it's fair when everyone who is qualified to speak has a chance to have his say. Any challenge to either of our stipulations will result in further stipulations (decisions are best when every citizen has participated in making them, or decisions are best when the forum is limited to those who are educated or who have been elected, or who are ordained or who are not ordained), which in turn will be subject to challenge because they are substantive.

This last word—substantive—is the key, for it is supposedly the virtue of neutral principles to be free of substantive commitments; it is within the space afforded by neutral principles, or so we are told, that substantive agendas can make their case without prior advantage or disadvantage, with the result that the best argument (best is never defined; or, if it is, it is vulnerable to the same questions I have put to fairness) will win. But what the example of fairness—and you could substitute impartiality or neutrality or any other formal universal and it would turn out the same—shows is that there are no neutral principles, only so-called principles that are already informed by the substantive content to which they are rhetorically opposed. And even if you could come up with a principle that was genuinely neutral—a notion of fairness unattached to any preferred goal or vision of life—it would be unhelpful because it would be empty (that, after all, is the requirement); invoking it would point you in no particular direction, would not tell you where to go or what to do. A real neutral principle, even if it were available, wouldn't get you anywhere in particular because it would get you anywhere at all.[1]

Curiously enough, this is what makes neutral principles so useful politically and rhetorically and gives them the capacity to do bad things. It is because they don't have the constraining power claimed for them (they neither rule out nor mandate anything) and yet have the *name* of constraints (people think that when you invoke fairness you call for something determinate and determinable) that neutral principles can make an argument look as though it has a support higher or deeper than the support provided by its own substantive thrust. Indeed, the vocabulary of neutral principle can be used to disguise substance so that it appears to be the inevitable and nonengineered product of an impersonal logic. There are many ways to play this game, but in all its versions the basic move is to turn historically saturated situations into situations fully detached from any specific historical circumstance and then conclude that a proposed policy either follows from this carefully emptied context or is barred by it.

An example (and it is an example of doing a bad thing) is the majority argument in *Plessy v. Ferguson* (1896), a case that turned on the constitutionality of a Louisiana law requiring railroad companies to provide separate but equal accommodations for whites and blacks.[2] The plaintiffs challenging the law argued that it violated the Thirteenth and Fourteenth amendments. The Supreme Court ruled that there was no such violation and chided the plaintiffs for assuming "that the enforced separation of the two races stamps the colored race with a badge of inferiority": "If this be so it is not by reason of anything found in the act but solely because the colored race chooses to put that construction on it."[3] Here the phrase that does the crucial work is "in the act," which means "in the act *itself*," that is, the act as it is, apart from the history that gave rise to it or the intentions of those who performed it. Abstracted from this background information, "the act" is indeed without the significance imputed to it by the plaintiffs; it is without any significance at all. And therefore it makes perfect sense to say, as the Court has said earlier in its opinion, that laws requiring the separation of the two races "do not necessarily imply the inferiority of either" (50). This is too weak; such laws, understood without reference to the conditions of their production, imply *nothing* necessarily but can be made to imply anything.

This is what happens when this or any other "act" is detached from the history that renders it intelligible; it becomes unreadable, or (it is the same thing) it becomes readable in any direction you like. But if you reinsert it into the historical context of its production, implications are easily and nonarbitrarily readable, as they were for Justice Harlan when he said in his dissent, "Everyone knows that the statute in question had its origin in the purpose, not so much to exclude white persons from railroad cars occupied by blacks, as to exclude colored people from coaches occupied by or assigned to white persons" (52). Harlan alerts us to the nature of the work "in the act" did for the majority; it removed the purpose—the motive, aimed-at outcome, political agenda—informing the legislation and rendered it entirely formal, empty of substantive historical content. It might as well have been the separation of molecules or quarks or jelly beans that the Court was speaking of.

Harlan also makes clear that the Court was doing its work under the cover of a neutral principle (although he doesn't call it that), the principle of nondiscrimination: "It was said in argument that the statute of Louisiana does not discriminate against either race, but prescribes a rule applicable alike to white and colored citizens" (52). As Harlan sees, this is disingenuous at best. It is true that mixing in the railroad cars is denied to both races and thus, on this point, the rule does not discriminate against either; but it is also true that the rule against mixing flows from the design of one of the races to keep the other down. That design is certainly discriminatory, and the present act is certainly its extension, but the majority is able to obscure (perhaps from itself) that fact by defining nondiscrimination formally, as a matter of principle, and one that is applied to parties assumed to have no histories or antecedent purposes, parties that might just as well have been identified as X and Y rather than as black and white. Once that abstracting gesture has been performed, once the origins of the Louisiana statute have been forgotten, the Court can declare with a straight face that it discriminates against no one (if only because there is now no one—no particular one—in sight).

A neutral principle that facilitates the forgetting of history is repeating the forgetting that allowed it to emerge *as* a neutral principle. Neutral principles, if they are to deserve the name, must be presented as if they came first, as if they were there before history, even if the inhabitants of history were slow to recognize them. A neutral principle, in short, can have a historical habitation but not a historical cause. Accordingly, the question one asks of it is analytic ("What is its essence?") rather than genealogical ("Where did it come from?"). But once the genealogical question is put and the principle is given a biography, the idea of regarding it as neutral—as without reference to substantive imperatives—will seem less compelling.

Ask, for example, where the principle of nondiscrimination comes from. It comes not from some a priori moral map—it did not come down with the Ten Commandments—but from a set of historical circumstances to which it was a response. Men did things to other men for a long time and without moral anxiety. At some point (and rather slowly) moral anxiety arose, and with it a new name for old activities: discrimination. Because the new name was understood to be a negative judgment, it generated an initiative of reform ("Let's do away with this unhappy practice"); and as the proponents of reform warmed to their task, they began to think of it as the Lord's work and as the extension of an absolute and pre-existing imperative, the imperative of nondiscrimination. Once this last move is made, it becomes possible (and tempting) to think of nondiscrimination in formal terms, as a principle that mandates policies favoring no group no matter who the group is or what it has done or what has been done to it. When that thought has taken hold, the principle has become a neutral principle to which you can be true only by abstracting away from the historical concerns that gave rise to it.

In his dissent, Justice Harlan is trying to recall his brethren to those concerns and that history, asking them in effect to remember why the Thirteenth and Fourteenth amendments were enacted in the first place. The standard story we tell one another is that while Harlan failed in 1896, he was vindicated in 1954 when the separate-but-equal doctrine was overturned in *Brown v. Board of Education*. But while that particular doctrine has been repudiated, the logic underlying it—the logic of neutral principles—has not been, and today the courts regularly issue rulings the *Plessy* majority would have recognized and approved. The vehicle of *Plessy*'s resurrection has been the notion of reverse discrimination, the assertion that any action tinged with race-consciousness is equivalent to any other action tinged with race-consciousness, an assertion that makes sense only if historical differences are dissolved in the solvent of a leveling abstraction. Armed with this neutral principle, this device for erasing the difference between oppression and the amelioration of oppression, the courts have undone the gains of affirmative action and issued rulings in which the Voting Rights Act, passed in order to enhance the voting power of blacks, is violated by any policy that is true to the act's purpose. Indeed, it would not be too much to say that the result of these rulings has been to declare the Voting Rights Act in violation of itself.

This is what I meant when I said at the beginning that many bad things are now being done in the name of neutral principles, and I hope it is clear by now that it is no paradox to say that bad things are being done by something which doesn't exist. Indeed, it is crucial that neutral principles not exist if they are to perform the function I have described, the function of facilitating the efforts of partisan agents to attach an honorific vocabulary to their agendas. For the effort to succeed, the vocabulary (of "fairness," "merit," "neutrality," "impartiality," "mutual respect," and so on) must be empty, have no traction or bite of its own, and thus be an unoccupied vessel waiting to be filled by whoever gets to it first or with the most persuasive force.

But while there is a strong relationship between the emptiness or nonexistence of neutral principles and the work that they do (again, the emptiness provides the space for the work), there is no relationship at all between the emptiness of neutral principles and the political direction of that work. I have labeled the things I see being done with neutral principles "bad" because they involve outcomes I neither desire nor approve. They are not "bad" simply because they were generated by the vocabulary of neutral principles, for that vocabulary has also generated outcomes I favor, especially in the areas of civil rights and the expansion of opportunities for women in the workplace and on the athletic field. The fact that the game of neutral principles is really a political game— the object of which is to package your agenda in a vocabulary everyone, or almost everyone, honors—is itself neutral and tells you nothing about how the game will be played in a particular instance. The truth, as I take it to be, that neutral principles, insofar as they are anything, are the very opposite of neutral, and are filled with substance, won't tell you what substance they are filled with or whether or not you will like it.

The fact that someone is invoking neutral principles will give you no clue as to where he is likely to come out until he actually arrives there and reveals his substantive positions.

And whatever *my* substantive positions are, they do not follow from the fact that I believe neutral principles to be the empty vehicles of partisan manipulation. Reading the previous pages will have given you no clue as to my views on any vexed question. It would have been perfectly consistent with my analysis of *Plessy* had I announced at the end of it that I was in agreement with the majority. My interest in the analysis was in the way the Court managed to turn a statute manifestly discriminatory into an exemplary instance of nondiscrimination. Any indignation I may have registered should be traced to my dislike of the outcome and not to my disapproval of the strategy. The passion I display when debunking the normative claims of neutral principle ideologues is unrelated to the passion I might display when arguing for affirmative action or for minority-enhancing redistricting. To be sure, there might be a contingent relation in a given instance if the outcome I dislike was brought about in part by neutral-principle rhetoric; I might then attack the rhetoric as part of my attack on what it was used to do. But I might turn around tomorrow and use the same rhetoric in the service of a cause I believed in. Nor would there be anything inconsistent or hypocritical about such behavior. The grounding consideration in both instances (whether I was attacking neutral-principle rhetoric or employing it) would be my convictions and commitments; the means used to advance them would be secondary, and it would be no part of my morality to be consistent in my handling of those means.

I know that some of my readers will think that I have revealed myself in the preceding sentence to be one of those horrible persons who profess a morality of ends rather than means. But that has been my stance from the beginning. The argument that neutral principles are either empty or filled with the substance they claim to hold at arm's length is an argument for the impossibility (despite many claims and hopes) of disentangling oneself from substantive agendas and therefore an argument that ends-based reasoning cannot be avoided. It is not, however, an argument *for* ends-based reasoning (arguing for something you can't avoid would be an odd thing to do), and in making it I am as usual offering no recommendation (you can't coherently recommend an inevitability), just pointing out, for the umpteenth time, that when all is said and done there is nowhere to go except to the goals and desires that already possess you, and nothing to do but try as hard as you can to implement them in the world.

No doubt this will be heard by some as the unhappy and suspect announcement that everything is politics. This would be a strong and damning point only if politics meant the implementation of naked preferences. Naked preferences, however, are a part of the neutral-principle picture of the world, where it is possible (and desirable) to distinguish between principle and substance. In that picture, naked preferences are the danger and neutral principles the bulwark erected against them. But there are no naked preferences for the same reason that there are no neutral principles: principle and substance come always mixed. Principle and its vocabulary of fairness, equality, and so on are already informed by substantive preferences (were they not, they would be incapable of giving direction), and preferences are always preferences in relation to some notion of the good; they are never naked. In fact, preferences (except for trivial cases like a preference for vanilla ice cream over chocolate) *are* principles (or at least principled)—not principles of the neutral kind but principles of the only kind there really are, strong moral intuitions as to how the world should go combined with a resolve to be faithful to them.

For liberal theorists, however, such principles are not enough because they are insufficiently general. But the demand for a general principle—for a principle to which one might turn when moral values clash and there is a need for adjudication—is once again the demand for a neutral principle. A principle would be general if it could be applied invariably to variable contexts and situations; a general principle resists appeals to the particular, resists statements like "You must take into consideration that he's had a hard life," or "You should bear in mind the practical effects of your decision," or "You should remember how important this project is to the goal of racial peace." You arrive at the identification of a general principle by putting any candidate to the test proposed by Herbert Wechsler (who introduced the term "neutral principles" to the legal community): "Would I reach the same result if the substantive interests were otherwise?"[4] If the answer is no, if the principle you are applying generates different outcomes when one or the other of the parties changes color, or the organization at the center of a case is the NAACP rather than the Ku Klux Klan, or the publication under attack is pornography rather than *The New York Times,* then it is not really general, is not really a principle, but is instead a policy weighted in the direction of a particular race or class of groups or type of expression.

The generality of a principle, then, is measured by the extent of what it ignores, and in human terms—the terms in relation to which most moments in our lives are led—a general principle ignores almost everything, not only race, gender, class, religious affiliation, ethnic identity, sexual orientation (the usual list), but accomplishments, failures, value to society, moral worth. These negative requirements for reaching the plateau of general principle are perfectly met by John Rawls's "original position," a position one occupies by willfully putting on a "veil of ignorance"—ignorance of "features relating to social position, native endowment, and historical accident, as well as to the contents of persons' determinate conceptions of the good" (79), or, as Rawls calls them, "comprehensive doctrines."[5] Comprehensive doctrines are an embarrassment to the hopes of generality because there are too many of them (two would be too many). This is a "serious problem," says Rawls, because a modern society "is characterized not simply by a pluralism of comprehensive religious, philosophical, and moral doctrines but by a pluralism of incompatible yet reasonable comprehensive doctrines," no one of which "is affirmed by citizens generally" (xii). Under such conditions, Rawls asks, what does one do? And the answer he gives is: "abstract from and not be . . . affected by the contingencies of the social world" (23); that is, "find some point of view, removed from and not distorted by the particular features of [any] all-encompassing background framework" (25).

Such a view is what Thomas Nagel calls the view from nowhere, and in Rawls's argument it is also the view from no one, from no particular one, from a one that is general. Achieving that view, he claims, "serves as a means of public reflection and self-clarification" (26), but it would be more accurate to name the result "self-evacuation," for the imaginative act of entering the original position involves a bracketing and (for the time of sojourn) forgetting of every affiliation and association that makes you what you are.

The trick is to regard social, political, and institutional investments as cosmetic. One sees how it is done when Rawls describes reasoning in the original position as proceeding "in accordance with the enumerated restrictions on information" (27). The restrictions are the sum of what you are not allowed to know under the veil of ignorance—everything from name, rank, and serial number to matters of gender, class, and race to memberships in churches and political parties to "various native endowments such as strength and intelligence" (25). By referring to these as restrictions on *information*, Rawls makes it clear that in his view the characteristics they remove from inspection are not essential to the person, who is what he is with or without these identifying marks of merely social relations: he is an agent with a capacity to imagine a condition of justice and a vision of the good (81); and it is this capacity, rather than any realization it happens to have, that defines him. Those who have this capacity, even if they realize it in different ways, are the same; and a person who realizes it differently at different times in his life is also the same: "For example, when citizens convert from one religion to another, or no longer affirm an established religious faith, they do not cease to be, for the questions of political justice, the same" (30). "For the purposes of public life, Saul of Tarsus and Paul the Apostle are the same person" (32n).

It would appear that by declaring Saul and Paul to be the same only in the public realm, Rawls gives the experience of conversion its due, but in fact he trivializes it by limiting its effects to the quarantined realm of the private, where religious commitment takes its place alongside commitment to the Elks Club or the New York Yankees or country music. One imagines that Paul would have a different view of the matter, and that if you told him it was all right to believe anything he liked (even that someone walked on water and rose from the dead) as long as he left his belief at home and didn't allow it to influence his actions in public, he might smile at you and say things like "You cannot serve two masters."

It is no accident that the question of religion surfaces often in Rawls's book, for religion is the very type of the substantive views that are to be banished, or at least set to the side, in a world ordered by neutral principles. Religion is the chief stumbling block in the way of the liberal dream of a public life cleared of the perturbations that arise when fundamental beliefs (liberal theorists rename them "opinions" on the way to marginalizing them) come into conflict. Rawls acknowledges this at the very beginning: "The most intractable struggles, political liberalism assumes, are confessedly for the sake of the highest things: for religion, for philosophical views of the world, and for different moral conceptions of the good" (4). He proposes to deal with this intractability as John Locke proposed to deal with it three hundred years ago, by removing issues of religion, philosophy, and morality from the public agenda. But if these are really the "highest things," a public realm purged of them would be diminished and thin and you will have bought your peace at the price of substance (a price liberal theorists are willing and eager to pay); and, on the other hand, if you think that public life emptied of religious, philosophical, and moral urgencies is robust and substantial, you don't believe that they are the highest things and you call them that only as a gesture on the way to dismissing them.

Political liberalism stakes its project on the possibility of at once being fair to religion, giving it its due, and preventing its concerns (the concerns of moral conviction in general) from interfering with the operations of the public sphere. But it can manage this only by turning the highest things into the most ephemeral things (higher in the sense of "airy") and by making the operations of the public sphere entirely procedural, with no more content than the content of traffic signals. In fact, neither of these strategies can be realized; the religious impulse will refuse to be confined (that's what makes it what it is), and matters of procedure will never be purely so, will always be touched by and touch on matters of substance. Rawls wonders whether, given the deep oppositions that have always divided men along religious, philosophical, and moral lines, "just cooperation among free and equal citizens is possible at all" (4). It isn't.

What is possible is cooperation achieved through the give and take of substantive agendas as they vie for the right to be supreme over this or that part of the public landscape. In the course of such struggles, alliances will be formed and for a time at least conflict of a deep kind will be kept at bay. Alliances, however, are temporary, conflict is always just around the corner (Hobbes was right), and when it erupts, all the muted claims of "comprehensive doctrines" will be reasserted, until, for largely pragmatic reasons, those claims are again softened and replaced (temporarily) by the conciliatory words of another vocabulary, perhaps the vocabulary of political liberalism. As a genuine model for the behavior of either persons or nations, as something you could actually follow and apply, political liberalism is hopeless. Like all projects based, supposedly, on neutral principles, it is either empty (you can't get from its abstractions to the nitty gritty of any actual real-life situation) or filled with an agenda it cannot acknowledge lest it be revealed as the limiting and exclusionary mechanism it surely is. That is, the project either doesn't exist or it exists on a level less general and considerably lower than the level of its polemic.

This does not mean that all is lost, for even in its (inevitably) failed and incoherent form, political liberalism, like any other engine of an impossible abstraction, is available to be quarried and manipulated for the kind of partisan effort from which it claims to be distanced. Political liberalism, in short, can be a resource for politics, not for politics in the rarified sense named by chimeras like fairness and mutual respect but for politics as it has always been practiced, and practiced honorably, in the wards and boroughs of ancient Rome, seventeenth-century London, and twentieth-century Chicago.

Such at least is the argument of this book, and it is an argument with many antecedents, in the pre-Socratics, in the rhetorics of Cicero and Quintilian, in the writings of Castiglione and Hobbes, in the pragmatism of James, Dewey, and Rorty, in the speech act theory of J. L. Austin. Perhaps the most obvious and pertinent antecedent is Machiavelli's *The Prince*. In the first paragraph, Machiavelli promises not to stuff his book "with pompous phrases or elaborate, magnificent words" or to decorate it "with any form of extrinsic rhetorical embroidery" (3).[6] In the long tradition in which rhetoric is the negative pole of a binary opposition, the other pole is always occupied by Truth or the Real or the Transparent or the Essential or the Normative or some other supracontextual universal. Rhetoric, on the other hand, is stigmatized as the realm of appearances, of surfaces, of fashion, of flux, of the local, of the parochial, of the contingent, of the "merely" historical, of language on holiday from its responsibilities, of everything that obscures and threatens to usurp the realm of pure forms and principles.

Machiavelli simply turns this on its head, for what he means by rhetorical embroidery and pompous phrases is the idealizing language of moral and political theory. It is that high-sounding and pious vocabulary that gets in the way of understanding the only knowledge worth having, "knowledge of the actions of men" (3). If you are after the "real truth of the matter"(44), he counsels, you should study and observe everything that utopian thought disdains and flees: "A great many men have imagined states and princedoms such as nobody ever saw or knew in the real world, for there's such a difference between the way we really live and the way we ought to live that the man who neglects the real to study the ideal will learn how to accomplish his ruin, not his salvation" (44).

A sure way to ruin is to identify an invariant rule and resolve to stick to it. "I can give no fixed rules" (30), Machiavelli declares. On any great matter, "there is no general rule," for everything "varies with circumstances" (61). Were he to have heard Wechsler's question—"Would I reach the same result if the substantive interests were otherwise?"—Machiavelli would have replied by saying something like "I hope not," for such rigidity would sacrifice the values and interests at stake in a particular moment to a formal consistency that valued nothing but itself—the consistency, in short, of neutral principle.

Those who stand on neutral principles often wish to be neutral in the political sense, and they avoid taking sides in deference to the pluralism of the forces in the field. It is for them that Machiavelli reserves his greatest scorn: "As a general thing, anyone who is not your friend will advise neutrality, while anyone who is your friend will ask you to join him, weapon in hand" (64). Taking sides, weapon in hand, is not a sign of zealotry or base partisanship; it is the sign of morality; and it is the morality of taking sides, of frank and vigorous political action, that is celebrated (not urged; it is inevitable) in the pages that follow.

Those pages rehearse and elaborate a number of related and finally equivalent lessons:

- no principle not already inflected with substance; no substantive agenda that is not (in the only appropriate non-neutral sense) principled
- no part of the self (deliberative reason, reflective self-consciousness) abstracted from substantive commitments, and therefore no vantage point from which to survey one's beliefs and revise them
- no *good* reason to set one's beliefs aside in favor of some higher order impartiality or ethic of mutual respect, unless these abstractions are what you believe in, unless, that is, they are substantive and available to challenge as such
- no vocabulary not already laden with substance and therefore no neutral observation language (Thomas Kuhn's phrase) on the basis of which nonbiased action can be taken
- no device, either representational or empirical, for quarantining politics, and therefore no hope of a procedural republic from which divisive issues have been banished and in which we can all just get along
- no straight line from these lessons to the solution of any real-life problem; they are of no help and do no work except the (non-directing) work of telling you that you are on your own and that the resources you need are within you if they are anywhere.

These lessons turn up in every one of the chapters below, although the materials and the emphases will differ. Hence the division into four sections. The first section sets out the argument against neutral principles and for (not in the sense of advocacy; none is needed) politics. The chapters in Part II focus on First Amendment jurisprudence as the arena in which the effort to install a regime of neutral principles has been the most concerted. In Part III I turn to the religion clause of the First Amendment and to the difficulties presented to the dream of liberal neutrality by a discourse that refuses to be confined within the precincts of the private. And in Part IV I allow myself some more general speculations and even say a few things about what I believe.

The main thing I believe is that conflict is manageable only in the short run and that structures of conciliation and harmony are forever fragile and must always be shored up, with uncertain success. I am tempted to turn this into an imperative—perhaps, with a nod to Fredric Jameson, "always politicize"—but the imperative would be unnecessary, for that is what we do all the time, whether we choose to or not.

POLITICS ALL THE WAY DOWN

1

AT THE FEDERALIST SOCIETY

The last time I stayed at the Mayflower Hotel in Washington was to see Dinesh D'Souza get married, and here I was coming to a Federalist Society meeting at which Dinesh, now under siege from some of his former allies, was to be a featured speaker, along with the likes of Clarence Thomas, Robert Bork, Gertrude Himmelfarb, William Kristol, Edwin Meese, Glenn Loury, Linda Chavez, Walter Berns, Laurence Silberman, and Alan Keyes. This crew was assembled on September 22 and 23, 1995, to discuss "Group Rights, Victim Status, and the Law," and they all knew their lines: an emphasis on group rights (I am entitled to special treatment because I am black or Hispanic or female or gay) leads to the de-emphasis of individual achievement (my fate is the result of my sex, race, or ethnic affiliation and not of my abilities or lack of ability) and to a society in which one competes not for prizes but for the status of most victimized (my disadvantages are greater than yours and therefore my rewards, or spoils, should be greater too).

It is because we now glorify victims rather than heroes and prize sensitivity over character (they continue) that we live in a world • of *affirmative action* (where you believe you deserve something before you have done anything); • of *multiculturalism* (where universal and objective norms are replaced by the local norms of insular groups, and anything you do is all right so long as everyone you hang out with does it too); • of *feminism* (where, in a new form of paternalism, your gender gives you a leg up rather than an equal chance); • of *criminal rights* (where the judiciary is more solicitous of the repeat offender than of the men and women he has robbed and killed); • of *welfare* (where, by removing incentives for effort, the state destroys the spirit of self-improvement and produces an ethic of dependency); • of *political correctness* (where you are penalized for calling a spade a spade and pressured to adopt a vocabulary that offends no one and says nothing); • and of *runaway damage awards* (where entrepreneurship is discouraged by a tort system that turns your every action into a potential lawsuit).

If you add all this up (and no opportunity to do so was missed), the result is an America full of whiners, freeloaders, and above all, professional victims—victims of bad luck, victims of racism, victims of sexism, victims of homophobia. In that America, no one takes responsibility for anything and everyone drinks at the public trough. Everyone, that is, except for the 500 or so gathered at the Mayflower Hotel. Here, there are only believers in the litany Clarence Thomas rehearsed early in his speech: self-reliance, home, school, church, and Horatio Alger.

Who *are* these people? In the course of the presentations, this question received two contradictory answers. One has the ring of Milton's "Among the faithless, faithful only hee":[1] the world may be going to hell (or to multiculturalism) in a handbasket, but we few are still hewing to the straight and narrow path. In the other answer, the same few are the representatives of the many, strong witnesses to universally known and objective truths from which a minority (in fact, several minorities) have unaccountably strayed.

Both postures have their advantages: the first ("we few") defines heroism as the participants in the conference repeatedly celebrated it; the second ("we normative") defines righteousness as every moment in the conference breathed it. But both also have their disadvantages. If the members of the Federalist Society are part of the true moral majority and heirs to a tradition of enduring truths, what are they afraid of? Why the rhetoric of alarm? And if the alarm is sounded because "our enemies" are all around us (in the White House, in the judiciary, in the universities, in the media) and are taking our jobs and robbing our children of places at Harvard and suing us for sexual harassment and inserting themselves into our St. Patrick's Day parades, then a conference called to decry "victimology" will turn out to be populated by self-proclaimed victims convinced that the world's deck is stacked against virtuous white guys. (It is this danger that Clarence Thomas warned against when, in the only moment of ideological caution in two full days and one night, he spoke against "angry white males" whose preoccupation with their "oppression" has become the defining fact of their existence.)

The question is, can you be a hero and a victim at the same time? And the answer is yes, if the conditions of your victimhood define the field of your heroism, if the ascendancy of the forces arrayed against you makes your steadfastness all the more remarkable. Then, with Robert Bork, you can despair at the present scene, yet look forward to the time "when the barbarians finally retreat." Meanwhile, you can keep the faith by witnessing to it at meetings like this, which are in a very real sense revival meetings, called simultaneously to lament and to rejoice.

The trick is to keep the lamenting and rejoicing from bumping into each other so that the vehemence of the one will not be undercut by the elation of the other. On the present occasion this meant taking care to put some distance between rehearsing the latest outrages ("Have you heard about the Asian children who couldn't transfer to a school with a program for the gifted because it would upset racial balance?") and crowing about the growing power of the Republican Congress and the virtual disappearance of liberals. And it also meant taking care not to say that circumstances are irrelevant (except as something you are supposed to rise above) too soon after you have said that circumstances are intolerable. You say that circumstances are intolerable when your point is that things have become so bad that the last light of liberty may be going out even as we gather. You say that circumstances are irrelevant when you want to heap scorn on those who use circumstances (rather than character) to explain why blacks and Hispanics are so disproportionally represented in the ranks of the poor, the ill-educated, and the incarcerated.

These two views of the role circumstances play bring with them two different notions of what it takes to keep going and persevere. In the "things are so bad" picture, the way is hard and it is all you can do to keep from being overwhelmed by political correctness, racial gerrymandering, the feminist gestapo, gay activists, and bleeding heart judges. In the "no matter how bad things are" picture, all you need is the resources you carry within you, for they, and not accidents of birth, class, or economic status, are responsible for what you can do and what you can become.

This latter note was sounded many times and most eloquently by Glenn Loury: "The social contingencies of race, gender, and class are but the raw materials from which an individual constructs a life . . . Whatever our race, class or ethnicity, we must all devise and fulfill a life plan. By facing and solving this problem, we grow as human beings, and give meaning and substance to our lives. Because we share this problem—identical in essentials, different only in details—we can transcend racial difference." In fact, in this vision, you can transcend *anything*. The devil is not in the details; the devil *is* the details or, rather, is the mistake of failing to look beyond the details (of race, class, gender, religion, economic status, disabled status, immigrant status, regional status, and on ad infinitum) to "conditions and feelings" that are "universally shared," to our "common humanity."[2] In this up-to-date version of Platonic Christian idealism (the world is but a blank tablet on which you inscribe your inner meaning, or lack of it) you are the master of your own destiny. Be right (with God and with the right set of values) and you'll do all right.

To be sure, there was an occasional dissenting voice to this Polonius-like advice, usually emanating from a small chorus of designated scapegoats invited to demonstrate how open and nonideological the meeting was. John Payton observed that the whole argument founders when you remember that the appallingly small representation of minorities in the construction industry in Richmond and other cities cannot possibly be attributed to lack of skills because no skills are required; skills are what is provided by a program of apprentice training, but you cannot acquire them if you are excluded from the program. Cass Sunstein wondered aloud why people who bring suits against those who may have harassed them or discriminated against them are thereby made victims; aren't they, he asked, exercising their rights as all of us are urged to do? Joan Williams declared that individual choice was of course a fine thing, but we should not forget that choices are exercised within constraints we did not choose, and that women, for example, who choose to live up to the "ideal worker norm" (hard work, long hours, short vacations) do so at the expense of "family values" and are therefore choosing (if that is the word) between economic marginality and poor parenting. And Jamie Raskin observed, in rapid fire order, that if you listened to this crowd, you would think that racial politics began on the left and you would forget that the doctrine of color-blindness received its first powerful articulation in *Plessy v. Ferguson,* and you might not see that the alternative to multiculturalism is white supremacy, and you would fail to be struck by how odd it is that strangely shaped congressional districts began to be viewed with suspicion only when the beneficiaries were minorities.[3]

But by and large these were minor and barely heard notes in a loud and booming song that was sung continuously and in perfect harmony. After a while you knew what someone was going to say thirty seconds after a talk began, and you had the leisure to look around and take note of those small things that mark an occasion more surely than anything on the formal program. There was the huge applause that greeted every black or woman who could be counted on to attack affirmative action or feminism and thereby provide not only one more confirmation of what everybody already knew but also reassurance that in knowing it and affirming it you weren't being racist or sexist. (Being homophobic was perfectly all right, and no maneuvers were needed to deny it while practicing it.) And then there was the extraordinarily theatrical moment when, upon entering the auditorium after a break, you saw Clarence Thomas sitting on the stage radiating the energy of an angry deity while in the front row Mrs. Thomas sat with a raised head that resembled in its fierceness and intensity the prow of a Viking ship.

And there were the questions, especially after Raskin's talk. One woman rose to compliment him for being able to defend bad ideas with such skill. A man began by saying, you just do not know how it is when they move into your neighborhood and things begin to deteriorate and you begin to be afraid. At that a rustle of nervousness went around the room, and you could sense the discomfort of people who were unexpectedly presented with a self-image they wanted to push away. The questioner quickly realized that he was off key, lowered the register of his words, and ended by saying that he did not know exactly what he thought and could Raskin help him. "We haven't got that much time," Raskin replied.

Later, at the very end of the day, I met the woman who had praised Raskin for being so good in a bad cause. We talked about the conference, and I said that what bothered me was the tone of rebuke directed against innercity youths, teenage mothers, and minorities in general. But that is why we came here, to rebuke them, she said, leaving me without a comeback.

So I gave my talk (which follows) and accompanied it with a handout placed on every chair. I was heard attentively and with applause and was the beneficiary of several good questions and one that was terrific. ("Although you bill yourself as being 'against principles,' doesn't your own argument suggest that you would have recourse to the vocabulary of principle if it suited your ends?" Right.) It was an altogether pleasant experience on many levels, but finally it made me tired in the way you get at a formal dinner party where the conversation is relentlessly serious and although you can certainly talk the talk, you'd rather not. And so I must confess that the time I enjoyed most was when I skipped the lunch (and Judge Silberman's address) and went across the street to have a bagel and a conversation with Jamie Raskin's father.

As I was composing and revising my remarks for this occasion, I was also reading Dinesh D'Souza's new book *The End of Racism,* and I was struck by the fact that while Dinesh and I both point to relativism as a prime source of moral and conceptual difficulties in the current scene, each of us identifies relativism with the other's position.[4] For Dinesh, it is relativism when you slide away from formal universal principles like equality and color-blindness and emphasize instead the norms, histories, and practices of different cultures and groups. For me, it is relativism when you slide away from the norms, histories, and practices of different cultures and groups and emphasize instead formal universal principles like equality and color-blindness. He thinks it's relativism when you take race, gender, and group history into account in your decisions about hiring and college admissions. I think it's relativism when you don't. The difference between us will become clear, I hope, in my discussion of affirmative action, a discussion I am going to ease into by way of another issue often debated in the political arena, regulation of speech under the First Amendment.

Although First Amendment jurisprudence is complicated and sometimes confusing, a few formulas are invoked so often that we are probably justified in regarding them as canonical. Here are two of them: (1) "One man's vulgarity is another's lyric."[5] (2) "Under the First Amendment there is no such thing as a false idea."[6] "One man's vulgarity is another's lyric" means that because arguments about taste are endless, and no mere mortal has the authority to resolve them, government should stay out of the fray and let the chips fall where they may. "There is no such thing as a false idea" extends this reasoning to the world of values. It says that because ideas are expressions of value and value is something perpetually in dispute, the government should neither embrace nor condemn a particular idea if only because tomorrow may bring a reversal of the judgment we make today.

This is an argument from principle, for it refuses to put the power of the state behind this or that point of view and insists that government maintain a strict neutrality between the various combatants in the wars of taste and truth. Right now, it says, this vulgarity may seem clearly distinguishable from a lyric poem, but what if it were embedded in a paragraph written by James Joyce or put between quotation marks as part of a technical report or someday made it into the *Norton Anthology of American Poetry*? Would you want to regulate it then? If the answer is no (and if it is not, your interrogator will think up another example), then the decision to regulate it now is not principled and shouldn't be made.

The logic is clear and apparently compelling until you realize that it is the logic of relativism and that it undermines the possibility of saying that some things are true and others false, or that some verbal expressions are beautiful and inspiring while others are ugly and potentially dangerous. Shakespeare or graffiti? Just different strokes for different folks. Jews are bagel-eating vermin and it's too bad Hitler didn't get the job done, or Jews are human beings worthy of our respect? Just a matter of viewpoint, and who is to say which is preferable to the other? If you think I exaggerate, just remember the Skokie case and the judgment of a three-judge panel that while most of us may find neo-Nazi propaganda repulsive, it is after all the expression of an idea, and, under the First Amendment, there is no such thing as a false idea. Besides, the judges suggest, Nazism may right now be an unpopular idea, but who knows what the next turn in the wheel of political fortune might bring?[7]

The Skokie example—and there are many that could be added to it—shows that one feature of an argument from principle is that it easily becomes a recipe for inaction, for not doing anything in the face of an apparent urgency, on the reasoning that sometime in the future that urgency might fade and we will find ourselves wishing we hadn't responded to it. That is why arguments from principle are typically marked by a failure to satisfy the demand they make, the demand for a judgment that would hold good not only for the present circumstances but for any circumstances that might be imagined by a resourceful intelligence. This is the chief currency of law school pedagogy. The professor gets his students to commit to a position and then watches them squirm as he poses hypothetical after hypothetical until each of them is forced to relinquish a judgment that was premature because it was unprincipled.

The postwar model for this technique in teaching and in argument is Herbert Wechsler's enormously influential essay, "Toward Neutral Principles," first published in 1959.[8] The title promises a journey toward a goal, but the goal is never reached, for in the end Wechsler declares himself unable to find the principle he has been seeking, a principle that would justify the Supreme Court's decision in *Brown v. Board of Education*. What troubles Wechsler about *Brown* is that the decision is result-driven—the justices don't like segregation and want to end it—rather than being driven by a principle indifferent to particular results and faithful only to the enforcement of its own abstract norm. The principle in the *Brown* opinion seems to be that segregation is a denial of equality because it places a "badge of inferiority" on blacks. But, asks Wechsler, if the separate facilities are in fact equal, where is the denial of equality? And as for the "badge of inferiority," is this not, as the majority in *Plessy v. Ferguson* declared, only the construction put on the practice of segregation by those who are opposed to it? After all, there is nothing "in the act" itself that implies inferiority or anything else (32–33). Where, Wechsler asks again and again, is the principle?

And then, in a moment of last-minute rescue, he seems to have found it, all by himself, in the right of freedom of association, which is a principle because its denial "impinges in the same way on any groups or races." In a word, it is neutral. But then in a last-minute reversal—the argument here anticipates the ending of so many slasher films when the heroine assumes prematurely that she is safe—the very neutrality of the principle makes it an instrument not for justifying *Brown* but for once again denying its legitimacy. For, Wechsler observes, "if the freedom of association is denied by segregation, integration forces an association upon those for whom it is unpleasant or repugnant"; and "given a situation where the state must . . . choose between denying the association to those individuals who wish it or imposing it on those who would avoid it, is there a basis in neutral principles for holding that . . . the claims for association should prevail?" (34).

This is a moment of intense clarity for Wechsler, but it makes clear more than he thinks, for it shows not only how severe the requirement of neutral principle can be but at what cost we are faithful to it, the cost of nothing less than the *moral*—not neutral—principles that lead us to judge one course of action better than another. When Wechsler characterizes the state's choice as one between those who wish to associate and those who wish not to, the two wishes are presented so abstractly, almost

POLITICS ALL THE WAY DOWN

algebraically, that any sense of the projects to which they were attached is entirely lost. They seem mere preferences, something out of a Gershwin song—you like association, I like isolation, let's call the whole thing off.

Deliberately obscured is the fact that one wish is born of the desire to escape a history of oppression and exclusion, while the other wish is born of a desire to retain the political and economic advantages that have been produced by that same history. You can see the two desires as equivalent only if you empty them of their historical and moral content, which is exactly what the doctrine of neutral principles demands that you do when it asks you to test your present intuition against all the permutations that might be imagined to occur. When your intuition fails that test—as it always will—you can then throw up your hands and say with Justice Harlan that there is no principled way to distinguish between lyrics and vulgarities, and say with Justice Powell that there is no principled way to distinguish between a true and false idea, and say with Professor Wechsler that there is no principled way to distinguish between those who want to be free to enter the school door and those who want to be free to keep them out.

And this is where affirmative action comes in, for it is the logic of neutral principles that generates the strongest anti-affirmative action argument, the argument from "reverse discrimination," the argument that, in Justice Thomas's words, "it is irrelevant whether . . . racial classifications are drawn by those who wish to oppress a race or by those who have a sincere desire to help those thought to be disadvantaged."[9] It is irrelevant because what controls is a principle—racial classifications are odious and inherently suspect—and in the blinding light of that principle, distinctions of motive, circumstance, power, and justice literally fade from sight. If race-consciousness is a component of a policy, it is the same as any other policy rooted in race-consciousness—Ku Klux Klanners the same as admissions officers at the University of California—just as Shakespeare and graffiti are the same because they are both speech, and the golden rule and neo-Nazi ranting are the same because they are both expressions of ideas.

The objection to this line of reasoning is not that it evacuates history—although it surely does that—but that it evacuates morality, by first taking away the usual measures by which we label one act abhorrent and another praiseworthy and then substituting for these measures a mechanical test like the question "Does it display race-consciousness?"

Moreover, in reducing the complexity of moral questions to a single question asked without nuance, the logic of neutral principles mirrors and reproduces the logic of multiculturalism when it refuses to distinguish between cultural practices on the reasoning that to do so would be to violate the neutral principle of diversity. The mentality that finds no difference between Jim Crow laws and minority set-asides is only the flip side of the mentality that finds no difference between wearing rings on your finger and inserting rings into your penis. In one case we suspend our everyday judgments about what is right and wrong in order to render easily distinguishable acts indistinguishably bad; in the other we suspend our judgments about what is right and wrong in order to render easily distinguishable acts indistinguishably good. On the one hand tarring everything with the same brush, on the other whitewashing everything.

This is the trouble with principles determined to be neutral: they operate by sacrificing everything people care about to their own purity. As Charles Krauthammer has said of the principle of diversity, it becomes "an end in itself" that blithely disregards any other value.[10] And the same can be said of the reasoning of the ACLU when it finds no difference between offering a nondenominational prayer to a middle-school audience free to disregard it and establishing a religion by state coercion. Here the neutral principle is not "If it displays race consciousness it is unconstitutional" but "If it displays consciousness of religion it is unconstitutional," and of *that* principle Justice Scalia has said, it "is conspicuously bereft of any reference to history" and relies instead on "formulaic abstractions," forgetting "Justice Holmes' aphorism that 'a page of history is worth a volume of logic.' "[11]

What happens when we close the book of formulaic abstractions and instead turn the pages of history? What are we left with? What we are left with is what Judge Richard Posner has termed "the messy world of empirical reality"—the world of facts, values, histories, choices, disputes. And in response to that world, no longer filtered out by principle, we will be moved to ask the kind of question Posner would have wanted Wechsler to ask in place of the question "Where is the principle?" "One might have supposed," says Posner, "that the central question in *Brown v. Board of Education* was not the scope of some abstract principle of freedom of association but whether racial segregation . . . was intended or likely to keep the blacks in their traditionally subordinate position."[12] One might have supposed, in other words, that you would ask a *real* question rather than a question asked just so that you could declare yourself unable to answer it.

Of course real questions—questions like "Does affirmative action work?" "Are there preferable alternatives?" "Do its benefits exceed its costs?"—do not predetermine their answers. There is no guarantee that if we reject the logic of neutral principles and deprive formulas like reverse discrimination of their facile force, the case for affirmative action will then have been made. I only argue against framing the issue in a certain way—a way that labels itself a higher morality but is finally so high that, from its lofty perspective, we are unable to see either the forest or the trees.

The arguments against affirmative action are now rehearsed so routinely that you can tick them off in a verbal shorthand and be immediately understood. Here they are: • it's not needed; • it's not working; • it's not fair; • it's not merit; • it's reverse racism; • it's group-think; • it's quotas; • it lowers self-esteem; • it provokes race-consciousness. There are many who believe these arguments to be unanswerable because they have never heard anyone attempt to answer them. Here is my attempt.

The argument that affirmative action is not needed comes in two versions: (1) It's not needed because discrimination is already illegal and nothing more is required. (2) It's not needed because the pendulum has already swung too far in the direction of women and minorities. The first version falls before the undoubted facts of systemic discrimination—glass ceilings and redlining practices that keep neighborhoods all white and deny loans to well-qualified African Americans; the second version is belied by every statistical survey that shows the pendulum just where it has been for years. As a *Los Angeles Times* news story put it, "The prevailing public sentiment that . . . preferences have had a huge effect on the workplace or in universities . . . is flatly untrue."[13]

The argument that affirmative action is not working also comes in two (contradictory) versions: (1) It's not working because the problems of the underclass have more to do with economics than with race. (2) It's not working because the gap between blacks and whites is genetic, not cultural, and we are only throwing good money after bad. The first version collapses under its own weight: if the problem has multiple causes, then a multiple strategy is required and it makes no sense to discard one prong of it. The second version is what many think of as *The*

Bell Curve argument (although the authors insist that their thesis is about intelligence, not race).[14] It says that blacks occupy inferior social and economic positions because they are naturally inferior. The fact that many believe this, despite the overwhelming scientific consensus that the concept of race has no biological foundation and cannot be correlated with anything, is a tribute to the appeal of any argument that can serve as a rationale for the status quo.

The third argument is a favorite. It's not fair because those who pay the penalty did not inflict the injury. Why should white males in 1995 be taxed for acts performed fifty or one hundred or two hundred years ago by people long dead? The question is its own answer: if today's white males do not deserve the (statistically negligible) disadvantages they suffer, neither do they deserve to be the beneficiaries of the sufferings inflicted for generations on others; they didn't earn the privileges they now enjoy by birth, and any unfairness they experience is less than the unfairness that smooths their life path irrespective of their merit.

Merit is the heart of the fourth argument. It goes like this: people should get jobs and places in college because they merit them, and neither race nor gender could be a component of merit. The trick here is to define merit narrowly—with test scores or examination results—and then stigmatize any other consideration as unwarranted preference or bad social engineering. But merit is just a word for whatever qualifications are deemed desirable for the performance of a particular task, and there is nothing fixed about those qualifications. Some medical schools now decline to certify aspiring doctors who have proven themselves technically but lack the skills that enable them to relate to patients. These schools are not abandoning merit but fashioning an alternative conception of it rooted in an alternative notion of what the job requires. In the same way, it may be a qualification for a policeman or policewoman in the inner city to be black or Hispanic; and it may be part of the merit of a worker in a rape crisis center that she is a woman. Merit is not one thing but many things, and even when it becomes a disputed thing, the dispute is between different versions of merit and not between merit and something base and indefensible.

The fifth argument is the big one and the most specious. If it was wrong for Jim Crow laws to penalize people just for being black, then it is equally wrong to give preference to some people just for being black. It's reverse racism. But the reasoning works only if the two practices are removed from their historical contexts and declared to be the same because they both take race into consideration. According to this bizarre logic, those who favor minority set-asides are morally equivalent to Ku Klux Klanners. It is just like saying (what no one would say) that killing in self-defense is morally the same as killing for money because in either case it's killing you're doing. When the law distinguishes between these two scenarios, it recognizes that the judgment one passes on an action will vary with the motives informing it. It was the express purpose of some powerful white Americans to disenfranchise, enslave, and later exploit black Americans. It was *what they set out to do*, whereas the proponents of affirmative action did not set out to deprive your friend's cousin's son of a place at Harvard.

The sixth argument—it's group-think—says that by focusing on group harms and remedies, affirmative action runs contrary to the American tradition of regarding persons as individuals. The "group perspective" is rejected both as a way of assigning responsibility (it is individuals who discriminate, not society or patterns of history) and as a way of identifying the victimized (it is individuals, not groups, who are harmed). But this insistence on what the *Adarand* decision calls an "individualized showing" of harm does not correspond to the manner in which the harms were inflicted and experienced.[15] Blacks were not historically discriminated against one by one but as a group, by persons who had the entire African-American population, not particular members of it, in mind. And those who experienced discrimination did not do so as the result of being individually targeted (although that of course happened more than occasionally) but as the result of living in a society whose general and impersonal structures worked ceaselessly to their disadvantage. It is ironic that after practicing "societal discrimination" for so long, the society would now decide to make amends by proceeding piecemeal and leaving the larger patterns of exclusion it had fashioned firmly in place. If "group-think" is a problem, it is not one originated by the proponents of affirmative action but by those who oppose it.

The seventh argument—it's quotas—is on one level easily dismissible because quotas are illegal. What is permitted under current affirmative action law are ranges, targets, and goals. But, reply those who oppose affirmative action, ranges, targets, and goals amount to quotas in the end because they require employees and school administrators to move toward proportions numerically defined. This is in fact a strong argument which should be answered not by reinvoking the distinction between quotas and goals but by asking the question "What's wrong with quotas anyway?" What's wrong with quotas, presumably, is that they require taking race into consideration when making hiring or admissions decisions. But that is precisely what affirmative action is all about. The objection against quotas is really an objection to the word "affirmative" in the phrase affirmative action; and as the historical record surely shows, without *affirmative* action the inequalities and inequities produced by massive legal and cultural racism would not be remedied. But isn't a quota that reserves a number of places for women and minorities the same as the old, now-despised quotas that prevented all but a few Jews and even fewer African Americans from entering colleges, law schools, and medical schools? The answer is no, because the objection fails to distinguish between quotas imposed to keep people out (what is often called first-order discrimination) and quotas designed to let previously excluded persons in, which might in some small measure have the secondary—not intended—effect of marginally disadvantaging members of the majority. Finally, the case against quotas is often misrepresented as the case against "strict racial quotas." But that is a misnomer; there are no strict racial quotas in the sense that a contractor or chairman or college admissions officer is told to go down to the mall and pick out the first ten minority-looking persons he sees, whether or not they are qualified. In fact, when quotas—or ranges or goals or targets—are in place, their implementation always occurs in relation to a pool of already qualified applicants. No one is telling anyone to hire or admit persons who are unqualified; rather, employers and admissions officers are being told that when the pool of qualified workers or applicants has been assembled (and new ways of assembling it are also a part of affirmative action imperatives), choices within it can take minority status into consideration in cases where gross, disparate representation is obvious and long-standing. This last sentence of mine is wordy and unwieldy and doesn't have the quick impact of "It's racial quotas," but at least it is accurate.

The eighth argument—affirmative action lowers the self-esteem of its clients—has little statistical support and is dubious psychology. Some beneficiaries of affirmative action will question their achievements; others will be quite secure in them; and many more will manage to have low self-esteem no matter what their history. Affirmative action is a weak predictor of low self-esteem, and even if there were a strong correlation, you might prefer the low self-esteem that comes along with wondering if your success is really earned to the low self-esteem that comes with never having been in a position to succeed in the first place. At any rate, low self-esteem is at least in part the product of speculation about it. People who never would have thought of questioning their accomplishments might begin to do so if the question was raised every night on the evening news.

The ninth argument—affirmative action provokes race-consciousness—is a variation on the blame-the-victim strategy. If there were no affirmative action, it tells us, whites would not be resentful and racial hostility would be dissipated. This might make sense were it not for the little fact that racial hostility antedates affirmative action, which is a response to its effects. To say that as a response it only creates more of what it would redress is like saying "Don't complain or agitate or we will hit you again." The affirmative action backlash is certainly real, but it reflects discredit on the backlashers and not on those who continue to press for justice.

There they are, the nifty nine arguments and the counter-arguments you may not have heard elaborated. Use them the next time the question of affirmative action comes up. But don't be surprised if some of those you talk to persist even when the reasons they have always relied on are challenged by reasons equally powerful and by the facts. Sometimes the principled reasons people give for taking a position are just window dressing, good for public display but only incidental to the heart of the matter, which is the state of their hearts.

SAUCE FOR THE GOOSE

2

There's a moment in *The Wizard of Oz* when Dorothy picks an apple off a tree and the tree protests, "Hey there! How'd you like it if someone came and tried picking things off of you?" Abashed, Dorothy replies, "I . . . don't know. I suppose I didn't think of that." A churlish response, one Dorothy doesn't give, might be "Why *should* I think of that? After all, I'm a person and you're just a tree. I'm supposed to pick things off of you." But it is the entire point of the scene to call into question a difference so casually assumed. Indeed, the exchange is a questioning of difference in general and especially of differences that are invoked to justify differential treatment of agents otherwise the same. Thus read, this little conversation is a compressed illustration of the tendency in liberal thought—a tendency one sees in the usually opposed philosophies of multiculturalism and libertarianism—to regard many, if not all, differences as superficial and therefore as an inappropriate basis for the unequal distribution of goods or the selective allocation of rights. You may be black and I may be brown, you may be Jewish and I may be an atheist, you may be a neo-Nazi and I may be a Republican, but when it comes down to the right to speak or the right to vote or the right to associate or the right not to have a limb picked off, we are the same.[1]

That last sentence has to most of us the ring of democratic truth. We have learned in the past 150 years to be ashamed of having once relied on distinctions we now think invidious, and we congratulate ourselves on looking past them to the essential something all of us share, no matter what color we may be or party we may belong to or religious belief we may profess. But how far does this extend? What differences are so deep that to ignore them would be to default on the imperatives of morality? And if there are such deep differences, as opposed to the differences we now regard as inessential, how is the difference between them to be determined? Where do you draw the line? Do you draw the line between persons and trees? Neither Dorothy nor the tree would think so, and there are deep ecologists who might agree with them, not to mention those in the animal rights movement who are halfway to embracing plant rights.

Now, it might seem a stretch to go from this fanciful speculation to the serious issues of today's political landscape, but in fact it is no distance at all, for theoretically there is no difference between the difference between Dorothy and the tree and the difference between anything and anything else. The question is always the same: is the difference real and therefore something that should be acted on, or is the difference cosmetic and therefore something we should either not pay attention to (as we don't pay attention to eye color) or celebrate (as we celebrate styles in clothing or art)? It is one insight of liberalism that there is no answer to this question (except the answers given by already interested parties), and so it has seemed prudent and even moral to not answer it, but to let differences flourish in the hope that eventually they will sort themselves out. In the world of the university, this hope is called academic freedom, and its logic is the logic of Dorothy and the tree: I'm all right, you're all right, judge not lest you be judged, extend respect to others so that you can receive it in turn.

In what follows I want to interrogate that logic and suggest that it may not be as attractive as it seems. In fact, I shall go so far as to suggest that academic freedom is a bad idea, a dubious principle that • confuses eccentricity with genius and elevates pettiness, boorishness, and irresponsibility to the status of virtue; • evacuates morality by making all assertions equivalent and, because equivalent, inconsequential; • empties history of its meaning so that actions proceeding from entirely different motives and agendas become indistinguishable as instances of individual preference and free choice; and • promotes a regime of relativism by refusing to make judgments, on the reasoning that one man's meat is another man's poison.

These are deliberately provocative statements, but before elaborating and defending them I want to complicate them by saying that I am in favor of academic freedom and would do anything in my power to protect it. But why would I want to protect something I have just called a "bad idea"? The answer is that it is the idea or ideology of academic freedom I oppose, not the practice. Or, rather, I oppose the rhetoric that usually accompanies it, the rhetoric of even-handedness, open-mindedness, neutrality in the face of substantive conflict, autonomy of thought and choice. It will be my contention that these honorific phrases are either empty and therefore incapable of generating a policy (academic freedom or any other) or are covertly filled with the very partisan objectives they supposedly disdain. I will argue, in short, that the vocabulary of academic freedom (or at least the vocabulary of its pious champions) is a sham and a cheat.

But the practice of academic freedom has nothing (causal) to do with that vocabulary (which comes to adorn it after the fact) and everything to do with a history in which certain forces—the church, the state, boards of trustees, influential alumni and parents—are always trying to control and police what academic professionals (teachers and administrators) do. I am an academic professional and, like any member of any profession, I want the norms governing my labors to be devised by me and people like me, not by outsiders. (Academic freedom *is* a sectarian agenda, but it is *my* sect.) I want, that is, to be free of interference, and if the mantra of academic freedom will help to keep my would-be wardens at bay, I'm all for it, not as a morality but as a guild practice; and I am for it even as I set myself the task of debunking the argument it offers to the public.

It is a complex argument. First it asserts fallibilism: we are all prone to error and to the overvaluation of our own opinions. From fallibilism follows the obligation to refrain from judging one another: for who among us is fit to cast the first stone? From the obligation to refrain from judging one another follows an ethic of mutual respect: since none of us is God and in full possession of the truth, we must allow others the freedom to pursue the truth by their own lights, and they must allow us to do the same. In Kantian terms this becomes the doctrine of the autonomy of free agents, who are to be regarded not as means but as ends, and the final flower of the entire sequence is the logic of reciprocal rights. If I claim a privilege—say, the privilege of speaking my mind without restrictions—I must accord the same privilege to my fellow autonomous agents; and if I seek to restrain the speech or action of my fellows, I must accept the same restraint on my own speech and action.

POLITICS ALL THE WAY DOWN

In Kant's words, "Each may seek his happiness in whatever way he sees fit so long as he does not infringe upon the freedom of others to pursue a similar end; that is, he must accord to others the same rights he enjoys himself." Or in the words of John Stuart Mill, "We must beware of admitting a principle of which we would resent as a gross injustice the application to ourselves."[2]

It would be hard to overestimate the power of this line of reasoning, which underwrites familiar statements like "You can't fight discrimination with discrimination," "Racism is racism, no matter what the color, ethnicity, or economic status of the perpetrator," "Speech should be freely allowed even when—no, especially when—we find the message loathsome," "What goes around comes around," "What's sauce for the goose is sauce for the gander." These and similar pronouncements are seldom inquired into—they constitute the end-limit of the open inquiry they otherwise mandate—but I propose to inquire into them with a view toward rendering them less comfortable than you may now find them. And I will begin with what might seem an unlikely topic, religion and religious discourse, which are to my mind the keys to understanding academic freedom, at least as it has developed in the United States.

I say this because of a famous passage in the declaration of principles of the American Association of University Professors, first published in 1915 and left in place (if only by silence) in subsequent declarations. In that passage the AAUP denies to religiously based institutions the name of "university" because "they do not, at least as regards one particular subject, accept the principles of freedom and inquiry." Such institutions, the association grandly allows, may continue to exist, "but it is manifestly important that they should not be permitted to sail under false colors," for "genuine boldness, and thoroughness of inquiry, and freedom of speech are scarcely reconcilable with the . . . inculcation of a particular opinion upon a controverted question."[3] It is not that controverted questions should not be asked, but answers to them should not be presupposed and insulated from the challenge of free rational inquiry.

Unfortunately, it is the nature of religious dogma to resist and even condemn challenges from perspectives other than its own, and accordingly it is to be feared that in an institution founded on dogma, some avenues of inquiry will have been closed off even before the classroom doors open. As Professor Walter Metzger put it in his brief history of academic freedom, "Academic freedom . . . was historically the enemy and is logically the antithesis of religious tests."[3] Although the dangers to unfettered inquiry can have many sources—in legislative actions, administrative biases, forms of political pressure including what has come to be known as "political correctness"—religion has always been considered the original and prototypical danger, and the fact that it is a danger whose force has diminished in the wake of the Enlightenment makes it a convenient reference point for its modern successors. Thus Philip Resnick refers, in passing, to the "long and hard struggle for the freedom of scientific inquiry . . . against very strong opposition from the adherents of religious orthodoxy" before going on to consider the more recent threats from powerful economic interests and various forms of identity politics.[4] And John Fekete, in *Moral Panic: Biopolitics Rising,* characterizes the emergence of campus speech-codes as "the New Religion"; speech codes are shots fired in a "holy war" in which universities are pushed in the direction of becoming "doctrinal institutions" bent on punishing "heresies" that deviate "from orthodox beliefs." This, Fekete goes on to say, is "the *fundamentalism* of biopolitics," the "new piety," a form of Calvinism not unlike the Inquisition, all leading to a "creed-state . . . on the model of Christendom."[5]

Now what makes these statements somewhat odd is the fact that whenever freedom is celebrated, freedom of religion is always high on the list of what the concept includes. Here is a sentence from an essay on academic freedom by the legal philosopher Ronald Dworkin: "Freedom of speech, conscience and religion, and academic freedom are all parts of our society's support for a culture of independence and of its defense against a culture of conformity."[6] Notice that religion occupies opposing positions in the two halves of this sentence. In the first half it is one of the freedoms; in the second it is, implicitly, the enemy of freedom because of its insistence on conformity (with doctrine, or received morality, or rigid theodicy). Of course in standard liberal thought this paradox—religion is honored, religion is condemned— is easily resolved by invoking the belief/action distinction, as the Supreme Court did when it rejected the claim by some Mormons that polygamy was essential to their religion and thus protected by the free-exercise clause. "Laws are made for the government of actions, and while they may not interfere with mere religious belief and opinions, they may with practices."[7] That is, Mormons are free to believe and say anything they like so long as they do not put their beliefs and words into actions of which the authorities disapprove.

One sees in this example what freedom of religion means in a liberal regime, and why the announcement of it can go hand in hand with the demonization of religion: you are free to express your religious views not because of their content but because of their status as expressions. Religious views in this understanding are just like other views—political views, aesthetic views, sexual views, baseball views—and what is valued about them is that they have been freely produced (no one forced you to utter them) and that they are freely broadcast (no one has censored them). What is *not* valued about them is the content of what they urge. As instances of a favored category—expression—religious utterances are cherished; as something you are asked to take seriously, they are feared and condemned.

I have lingered over the example of religion because it can stand for what liberalism, in the name of academic freedom, does to any form of strong conviction that refuses to respect, or even recognize, the line between the private and the public, between the cerebral and the political, and moves instead to institutionalize itself in the rule of law. The Trent University "Statement of Free Inquiry and Expression" claims that "academic freedom makes commitment possible." No, it makes commitment, except to expression, suspect; or rather, it makes possible and *mandates* commitment to academic freedom, which requires as the price for your being able to proclaim your views that you tolerate the views of others, even those "you do not condone and, in some cases, deplore."

Now it is hard in a statement like this to know exactly what "deplore" means. For the ethic of toleration to make sense, "deplore" must indicate a revulsion that is *merely* personal, as in I deplore the ties he wears or the music she listens to. Deploring something on that level does not involve the determination to stamp it out, root and branch. If, however, by "deplore" you mean "fear" or "think dangerous" or "find evil," then it is not so clear why you would be so willing to allow what you deplore to flourish. Academic freedom is coherent only if you assume that the things you freely allow will be innocuous and containable, which they will be if they are regarded not as calls to action but as material for discussion, preferably in the setting of a seminar. However, if a form of speech or advocacy will not offer itself as material for discussion but simply declares itself to be the truth to which all must bend, academic freedom will reject it as illiberal, just as it rejects religious speech seriously urged.

What this means is that academic freedom, rather than being, as Resnick claims, "open to all points of view," is open to all points of view only so long as they offer themselves with the reserve and diffidence appropriate to Enlightenment decorums, only so long as they offer themselves for correction. In short, academic freedom places severe limits on what can go on in its playground and is in fact a form of closure. Academic freedom is not a defense against orthodoxy; it *is* an orthodoxy and a faith. The orthodoxy is rational deliberation, and the faith—somewhat paradoxical—is that through rational deliberation we shall arrive at the truth of whose existence rational deliberation is so skeptical.

Now, to say that academic freedom is an orthodoxy is not to score a fatal point against it. For even if academic freedom is deprived of the claim to be hostage to no point of view, it survives as a point of view you might reasonably want to embrace. And the question to be put to it, *as* a point of view, is what does it urge and what does it exclude? The answer to that question has already been partly given by the example of religion. Academic freedom urges the interrogation of all propositions and the privileging of none, the equal right of all voices to be heard, no matter how radical or unsettling, and the obligation to subject even one's most cherished convictions to the scrutiny of reason. What academic freedom excludes is any position that refuses that obligation, any position which rests, for example, on pronouncements like "I am the way" or "Thou shalt have no other gods before me."

To be sure, a champion of academic freedom would say that such positions are not excluded at all; rather, they are invited into the seminar, where they can be discussed, interrogated, reasoned with, analyzed. But of course that is not what the proponents of doctrinaire agendas want. They want to win; they want to occupy, and be sovereign over, the discursive space, and expel others from it. And *this* academic freedom will not permit (it wants to win, too, and does by exiling from its confines any discourse that violates *its* rules). In short, academic freedom invites forceful agendas in only on its terms, and refuses to grant legitimacy to the terms within which such agendas define themselves. We are right back to the 1915 AAUP declaration with a slight modification: religion can be part of university life so long as it renounces its claim to have a privileged purchase on the truth, which of course is the claim that defines a religion as a religion as opposed to a mere opinion.

It's a great move whereby liberalism, in the form of academic freedom, gets to display its generosity while at the same time cutting the heart out of the views to which that generosity is extended. Not only is it a great move; it is a move that works, and it works in part because it comes packaged in the vocabulary of rights, which is also a theory of personhood. In that theory, you are defined by your rights and not by the content of their exercise; you are defined, that is, as the bearer of rights—the right to believe, the right to speak, the right to choose—and those capacities, rather than what you happen to believe, or happen to say, or happen to choose, are what is important and what must be protected.

From this definition of personhood follows what I called at the beginning the logic of reciprocal rights. For if what makes you what you are is your capacity for speech, belief, and choice and not what is believed and spoken and chosen, then you are obligated, as a mark of self-respect—since you define yourself by general capacities that belong equally to everyone—to respect the beliefs, utterances, and choices of others. If your neighbor's meat is your poison, then you should just refrain from eating it while leaving him to eat what he likes. If your colleague's positions on abortion or affirmative action are anathema to you, debate them while upholding his right to have them so long as he upholds your right to have yours. What is sauce for the goose is sauce for the gander.

It all sounds fine and highly moral, but in fact it displaces morality by asking you to inhabit your moral convictions loosely and be ready to withdraw from them whenever pursuing them would impinge on the activities and choices of others. In short, the what's-sauce-for-the-goose-is-sauce-for-the-gander argument asks you to be morally thin; and it does this by asking you to conceive of yourself not as someone who is committed to something but as someone who is committed to respecting the commitments of those with whom he disagrees. Again, this sounds fine until you realize that what it requires is that you suspend those very urgencies that move you to act in the world, and to regard them as no different than the urgencies of your enemies.

To put the matter from the other direction: the logic of what's sauce for the goose is sauce for the gander requires that you redescribe your enemy as someone just like you. Indeed, in this vision, there are no enemies (except religious zealots), just persons with different preferences. And if that's all there is to it, you certainly don't want to silence, or penalize, or even imprison people just because they don't share your preferences. Again, for the third time, this sounds fine if you don't detect the slippery logic whereby convictions and life allegiances are turned into preferences, much as free speech doctrine turns all utterances into opinions. In this profoundly reductive scenario, everything is like everything else, neither something to live for nor something to fight for.

Once moral stances have been turned into individual preferences and assertions into opinions, it makes perfect sense that you refrain from acting on them in ways that would interfere with the freedom of others to prefer differently. I think the Holocaust really happened; you think it didn't; let's agree to disagree, that's what makes horse races, and who's to judge anyway? Any tendency to judge and to enforce your judgment by an act of coercion will be met by someone asking "How would you like it if someone did that to you?" This question assumes (a) that you and the hypothetical someone are interchangeable, exactly alike except for a few moral, political, or religious views, and (b) that the "that" that you wouldn't want done to you is an abstract act identifiable apart from any set of circumstances or motives—a violation of right, no matter who does it to whom.

The result is not only a self rendered morally thin but a society rendered morally thin when the logic of reciprocal rights is invoked to forbid the state from taking any action that endorses or seems to endorse one point of view over another. In a landmark case, *American Booksellers Association, Inc. v. Hudnut,* the U.S. Appeals Court for the seventh circuit struck down an antipornography ordinance because it enshrined in law a particular view of women—the view that they are human beings and not sex objects—over against the alternative view found in pornography.[8] After all, who is to say; live and let live; different strokes for different folks. The same withdrawal from moral judgment and from morality, on the basis, supposedly, of principle, is the content of the phrase "reverse racism"—the idea that any action taken on the basis of a racial classification is equivalent to any other action taken on the basis of racial classification. Armed with the scalpel of race-consciousness, you can find Ku Klux Klan lynchings no different from efforts to deny the Klan representation in public spaces; you can find the exclusion for centuries of minorities from the construction industry no different from minority set-aside programs; you can find quotas designed to exclude races from institutions of higher education no different from admissions procedures that take race into account as one of many factors; you can find that the voting rights act, passed in order to grant blacks a share of the franchise, can be invoked by whites who declare themselves disenfranchised by the voting rights act; and you can find the rantings of neo-Nazis no different from—indeed, more legitimate than—the proclamation of the golden rule, on the reasoning, first, that they are both expressions and, second, that the golden rule is an expression of a religious viewpoint and therefore out of bounds in a forum dedicated to academic freedom.

This is where liberal neutrality, academic freedom, and the principle of what's sauce for the goose is sauce for the gander get you, to a forced inability to make distinctions that would be perfectly clear to any well-informed teenager—distinctions between lynchings and set-asides, between a Shakespeare sonnet and hard-core pornography, between (in Justice Stevens's words) a welcome mat and a no-entry sign. This inability follows from the removal of situations from the historical context that gave them meaning to an abstract context in which they have no meaning or any meaning.

Here is another example. Samuel Walker, writing as a member of the American Civil Liberties Union—that curious organization whose mission it is to find things it hates and then to grow them—complains because at different times the U.S. Supreme Court protected the National Association for the Advancement of Colored People from acts of harassment but declined to protect the Ku Klux Klan from similar acts. The only difference, says Walker, is the "reputation of the organization under attack."[9] Right. The only difference is the difference between the Klan and the NAACP, and if that's not a difference, then I don't know what it is.

The question is, why would anyone reason in this "principled" way? And the answer is, because reasoning *that* way has a pay-off in outcomes someone desires: the rollback of affirmative action, the perpetuation of male dominance, the flourishing of arguments for racial superiority. The way of thinking that produces an inability to make otherwise obvious distinctions is not politically innocent; it is a political weapon wielded self-consciously, and often skillfully, by persons and groups with definite goals in mind; and those goals are not free speech, open inquiry, mutual respect, etc., but sales of pornography, maintenance of lily-white construction crews, the disadvantaging of minority religions, and so on. If liberal neutrality cannot make good on its claim to be above the fray (and it certainly cannot), then it is of necessity embroiled in the fray, coming down on one side rather than another, and doing so with an effectiveness that is indirectly proportional to the plausibility of the claim it cannot make good on. Liberal neutrality does political work so well because it has managed to assume the mantle of being above political work; and if you don't like the political work it is doing, you must labor to take the mantle away, strip off the veneer of principle so that policies that wear the mask of principle will be forced to identify themselves for what they are and for what they are not.

In your efforts to do this, the vocabulary and rhetoric of multiculturalism will not help. After a life-long search, I may have found a position no one likes. Liberal defenders of academic freedom won't like it, but neither should multiculturalists, if only because they are liberal defenders of academic freedom in only slightly different clothing. Whereas the watchwords of liberal defenders of academic freedom are neutrality and impartiality, the watchwords of multiculturalists are difference and diversity. But just as neutrality and impartiality mandate the exclusion from their circle of strong religious views, so do difference and diversity mandate the exclusion from their circle of views alleging racial superiority or the immorality of homosexuals. Liberal neutrality and multiculturalism are both engines of exclusion trying to fly under inclusive banners.

That is why people on the wrong side of these respective engines feel suffocated when they get going, why minorities protest that neutrality is a sham, and middle-aged white professors, like me, protest that diversity reaches out to include everyone but them. Both sides are right. They *are* being excluded. Where they are wrong is to think that inclusion, of a truly capacious kind, is possible. All that is possible—all you can work for—is to arrange things so that the exclusions that inevitably occur are favorable to your interests and hostile to the interests of your adversaries.

Inclusion, in the university or anywhere else, is not an attainable goal. It is not even a worthy one, for to attain it would be to legitimize all points of view and directions of inquiry and thereby to default on the responsibility of the university to produce knowledge and to refine judgment. The debate is never between the inclusive university and a university marked by exclusions; the debate is always between competing structures of exclusion. And the debate is over, at least for a time, when one structure of exclusion has managed to make its interests perfectly congruent with what is understood by the term "academic freedom."

The assertion of interest is always what's going on even when, and especially when, interest wraps itself in high-sounding abstractions. This is not an indictment of anyone, certainly not an indictment of anyone for having forsaken principles for politics; politics is all there is, and it's a good thing too. Principles and abstractions don't exist except as the rhetorical accompaniments of practices in search of good public relations. This is not an indictment either, just an observation, and perhaps a piece of advice: be alert to those moments when your opponents have a public relations machine so good that it's killing you, for then you're going to have to stop and try to take it apart.

Right now the public relations machine that rides on the tracks of the ethic of mutual respect and the mantra of academic freedom is in such high gear that those whose interests are likely to be rolled over by it had better do something. That's what I have been trying to do here by explaining, over and over again, how these formulas work, the kind of work they do, and why, if you look beneath them, you may not like what you see. Perhaps when you next hear someone say what's sauce for the goose is sauce for the gander, or are tempted to say it yourself, you will at least hesitate and remember that a goose *is* a goose and *not* a gander, before surrendering to the satisfactions of liberal complacency.

3

OF AN AGE AND NOT FOR ALL TIME

Liberal complacency is not merely a descriptive term of political analysis; it can do actual harm in the real world, as I shall try to show by interrogating a moment in cultural history that owes its power to the convergence of literary and legal canons and to an even deeper canon that underlies both. The moment I have in mind occurs in the midst of *Collin v. Smith,* or, as it is more familiarly known, the Skokie case. The case turned on an ordinance prohibiting "the dissemination of any material within the Village of Skokie which promotes and incites hatred against persons by reason of their race, national origin, or religion, and is intended to do so." In the course of affirming a district court finding that the ordinance is unconstitutional because it violates First Amendment rights, Appellate Justice Pell, writing for a two-person majority, declares, in the tone of someone who is delivering a knock-out blow, that the judgment of the lower court is "supported by the fact that the ordinance could conceivably be applied to criminalize dissemination of *The Merchant of Venice.*"[1]

Now several things mark this moment as one in which canonical power is being exercised. First of all, Judge Pell feels no need to identify the author of *The Merchant of Venice.* He assumes that it goes without saying that it is Shakespeare's *Merchant of Venice,* and not, for example, Homer Simpson's *Merchant of Venice* (a play I would dearly love to read). And because it goes without saying, he can make his point without actually making it—point being that any policy which might conceivably deprive us of *The Merchant of Venice* is by definition, and without any further elaboration, unacceptable.

Here we see two features possessed by canonical materials. (1) They carry their authority with them, seeming to have acquired it by natural right. And (2) they function not to encourage thought but to stop it. Canonical materials, when they are exerting their full force, draw a line in the sand, but with an air suggesting that the sand is a monument of steel. When a piece of the canon is invoked in this way, it is assumed that there is nothing more to say. In fact, there is always more that could be said; it is just that the structure of canonical authority is such that one is discouraged from saying it, or even from thinking it.

Let me, however, be characteristically perverse and imagine what one might reasonably say to Judge Pell when he cites as the most powerful of arguments against the ordinance the danger it carries, at least hypothetically, of losing *The Merchant of Venice.* One might begin by saying, "So what? After all, the guy wrote 36 other plays, 154 sonnets, and several rather tedious narrative allegories, and the loss of a single play, especially of one rarely performed (now that Laurence Olivier is dead) would·hardly seem to be a matter of great concern." Or if that is too flip, consider this more philosophical formulation of the same line of argument: "Are we really to believe that if *The Merchant of Venice* were to be placed in one of a pair of balancing scales, that *nothing* could be placed in the other scale that would outweigh its loss? Is no price too high to pay for the protection of *The Merchant of Venice?*"

I know *my* answer to that question, but if you are a practicing literary critic, the answer is likely to be yes, for as a work of Shakespeare's the play instantiates everything in the name of which you labor. It is not simply that Shakespeare is canonical; he is the very canon—rule, norm, measure, standard—in relation to which canonicity is established. The crucial judgment was put in place only seven years after his death by Ben Jonson in his celebratory poem in the First Folio: "He was not of an age, but for all time."[2] In this opposition between the merely historical and the transcendent one finds the essence of canonicity—an authority that can be invoked in the face of almost any counter-evidence because it is its own evidence and stronger in its force than any other. If Shakespeare is on your side in an argument, the argument is over. His name stops inquiry in much the same way as when, in response to a question about the nature of his identity, Jehovah replies, "I am what

I am." Shakespeare and God—one and the same in literary circles—occupy the position reserved by H. L. A. Hart for the "ultimate" rule, a rule that brings "a stop in inquiries concerning validity" because while it "provides criteria for the assessment of the validity of *other* rules . . . there is no rule providing criteria for the assessment of its own validity."[3]

One of Shakespeare's qualifications for this position is that we know almost nothing about him, and in fact do not even know who he was. The history rehearsed in a 1992 publication, *The Shakespeare Controversy: An Analysis of the Claimants to Authorship and Their Champions and Detractors*, is driven by the inability of many to believe that an ignorant poacher from Stratford could have written the elegant and learned verse that fills the plays.[4] No less a person than Henry James declared that "the divine William is the biggest and most successful fraud ever practised on a patient world," and in James's short story "The Birthplace," the curator of Shakespeare's cottage, growing weary of the myth he is paid to refurbish, cries out, "We don't know. There's very little *to* know. He covered His tracks as no other human being has ever done." To which his more credulous and faithful wife replies sarcastically, "Don't you think that he was born *anywhere*?"[5]

Given Shakespeare's canonical status, the correct answer to her question is no, because if He (capitalized in the text) were born in a particular place and lived a particular life, the productions of his pen would be the object of a *historical* explanation; and to the extent that such an explanation localized his achievement, its claim to transcendence would be compromised. A writer in *Publishers Weekly* reports that Shakespearean scholars by and large do not respond to the various efforts to give Shakespeare a local habitation; they just reject the idea as "impossible" and "unfathomable"; they "can't stand the very thought of it."[6] What they can't stand is the thought that the literary measure of all measures was a human being, a man of his age and not of all time, a man whose motives might be as variable and base as the motives of those who want to worship him.

Shakespeare idolaters draw back from the controversy because they sense, and sense correctly, that even to argue the matter would be to acquiesce in the assumption that the truth about Shakespeare could be established by evidence external to his plays. From that assumption it is only a short step to the reversal of the relationship between the plays and their "background." Before you know it, background has become foreground, displacing the plays as the measure of themselves, and pretty soon someone is arguing—as has one supporter of Edward de Vere, Seventeenth Earl of Oxford (the current favorite)—that the plays are "works of political propaganda, directed against internal and external enemies of the government, written often at the direction of the monarchy."[7] Once Shakespeare is deprived of his self-validating status and is referred for both description and evaluation to the contexts of economic calculation and power politics, he can no longer serve as a guiding light to those who wander in the perilous woods of human error, for he has been revealed to live and move and have his being in those very same woods.

That is why the preferred explanation of Shakespeare's achievement remains that of "inspiration" and "genius," two categories defined by the immediacy with which the vessel receives illumination from on high. Rather than negotiating the contorted pathways of social and political influence, inspiration bypasses them and simply pours its treasure into the vehicle of its magisterial choice, a vehicle who is then certified as a genius precisely because nothing in the circumstances of his merely historical life explains his eloquence and wisdom. *Of course* Shakespeare seems to spring fully grown from a soil that could not have nurtured him; that's why he is a genius.

This explanation—or, rather, refusal of explanation—has the advantage of confirming and being supported by the most general assumption informing the literary culture—the assumption that literary value, both in its creation and its reception, is realized in the realm of the mind, first in the minds of those designated by grace to be its vehicle and then in the minds of those select readers whose sensibilities are so refined that they are able to recognize, without reflection and independently of the vagaries of their personal histories, the very best that has been thought and said. "Fit audience, though few" is the way Milton put it, and in his phrase (which has many antecedents and successors) one sees that the restricted universe of similarly constituted minds is as much social as it is aesthetic. Participation in the making and sustaining of canons loses its attraction if it does not include the power to *ex*clude, to cast out into an undifferentiated outer darkness all of those who neither receive nor respond to the light.

It is in this spirit (if I may use that word innocently) that Judge Pell implicitly dismisses as not worth taking into account all those (surely the majority) who would think that *The Merchant of Venice* sells surfboards in a California beach town. It is not that persons ignorant of Shakespeare are to be denied rights; presumably few if any of the neo-Nazis whose right to march in Skokie is at this moment being protected are readers of the plays. Yet while Pell may rule in their favor, he has no real interest in them and several times deplores the very fact of their existence. He defends what they are doing only because he fears that a policy which silences them could lead down the road to the silencing of voices that really matter, voices like Shakespeare's, whose appeal is not to the prejudices and fears of ignorant rabble but to the aspirations and idealism of those who spend their lives watching *Masterpiece Theater*. It is those people—the Shakespeares and the fit-though-few audience they seek—that constitute the core of his concern, for they are living the "life of the mind," a life that is about as far from the miserable existence of goose-stepping malcontents as one can get.

And it is here—in the valorization of the life of the mind—that literary and legal canons find a meeting place and forge a particularly powerful alliance. The link is the tendency of liberalism to value the rights of individuals above all else and to identify an individual with his or her mental processes, in isolation from, if not opposition to, the processes of the body and the body politic. In the literary culture, what counts is the moment of private inspiration in which the superior consciousness rises above its surroundings and proclaims an atemporal truth. In the legal culture, as crystallized in First Amendment jurisprudence, what counts is the moment in which a lone speaker rises and, in defiance of the forces that press in on him, gives utterance to the inner voice of conscience. In both scenarios, as heroic as anything John Wayne ever imagined, the person is reduced, or exalted, to the status of pure mind, a bodiless agent whose paradigmatic act is the act either of forming an expression or expressing it. Everything else is accidental, in the strict philosophical sense; everything else is dross.

That is why more than a few First Amendment opinions will exhibit the pattern displayed in an exaggerated form by *Collin v. Smith:* first an acknowledgment of how grievous are the harms caused by certain kinds of speech, followed by a declaration that these harms, while regrettable, are finally beside the point, because the point, and the only point, is to preserve the autonomy of individual moral choice. In the contexts informed by high liberal thought, it is not the consequences of an action—its real-world community effects—that matter but the extent to which the action is free, that is, the product of an uncoerced will. A

POLITICS ALL THE WAY DOWN

speech delivered out of fear or in deference to power and not in response to the heart is the issue of an enslaved consciousness. A poem written for hire rather than for the Muse is an act of literary prostitution. When Charles Fried declares that "no conviction forced upon us can really be ours" (225), he is saying pretty much the same thing a high aesthetician says when he declares that if a work can be adequately explained by the historical circumstances of its production, it is not really literary.[8]

Hence the *double* force of Pell's invocation of *The Merchant of Venice:* not only does he draw upon the cultural capital of a literary icon but he taps into the even deeper cultural capital of the assumption that underwrites the status both of the icon and of the legal doctrine he is presently enforcing, the assumption that autonomy is the defining feature of genuine action in a democratic society. That assumption grounds the entire structure of canonicity in both disciplines and lends its prestige to the other forms of canonicity that operate at less embedded levels.

At the surface level we have the canons of institutional authority in its present shape—the opinions of prominent critics or of well-placed law professors, the weight of frequently assigned anthologies of poetry or of frequently used casebooks and hornbooks. At a level somewhat below the surface but always in sight, we have the canon of authorized, even sacred, texts—Shakespeare, Milton, the Constitution, the Bill of Rights, *Brown vs. Board of Education*—and along with these texts an array of taxonomies and binaries through which they are read and given shape (epic, tragedy, lyric, satire; tort, contract, private/public; legislative law/administrative law).

When these binaries and taxonomies are put into play, they are sometimes accompanied by disciplinary mantras designed to assure both practitioners and the lay audience that everything is proceeding according to Hoyle: a court does not substitute its own terms for the terms agreed to by the contracting parties; a critic does not substitute his own meaning for the meanings intended by the poet. And if the system should prove resistant to an outcome desired by the majority, formulas of flexibility will be invoked, but with an insistence that in their apparent irregularity they are true to the core values of the enterprise. You say, "After all, it is the essence of poetry to be available to many interpretations"; you say, "After all, we must always keep in mind what equity or justice requires." And when these formulas are invoked, you are very close to naming your core values—beauty, form, complexity, justice, freedom, autonomy—although for the most part naming them is unnecessary because they are presupposed and need be brought in only in a ceremonial way at the end of an explication or at the conclusion of an opinion after all the work has been done.

These varied materials, and many more that I have not instanced, make up the canon, which is neither stable nor homogeneous but is rather a rag-tag and shifting collection of quotations, precedents, statements of principle, talismanic phrases, charismatic practitioners, exemplary accomplishments, all of which carry authority in the sense that you can be fairly certain that by deploying them your agenda will be advanced. I say "fairly certain" because as components of a shifting canon, of a canon always re-forming itself on the wing, their force is vulnerable to challenge and to the emergence of new exemplary acts and actors. In general that vulnerability does not touch the heart of the enterprise—the values so defining of its purpose that to question them is literally unthinkable, or the texts to which members of the enterprise pledge allegiance—but there are times when a challenge goes that deep. And at those times the guardians of orthodoxy rise up in a combination of outrage and incredulity—outrage at the very fact of an assault on truths so perspicuous that no one could, or should, deny them; incredulity at the spectacle of intelligent, credentialed men and women who seem unaccountably to have forgotten what everyone knows and shouldn't have to say.

The resulting discourse is at once regretful, hectoring, chiding, and above all, condescending, in the exact sense of "coming down voluntarily to the level of inferiors." Charles Fried's essay is all of these things, even in its title, "The New First Amendment Jurisprudence: A Threat to Liberty." "One would think," he declares in the first sentence, "that there is nothing new to say about the First Amendment," for "the principle lines of doctrine are clear" (225). Yet, unbelievable though it may be, new things *are* being said, and being said in "classrooms and law reviews," of all places, and being said by people who apparently don't realize that they are participating in an "attack on the great liberal ideal of free expression." "I sound the alarm," Fried announces as he promises to "identify and catalogue, to analyze and explain and I hope exorcise this new intellectual attack on liberty" (226).

Now Fried is not just whistlin' "Dixie" here; from his perspective, which is shared by many, perhaps by most, there really is something to sound the alarm about. For in the past twenty years or so, there have arisen forms of thought—call them antifoundationalist—whose effect, were they to triumph, would be to take away much of the authority Judge Pell relies on when he confidently cites the possibility of losing *The Merchant of Venice* as a knock-down argument against the Skokie ordinance. First of all, not only is liberty under attack but (and it finally amounts to the same thing) Shakespeare is under attack, and what he is being attacked by is the same enemy Fried identifies as the threat to First Amendment freedoms—politics.

Under the banner of the new historicism and cultural materialism, a legion of academics has been busily removing Shakespeare from the pedestal of timeless value and re-embedding him in the social, economic, and political histories not only of his own time but of later times in which his name and works have been appropriated for a wide variety of polemical purposes, most of them supportive of the status quo. A book like Graham Holderness's *The Shakespeare Myth* does not take up the question of authorship (now thought profoundly uninteresting) but rather provides massively detailed accounts of the many ways in which the figure of Shakespeare (as opposed to "Shakespeare himself," an idealized and ideological personage who now tends to disappear) has been reconfigured in the service of any number of projects, including the projects of colonial apologists, educational conservatives, ministers of tourism, propagandists of national unity, and so on.[9] The word used to describe this continual reinvention of Shakespeare is "reproduced," which does not mean "given a new realization on the contemporary stage" but literally *re*-produced, made over into an entirely new form, in effect, reborn. The Shakespeare who in an idealist vision was never born but floated serenely above the vicissitudes of the sublunary world is now the creature of those vicissitudes. Rather than standing behind the uses made of him, he *is*, at any one moment, the uses made of him; and it is in response to Judge Pell's invocation of him as a timeless icon that one could reply as I did earlier, "So what?" Or, perhaps, "Which *Merchant of Venice* were you thinking of? Perhaps we could do very well without it."

Quite obviously, this line of argument, which is now endemic, takes away Shakespeare's autonomy by inscribing him (as the saying goes) in the variable and fluctuating histories to which his transcendental greatness has traditionally been opposed. But this is hardly the worst of it, for the same line of argument, when pursued to its inevitable conclusion, takes away *everybody's* autonomy by refusing to recognize, never mind privilege, a core self whose integrity survives the sea changes of mortal existence. If Shakespeare's "identity" is continually rewritten by the historical forces that rewrite him, so too are the identities of each of us rewritten by the same forces. (We don't have to die before we become texts.) This thesis goes under the rubric of "the social construction of the self," and it is not merely a "threat" to liberty; it is a denial that liberty—the condition in which one freely makes rational choices uncoerced by external circumstances—even exists.

The principal lines of First Amendment doctrine may be clear, as Fried says they are, but if the antifoundationalists are right, it is a wholly artificial clarity, a clarity rooted in an illusion and a delusion. Shakespeare, the very emblem of humanity's essence, is an illusion; the freedom of which he is the highest realization—the freedom (in Fried's words) to determine "for myself what is good and how I shall arrange my life" by exercising the powers of my own free mind—is an illusion, because the mind's powers are shaped and constrained by influences external to them (the mind's inside is always a function of its supposed outside); and the free speech that supposedly issues from such a mind is an illusion because its production, like the production of the thoughts it expresses, is constrained and determined by those same influences.

It would seem that in the wake of so corrosive a thesis (which I do not here endorse but merely report), nothing remains of the structure of canonicity, since the infection of politics and relativism has spread throughout its components, tainting first the fundamental values of autonomy and self-governance and then claiming all of the materials— texts, precedents, exemplary achievements, etc.—given intelligibility and authority by those values. But in fact the structure has not been destroyed; it has merely been historicized; and its authority is left pretty much intact, lessened only to the extent that it is thought to require a pedigree independent of history, a pedigree of divinity or at least of reason with a capital R.

And that is the real question about canons, not "Do we have them?"—we always have them; they are all around us—but "Where do they come from and on what do they rest?" This is the question that has acquired such urgency in recent years (partly in response to the strong emergence of antifoundationalist forms of thought), and it is asked in the legal academy by critical legal studies, feminist jurisprudence, critical race jurisprudence, and outsider jurisprudence.

It is not, however, a new question. It is coterminus with the idea of canonicity itself. Our current debates replicate the debates engaged in by our predecessors, including, preeminently, the armies of theologians who have for centuries argued as to whether the canon is to be located in "a codified set of rules" or in "the charismatic possibility offered by the example of Jesus."[10] *That* is the deepest question: are canons man-made or are they divine? I have an answer for that question, and I shall offer it in true canonical style, without argument or elaboration. Canons are *both* human and divine; or to be more precise, canonicity is the process by which human achievements—whether the achievements of Shakespeare, James Madison, or Sarah Vaughan—shed their humanity and become the regulative ideals by which mere human actions are henceforth measured. Is this process good, or does it mark the path by which men and women enslave one another? That is a question only a God could definitively answer, and therefore I will take evasive action and refer it to, of all things, a poem.

It is a poem in which an unidentified agent imposes a canonical mea-sure and then immediately withdraws, leaving us to ponder its effects in ignorance of its origin, uncertain as to whether the force of the measure is benign or the extension of an oppressive agenda that does not bring life but destroys it. The poem, which is a meditation on canons and is itself canonical, does not resolve the uncertainty, and I leave you with its troubling echoes. It is Wallace Stevens's "Anecdote of the Jar":

> I placed a jar in Tennessee,
> And round it was, upon a hill.
> It made the slovenly wilderness
> Surround that hill.
>
> The wilderness rose up to it,
> And sprawled around, no longer wild.
> The jar was round upon the ground
> And tall and of a port in air.
>
> It took dominion everywhere.
> The jar was gray and bare.
> It did not give of bird of bush,
> Like nothing else in Tennessee.

4

BOUTIQUE MULTICULTURALISM

Stevens's poem, hesitating as it does between a lush and variegated wilderness and the imposition of order from the outside, might be read as an allegory of the debates about multiculturalism. Multiculturalism comes in at least two versions, boutique multiculturalism and strong multiculturalism. Boutique multiculturalism is the multiculturalism of ethnic restaurants, weekend festivals, and high-profile flirtations with the other in the manner satirized by Tom Wolfe under the rubric of "radical chic."[1] Boutique multiculturalism is characterized by its superficial or cosmetic relationship to the objects of its affection. Boutique multiculturalists admire or appreciate or enjoy or sympathize with or (at the very least) "recognize the legitimacy of" the traditions of cultures other than their own; but boutique multiculturalists will always stop short of approving other cultures at a point where some value at their center generates an act that offends against the canons of civilized decency as they have been either declared or assumed.

The death sentence under which Salman Rushdie lived for many years is an obvious example, although it is an example so extreme that we might do better to begin with a few that are less dramatic. A boutique multiculturalist may find something of value in rap music and patronize (pun intended) soul-food restaurants, but he will be uneasy about affirmative action and downright hostile to an afrocentrist curriculum. A boutique multiculturalist may enjoy watching Native American religious ceremonies and insist that they be freely allowed to occur, but he will balk if those ceremonies include animal sacrifice or the use of a controlled substance.[2] A boutique multiculturalist may acknowledge the diversity of opinions about abortion, but he is likely to find something illegitimate in the actions of abortion opponents who block the entrance to clinics and subject the women who approach them to verbal assaults. A boutique multiculturalist may honor the tenets of religions other than his own, but he will draw the line when the adherents of a religion engage in the practice of polygamy.

In each of these cases (and in the many analogous cases that could be instanced) the boutique multiculturalist resists the force of the culture he appreciates at precisely the point at which it matters most to its strongly committed members—the point at which the African American tries to make the content of his culture the content of his children's education, the point at which a Native American wants to practice his religion as its ancient rituals direct him to, the point at which antiabortionists directly confront the evil that they believe is destroying the moral fiber of the country, the point at which Mormons seek to be faithful to the word and practices of their prophets and elders.

Another way to put this is to say that a boutique multiculturalist does not and cannot take seriously the core values of the cultures he tolerates. The reason he cannot is that he does not see those values as truly "core" but as overlays on a substratum of essential humanity. That is the true core, and the differences that mark us externally—differences in language, clothing, religious practices, race, gender, class, and so on—are for the boutique multiculturalist no more than what Milton calls in his *Areopagitica* "moderat varieties and brotherly dissimilitudes that are not vastly disproportionall."[3] We may dress differently, speak differently, woo differently, worship or not worship differently, but underneath (or so the argument goes) there is something we all share (or that shares us) and that something constitutes the core of our identities. Those who follow the practices of their local culture to the point of failing to respect the practices of other cultures—by calling for the death of an author whose writings denigrate a religion or by seeking to suppress pornography because it is offensive to a gender—have simply mistaken who they are by identifying with what is finally only an accidental aspect of their beings.

The essential boutique multiculturalist point is articulated concisely by Steven C. Rockefeller: "Our universal identity as human beings is our primary identity and is more fundamental than any particular identity, whether it be a matter of citizenship, gender, race, or ethnic origin" (88).[4] Taking pleasure in one's "particular identity" is perfectly all right so long as when the pinch comes and a question of basic allegiance arises, it is one's universal identity that is affirmed. For as "important as respect for diversity is in multicultural democratic societies, ethnic identity is not the foundation of recognition of equal value and the related idea of equal rights" (88). That is to say, we have rights not as men or women or Jews or Christians or blacks or Asians but as human beings, and what makes a human being a human being is not the particular choices he or she makes but the capacity for choice itself, and it is this capacity rather than any of its actualizations that must be protected.

It follows, then, that while any particular choice can be pursued at the individual's pleasure, it cannot be pursued to the point at which it interferes with or prescribes or proscribes the choices of other individuals. (This is of course a reformulation of John Stuart Mill's "harm principle" in *On Liberty*.) One may practice one's religion, even if it is devil worship, in any manner one likes, but one may not practice one's religion to the extent of seeking to prevent others from practicing theirs by, say, suppressing their sacred texts or jailing their ministers. Women may rightly insist that they receive equal pay for equal work, but they cannot rightfully insist that they be given extra compensation or preferential treatment just because they are women. One may choose either to read or to disdain pornography, but one who believes in pornography's liberatory effects cannot compel others to read it, and one who believes that pornography corrupts cannot forbid others to publish it.

Of course it is just those two actions (or some versions of them) that pro- and antipornography forces will most want to take, since they flow logically from the beliefs of the respective parties and will be seen by those parties as positive moral requirements. This is what I meant earlier when I pointed out that the boutique multiculturalist will withhold approval of a particular culture's practices at the point at which they matter most to its strongly committed members: a deeply religious person is precisely that, *deeply* religious, and the survival and propagation of his faith is not for him an incidental (and bracketable) matter but an essential matter, and essential too, in his view, for those who have fallen under the sway of false faiths. To tell such a person that, while his convictions may be held, he must stop short of fully implementing them is to tell him that this vision of the good is either something he must keep to himself or something he must offer with a diffidence that might characterize his offer of canapés at a cocktail party.[5] Rockefeller might say that "respect for the individual is understood to involve not only respect for . . . universal human potential . . . but also respect for . . . the different cultural forms in and through which individuals actualize their humanity" (87), but it is clear from his commentary that the latter respect will be superficial precisely in the measure that the cultural forms that are its object have themselves been judged to be superficial, that is, not intrinsic to universal identity.

The politics generated by views like Rockefeller's has been called by Charles Taylor "a politics of equal dignity" (38).[6] The politics of equal dignity, Taylor explains, ascribes to everyone "an identical basket of rights and immunities," identical because it is limited to that aspect of everyone that is assumed to be universally the same, namely, "our status as rational agents" (41), agents defined by a shared potential for deliberative reason. The idea is that so long as that potential is protected by law, particular forms of its realization—cultural traditions, religious dogmas, ethnic allegiances—can be left to make their way or fail to make their way in the to-and-fro of marketplace debate. A tradition may die, a religion may languish, an ethnic community may fail to secure representation in the classroom or the boardroom, but these consequences are of less moment and concern than the integrity of the process that generates them, a process that values deliberation over the results of deliberation, results that are, from the perspective of this politics, indifferent.[7]

Results or outcomes are not at all indifferent in another politics, named by Taylor the "politics of difference" (38). The politics of difference, as Taylor explains it, does not merely allow traditions a run for their money; it is committed to their flourishing. If the politics of equal dignity subordinates local cultural values to the universal value of free rational choice, the politics of difference names as its preferred value the active fostering of the unique distinctiveness of particular cultures. It is that distinctiveness rather than any general capacity of which it is an actualization that is cherished and protected by this politics. Whereas the politics of equal dignity "focuses on what is the same in all" and regards particularity as icing on a basically homogeneous cake, the politics of difference asks us "to recognize and even foster particularity" as a first principle (43).

In practical terms, fostering particularity requires that we make special adjustments to the special requirements of distinctive groups, for if we refuse such adjustments in the name of some baseline measure of rational potential, we weaken the distinctiveness recognition of which is our chief obligation. "Where the politics of universal dignity fought for forms of nondiscrimination that were quite 'blind' to the ways in which citizens differ, the politics of difference often redefines nondiscrimination as requiring that we make these distinctions the basis of differential treatment" (39).

It is the politics of difference that gives us campus speech codes (like Stanford's before it was struck down) that judicialize racist epithets directed against minorities but do not consider epithets (honkey, redneck, whitey) directed against Caucasian males a form of racism (on the reasoning that racism is defined as hostility plus power rather than as mere hostility). It is the politics of difference that leads to the establishment of schools for young black males in our inner cities (on the reasoning that the maintenance of cultural and gender homogeneity will bolster confidence and stimulate learning). It is the politics of difference that produces demands by blacks, Asians, and Native Americans that they be portrayed in films and plays by actors who are themselves blacks, Asians, and Native Americans. It is the politics of difference that asks for proportional representation of various cultural traditions in the classroom and in faculty hiring. The politics of difference is the equivalent of an endangered species act for human beings, where the species to be protected are not owls and snail darters but Arabs, Jews, homosexuals, Chicanos, Italian Americans, and on and on and on.

The politics of difference is what I mean by strong multiculturalism. It is strong because it values difference in and for itself rather than as a manifestation of something more basically constitutive. Whereas the boutique multiculturalist will accord a superficial respect to cultures other than his own—a respect he will withdraw when he finds the practices of a culture irrational or inhumane—a strong multiculturalist will want to accord a *deep* respect to all cultures at their core, for he believes that each has the right to form its own identity and nourish its own sense of what is rational and humane. For the strong multiculturalist, the first principle is not rationality or some other supracultural universal but tolerance.

The trouble with stipulating tolerance as your first principle, however, is that you cannot possibly be faithful to it because sooner or later the culture whose core values you are tolerating will reveal itself to be intolerant at that same core. The distinctiveness that marks it as unique and self-defining will resist the appeal of moderation or incorporation into a larger whole. Confronted with a demand that it surrender its viewpoint or enlarge it to include the practices of its natural enemies— other religions, other races, other genders, other classes—a beleaguered culture will fight back with everything from discriminatory legislation to violence.

At this point the strong multiculturalist faces a dilemma: either he stretches his toleration so that it extends to the intolerance residing at the heart of a culture he would honor, in which case tolerance is no longer his guiding principle, or he condemns the core intolerance of that culture (recoiling in horror when Khomeini calls for the death of Rushdie), in which case he is no longer according it respect at the point where its distinctiveness is most obviously at stake. Typically, the strong multiculturalist will grab the second handle of this dilemma (usually in the name of some supracultural universal now seen to have been hiding up his sleeve from the beginning) and thereby reveal himself not to be a strong multiculturalist at all. Indeed, it turns out that strong multiculturalism is not a distinct position but a somewhat deeper instance of the shallow category of boutique multiculturalism.

To be sure, there will still be a difference, but it will be a difference in degree. When the novelist Paul Theroux encounters a Pakistani with an advanced degree in science who nevertheless declares "Rushdie must die," Theroux responds in true boutique multiculturalist fashion by setting him "straight" and informing him (as if he were a child) that his are "ignorant and barbarous sentiments."[8] (I bet that really convinced him.) Contrast this with M. M. Slaughter, a strong multiculturalist who, in the place of name calling, offers an explanation of why an educated Muslim whose sense of identity "is inseparable from the community of believers" might think himself mortally wounded by something written in a book (198).[9] For Slaughter, the issue is properly understood not as a simple contrast between civilization and barbarity but as a tension between "essentialist ideologies that inevitably and irreconcilably conflict . . . The concept of the autonomous self requires the free speech principle; the socially situated self of Islamic society necessarily rejects free speech in favor of prohibitions against insult and defamation" (156). Yet even while she elaborates the point, Slaughter declines to extend her act of sympathetic understanding into a statement of approval, and she is careful to declare at the beginning of her essay that "the placing of a bounty on Rushdie's head" (155) is "a terroristic act"

(154). Slaughter's judgment, in short, is finally not all that different from Theroux's, although it comes accompanied by an analysis the novelist has no interest in making. Both Theroux and Slaughter—one of whom sees the fatwa as an instance of fanaticism bordering on insanity while the other pushes through to a comprehension of the system of thought in which the fatwa might constitute a moral obligation—stop far short of going all the way, that is, of saying, with Theroux's Pakistani, "Rushdie must die."

In the end neither the boutique multiculturalist nor the strong multiculturalist is able to come to terms with difference, although their inabilities are asymmetrical. The boutique multiculturalist does not take difference seriously because its marks (quaint clothing, atonal music, curious table manners) are for him matters of lifestyle, and as such they should not be allowed to overwhelm the substratum of rationality that makes us all brothers under the skin. The strong multiculturalist takes difference so seriously as a general principle that he cannot take any particular difference seriously, cannot allow its imperatives their full realization in a political program, for their full realization would inevitably involve the suppression of difference. The only way out for the would-be strong multiculturalist is to speak not for difference in general but for *a* difference, that is, for the imperatives of a distinctive culture even when they impinge on the freedom of some other distinctive culture.

But if he did that, the strong multiculturalist would no longer be faithful to his general principle. Instead, he would have become a *really strong* multiculturalist, someone whose commitment to respecting a culture was so strong that he will stay its course no matter what. But that would mean that he wasn't a multiculturalist at all since if he sticks with the distinctiveness of a culture even at the point where it expresses itself in a determination to stamp out the distinctiveness of some other culture, he will have become (what I think every one of us always is) a uniculturalist. It may at first seem counterintuitive, but given the alternative modes of multiculturalism—boutique multiculturalism, which honors diversity only in its most superficial aspects because its deeper loyalty is to a universal potential for rational choice; strong multiculturalism, which honors diversity in general but cannot honor a particular instance of diversity insofar as it refuses (as it always will) to be generous in its turn; and really strong multiculturalism, which goes to the wall with a particular instance of diversity and is therefore not multiculturalism at all—no one could possibly *be* a multiculturalist in any interesting and coherent sense.[10]

The reason that this will sound counterintuitive is that multiculturalism and its discontents are all people are talking about these days. Is everyone arguing about something that doesn't exist? An answer to that question will require a fresh beginning to our analysis and the introduction of a new distinction between multiculturalism as a philosophical problem and multiculturalism as a demographic fact. Multiculturalism as a philosophical problem is what we've been wrestling with in the preceding passages, with results not unlike those achieved (if that is the word) by Milton's fallen angels who try to reason about fate, foreknowledge, and free will and find themselves "in wandering mazes lost."[11] We too become lost in mazes if we think of multiculturalism as an abstract concept that we are called upon either to affirm or reject. But if we think of multiculturalism as a demographic fact—the fact that in the United States today many cultural traditions flourish and make claims on those who identify with them—the impulse either to affirm or reject it begins to look rather silly. Saying yes or no to multiculturalism seems to make about as much sense as saying yes or no to history, which will keep on rolling along irrespective of the judgment we pass on it.

Not that there is nothing to say once you have recognized that multiculturalism is a demographic fact; it is just that what you say will have more to do with the defusing of potential crises than the solving of conceptual puzzles. We may never be able to reconcile the claims of difference and community in a satisfactory formula, but we may be able to figure out a way for *these* differences to occupy the civic and political space of *this* community without coming to blows. "All societies," Taylor observes in "The Politics of Recognition," "are becoming increasingly multicultural"; as a result, "substantial numbers of people who are citizens" of a particular country are also members of a culture "that calls into question" that country's "philosophical boundaries" (63). What we "are going to need . . . in years to come," Taylor predicts, is some "inspired adhoccery."[12]

I want to take the phrase "inspired adhoccery" seriously. What it means is that the solutions to particular problems will be found by regarding each situation-of-crisis as an opportunity for improvisation and not as an occasion for the application of rules and principles (although the invoking and the recharacterizing of rules and principles will often be components of the improvisation). Any solution devised in this manner is likely to be temporary—that is what ad hoc means—and when a new set of problems has outstripped its efficacy, it will be time to improvise again. It follows then that definitions of multiculturalism will be beside the point, for multiculturalism will not be one thing but many things, and the many things it will be will weigh differently in different sectors of the society. In some sectors multiculturalism will take care of itself; in others its problematic will hardly register; and in others it will be a "problem" that must be confronted.

It will not, however, typically be a philosophical or theoretical problem. Multiculturalism in the workforce? Projections of demographic patterns indicate that in the foreseeable future the workforce will be largely made up of women and minorities; accordingly, corporations have already begun to change their recruiting patterns. It is clear, Corning CEO James Houghton has said, that no company can afford a predominantly white, male workforce. Neither can a company afford a workplace driven by racial and ethnic tensions; and therefore the same bottom-line consideration that is altering hiring and promotion policies is also mandating sensitivity programs, a more consultative organizational structure, and decentered management. In short, for the business world it's multiculturalism or die.

The same formula applies, for different reasons, to colleges and universities. When the college population was relatively small and homogeneous, it was a matter of neither concern nor surprise that the range of cultural materials studied was restricted to the books produced by earlier generations of that same homogeneous population. But when the GI bill brought many to college who would otherwise not have thought to go, and when some of those newly introduced to the academy found that they liked it and decided to stay on as faculty members, and when the rising tide of feminist consciousness led women to no longer be willing to sacrifice their careers to the ambitions of their husbands, and when a college degree became a prerequisite for employment opportunities previously open to high school graduates, and when immigration after the Korean and Vietnam Wars added large numbers of motivated students to a growing cultural mix, and when pride in ethnic traditions (stimulated in part by the extraordinary impact of the television miniseries *Roots*) weakened the appeal of the "melting pot" ideal, the pressures to include new materials in the classroom and to ask that they be taught by members of the cultures or subcultures from which they were drawn seemed to come from all directions. Although multiculturalism is sometimes characterized as a conscious strategy devised by insurgent political groups desirous of capturing America's cultural space so that it can be turned over to alien ideas, in fact it is a development that was planned by no one. As an effect it was decidedly overdetermined; and now that it is here, those who wish to turn the clock back will find themselves increasingly frustrated.

To be sure there will always remain a few colleges (like Hillsdale in Michigan) that set themselves up as the brave defenders of the beachheads others have ignominiously abandoned, but by and large, at least in the world of education, multiculturalism is a baseline condition rather than an option one can be either for or against. Indeed, in many facets of American life there is no multiculturalism issue despite the fact that it is endlessly debated by pundits who pronounce on the meaning of democracy, the content of universal rights, the nature of community, the primacy of the individual, and so on. These mind-numbing abstractions may be the official currency of academic discussion, but they do not point us to what is really at stake in the large social and economic dislocations to which they are an inadequate (and even irrelevant) response. In and of themselves they do no genuine work and insofar as they do any work it is in the service of the adhoccery to which they are rhetorically opposed.

I would not be misunderstood as recommending adhoccery; my point, rather, is that adhoccery will be what is going on despite the fact that the issues will be framed as if they were matters of principle and were available to a principled resolution. As we have seen, there are principles aplenty—autonomy, respect, toleration, equality—but when they are put into play by sophisticated intelligences, the result is not resolution but a sharpened sense of the blind alleys into which they lead us. Here, for example, is Amy Gutmann asking a series of questions to which she apparently thinks there are answers: "Should a liberal democratic society respect those cultures whose attitudes of ethnic or racial superiority . . . are antagonistic to other cultures? If so, how can respect for a culture of ethnic or racial superiority be reconciled with the commitment to treating all people as equals? If a liberal democracy need not or should not respect such 'supremacist' cultures, even if those cultures are highly valued by many among the disadvantaged, what precisely are the moral limits on the legitimate demand for political recognition of particular cultures?"[13]

You will recognize in these questions the interlocking quandaries that led me to conclude that multiculturalism is an incoherent concept that cannot be meaningfully either affirmed or rejected. But this is not Gutmann's conclusion. In good liberal-rationalist fashion, she regards the difficulties she uncovers as spurs to a greater conceptual effort, and she sets herself the task of coming up with a formulation that will rescue us from a world of entrenched "political battlefields" and point the way to "mutually respectful communities of substantial, sometimes even fundamental, intellectual disagreement" (20). What is remarkable about this statement is its reproduction of the dilemmas it claims to resolve and the determined (if unintentional) evasion of the difficulties these dilemmas present. The vocabulary will not stand up to even the most obvious lines of interrogation. How respectful can one be of "fundamental" differences? If the difference is fundamental—that is, touches basic beliefs and commitments—how can you respect it without disrespecting your own beliefs and commitments? And on the other side, do you really show respect for a view by tolerating it, as you might tolerate the buzzing of a fly? Or do you show respect when you take it seriously enough to oppose it?

It is these and related questions that Gutmann begs and even hides from herself by inserting the word "intellectual" between "fundamental" and "disagreement." What "intellectual" does is limit disagreement to matters that can be debated within the decorums of Enlightenment rationalism. Fiercer disagreements, disagreements marked by the refusal of either party to listen to reason, are placed beyond the pale where, presumably, they occupy the status of monstrosities, both above and below our notice (above our notice when they are disagreements over matters of religion, below our notice when they are disagreements between groups that want not to talk to each other but to exterminate each other). As a result, the category of the fundamental has been reconfigured—indeed, stood on its head—so as to exclude conflicts between deeply antithetical positions, that is, to exclude conflicts that are, in fact, fundamental.

The sleight of hand involved here is nicely illustrated by Gutmann's example of a disagreement that she says can be pursued in the context of mutual respect, the disagreement between the prochoice and prolife parties in the abortion debate. It is an example that tells against the principle it supposedly supports; for as everyone knows, strong prolife advocates regard prochoicers as either murderers or supporters of murderers, while in the eyes of prochoicers, prolife advocates are determined to deprive women of the right to control their own bodies. The disagreement between them is anything but intellectual because it is so obviously fundamental. In an intellectual disagreement the parties can talk to one another because they share a set of basic assumptions; but in a fundamental disagreement, basic assumptions are precisely what is in dispute. You can either have fundamental or you can have intellectual, but you can't have both, and if, like Gutmann, you privilege intellectual, you have not honored the level of fundamental disagreement—you have evaded it.

Gutmann does it again when she turns to the vexed issue of campus hate speech. Here the question is "How can we have a community of mutually respectful cultures when it is a practice in some cultures to vilify the members of others?"[14] It looks like an intractable problem, but Gutmann solves it, she thinks, by distinguishing between differences one merely tolerates and differences one respects. You respect a difference when you see it as a candidate for serious moral debate; it has a point even though it is not your point. But some differences are asserted so irrationally that debate is foreclosed, and those differences, while they must be tolerated in a free society, must also be denounced by all right-thinking persons. Hate speech—speech directed against women, Jews, blacks, and gays—falls into the second category; it is "indefensible on moral and empirical grounds" (23).

This seems neat and satisfying until one realizes that the "moral and empirical grounds" on the basis of which the arguments of certain speakers are judged "indefensible" have not been elaborated. Rather, they are simply presupposed, and presupposed, too, is their normative status. In effect Gutmann is saying, "Well, everybody knows that some assertions just aren't worth taking seriously." This is the result of withdrawing the offending opinions from the circle of rationality: a blind eye is turned toward the impact they might have on the world by assuming—without any empirical evidence whatsoever—that they will have none, that only crazy people will listen to crazy talk. With that assumption in place—and it is in place before she begins—the community of mutually respectful disputants has been safely constituted by the simple strategy of exiling anything that might disturb it.

No wonder that within its confines disputants exercise mutual respect, since mutuality (of an extremely pallid kind) has been guaranteed in advance, as problems are solved by being defined out of existence.[15] Once hate speech (a designation its producers would resist) has been labeled "radically implausible" (22) (and plausibility is added to the abstractions whose essentialist shape Gutmann blithely assumes), it is no more threatening than a belch or a fart—something disagreeable, to be sure, but something we can live with, especially since the category of the "we" has been restricted to those who already see things as Gutmann does.

In the end, the distinction between what is to be respected and what is tolerated turns out to be a device for elevating the decorum of academic dinner parties to the status of discourse universals while consigning alternate decorums to the dustbin of the hopelessly vulgar. In the expanded edition of the volume she edits, Gutmann is joined by Jürgen Habermas, who declines to admit religious fundamentalists into his constitutional republic because they "claim *exclusiveness* for a privileged way of life" and are therefore unfit for entry into "a civilized debate . . . in which one party can recognize the other parties as co-combatants in the search for authentic truths."[16] Of course, religious fundamentalists begin with the conclusion that the truths they hold are already authentic, but that is precisely why they will be denied entry to the ideal-speech seminar when it is convened. (I hear you knocking but you can't come in.) Fundamentalists and hate speakers might seem an odd couple; what links them and makes them candidates for peremptory exclusion is a refusal to respect the boundaries between what one can and cannot say in the liberal public forum. (You can't say kike and you can't say God.) Although the enemies named by Gutmann and Habermas are different, they are dispatched in the same way, not by being defeated in combat but by being declared ineligible before the fight begins.

The result is the kind of "civilized" conversation dear to the hearts of academic liberals who believe, on the model of the-world-as-philosophy-seminar, that any differences between "rational" persons can be talked through. It is finally a faith in talk—in what liberals call open and inclusive dialogue—that underwrites a program like Gutmann's. But the dialogue is not really open at all, as we can see when she sets down the requirements for entry: "Mutual respect requires a widespread willingness and ability to articulate our disagreements, to defend them before people with whom we disagree, to discern the difference between respectable and disrespectable agreement, and to be open to changing our own minds when faced with well-reasoned criticism" (24). Words like "widespread" and "open" suggest a forensic table to which all are invited, but between them is the clause that gives the lie to the apparent liberality—"to discern the difference between respectable and disrespectable disagreement"—which means of course to decide in advance which views will be heard and which will be dismissed. It is a strange openness indeed that is defined by what it peremptorily excludes.

It is not my intention, however, to fault Gutmann for not being open enough. Quite the reverse. It is her desire to be open that is the problem, because it prevents her from taking the true measure of what she recognizes as an evil. If you wish to strike a blow against beliefs you think pernicious, you will have to do something more than exclaim, "I exclude you from my community of mutual respect." That kind of exclusion will be no blow to an agenda whose proponents are not interested in being respected but in triumphing. Banishing hate speakers from your little conversation leaves them all the freer to pursue their deadly work in the dark corners from which you have averted your fastidious eyes.

Gutmann's instinct to exclude is the right one; it is just that her gesture of exclusion is too tame—it amounts to little more than holding her nose in disgust—and falls far short of wounding the enemy at its heart. A deeper wound will be inflicted only by methods and weapons her liberalism disdains: by acts of ungenerosity, intolerance, perhaps even repression, by acts that respond to evil not by tolerating it—in the hope that its energies will simply dissipate in the face of scorn—but by trying to defeat it. This is a lesson liberalism will never learn; it is the lesson liberalism is *pledged* never to learn because underlying liberal thought is the assumption that, given world enough and time (and so long as embarrassing "outlaws" have been discounted in advance), difference and conflict can always be resolved by rational deliberation, where by rational deliberation is meant the kind of deliberation routinely engaged in by one's circle of friends.

I remarked earlier that producers of what is called hate speech would not accept that description of their words, words they would hear as both rational and true. In arguments like Gutmann's and Habermas's, rationality is a single thing whose protocols can be recognized and accepted by persons of varying and opposing beliefs. In this model (as in Rockefeller's), differences are superficial, and those who base political and social judgments on them are labeled irrational. But if rationality is always differential, always an engine of exclusion and boundary-making, the opposition is never between the rational and the irrational but between opposing rationalities, each of which is equally, but differently, intolerant.

What this means, finally, is that there is no such thing as hate speech, if you mean by that designation speech that would be judged hateful by an *independent* norm. Instead, there is speech that is hateful to some persons because it offends the ideals to which they pledge allegiance. To those who produce the speech, however, it is not hateful but needful, and they will hear as hateful (or perverse or dangerous) speech that offends against *their* ideals. An utterance is hate speech so long as someone or group will find it objectionable, and since this is a requirement almost any utterance will meet, hate speech is not a limitable category and can be anything (that's why it is no thing), even the Declaration of Independence or the Golden Rule. It follows, then, that hate speech and rationality cannot be *generally* opposed, for whether a form of speech is one or the other will depend on the prior investments of those who produce and receive it. Hate speech, so called, is always at once someone's rationality and someone else's abomination.

This leads to the perhaps startling but inevitable conclusion that hate speech (or rather speech hateful to some) is rational and that its nature as a problem must be rethought. Indeed, it is only when hate speech is characterized as irrational that the label "problem" seems appropriate to it, and also comforting, because a problem is something that can be treated, either by benign neglect (don't worry, it's a fringe phenomenon that will never catch on) or by education and dialogue (the answer to hate speech is more speech: remember Theroux and the Pakistani) or, in a darker view of the matter, by quarantine and excommunication (you have a disease and while we won't exterminate you, neither will we have anything to do with you). This is the entire spectrum of remedies in the liberal pharmacy, which can only regard hate speech as something we can live with or something we can cure or something we can't cure but can avoid by refusing to join a militia.

It is in relation to this spectrum that speech codes seem obviously counterproductive, either because they are an overstrong response to a minor irritant, or because they stand in the way of the dialogue that will lead to health, or because they will only reinforce the paranoia that produced the problem in the first place. Everything changes, however, once hate speech is seen not as evidence of some cognitive confusion or as a moral anomaly but as the expression of a morality you despise, that is, as what your enemy (not the universal enemy) says.[17] If you think of hate speech as evidence of moral or cognitive confusion, you will try to clean the confusion up by the application of good reasons; but if you think that hate speakers, rather than being confused, are simply wrong—they reason well enough but their reasons are anchored in beliefs (about racial characteristics, sexual norms, and so on) you abhor—you will not place your faith in argument but look for something stronger.[18] The difference between seeing hate speech as a problem and seeing it as what your enemy says is that in response to a "problem" you think in terms of therapy and ask of any proposal "Will it eliminate the pathology?" whereas in response to what your enemy says, you think in terms of strategy and ask of any proposal "Will it retard the growth of the evil I loathe and fear?"

The advantage of this shift is that it asks a real question to which there can be a variety of nuanced answers. When you ask, as liberals always do, "Will speech codes dispel racism and remove prejudice from the hearts of those who now display it?" the answer can only be no, which, I would say, points not to the inadequacy of speech codes but to the inadequacy of the question. The demand that speech codes dispel racism trades on the knowledge (which I share with antiregulation liberals) that racism cannot be altered by external forces; it is not that kind of thing. But the fact that it is not that kind of thing does not mean that there is nothing to be done; it merely means that whatever we do will stop short of rooting out racism at its source (as we might succeed in doing if it were a disease and not a way of thinking) and that the best we can hope for is a succession of tactical victories in which the enemy is weakened, discomforted, embarrassed, deprived of political power, and on occasion routed.[19]

This, however, is not a small basket of hopes, and, what's more, the hopes are realizable. If you think of speech codes not as a magic bullet capable of definitive resolution but as a possible component of a provisional strategy, you no longer have to debate them in all-or-nothing terms. You can ask if in this situation, at this time and in this place, it would be reasonable to deploy them in the service of your agenda (which, again, is not to eliminate racism but to harass and discomfort racists). The answer will often be no, and, in fact, that is my usual answer; for in most cases speech codes will cause more problems than they solve, and, all things considered, it will often be the better part of wisdom to tolerate the sound of hate and murmur something about sticks and stones and the value of free expression.

At that moment you will be talking like a liberal, but there's nothing wrong with that as long as you don't take your liberalism too seriously and don't hew to it as a matter of principle. Just as speech codes become thinkable once they are no longer asked to do impossible things, so do liberal platitudes become usable when all you want from them is a way of marking time between the battles you think you can win. Switching back and forth between talking like a liberal and engaging in distinctly illiberal actions is something we all do anyway; it is the essence of adhoccery, which is a practice that need not be urged because it is the only one available to us.

FISH ON THE FIRST

II

5

THE RHETORIC OF REGRET

My argument against hewing to liberal platitudes as a matter of principle is also an argument against the dream of procedural justice. In a system of procedural justice—by which I mean what everyone else means: justice which in its unfolding is neutral between competing moralities or lifestyles or visions of the good—the fact that you are a man or woman, rich or poor, black or white, straight or gay, Democrat or Republican, theist or atheist will be irrelevant to the determination of whether your rights have been abridged or whether you have committed a crime. It follows, then, that rights themselves are defined independently of those same variables (you have them no matter who you are or what you believe) and that crimes are defined in relation to rules (thou shalt not kill, thou shalt not steal, thou shalt not bear false witness) that are general in the sense of not being hostage to a particular and contestable point of view. It is not "You have rights to property legally acquired if you are Christian and a man" but "You have rights to property legally acquired, period." It is not "Thou shalt not kill, except if you kill a nigger or an Indian or a queer" but "Thou shalt not kill, period."

Of course these very examples alert us to the unhappy fact that in our own history, procedural justice has been contaminated by the very value judgments it supposedly brackets. There was a time, and it was a long time, when women did not enjoy the free use of their property, in part because they were considered by those who made the laws—that is, by men—not fully capable of ordering their affairs. And there was a time, within my living memory, when crimes against African Americans were either condoned or ignored. And many Americans do not need the recent controversies about gays in the military to remind them that in some states in the nation, homosexuals are even now regarded by the law as either criminals or as potential criminals should they decide to translate their sexual orientation into actions. These examples do not necessarily embarrass the champions of procedural justice, who will acknowledge the mistakes that have been made along the way but insist that, however distressing some aspects of our past performance may be, we are nevertheless going in the right direction, as the law, in Ronald Dworkin's words, continues to "work itself pure," where pure means *procedurally* pure, unadulterated by substantive biases, a law that is truly blind: color-blind, gender-blind, race-blind, ideology-blind, sexual-orientation-blind.

One place where this goal seems at least to have been approximated is in First Amendment jurisprudence, which after many false starts—or so the standard histories tell us—has arrived at what the framers meant when they said that Congress shall make no law abridging freedom of speech. They meant that *all* forms of speech, like all colors or genders or races, are to be tolerated indifferently, no matter what their content. Perhaps the strongest formulation of this mature understanding is a pronouncement by Justice Powell in a 1974 case, *Gertz v. Robert Welch, Inc.*: "Under the First Amendment there is no such thing as a false idea. However pernicious an opinion may seem, we depend for its correction not on the conscience of judges, but on the competition of other ideas."[1] The word "seem" in the second sentence is the key to the logic here: an idea may *seem* pernicious, even to persons in high positions, but the First Amendment prohibits us from making such judgments, which must be left to time and the marketplace of ideas. Thus interpreted, the First Amendment is an exemplary instance of procedural justice: it identifies an activity—speech or expression—in minimally physical terms and without reference to substantive determinations; and then it puts the majesty of the law squarely behind the right of anyone saying anything to engage in that activity.

In what follows I shall be asking two related questions. First, is this a possible thing to do? Can one in fact devise a procedural mechanism that is no way hostage to judgments of substance? And, second, is it a *good* thing to do? My answer to both questions will be no, and I propose

FISH ON THE FIRST

to begin developing that answer by examining a sentence from a recent book, *Free Speech in an Open Society,* by Rodney Smolla. Here is the sentence: "A professor should have the right to espouse bona fide academic opinions concerning racial characteristics or capabilities, even though most people of good will and good sense on the campus would find the opinions loathsome."[2] Every time I read this sentence I am moved to ask "What does Smolla mean by 'bona fide?'" What could he *possibly* mean by it? The problem is not the phrase itself, which bears the perfectly ordinary meaning of "authentic" or "genuine"; the problem is the opposition established in the sentence between the judgment of value inherent in "bona fide" and the collective judgments of "most people of good will and good sense on the campus." If such persons are joined in their rejection of the opinions in question, in what sense are they bona fide? Or, to pare the question down to its core, what is the *content* of bona fide?

There are two possible answers. On the one hand, bona fide may be a purely formal requirement that has no content whatsoever, in which case a bona fide *academic* opinion would be any opinion that came out of the mouth of someone who had a degree and an appointment in a department. (Or, in an alternative, internal, formalistic reading, the "good faith" sense of "bona fide" could be emphasized and a professor could freely say anything—"the trouble with the Holocaust is that it didn't kill more Jews"—so long as he sincerely believed it.) This would square with the sentence's severing of bona fide from the properties of good will and good sense, but it would imply an oddly impoverished notion of what it means to be an academic and one that certainly would not be ratified by deans and tenure committees, for whom good sense—as defined by the prevailing norms in a discipline—is a bottom-line criterion. The alternative is to read bona fide as if it had a content, as if it marked a distinction between the legitimate and the illegitimate, between opinions worth paying attention to and opinions that are not. This would have the advantage of putting some life into the phrase— bona fide would now have some substantive bite—but at the expense of the disjunction between academic freedom and good sense that makes the assertion of freedom as strong as Smolla apparently wants it to be.

Smolla is thus in a perfect bind; either he really means something by bona fide, in which case professors are constrained in what they are able to say—they can't freely and without fear of disciplinary action say things that aren't bona fide—or bona fide is without its usual honorific significance and will be the imputed property of anything said by a professor, no matter how outlandish, uninformed, and nonsensical. The bind is not of Smolla's making but is given to him by a view of the First Amendment in which what the amendment protects is the production of noise (because it is indifferent to what the noise means or to whether or not it means anything). In the context of that view it is hard to make coherent sense, since coherence and sense have been dispensed with as criteria of judgment. The result is the embarrassment of a phrase like "bona fide," which is a vestigial survivor in the sentence of a value system that the sentence is in the process of abandoning.

This is a nice example of what Alisdair MacIntyre is referring to when he talks (in *After Virtue*) about the shards of a moral vocabulary that no longer has a point of reference in relation to which it might be intelligible. A literary analogue would be the inability of the fallen angels in Milton's *Paradise Lost* to produce sentences that do not fall apart in their mouths. Having severed their connection with the only source of value in the universe, they are reduced to saying things like we are "Surer to prosper than prosperity/ Could have assur'd us" (II, 39–40); one would be as hard put to assign a meaning to "sure" or "prosperity" in Satan's utterance as we are to assign meaning to "bona fide" in Smolla's.

Smolla, however, is not Satan. (He does not declare, "evil be thou my good.") He is just a liberal, and as a liberal he does not want to abandon the perspective of morality, of substantive justice; he wants merely to remove it from the precincts of First Amendment determinations. When he insists that the possibly racist opinions of professors must be tolerated in the name of academic freedom, he does not tolerate them personally and he would no doubt include himself on the side of those with good will and good sense. He states unequivocally that "hate speech should be fought by all citizens of good will" because "it is an abomination, a rape of human dignity" (169) and because "the elimination of racism is *itself* enshrined in our Constitution as a public value of the highest order" (156). If he were asked, I am sure Smolla would see no contradiction between these strong expressions of value and his extension of First Amendment protection to racist views; rather, he would see their conjunction as evidence of the strength of his First Amendment position, which commits him to the defense of speech acts he despises.

The stance is a familiar one, whether it derives from Voltaire or the ACLU, and those who strike it often imagine themselves as First

Amendment heroes, bravely rising above their mere preferences and prejudices in order to stand up for an abstract principle. The principle is that under the constitution there is no such thing as a false idea, and that therefore ideas are to be let into the public air indiscriminately. The problem is that everyone, including the strong defenders of the principle, discriminates between ideas all the time, not because of a failure to live up to a principle but because the formulation of expression is itself a discriminatory activity: you only say something against the background of things you could have said and chose to suppress. The fact that a phrase like "bona fide" finds its way into Smolla's disavowal of value judgments does not mean that he should have cleaned his sentence up; it means that *he couldn't have,* because neither he nor anyone else could write a sentence or have a thought purged of the discriminatory impulses he would have us bracket or suppress.

Someone like Smolla is laboring under an impossible (self-imposed) requirement: he must continue to be full of the values that make him what and who he is—he must continue to be a person of substance—and at the same time enact the supposedly higher value of setting his values aside in the name of procedural purity. The resulting strain (not to say schizophrenia) produces the awkwardness of "bona fide," but it has far more consequential effects in the decisions of appellate and Supreme Court judges, where it takes the form of what I call the rhetoric of regret.

You know you are hearing the rhetoric of regret when a judge tells you that he hates the activity he is about to allow, has contempt for those who are engaging in it, and profound sympathy for those who are its victims. This stuff is really terrible, the people trafficking in it are really awful, and you are their innocent victims, but nevertheless . . .

That is the sound of regret being performed, and never has the performance been so elaborate and "heartfelt" as in the case of *Collin v. Smith,* the Skokie case.[3] The facts of the case are well known: as part of a campaign of provocation, a neo-Nazi group called the National Socialist Party of America led by Frank Collin announced its intention to demonstrate in the village of Skokie, Illinois, the home, not incidentally, of many survivors of the Holocaust. The purpose of the demonstration was clear. Collin spoke of using the First Amendment against "the Jew"; that is, he counted on provoking a response from the Holocaust survivors that would allow him to portray himself as a First Amendment hero. "I planned the reaction of the Jews," he boasted, and one of his followers was even more forthright: "I hope they're terrified . . . I hope they're shocked. Because we're coming to get them again. I don't care if someone's mother or father or brother died in the gas chambers. The unfortunate thing is not that there were six million Jews who died. The unfortunate thing is that there were so many Jewish survivors."[4]

Not surprisingly, statements like this one, reported in the *Chicago Sun Times,* produced the desired reaction, and the village elders (in this case a literal, not a metaphorical, descriptive) passed several ordinances (including an insurance requirement the NSPA would have been unable to meet) designed to block the demonstration. Their efforts failed when two members of a three-judge panel held the ordinances unconstitutional under the First Amendment, saying among other things that it was the business of the court to protect "the activity in which appellees wish to engage, not to render moral judgment on their views or tactics" (1201). That is to say, the court declares itself to be neutral with respect to moral questions because (and the citation is inevitable) "under the First Amendment there is no such thing as a false idea" (1203).

Like Smolla, however, the majority judges know a false idea when they see one; and, again like Smolla, they want to assure the world that they are on the right side. Hence the rhetoric of regret, which begins in the second sentence of the opinion's first section, just after the recital of facts: "We would hopefully surprise no one by confessing personal views that NSPA's beliefs and goals are repugnant to the core values held generally by residents of this country, and, indeed, to much of what we cherish in civilization. As judges sworn to defend the constitution, however, we cannot decide this or any other case on that basis. Ideological tyranny, no matter how worthy its motivation, is forbidden as much to appointed judges as to elected legislators" (1200).

This is an amazing sequence. It begins with Judge Pell, speaking for himself and his fellows in the majority, announcing his "personal" morality, which is, he says, wholly opposed to the morality of the NSPA. The word "personal" is not casually used here; it contains a familiar First Amendment argument: each of us has his or her strong views, but we should be wary of imposing those views as if they were everyone's. But as the sentence unfolds, it turns out that in this instance Pell's views *are* everyone's; they are not, strictly speaking, personal at all, for they correspond (as he says) to the core values held generally by residents of this country. "Core" values are values that sustain an enterprise, and in this case what they sustain is the enterprise of American democracy.

In the next part of the sentence the ante is upped even higher when the enterprise is reidentified as *civilization* itself and all we cherish in it. If this is what is endangered by "NSPA's beliefs and goals," then it is hard to see the rationale for tolerating the organization's activities, for as a lower court acknowledged in passing, "If any philosophy should be regarded as completely unacceptable to civilized society, that of the plaintiffs, who . . . have . . . deliberately identified themselves with a regime whose record of brutality and barbarism is unmatched in modern history, would be a good place to start" (1203).

But Pell declines to start there because, he says, to do so would be to commit "ideological tyranny," which is forbidden no matter how worthy its motivation. "Worthy" here is like "bona fide" in Smolla's sentence; it belongs to a vocabulary of moral judgment that is being discounted, and therefore it produces a logical puzzle: how can something worthy in its motivation be "tyranny"? One knows what Pell means: the desire to prevent further harm to those who have already suffered extraordinary physical and psychological pain is a worthy one, but in order to realize that worthy desire we would have to suppress a viewpoint, and that is tyranny. This makes a certain kind of sense until you remember that Pell himself has characterized this "viewpoint" as the very *type* of tyranny and implied that his judgment is pretty much (the NSPA would of course be the exception) a universal one. He is drawing on the (sociological) fact that if you want a short-hand way of demonizing an agenda, you associate it with Nazism, and if you want to establish the enormity of a disaster, you call it a Holocaust. These equivalencies are not parochial; they embody the considered judgment of civilization, and it is only when civilization's values are bracketed that a determination to preserve them can be called "ideological tyranny." It is only by taking the content out of tyranny and making it an epistemological crime—a crime one commits against Immanuel Kant—that tyranny can be equated with the protection of defenseless men and women.

It might seem that the example is too easy a one, and that I am trading on Nazism's status as an ideology no one (or almost no one) would want to be associated with. What if the demonized agenda in an analogous situation were affirmative action or planned parenthood or the right to die or gun control? Would I still be happy to see those who favored it prevented from marching in Skokie?

The question (which will surely arise) misses my point, which is not that *I* regard neo-Nazi propaganda as a threat to civilization but that

Pell believes it to be one and yet decides to allow its dissemination. As usual my own position on the substantive issue cannot be deduced from my analysis. It might well be that had I been on the bench that day I would have decided to permit the march, on the reasoning, perhaps, that the NSPA posed no real danger or that the danger presented by the march was outweighed by the danger (in present and future costs) of stopping it. Any such decision would have been made on empirical grounds, on a calculation of likely outcomes, and not on the grounds of principles thought to be indifferent to outcomes. It is the illogic of Pell's argument as he makes it—the illogic of first finding a discourse terribly dangerous and then encouraging its proliferation—and not the policy he finally settles on that is the object of my criticism. The message of this chapter is not that Nazi voices must be silenced but that the Court's argument for refusing to do so is incoherent.

That incoherence is on display in one of the opinion's most honest and affecting moments, when Pell acknowledges that "the proposed demonstration would seriously disturb, emotionally and mentally, at least some and probably many of the Village's residents" (1206). The acknowledgment is significant because it takes note of what many First Amendment arguments fail to recognize—the cognizable harms pro-duced by some forms of speech. But the harms are finally not taken seriously and serve only to heighten the rhetoric of regret and render it even less intelligible: "We . . . feel compelled once again to express our repugnance at the doctrine which the appellees desire to profess pub-licly. Indeed, it is a source of extreme regret that after several thousand years of attempting to strengthen the often thin coating of civilization with which humankind has attempted to hide brutal, animal-like instincts, there would still be those who would resort to hatred and vili-fication of fellow human beings because of their racial backgrounds or their religious beliefs or, for that matter, for any reason at all" (1210).

Here is the reference to civilization again, but with an added phrase—thin coating—that points up the oddness of the court's logic. If civiliza-tion is in fact only a thin coating, then why is it the obligation of civilization's chief officers—members of the judiciary—to protect an activity whose professed aim and historically achieved intention is to wear that coating away and thereby release the "brutal animal-like instincts" it holds down? The paragraph tells a powerful, even dramatic, story of val-ues under siege, but the tellers of that story decline to come to the defense of the values they so obviously cherish. What holds them back?

The short answer to this question is "the demands of procedural justice," which require that the state neither favor nor disfavor any particular conception of the good life. Nazism is such a conception, and no matter how distasteful it might be to Judge Pell or to you or to me, we must be wary of institutionalizing our own views in the form of laws or judicial decisions. But the logic of procedural justice loses some of its persuasiveness when it comes clothed in the rhetoric of regret. A procedural view of the First Amendment is appealing only if you assume that speech-induced harms, unlike the harms caused by a physical assault, are relatively minor, barely skin-deep inconveniences for which a ready remedy is available in the form of counterspeech. But that assumption cannot be squared with the rhetoric of regret as it unfolds here.

The court is not saying "It's too bad that we have to endure the experience of being subjected to such boorish sentiments, but our way of life is strong enough to survive them and will in fact be stronger if we tolerate them." Rather, it is saying that our way of life is a fragile achievement, no stronger than the thin coating that covers brutal instincts; and what's more, the court is identifying the NSPA's doctrine as an expression of the barbarity we have barely escaped. The court's regret, in short, is deep and reflects deep fears which strain against the confidence that underlies procedural justice, the confidence that by refusing to engage in value judgments the state assures the flourishing of values, at least of the values it most prizes.

Here in this passage Judge Pell comes close to acknowledging that this confidence is baseless and that a strong procedural view of the First Amendment may be subversive of everything the First Amendment supposedly protects. But in other sentences, this acknowledgment is kept at bay when the neo-Nazi agenda is redescribed in ways that diminish its threat. Only two paragraphs after having characterized the NSPA's goals as "repugnant" to the values of this country and of civilization in general, the organization is referred to as an "unpopular minority," and we are admonished to remember that it is the resolve to protect unpopular minorities "that distinguishes life in this country from life under the Third Reich" (1201).

Now I would have thought that what distinguished this country from the Third Reich was the fact that the Third Reich was dedicated to the extermination of the Jews and we weren't; and that such a policy, and the beliefs supporting it, were contrary to everything this country stands for and that therefore we were obliged to take negative note of the rise of neo-Nazi views. But if I were to say that, Pell would no doubt respond that what this country stands for is neutrality before all beliefs—that is, for procedural justice—and we stand up for *that* by allowing Nazis to have their say and make their case.

This makes sense, however, only if we believe either that Nazism is just another idea no different from other ideas which vie for our approval—in which case one wonders why we fought World War II—or if we believe that the differences will sort themselves out in the right direction without anyone's help. Either the eventual triumph of Nazism is something we can contemplate with equanimity, or we believe that Nazism is something especially horrendous but believe too that the world is so arranged that Nazism will wither under a policy of indifference and benign neglect. These views of Nazism are mutually exclusive, but they are simultaneously asserted when the Skokie Nazis become members of an "unpopular minority"—that is, they are either members of a group too marginal to fear or members of a group presently despised but perhaps destined, like the early Christians, to move into the center and become our truth. The curious thing is that Judge Pell believes neither of these things. He believes that Nazism is repugnant to civilization *and* that civilization is a precarious achievement in need of continual maintenance and protection; but as the guardian of procedural justice, he must contrive to forget his beliefs or to hide them from himself in the folds of a bland and softened vocabulary.

It is not, however, so easy as all that to detach yourself from your convictions, and they well up even in sentences from which they have supposedly been purged. Here is the concluding sentence of the majority opinion: "The result we have reached is dictated by the fundamental proposition that if these civil rights are to remain vital for all, they must protect not only those society deems acceptable, but also those whose ideas it quite justifiably rejects and despises" (1210). Pell's intention here is to restate for the last time the fundamental tenet of procedural justice: the protection of individual rights must not vary with the ideological commitments of particular citizens; rights are to be extended to everyone, not merely to those whose views society happens to approve. "Deems acceptable" strikes just the right skeptical note: what is deemed acceptable today may not be deemed so tomorrow when a view currently despised—Nazism perhaps?—will have replaced it. But the note is not sustained because when it comes time to relativize today's hated viewpoint, Pell cannot do it and instead of saying of Nazism that it is *currently* despised, he says that it is "quite justifiably" despised, where "quite justified" is not a qualified judgment, as in "justified given current and revisable norms," but means just plain justified, now, then, always. "Quite justifiably" is like "bona fide" in Smolla's sentence; it gives the lie to the assertion of content neutrality and acknowledges a perspective of certainty and judgment that has supposedly been repudiated.

Here one might object that my account of these matters is perverse because it leaves out the essential point: when strong First Amendment advocates like Smolla and Pell discount their personal values, they do so in the name of a higher value whose flourishing requires this act of self-abnegation. Just what that higher value is has often been a matter of dispute, but Pell's account of it (which he takes from *Police Department of Chicago v. Mosley*) is fairly representative: we must allow the expression of all speech, no matter what its content, in order to facilitate "the continued building of our politics and culture, and to assure self-fulfillment for each individual" (1202). This statement imagines democracy as an experiment always in process and asserts that the health of the process depends on not closing off any of the pathways it might want to explore, even if they are pathways that seem to most of us ("of good will and good sense") to be dark and forbidding.

Moreover, keeping the flow of information open is important not only to the growth of the culture but to the growth of its individual members, whose development or self-fulfillment requires a ready supply of contending viewpoints from which to pick and choose. Like the political culture he inhabits, the individual is himself in process and, again like the political culture, he must be protected from his own tendency to assume that the opinions he now holds are the right ones. He must experience the frustration of his present desire—the desire to see his opinions enacted into law—in order to achieve the maturity that awaits him in a future that will emerge only if he resists the attractions of premature judgment.

This account of the benefits to be derived from a strongly procedural view of the First Amendment—a view that forbids discrimination according to content—is coherent and powerful and is essentially the account offered 350 years ago by Milton in the *Areopagitica*. There is, however, one crucial difference: Milton, in a passage that has given his First Amendment admirers fits, announces that there is one form of doctrine, one idea, that will not be welcome in his marketplace. You understand, he says, that when I speak of a general toleration, I don't mean Catholics: "I mean not tolerated popery and open superstition, which as it extirpates all religious and civil supremacies, so itself should be extirpate," that is "destroyed" or "pulled up by the roots."[5] There might seem to be a contradiction between this discriminatory judgment and Milton's tract-long plea for toleration, but in fact, he would say, the maintenance of toleration requires this exception to it. Earlier he has told us that the toleration of many opinions is necessary if the waters of truth are to flow "in a perpetual progression" and not "sicken into a muddy pool of conformity and tradition" (310). But conformity and tradition, he has also told us, are exactly what is taught and urged by Catholicism, and therefore to tolerate the propagation of Catholic doctrine would be to endanger the goal—of perpetual progression—toleration serves. No law, Milton points out, can permit activity that constitutes an assault on it, no law, that is, that "intends not to unlaw itself."

Milton's point holds for any law that is purposive, any law that has a goal in the form of hoped-for consequences, whether that goal is the flourishing of the search for truth or the continual building of our culture or the self-fulfillment of the individual. There will always be a form of speech that is subversive of the goal speech is supposed to further, a form of speech whose effect is to impede the search for truth, or frustrate the building of our culture or block the self-fulfillment of the individual; and to those speech acts one will say what Milton says to Catholics: "I mean not tolerated _____." A strongly procedural First Amendment will always have a substantive kicker up its sleeve, one that will emerge in times of crisis. The higher value in whose name you are to refrain from content discriminations itself requires (because *it assumes*) a content discrimination if it is to be honored and maintained.

The only way out of this corner, the only way for procedural justice to be truly procedural and not covertly substantive, is for the First Amendment to have no goal or purpose whatsoever. This is a position almost no one holds, but it is held, apparently, by William Van Alstyne, who writes, "The First Amendment does not link the protection it provides with any particular objective and may, accordingly, be deemed to operate without regard to anyone's view of how well the speech it protects may or may not serve such an objective."[6] Or, in other words, "Ask not what the First Amendment does for you"; it is a principle which brooks no interrogation and welcomes no inquiry into the absoluteness of its ways. If you ask the First Amendment to explain itself or provide a pedigree for its authority, it will not answer, saying in effect, "I am what I am."

This of course is the language of divinity, and it is at least ironic that a secularist like Van Alstyne would lay bare the theological claims implicit in a strong First Amendment position. For if you sunder the First Amendment's operation from the determination of value (on the reasoning that values are relative to persons and therefore not an appropriate basis for a general rule), then that operation is pointing in no direction except back at itself; it becomes its own value, unaccountable and unassailable. It becomes God.

Here then is the choice: either a true proceduralism that disallows any inquiry either into its rationale or its effects, or a Milton-like exercise of substantive judgment in which it is determined that the meaning of free speech can be honored only by suppressing an instance of it. I obviously prefer the second of these alternatives, but merely to articulate it is to provoke two strong (and, for many, conclusive) objections. The first usually takes the form of a series of questions. Who is to make the determination that a particular kind of speech is subversive of the value speech is supposed to support? Will not any such determination reflect preferences, moral or political, of some individual or group? Does not that person or group become vulnerable to the same act of suppression should there be a change in the structure of power? These questions point us to the second objection: once substantive considerations are allowed to inflect and infect First Amendment decisions, once you protect or suppress a particular form of speech because you either favor or fear the agenda it urged, you have no argument of *principle* against a speech policy motivated by a politics opposed to your own. Suppress Nazi rantings today and it will be Shakespeare tomorrow, which is exactly what Judge Pell says at an appropriately dramatic point: the ordinance designed to prevent the NSPA demonstration "could conceivably be applied to criminalize dissemination of *The Merchant of Venice*" (1207).

Notice here the usual double game of First Amendment argument: on the one hand Pell is saying that there is no way of distinguishing between neo-Nazi rantings and Shakespeare; but at the same time his warning—that we risk losing *The Merchant of Venice*—has force only if the distinction is assumed and if it is assumed, too, that everybody recognizes it (just as everyone recognizes that "NSPA's values and goals are repugnant" to everything we cherish). My point is a double one. First, the slippery-slope fear will not be realized because a society that values Shakespeare will act to prevent his disappearance; slippery-slope arguments work only in a vacuum, and in the real world the slide will be retarded by all the in-place investments that a slippery-slope argument rhetorically suspends. And, second, it is Shakespeare or some other already honored and preferred discourse that we wish to protect and *not* a principle in relation to which Shakespeare and neo-Nazi rantings are valued indifferently. Indeed, I would go further and say that what is at stake in First Amendment disputes is almost never a principle, even though it is in the vocabulary of principle that the argument is conducted.

Moreover, it is the habit of framing everything in terms of principle that makes people confused about what they really want and renders them vulnerable to certain argumentative ploys. In recent years, liberals have been discombobulated when a practice they abhor is defended by invoking the same principle they had themselves invoked in order to argue for a practice they favor. How can you, who so vigorously opposed the McCarthyite suppression of Marxists on certain campuses, now urge the suppression of neo-Nazis or anti-Semites or pornographers on those same campuses? By what principle can you be on one side of the free speech question in 1964 and on the other side in 1994? Or, how can you who worked for integration in the great civil rights struggles now condone all-black fraternities or separate dining tables or schools for young black males in the inner cities? The strategy that joins these questions is powerful because it renders your own history an obstacle to your present goals and purposes. In the past you have taken a stand and referred it to a principle, and now you are told that by the logic of that very principle you are committed to supporting the agenda of your enemy.

A nice illustration of the strategy and the problem it raises for liberals is provided by a front-page *New York Times* story in the issue of June 11, 1994. The story concerns a provision attached to a Senate crime bill that makes it unlawful for anyone "to obstruct, impede or otherwise interfere with hunters." Those opposed to the provision, usually liberals, point out that interference could be defined to include vigorous verbal criticism and that this would be an unconstitutional restriction on free speech; those supporting the provision, usually conservatives, retort that its language mirrors the language of a recently passed bill outlawing certain forms of demonstration at the entrance of abortion clinics. At the time the abortion-clinic protection bill was being debated, antiabortion groups predicted "that it would set a precedent that would later trip up the liberals who supported it," and it would now seem that this prediction has come true. If you are *for* restricting the speech of abortion protestors, how can you, in principle, be *against* restricting the speech of those, like animal rights activists, who protest against hunters?

Predictably, liberals who find themselves on the horns of this dilemma try to wriggle off by drawing distinctions between the two measures, arguing that one—the one they favor—is less an encroachment on speech rights than the other. But just as predictably, this drawing of ever-finer distinctions is unpersuasive and sounds just like what it is, an attempt to fudge a principle on which they have stood four-square in the past. That is, you know as you listen to these people that they are trying, desperately, to bring under a single umbrella of principle two policy preferences—being *for* protecting abortion clinics and *against* protecting hunters—that simply will not fit together.

What's a liberal to do? My answer is simple: forget about the principle (and therefore stop being a liberal), which was never what you were interested in in the first place, and make an argument for the policy on policy grounds, that is, on the grounds that you think it is good and right. Argue that civil rights supporters were not working for a color-blind society (even though it may have been rhetorically effective to use that language) but for better conditions for African Americans, and that today the achieving of better conditions might involve practices of voluntary segregation. Argue that in your view the presence of Marxists on campus is beneficial to education and the presence of bigots and racists is not, and that's all there is to it. Point out that there is no reason to afford protection to hunters, given the facts rehearsed in the *Times* story: that the "abortion bill was deemed necessary after more than 1000 acts of violence . . . at abortion clinics since 1977. They included at least 36 bombings, 81 cases of arson, 131 death threats, 84 assaults, two kidnappings and the shootings of two doctors, one of whom was killed." (More killings have since been added to the tally.) As for the hunters, the only known incident in the past fifteen years is one in which "a protestor in Montana jabbed a hunter with a ski pole," and he was quite appropriately prosecuted for assault.

In short, the so-called "hunters' rights" bill doesn't respond to any existing social conditions; it is an artifact of the obsession with principle.

It is only because we are so accustomed to justifying our political preferences by baptizing them in the waters of principle—of abstract rights and obligations—that some persons have been able to fashion a superficially appealing case for legislating remedies against harms that have never occurred. In fact there is evidence that the goal of the hunter-protection legislation is not the protection of hunters—how could it be, since no one is harassing them?—but the hoped-for invalidation of the abortion clinic protection legislation when the challenge to it reaches the Supreme Court. For if the empirical differences between the threat to abortion clinics and the threat to hunters can be overridden by an argument that makes them equivalent in principle, liberal judges might see no way of approving the one without approving the other and might decide to approve neither.

This is what almost always happens when the courts hand down a principled First Amendment decision: the issues that truly concern the parties disappear in the solvent of a so-called "higher" argument—an argument pitched at a level that refuses to recognize the legitimacy of what actual persons either fear or desire—with the result that substantive matters are displaced by the attenuated and attenuating logic of abstraction. When principle enters the picture and takes it over, no one is able to talk about what is really on his mind. A good example is the 1992 cross-burning case in Minneapolis, in the course of which it was repeatedly said that the plaintiffs (a black family, the only one in the neighborhood, on whose lawn a cross was burned) could have won on simple trespass and that there was therefore no need for a hate-crime law.[7] But it was not the trespass on its property by which the black family felt wounded, nor was trespass the crime the cross-burners wanted to commit.

That is what I meant earlier when I said that what is at stake in First Amendment disputes is never a principle, even though it is in the vocabulary of principle that the argument is usually conducted. Pornographers, Holocaust deniers, and cross-burners are not for free speech but for pornography, the denial of the Holocaust, and the intimidation of minorities. And on the other side, the homeless advocates who wish to sleep in federal parks, animal rights activists who heap scorn on fur-clad women, and antigovernment protestors who burn American flags are not for free speech either but for housing for the homeless, humane treatment of animals, and a change in U.S. policies.

In all these instances, the fact that free speech arguments migrate from one side of the debate to the other—"You are subverting the right of free expression"; "No, you are"—is a clear indication that the employment of free speech arguments is a strategy in the service of some agenda that is not identical with and does not follow from any free speech principle. Even when a free speech principle is being invoked "for itself" and not as a cover for a substantive politics—even, for example, when a court sincerely decides that a form of abusive or repugnant speech must be allowed in order to promote the search for truth—that principle, as we have seen, will contain its own substantive qualification. For if some form of speech is later found to be antithetical to the search for truth, the consequential logic of the principle will require that it be judged unworthy of protection.

But, again, who is to judge? By now you should see that this question, which I raised earlier, is simply another form of the strategy by which the everyday context in which judgments are made all the time is replaced by the abstract (principled) and substantively empty context in which judgment is by *definition* always impure. Who is to judge? Who is to draw the line? These are not serious questions, for those who pose them would be satisfied only if the judge were infallible and the line could be drawn once and for all; and all the while they know that there are no such judges and that a line drawn once in the context of this situation with these participants will have to be drawn again when the situation and the participants change. The questions, in short, are asked with the expectation (and hope) that they will not be answered, for then those who ask them can throw up their (clean) hands and say, "See, there is no *principled* way to do this, so let's not go down that road." Well, let's stipulate to the fact: there is no principled way to do this, but let's remember too that the principle upheld in *not* doing it—in not standing up for substantive justice when speech is productive of harms—is the principle of doing nothing, the principle, as the dissenting judge in *Collin v. Smith* put it, of "paralysis" (1211).

Who is to judge? How about the people whose job it is to judge—judges, administrators, mayors, governors, college presidents—all of those who by virtue of the positions they occupy have been assigned, and have accepted, the task of making decisions even when the lines are not perfectly clear and they are less than infallible. Exercising this responsibility is, of course, a risk, and the risk if it goes badly may have dire consequences. But there are also consequences to not exercising that responsibility, especially when, as in the Skokie case, there is no acknowledgment of the relative costs and benefits of deciding not to decide. "One might have hoped," writes Lee Bollinger, "for a full and rich appreciation of the gains to be had by protecting speech of that kind, a clear sense of the purpose or purposes behind the concept of free speech . . . and a consciousness of the costs of pursuing those purposes at the expense of other possible aims." But all we got, Bollinger laments, is a "tight doctrinal"—that is, procedural—"analysis that avoided rather than confronted the social meaning of what was being done." Bollinger then notes, as I have here, the presence of the rhetoric of regret: "When the judges peered out from behind the wall of doctrine, it was only to plead further helplessness through an argument about the inability to draw the distinctions required to decide the case the way they said they would personally have done."[8]

In the end what they said was we will not decide because we are not gods, to which I would reply, because none of us is a god some of us must decide, lest the imperatives of the moral life be given over to forces—called the marketplace of ideas—that are accountable to no one and bound to no vision except the antivision of chance and random fate.

6

FRAUGHT WITH DEATH

My analysis of the Skokie case is an extension of an argument I first made in an essay entitled "There's No Such Thing As Free Speech and It's a Good Thing Too."[1] By "there's no such thing as free speech," I meant three things. First, the act of speech, unless it is understood as the production of mere noise, is always at once constrained and constraining. Speech is constrained because one does not think to speak (or write) independently of some vision or agenda that, quite literally, *compels* assertion; speech therefore is not free because one is in the grip of compulsion—the softer word would be belief or conviction—at the moment of its production. Speech constrains because as an action impelled by belief and conviction it is always in the business (implicitly if not explicitly) of rejecting and stigmatizing the beliefs and convictions of others. You go to the trouble of asserting X because some other persons have been asserting Y, and in your view Y is false and perhaps dangerous; or you go to the trouble of asserting X because you think X is a truth insufficiently recognized and, again in your view, a world deprived of it is a world that is impoverished and perhaps diseased. You do not, in short, speak in order to encourage others to speak freely but in order to discourage others from disseminating or hearkening to error. You do not seek to enfranchise the community but to bind it to the truths you take to be salutary.

The second sense in which there is no such thing as free speech is captured in the proverbial saying "There is no such thing as a free lunch." Speech, like lunch, costs, and it costs for a reason that follows logically from sense #1: if utterance always works to advance some interests as defined by some agenda, its effectiveness will always be achieved at the expense of some other interests as defined by some other agenda. Someone always pays when speech takes.

And this leads directly to the third sense in which there is no such thing as free speech. There is no speech that is free of consequences—no speech, that is, whose impact can be confined to the sterilized and weightless atmosphere of a philosophy seminar (assumed as a model for the entire world by free speech ideologues). And because there is no speech free of consequences, a jurisprudence based on the identification of such a category of speech—a jurisprudence strongly invested in some form, however qualified, of the distinction between speech and action—will be fatally confused and engaged in activities it is incapable of acknowledging or even recognizing. It will be protecting something that doesn't exist, and therefore it will not be doing what it thinks and says it is doing.

It will, however, be doing something (it's hard not to), and the conclusion that follows from the several senses in which there is no such thing as free speech is that what it will be doing is enacting a politics. It is that conclusion that accounts for the hostile reception of my piece by First Amendment watchdogs. For it is axiomatic in the free speech community that the purpose of the First Amendment is to insulate the discussion and dissemination of ideas from political interference, a purpose that is supposedly realized when politics, in the form of governmental regulation, is forbidden to enter the precincts where speech is produced and consumed. It is my argument, however, that politics is already *inside* those precincts; for since speech is unimaginable apart from consequences and since the consequences of any piece of speech will be friendly to some interests and inimical to some others, the decision to draw a line between protected and regulated speech will always be a decision to advance some interests and discourage others, will always, that is, be a political decision. This does not mean that a First Amendment actor, once the line is drawn, will be performing politically; he or she will (or should) try to respect that line rather than manipulating it in order to serve a partisan purpose. It is just that the line being respected will itself be a contestable one, and it is in this (inevitable and incorrigible) sense that any First Amendment decision will be political.

One way of replying to this argument would be to declare *all* speech protected (draw *no* lines) and then step back and wait to see what happens (this is the "Time will tell" strategy). To this I would say, first, that while people are always declaring that they want to protect all speech, in practice they never follow through, for sooner or later some piece of verbal behavior will turn up and the would-be free speechers will protest "But we didn't mean *that*" and then invoke (or invent on the spot) some way of denying the label "speech" to the offending utterance. And even if it were the case that all speech was completely protected (including obscene speech, speech giving information to the country's enemies, low-value speech, fighting words, threatening words, etc.), it is not at all clear what would be the benefits of a policy that trusted everything to a future whose outlines were entirely obscure. In the rest of this chapter I shall analyze and critique this orientation-toward-the-future characteristic of First Amendment rhetoric in order to see if it is any more coherent than the other components of strong free speech polemics.

Let us begin with the thesis one is likely to find at the beginning of almost any First Amendment explication: *It is the function of the marketplace of ideas (and therefore of the toleration of expression) to allow the truth to emerge, and this end will not be furthered by the premature pronouncements of legislatures or courts.* Behind this thesis is what has been termed the "skeptical premise" underlying marketplace theory, the premise that the First Amendment protects (in the words of McGowan and Tangri) "the public interest in being free from potentially erroneous governmental determinations of speech" (888).[2] The premise is skeptical because it says that all determinations of truth, not only those made by the government, are, at best tentative, based as they necessarily are on nothing firmer than, in Robert Post's words, "the particular standards of a specific community" (CC, 659).[3] Since, as Post observes, the judgment of a community will always be biased, reliance on it will be fraught with long-run danger: "Whenever the state attempts definitively to determine the truth or falsity of a specific factual statement, it truncates a potentially infinite process of investigation, and therefore runs a significant risk of inaccuracy" (CC, 659).

The question I would ask is, "When will this risk be overcome?" And the answer, dictated by the skeptical logic of the premise, is "Never," at least if we remain within the secular precincts of First Amendment discussions. For if the process of investigation is "potentially infinite," cutting it off at *any* point short of revelation will truncate it and court the feared risk. And what exactly is that risk? It is the risk of proceeding on the basis of something less than the whole truth, of proceeding on the basis of the merely partial vision available to any "specific community." The problem is that the condition of partial vision is the condition of humanity; and if we are to be ruled by the fear of partiality (and this fear is the *content* of marketplace skepticism), then we would seem to preclude the possibility of decision and action altogether. If the marketplace will render its verdict only at the end of time (or, as Milton would have it, at Christ's second coming), the resolution of *timely* matters will be deferred forever.

In strong First Amendment arguments this conclusion is avoided by positing a realm of public discourse that somehow escapes, or is significantly insulated from, the pressures of partiality. As Post observes, this notion of public discourse "rests upon a very abstract logic" that requires "a constant effort to distance oneself from the assumptions and certitudes that define oneself and one's community" (CC, 637). Indeed, so abstract is the logic that, as Post acknowledges, "its value as an empirical description may be questioned" since no concrete practical solution of the kind that demands immediate action could link up with it. It is precisely in relation to context-specific "assumptions and certitudes" that moments of conflict arise, and the usefulness to such moments of a zone purged of everything that gives them urgency is at the very least questionable.

Public discourse theorists respond to this criticism by claiming (not surprisingly) an abstract usefulness that goes along with the abstract quality of their favored forum: the idea of "speech as pure communication . . . severed from its social context" must be regarded "as articulating" not a present reality but "a regulative ideal for the legal structure of public discourse" (CC, 641). The ideal, that is, does not correspond to any form of social organization now extant, and that is exactly why it can be urged as the condition to which all forms of social organization should aspire. To put it in another (unappetizing) way, the chief recommendation of the regulative ideal is that it is empty; it is unencumbered by any commitments or desires that might recommend themselves to politically situated agents. It is, in Post's words, formal and "extremely thin" (CH, 297).[4] Its values are "bloodless"—that is, they have insufficient substance to arouse anyone either to passionate affirmation or passionate denial—and perform "the wholly negative function of shielding speakers from the enforcement of community standards" (CC, 638). Yet despite, indeed because of, this thin bloodlessness, we are exhorted to prefer the abstraction of the ideal to "the experience of political participation by members of victim groups."[5] What this means is that, however many instances of injury harm can be demonstrably linked to verbal action, the temptations of regulation and discipline must be resisted in the name of a future that can have only the most formal—that is, substanceless—description.

This resolution to sacrifice the needs of men and women now suffering documentable harm to a bodiless hope explains the cheerful (almost gleeful) rehearsal of speech-related harms in opinions that finally rule against any remedial action. Thus in the landmark pornography case *American Booksellers Association, Inc. v. Hudnut*, the court gives eloquent testimony to the (often harmful) power of ideas expressed in speech: "A belief may be pernicious—the beliefs of Nazis led to the deaths of millions, those of the Klan to the repression of millions. A pernicious belief may prevail. Totalitarian governments today rule much of the planet, practicing suppression of billions and spreading dogma that may enslave others" (328).[6] These and other instances of the effects produced by speech ("Racial bigotry, anti-semitism, violence on television, reporter's biases") are marshaled *in support* of the contention by the drafters of an Indianapolis antipornography ordinance that "pornography affects thoughts, . . . is an aspect of dominance, . . . does not persuade people so much as change them, . . . works by socializing," and is therefore "not an idea" but "the injury" (328).

The court concedes that "there is much to this perspective" and goes so far as to declare, "We accept the premises of this legislation" (328–329). Nevertheless, the court proceeds to set its own conclusion aside under the reasoning that the evidence it has just cited with approval "simply demonstrates the power of pornography as speech" (329). That is to say, the fact that pornography has effects does not distinguish it from any other form of speech, which also has effects—"If pornography is what pornography does, so is other speech" (329)—and this general capacity of speech to be consequential is a reason for not attending to the consequences, however well documented, of pornography.

As a reason, however, this general capacity of speech to produce harmful effects is a two–edged sword; for it undermines the speech/action distinction on which the case for the nonregulation of speech rests. If speech is characterized (as the court characterizes it here) as inevitably productive of power, it loses the special status that exempts it from regulation, and the assimilation of pornography to other forms of speech—to *all* forms of speech—becomes an argument for the possible regulation of everything. It is not that the court fails to see this possibility; rather, it is this very possibility from which it recoils: "If the fact that speech plays a role in a process of conditioning were enough to permit governmental regulation, that would be the end of freedom of speech" (330).

This is an instance of one of the most interesting (and least commented on) moments in intellectual discourse, the moment (not at all unique to legal discourse) when the path of inquiry a practitioner is following points in a direction that fills him (or her or it) with horror, and as a result the inquiry is abandoned, short of its potentially distressing conclusion. Here the refused conclusion is not only "the end of freedom of speech" but the realization (implicit in everything the court says) that freedom of speech never had a beginning, because the condition that made it a coherent notion—the condition of speech as either behavior that is not action or as action without immediate worldly consequences and hence action that can take its purely cognitive course unencumbered by the world's pressures—does not obtain. If pornography is defined by what it *does* and is in this like all "other speech," then by an inevitable logic speech in general, also defined by what it does, is indistinguishable from action, and there is no rationale for not regulating it in the same pragmatic ways that other actions are regulated. Or, to put it another way (which brings us back to the formal, thin, bloodless nature of the free speech interest), if speech is in every sense an action, then the category of speech concerned only with the expression and assaying of ideas apart from any particular political agenda is empty, and in giving it up one would be giving up nothing.

In more than one place, Post comes very close to saying as much, and it is instructive to watch him as he endeavors to give some content to the abstraction he feels compelled to defend. Taking up the argument (central to the Indianapolis ordinance) that pornography is not expression "but is the *practice* of subordination itself," Post finds confirmation in J. L. Austin's notion of performatives—utterances that perform actions—and concludes that the recharacterization of pornography as a performative makes perfect sense, resting as it does "on rather profound insights into the manner in which social actions are constituted by speech" (CH, 327). No sooner has he reached this conclusion, however, than he turns away from it because it is "incompatible with any viable

FISH ON THE FIRST

notion of free speech." "The argument that pornography can be regulated because it is the practice of subordination . . . proves too much to be useful for First Amendment purposes" (CH, 328), he explains; for given the fact that *all* speech can be thus recharacterized, there is no principled way in which the argument "can be confined to pornography and not applied to expression generally" (CH, 333)—no way, that is, of avoiding the conclusion that all speech is a possible candidate for regulation. It is a remarkable sequence (exactly reproducing the sequence in *American Booksellers*) in which Post first finds the antipornography logic powerful and persuasive but then feels compelled to reject it in the name of something—a "viable notion of free speech"—that he himself has shown to be a chimera.

Moreover, the logic, as Post sees it, can be pressed in the opposite direction, where it leads not to the conclusion that all speech should be regulated but to the equally distressing (and counterintuitive) conclusion that no speech should ever be regulated. For if speech is an indissoluble mix of expression and action, then all forms of speech (and indeed all action) are involved in the communication of ideas, and it would follow that the regulation of any speech, whatever its context or social impact, should be prohibited.[7] Post confronts just this dilemma when he considers the decision of the Supreme Court in *Hustler Magazine v. Falwell* to privilege the public ridicule of television evangelist Jerry Falwell's mother.[8] "It cannot be," he exclaims, "that *Falwell* absolutely protects all verbal means of intentionally inflicting emotional distress, all forms of racial, sexual and religious insults" (CC, 662). The problem, again, is to find a principled way of drawing a line between protected and regulated speech, but the fear this time is not of wholesale regulation but of wholesale privilege.

For some pages, Post relies on the distinction between public speech—speech contributing to the ongoing dialogue of the marketplace—and speech privately communicated, which because it does not contribute to that dialogue can be disciplined if it causes harms: "If [*Hustler* publisher Larry] Flynt were to call up Falwell's mother and ridicule her in the words of the *Hustler* parody, it seems to me unimaginable that the ridicule would be constitutionally privileged" (CC, 662). But even as he invokes this distinction, Post acknowledges that in practice it has proven impossible to maintain. First of all, as he notes, "the prevailing contemporary interpretation . . . privileges statements of opinion regardless of whether or not they occur in public discourse"

(CC, 661–662). And even if it were accepted that only in the realm of public discourse was speech, however vehement and scurrilous, to be privileged, we would then be confronted by the difficulty of determining the shape and extent of that realm.

Is gossip about prominent celebrities who are not in any way involved in making public policy a part of "public discourse" (because its objects are in some sense public figures) and therefore privileged? In the context of recent decisions the answer would seem to be yes. Is the matter of public discourse anything at all in the public domain? If so, we veer strongly in the direction of privileging everything, for, given world enough and time, it would be possible for a skilled advocate to link up any utterance, no matter what the circumstances of its production, to something of interest to the public. Even the midnight telephone call to Falwell's mother might be said to be the conveyance by a public medium of views that bear on a topic of public concern (the trustworthiness of television evangelists), and it could also be argued that Flynt's intention in this hypothetical scenario would be not to wound Mrs. Falwell but to enlist her in the project of discouraging her son's political activities. The case could then be analogized to cases in which the court classifies a communication as public even though it reaches very few people, on the grounds that influencing the public was a large part of the speaker's or writer's intention (CC, 676).

The point is that what is and is not of public concern is a wholly indeterminate matter and one whose specification will mark the (temporary) ascendance of some private (partial, not-common-to-all) agenda. This is what Post means when he says that "the criterion of 'public concern' lacks internal coherence" (CC, 678–679); although the category is offered as a way of marking off discourse related to the workings of democracy from discourse of merely personal (and hence regulatable) concern, its own boundaries shift in relation to the success various private groups have in getting their concerns labeled "public" or "private." The forum of public discourse, designed supposedly to be a place where contending political agendas fight it out on a level playing field, is itself politically constituted.

That is the insight Post strives to push away by stressing the requirement that the forum of public discourse must transcend "the bounds and perspectives of any particular community" (CC, 629); it must embody "an impartial and overarching public order" (CC, 630) and constitute (in Alvin Goudlner's words) "'a safe and cleared space'"

(CC, 636) that is "independent from the general context in which social action is routinely assessed" (CC, 639–640). It must, in short, display "neutrality among differing definitions of community identity" (CC, 648) and resist the desire of any community to have its own interests equated with the public good.

But so scrupulously does Post interrogate the phrases and formulas that accompany the invocation of the public forum that he repeatedly reveals its incoherence, and in the end he himself comes to the conclusion to which his analysis has long pointed. The fact that "the genre of public speech" is defined by "competing value commitments" and "pre-existing social norms" leads, he says, to "the startling proposition that the boundaries of public discourse cannot be fixed in a neutral fashion," and even more explicitly, "the boundaries of a discourse defined by its liberation from ideological conformity [that is, from politics] will themselves be defined by reference to ideological [political] presuppositions" (CC, 683).

And yet, so powerful is the appeal of the apolitical neutrality he has declared unavailable that Post immediately resurrects it, albeit in a somewhat weaker (and disguised) form: "This kind of ideological regulation of speech is deeply distasteful and it is best that it remain so. Democratic self-governance could easily be eviscerated if such regulation became the rule rather than the exception" (CC, 683). But as he himself has just demonstrated, it *is* the rule; any program of regulation in the name of a sanitized public discourse will rest on an ideological specification of what that discourse is. The most that one could do is be aware of that fact (which may be what Post is counseling), but awareness of it will in no way neutralize or mitigate it. Even if you pledged yourself to watch out for it, the part of your mind that was doing the watching would itself still be informed by some "value commitment," some ideology. You can no more *watch* neutrally than you can speak or deliberate neutrally; it is ideology (and politics) all the way down.

The fact that it is ideology and politics all the way down is another way of saying that the notion of public discourse and therefore of free (cleanly discursive and argumentative) speech is empty and is thus, at the very least, a questionable counterweight to the harms and injuries permitted in its name. Nevertheless, it is almost always the case that this negligible counterweight—formal, thin, abstract, and bloodless—tips the scales no matter how substantial the competing considerations.

Post's performance is only a particularly perspicuous instance of a pattern one finds everywhere in the history of the modern First Amendment. The sequence enacted in Post's essays—the sequence in which a spectral and ever-receding future hope is preferred to the claims of presently feeling human beings—is writ large in the history of modern First Amendment doctrine and is already fully on display in Oliver Wendell Holmes's oft-cited dissent in *Abrams v. United States* (1919).[9] The final and key paragraph of that dissent begins by acknowledging that, given the nature of conviction—the fact that people *believe* in the things they assert (else what would assertion be for?)—tolerating the expression of beliefs you think pernicious is illogical; for were you cheerfully to "allow opposition by speech," it would "indicate that you think the speech impotent, as when a man says that he has squared the circle, or that you do not care wholeheartedly for the result, or that you doubt either your power or your premises" (630).

The point is a profound one whose implications have not always been so clearly seen, and it is the point I have already made: total toleration of speech makes sense only if speech is regarded as inconsequential and unlikely to bring about a result you would find either heartening or distressing. If, on the other hand, speech is, as Holmes clearly believes it to be, potent, indifference to speech inimical to your deepest convictions would raise suspicions about the strength of those convictions. It would seem, then, that as a matter of moral and political obligation you would do everything in your power to legitimate speech supportive of your beliefs and to stigmatize (and perhaps suppress) speech supportive of the beliefs you consider false and dangerous.

Holmes avoids this conclusion in what is now standard First Amendment fashion by posing against the beliefs you now hold a recognition of their revisibility: "But when men have realized that time has upset many fighting faiths, they may come to believe even more than they believe the very foundations of their own conduct that the ultimate good desired is better reached by free trade in ideas—that the best test of truth is the power of the thought to get itself accepted in the competition of the market, and that truth is the only ground upon which their wishes safely can be carried out" (630). This famous sentence has echoed through the literature, but those who quote it might do well to examine it a bit more closely, to notice, for example, how the issue of agency is fudged in the phrase "get itself accepted"; the competition of the market seems to be driven by nothing but itself; no ideological motives corrupt its workings; with a sublime blindness to motive, it simply (we are never told how) generates the "ultimate good." The entire undertheorized process bears an uncanny relationship to what the writers of pagan epic called "fate"; and although Holmes urges it as the course of true responsibility, it could easily be seen as the *abandonment* of responsibility to impersonal, and perhaps terrible, forces.

There are other problems as well, problems in philosophical logic. The sentence suggests that the repeated experience of a change in belief will lead you to be wary of acting on the beliefs you presently hold—suggests, in short, the wisdom, and the possibility, of resisting the pull of your beliefs in the name of something more firmly ("safely") authoritative. But as Holmes's own language acknowledges, the something you would prefer to your present beliefs is itself a present belief, to wit, the belief that all your beliefs except this one are unreliable. But why should this belief be exempt from the general skepticism it announces? Why should it not fall by the very logic it declares and leave us once again where we were before its emergence, struggling through to conclusions and decisions on the basis of what we now think to be the case? (It is a subject for another time, but let me offer in passing the proposition that the greater the scope of skepticism, the less consequential it is because it leaves one with no basis for either accepting or rejecting a course of action.) And why as a matter of psychology should a belief in the revisibility of our beliefs make the edifice of our beliefs tremble? The only thing that will have changed when we reach the conclusion that time has upset many fighting faiths is the belief we may have previously had that our beliefs are not corrigible, and the rest of our beliefs could easily survive the experience of that one change. Knowing that what we know today we may not know tomorrow doesn't mean that we don't know (and therefore don't rely on) what we know today.

And even if we put these questions aside and accept the argument by which skepticism leads inevitably to the deferral of action in order that the truth might be allowed to freely emerge, new questions arise. How would we know when the promised moment (a consummation devoutly to be wished) had arrived? Who would be authorized to mark it, since the persons living in some unnamed future would be no less partial in their visions than we are now? It is only if we affirm a progressivism so strong that it issues in a race (or even a remnant) of bias-free observers that these questions could find an answer, and while a progressivism of that strength might be defensible in a theological context ("Now we see through a glass darkly, but then face to face . . ."), in the context of our militantly secular democratic (as opposed to theocratic) politics, there is no reason to believe that a future generation will have acquired the requisite unclouded vision.

This leaves us with the scenario I described earlier, the endless deferral of presently felt urgencies on behalf of something so vague that we can only characterize it negatively. "But you miss the point," someone might say. "Of course individual men and women will be free, as they have always been, to form strong convictions as to the way things should go in our society, and free also to urge their views on others; it is just that government should take no side in the resulting disagreement, but should stand as the guarantor of equal access to the market that will, in time, render its verdict." This, however, assumes that the market—the forum of public discourse—can be so constructed as to be neutral "among differing definitions of community identity," and that the tools it employs, such as the distinction between speech and action or between public and private concerns, are clean (internally coherent) and nonideological. But it is this assumption that will not stand up to scrutiny, as Post's anguished analysis shows, and it would seem that we are being asked to prefer to our sense of political imperatives the slow workings of a process that is no less political. In short, there isn't a disinterested or detached forum in sight, no "cleared and safe space," no matter how often and how resonantly it is invoked.

But even if the strong First Amendment position is deprived of its abstract rationale, it can avail itself of a prudential argument: "Simply put," according to McGowan and Tangri, "the marketplace theory rests ultimately upon the consummately libertarian belief that individuals are better judges of what is best for them than is the government. Marketplace theory therefore rests ultimately upon the relative risks of oppression involved" (838). One could respond to this by mounting a philosophical inquiry into the notion of "individual" and arguing (as many have) that the scenario here implied in which individuals free of governmental pressures make correspondingly free choices is an impossible one because individuals are not free but socially constructed by the same forces and pressures embodied in their governments. But I will decline the philosophical gambit (if only because the topic is now such a tired one) and read McGowan and Tangri's declaration as if it were an empirical observation to the effect that government regulation of speech produces more harms than the harms produced by unregulated individuals.

This is a historical assessment and one that would command my attention were it sufficiently documented. Yet even if it were documented, it would be a rule of thumb rather than a rule: it would amount to saying that in the past it has turned out that when governments get the power to regulate speech, they do bad things with it, and, all things being equal, it would be better not to grant them that power. All things, however, are not always equal, and it could still be the case that in some particular situation—perhaps in our situation today—the risk of not regulating speech will outweigh the risk of regulation. It is, in short, a judgment call, and while the experience of the past may be an ingredient in that judgment, it need not be any more dispositive than the spectral hope of a miraculously luminous future, especially when the present stakes are seen to be high.

Something of the spirit of this pragmatic emphasis on weighing the relative risks appears in Holmes's dissent, with which we are not yet done. Holmes seems to put his case in the strongest terms possible when he urges that "we should be eternally vigilant against attempts to check the expression of opinions that we loathe and believe to be fraught with death" (630). The strength of this inheres in Holmes's pushing on past "loathe"; for if he had stopped with that word (as many who quote or echo him do), he would have reduced the question (and the problem) to one of sensitivity or taste, to a loathing of opinions because they seem to us to be "vulgar" or because they reflect habits of mind and speech we would rather not encounter in polite society. Loathing in this sense would be no more serious than an intense dislike of romance novels or fast food.

But when Holmes adds to "loathe" the phrase "and believe to be fraught with death," he raises the stakes to a level that makes the *passion* of First Amendment debate intelligible. For if we believe something to be fraught with death, our fears about it extend far beyond peripheral or cosmetic matters; they go to the very survival of whatever it is we think vital to a truly human existence. By adding "fraught with death" to "loathe," Holmes acknowledges the awful consequentiality (at least in potential) of speech at the same moment that he enjoins us to stare that consequentiality in the face and not flinch.

This is strong stuff, but the sentence has not yet run its course, and the next turn it takes undercuts the apparent stringency of Holmes's pronouncement: "unless they so immanently threaten immediate interference with the lawful and pressing purposes of the law that an immediate check is required to save the country" (49). This introduction of the clear-and-present-danger test may seem a small concession to the basic absolutism of Holmes's position, but as David Kairys points out, "since the scope of the dangers referred to has never been meaningfully defined . . . the clear-and-present-danger formulation amounts to the notion that speech loses its protection when it becomes persuasive . . . concerning something a judge views as dangerous."[10] Kairys, writing from a critical legal studies perspective, reads Holmes's qualifying "unless" as an unhappy restriction on an absolute right. But I would read it as a recognition on Holmes's part that the right to speak cannot be abstracted from the political conditions in the context of which its exercise is meaningful. If speech is allowed to corrode those conditions, it participates in its own undoing, in its own death, and it is Holmes's point (at least in this part of his sentence) that in order to save speech (and the country), there are times when we must act to restrict it.

The question, of course, is when? That is, how long do we delay before acting? In another famous dissent *(Gitlow v. People of New York)*, Holmes seems willing to delay forever. The case involves the prosecution of a socialist who had superintended the publication of a manifesto advocating (among other things) a "revolutionary dictatorship of the proletariat." Responding to the majority point that "this manifesto was more than a theory . . . it was an incitement," Holmes replies: "Every idea is an incitement" in that "it offers itself for belief and if believed it is acted on unless some other belief outweighs it or some energy stifles the movement at birth" (673).[11]

As in *Abrams*, Holmes begins by strongly affirming speech's potency and adds that even in the absence of explicit words of incitement, the incendiary effect may occur, since "eloquence may set fire to reason" (673). But then, again as in *Abrams,* the acknowledgment of speech's consequentiality (and hence of its status as action) is followed by a disinclination, at least in the present circumstances, to attend to the consequences: "But whatever may be thought of the redundant discourse before us, it has no chance of starting a present conflagration. If in the long run the beliefs expressed in proletarian dictatorship are destined to be accepted by the dominant forces of the community, the only meaning of free speech is that they should be given their chance and have their way" (673). Although the second sentence follows the first in this passage, the two point in antithetical directions. The first takes the clear-and-present-danger test seriously by hypothesizing a state of near conflagration that would be sufficiently alarming to warrant regulatory action; but the second seems to contemplate with equanimity, and even with a kind of satisfaction, the eventual emergence of that very same conflagration.

To be sure, there is a good First Amendment way of distinguishing between the scenarios. In the first, the overthrow of our present political arrangements is attempted by force, and in that (hypothetical) event Holmes seems willing to urge judicial approval of a governmental response. In the second, by contrast, the overthrow (again hypothetical) is accomplished by the operation of ideas in the fabled free marketplace, and that prospect is one that Holmes views as definitive of the very purpose of the First Amendment. But the distinction seems to be largely without a difference. Why should the very same event—the triumph of dictatorship—be alternately feared or welcomed, depending on whether it has been brought about by force or by the force (somehow regarded as the antithesis of force) of speech?

The answer is to be found in the indifference of liberal democracy (in its more libertarian forms) to outcomes. Unlike other political systems, democracy, as Holmes envisions it here, is willing to contemplate (and even connive in) its own demise. Committed to procedure rather than to substance, to the principle of autonomy rather than to the consequences autonomous action might produce, liberal democracy enforces no orthodoxies, not even the orthodoxies constitutive of its deepest aspirations. The maintenance and flourishing of those aspirations are left to the blind workings of history, which of course may have other eventualities "in mind," including the emergence of dictatorship. As McGowan and Tangri put it with admirable candor, the marketplace theory "provides no way to defend against a population that willingly adopts objectively destructive and repugnant beliefs, and would prohibit the government from regulating against them" (837).

One suspects that many who declare themselves willing to risk that prospect do not believe that it is a real one and subscribe (as Holmes seems to at some moments) to some undertheorized form of progressivism rooted in an Enlightenment view of history. Pressed, they would point to the disappearance in the "civilized" world of slavery, to the improved political condition of women, to the more humane treatment of animals, and so on. But for everyone of these advances a skeptical observer could instance the appearance of new and renewed horrors— gay bashing, which has increased by a factor of five in recent years, violence against women, assaults on the environment (even in the context of a raised environmental consciousness). It is by no means clear that history's trajectory is benign, and even the most apparently heartening developments display a disturbing underside. For a brief moment, the breakup of Communist governments in Eastern Europe seemed to usher in a "new world order" marking the triumph of "freedom." But within a short time (some say twenty minutes) it was seen that the removal of one evil (totalitarian rule) opened the way for the re-emergence of others (virulent anti-Semitism, equally virulent nationalism, militant religious intolerance). History seems to have gone backward, not forward, leaping in the twinkling of an eye from 1990 to 1917, and it is instructive to observe how quickly the fear of overly strong centralized regimes has given way in the popular mind and in the press to the fear of Balkanization.

A sophisticated progressivism, one that does not tie its vision to any specific hopes, will not be embarrassed by such examples but will turn them to its advantage by making a virtue of the future's indeterminacy. Instead of arguing that a robust and uninhibited marketplace of ideas will bring us to a place we would now like to be, this progressivism takes comfort in the fact that we could not now recognize that place were we brought to it and would probably decline to choose it were it offered to us in a referendum. Not only will things have changed when that future arrives, the argument goes, but we too will have changed (as caterpillars change into butterflies) into beings responsive to ideals and imperatives we cannot now comprehend. In this version of "future-hope" (which has not been fully articulated and is only hinted at in some of the more rhapsodic critical legal studies and feminist prophecies), the passage of time will bring not only purified reasons but purified selves. The willingness to be undone is thus not as counterintuitive as one might have thought, for when the way of life we now know and instantiate has been swept away, it will be succeeded not only by a better way of life but by better persons who will be living it.

The trouble with this form of progressivism is that it does not fit coherently with the skepticism with which most strong First Amendment doctrine begins. As Mary Ellen Gale has said, "The thrust toward liberty and individualism that . . . characterizes American life . . .

springs from a . . . blend of optimism and pessimism about human nature and organization" (129–130).[12] The pessimism is emphasized at the entry level when we hear from Holmes and his followers the tale of a humanity each of whose members is wholly committed to a partial and partisan version of the truth; given the firmness of the grasp in which belief holds every one of us, there is no one person or group of persons who could be trusted to pass a disinterested judgment on the many beliefs that vie for our collective approval; hence the necessity of disallowing the claim of any private judgment (and in this story all judgments are, strictly speaking, private) to be affirmed as public policy, and the apparent wisdom of shifting the burden of judgment to the marketplace.

One might think that the logic of such a deep skepticism would generate a vision of life not unlike that of Hobbes: a perpetual war of all against all, an ever-shifting and never-ending struggle between irreconcilable factions. But somehow, in that indeterminate span in which the marketplace is open for business, the war turns into a cooperative effort by selfless, clear-eyed citizens to seek out and establish the truth. Somehow pessimism turns into optimism; and, as Gale puts it, "flawed moral selves," selves so in bondage to their views that they cannot be trusted to ordain wisely, are transformed into the "imagined model or archetype of the free person, integral, bold, active, and in control of his (or possibly her) destiny" (129).

The question is, how does this happen? How does a procedure designed to restrain the tendency of ideologically blinkered persons to institutionalize their personal agendas end up producing persons free of ideology and therefore capable both of recognizing and embracing a truth to which they were previously blind? In general the literature offers no answer to this question, but one is, I think, implicit and it involves what Ellen Rooney has called the "possibility of general persuasion," the assumption by liberal "pluralists" that everyone is capable of being persuaded or, to put it from the other direction, that no one is so obdurately committed to a point of view that he or she will not, as the phrase goes, listen to reason (5).[13] The rhetoric of general persuasion is the rhetoric of openness, but in fact, as Rooney points out, the logic of general persuasion is strongly exclusionary. What it excludes (declaring them beyond the pale) are those who refuse to submit their core principles to the scrutiny and play of the marketplace; such persons are labeled "irrational" or "fanatical" and in the name of inclusiveness they are read out of the community. "This 'pluralist' rhetoric accuses its opponents . . . of a monolithic totalitarianism . . . precisely in order to exclude them" (27). That is to say, liberal pluralism accuses its opponents of having a politics, and in making the accusation claims that it has no politics at all.

In fact, however, liberal pluralism is most definitely a politics, and its agenda has been well summarized by Ronald Beiner: "The maximization of social productivity, the organization of social life so as to enhance efficiency and technological control, the privileging of scientific over other forms of knowledge, the favoring of ways of life consistent with maximal individual mobility" (78).[14] The project of general persuasion works by naturalizing this agenda—regarding its components not as contestable theses but as obvious truths—and declaring all who do not affirm them to be not fully human. It then generates conclusions with which "everyone" (a strategically reduced everyone) agrees, if only because what everyone agrees to is what he or she already believes (that individual mobility should be maximized, etc.).

It is a nice piece of legerdemain, and it makes clear how the passage from a present riven by ideological conflict to a future marked by rational cooperation is managed: that future is identified with one of the contending ideologies (claiming of course to be the antithesis of ideology), which can then discover itself at the conclusion of a process (the "free" marketplace of ideas) it has carefully designed. The gap between the present and the future is closed when the future is imagined simultaneously as the time when ideology will have worked itself pure and as the time in which the presuppositions of one ideology—the ideology of liberalism—are fully realized. It is this piece of double-think, unrecognized by those who indulge in it, that allows the discourse of general persuasion—of marketplace liberalism—first to acknowledge the intractability of difference and then immediately to overcome it.

It is, as I have said, a nice trick, and the ease with which it is accomplished (how could it be otherwise given the pre-removal of any obstacle) is nicely illustrated in an essay by Calvin Massey, "Hate Speech, Cultural Diversity, and the Foundational Paradigms of Free Expression."[15] Early on Massey declares that "free expression law derives from the belief that autonomous self-governance can be achieved only by a dialogue open to all points of view" (112). And a little later he adds that the reason for open debate is "to enable every person within the polity to express his or her view in the hope that it will convince others" (118).

Although these two sentences seem at first glance to fit together nicely, they in fact point to a tension (perhaps a contradiction) that pervades the entire essay and is never resolved. The first sentence specifies autonomy as the end-product of open debate, while the second sentence assumes the autonomy of those who participate in the debate. That is, the "hope" that a debate "will convince others" can only be realized if the "others" are open to all the views they are asked to consider, where "open" means not already so strongly attached to (and owned by) a particular view that arguments against it will be dismissed out of hand.

But since just that openness is the goal of the process, it hardly seems right (or logical) to require it as a ticket of entry. By positing an audience *already* available to persuasion on any point, Massey renders strong First Amendment doctrine either superfluous or incoherent or both. It is superfluous if its end—autonomous self-governance—has already been achieved, and it is incoherent if its achievement requires persons free of the very liability (obdurate allegiance to a belief or set of beliefs) it is designed to remove. And indeed a version of this incoherence can be found in the two parts of the second sentence. The first part imagines some members of the population putting forward the views to which they are bound, and the second part imagines other (presumably more healthy) members of the population who are bound to (and by) nothing and who are therefore genuinely capable of being convinced. Just who these First Amendment saints are and by what mechanism (aside from some secular form of predestination) they have been brought to their happy ideology-free state Massey never says. Instead, he leaves the matter mysterious, as he must if he is to continue complacently on with his exposition.

At one point in that exposition Massey does attempt to give some content to the mystery, but he succeeds only in deepening it. He is discussing what seem to him to be the beneficial effects of hate speech: "By tolerating abhorrent and hateful speech, we are able to see more clearly our societal biases and thereby hasten the process by which we purge ourselves of hidden intolerance" (127). This unexpected piece of casual psychology is followed by a reference to Carl Jung, but the support supposedly given by Jung to Massey's account of self-purgation fails to shore up its incoherences. If we begin with biases so strong that they necessitate the restraining mechanism of First Amendment safeguards, what is it in us that will resist the sway of those biases and allow us to see through them? If Massey's were a theological discourse, an answer would be available in the traditional notions of conscience as the voice of God residing within or of the spirit of Christ struggling with the devil for possession of our souls. But in the militantly secular context of First Amendment thought such notions clearly have no place, and without them, or some plausibly elaborated secular proxy, there is a large hole right in the middle of the "process of transforming and transcending [our] inner demon[s]" (128).

It is the same difficulty I have analyzed above. Either there is already something within us that enables us to look askance at our own biases and intolerances (enables us to get to the side of our selves), in which case the goal of First Amendment restrictions is already achieved. Or we are, as the skepticism of First Amendment doctrine declares, wholly in the grip of our biases and intolerances, in which case there is no bridge between our present, fallen state and the first step on the path to transcendence. (I can imagine a Milton-like argument that views the marketplace of ideas as a mental gymnasium in which our critical faculties are being exercised and honed, but this would still leave unanswered the question of where these critical faculties, even in a stage of under-development, came from, since the strong pessimism informing the libertarian/marketplace position leaves no room for them to emerge.)

That is why the first step, as Massey and other liberals imagine it, is also (and mysteriously) the achievement of the putative goal. You *begin* by setting aside your convictions as to what is right or wrong, desirable or dangerous, true or false, so that they can be submitted to the ongoing (and impartial) scrutiny of the marketplace of ideas. But if you were able to do *that*, there would be no need for the marketplace's mechanisms. After all, the condition of being abstracted from your (partial) convictions is what the marketplace is supposed to produce, and if you are already able to set them aside, you are, without any further direction or compulsion, your own marketplace.

And even if it were an action that could coherently be enjoined—even if we hurry past the difficulty of the first step being the last and being, also, a step without a ground—setting aside one's convictions would be *in*coherent on its own terms. For in order to perform it, there is one conviction—the conviction that no conviction is to be privileged—that cannot be set aside, which means that at the moment of performance your mind will *not* be "open to all points of view" because you will have ruled out of court any point of view that refuses to acknowledge its own provisionality by putting itself on the table. Of course the fact that the project of being open to all points of view is itself closed to some points of view will constitute a criticism only from the perspective of its own impossible demand, the demand that one float free of the attachments that are the content of one's history and the motor of one's desires.

Not only is this demand impossible; it is unworthy. To say that one's mind should be open to everything sounds fine until you realize that it is equivalent to saying that one's mind should be empty of commitments, should be a purely formal device. As Beiner observes, the liberal ethos is "lack of ethos" (22), and therefore the life lived under its aegis (if a life could be lived under its aegis) is "episodic or haphazard" rather than moral (51). "What defines liberalism," Beiner explains, "is its desire *not* to be a regime, an organized social and political ordering of ends" (140). "The liberal regime is a regime of producers and consumers" where *what* is being produced or consumed is irrelevant (140). His point is mine—that such a life, lived in indifference toward the implications and effects of one's free exercise of will (a will without content), "may without absurdity be claimed to be a less than properly human existence" (51).

This may be the deepest irony embedded in strong First Amendment doctrine: that the disinterestedness it posits as an ideal and goal would, if it could be achieved (and of course it could not be), produce persons incapable of moral judgment at all. Is that what we really want? First Amendment ideologues would reply, "No, that's not what we want at all; we want a moral judgment—an ethics of choice—that is purified of its partialities." But as I have attempted to show, judgment without partiality—judgment delivered from nowhere and everywhere—is not an option for human beings and is available only to Gods and machines. The strong First Amendment promise is the promise that Satan made to Adam and Eve, that we shall be as Gods; it is not a promise the marketplace (which can deliver information but not vision) can redeem, but if we cling to it, the condition of being machines—engines of will unconnected to anything except the emptiness of repeated and directionless desire—may be the fate we make love to.

Nothing I say in this chapter should be taken to endorse a particular outcome or make a particular recommendation. That is, no one should think that my position on such issues as hate-speech codes, the regulation of pornography, school prayer, soliciting funds in airports, or enhanced sentencing for race-motivated crimes could be predicted from what I have written here. My intention is not to push First Amendment law in this or that direction but to inquire into the mechanisms by means of which First Amendment law goes in whatever direction it takes. Nor should the fact that in my account those mechanisms (stipulative definitions, obligatory binaries, routinely invoked aspirations) are unstable, incoherent, and empty be taken as an argument for abandoning or even revising them. I myself could make a plausible case for retaining every feature of current First Amendment jurisprudence even though, indeed *because,* its foundations have been shown to be built on sand. A demonstration that the reasons usually given for engaging in and maintaining a practice will not hold up under certain kinds of analysis says nothing conclusive about the wisdom of continuing to employ those reasons, which may be valued because of their power (independent of their philosophical cogency) to induce behavior we think desirable.

THE DANCE OF THEORY

One of the first questions I always ask students and audiences is "What is the First Amendment *for?*" I ask the question not because I want to recommend a particular answer but because I want to say that if you have *any* answer to the question, any answer at all, you are necessarily implicated in a regime of censorship. The reason is that when you say that the First Amendment is *for* something—perhaps for giving the truth the chance to emerge, or for providing the minds of citizens with the materials necessary for growth and self-realization, or for keeping the marketplace of ideas open in a democratic society—it becomes not only possible but inevitable that at some point you will ask of some instance of speech whether it in fact serves its high purpose or whether it does the opposite, retarding the search for truth, stunting the growth of mature judgment, fouling the marketplace.

This is not an empirical but a logical inevitability; for if you have what has been called a consequentialist view of the First Amendment— a view that values free speech because of the good effects it will bring about—then you must necessarily be on the lookout for forms of action, including speech action, that threaten to subvert those effects. Otherwise you would be honoring the means above the end and cutting the heart out of your moral vision. And to continue the logic, at the point you discern such a threat and move against it, you will not be compromising the First Amendment; you will be honoring it by performing the act of censorship that was implicit in it from the beginning.

By placing censorship inside the First Amendment, I join those who have been chipping away at First Amendment theory. For most of the twentieth century the dance of First Amendment theory was a two-step. The first step was to identify the essence or center of First Amendment freedoms; the second step was to devise a policy that protected and honored the center so identified. Within this general structure of analysis and argument there was considerable room for disagreement. One might disagree as to whether the free speech center should be defined in relation to some desired consequence (the emergence of truth, the free flow of ideas and information in a democratic society, the fashioning of well-informed citizens capable of independent judgment, the encouraging of dissent as a check against the tendency of state power to perpetuate itself) or whether a free speech regime follows from a moral imperative (autonomous agents should be accorded the liberty of expressing their own views and making their own choices without interference from the state) that is indifferent to consequences and cannot be relaxed just because a particular consequence is either feared or sought.

If one is a consequentialist, one will still debate which of the consequences is primary in the sense that the hope of its realization should guide policy. And if one is a nonconsequentialist, one will still debate which of the proffered moral imperatives (liberty, autonomy, equality, tolerance) is so strong that it should trump any policy considerations (the elimination of racism, the suppression of error, the fostering of civility) a would-be regulator might invoke. Even when consequentialists or nonconsequentialists settle in the same doctrinal corner, they can still debate whether the historical record of court decisions reflects and confirms their preferred view or whether that history displays a regrettable departure from the principle they have now revealed to be the true one. Obviously, then, the field will always be full of contest, but everyone will pretty much agree about the point of the contest and the prize to be won—the right to specify the correct free speech principle and the policy that follows from it.

In the past fifteen or twenty years, however, a number of commentators have begun to tell a different story. They say things like "There is no free speech principle," or "There is no such thing as free speech," or "There is no such thing as speech," or "There is no such thing as a principle." They reach these provocative conclusions through a variety of routes: • by undoing the distinction between speech and action and thus depriving First Amendment theorists of an object to clarify; • by declaring that any so-called procedural value is always and already hostage to a substantive vision and thus making viewpoint discrimination (a fancy name for politics) the *content* of the First Amendment rather than the evil it is supposed to keep at bay; • by arguing that First Amendment mechanisms do not, as is claimed, neutralize power by giving everyone an equal chance to speak but instead work to consolidate the power of those who benefit from the maintenance of the status quo and to disempower those already marginalized and silenced; • by insisting that words do not simply describe the world but make it and that, therefore, one cannot expect the world to remain what it always was no matter what is or is not said; • by pointing out the manifest incoherence and absurdity of current First Amendment doctrine which regulates in the name of nonregulation, draws bright lines no one can clearly see, and recognizes so many exceptions to its rules that it is finally as ad hoc and haphazard as the world it fails to order.

What is remarkable, however, is that after having demonstrated (at least to themselves) that the first step of identifying the free speech center cannot be taken, these same revisionists still believe they can take the second step and derive a policy from the unavailability of what the traditionalists have sought in vain. They believe, in short, that something follows from the fact (if it is a fact) that there is no principle or doctrine or overriding value for a First Amendment policy to follow. They contrive to turn the absence of a normative grounds into a ground for making normative decisions. They think to substitute for the (discredited) sequence "Because the essence of X is Y, we should do Z" the brave new sequence "Because X does not exist, we should do Z."

What they refuse to see is that if step one is a nonstarter, there is no basis for taking step two other than the prudential basis that recommends itself to a situated political agent. What they refuse to see is that the only alternative to a principled consequentialism—a consequentialism tied to an outcome (such as self-realization) that everyone desires or should desire—is a consequentialism tied to an outcome some particular one (or group) desires. What they refuse to see is that rather than *shaping* circumstances, policies *arise* from circumstances which also generate the abstractions that can then be used to give those same policies a timeless pedigree.

One suspects that Robert Post knows all this, although he will be my first example of a theorist who cannot let go of his theory even after he has cut away its ground. Post begins his 1995 article, "Recuperating First Amendment Doctrine," by declaring that First Amendment doctrine is "striking chiefly for its superficiality, its internal incoherence, its distressing failure to facilitate judicial engagement with significant contemporary social issues" (1250).[1] Post attributes this unhappy situation to a disconnect between the doctrinal pronouncements of the Supreme Court and its behavior in particular cases, and he attributes this disconnect to the fact that the Court often speaks as if it were defending speech "per se" (1272)—an abstract entity prior to any of the social contexts in which it might occur—and therefore couching its justifications in terms (like the intent to communicate a message) appropriate to that level of generality.

But, says Post, there is no such thing as speech per se, only speech uttered (or written) in "the social contexts that envelop and give constitutional significance to acts of communication" (1255). Rather than being an independent value whose primacy is to be honored no matter what the circumstances, speech is of consequence only in circumstances, and the value we assign to it (not as an abstract category but as a particular instance) is a function of the value already assigned the circumstance. In so-called "open forums" (town meetings, Hyde Park corners, radio talk shows) speech will be largely unfettered and unregulated (except for the regulation requiring each to wait his or her turn) not because we revere speech in and of itself but because the very point of open forums is to encourage as much varied expression as possible. In other contexts (Post cites the military, the medical, and the classroom contexts), the production of speech is incidental to the institutional or social point, and it makes no sense to prefer speech interests to the interests that give such contexts their reasons for being.

Post's conclusions to this analysis are sweeping. Because speech "does not itself have a general constitutional value" but attaches itself to the values already "allocated to . . . discrete forms of social practice," "the search for any general free speech principle is bound to fail" (1272). That failure is only thinly disguised by the contortions the Court has recourse to when it attempts to "force the entire spectrum of state regulation of forms of social interaction into conformity" with a chimerical "single value." The better course, the one Post is recommending, would be to make "the unit of First Amendment analysis . . . not . . . speech, but rather particular forms of social structure," with their particular purposes and goals (1273).

This suggests a new and urgent project, "a kind of interpretive charting of the ambient social landscape. Such a charting is necessarily creative and dialectical: Values already recognized as constitutional may precipitate the perception of practices deemed prerequisite for their realization, while actual but untheorized practices may spur the explicit articulation of new constitutional values" (1275). Such a charting would also, I think, be provisional and ever in need of revision and updating, because what it would be charting is the *political* process whereby specific practices move in and out of the category "worthy of constitutional regard." There is no end (as there was no beginning) to the creation of new constitutional values in the wake of the decision (a word that suggests more rationality than may be present) to find constitutional value in a practice that previously was not seen to contain it. When Post says that if someone were to deface public property by inscribing on it (or into it) "a particularized message that is likely to be understood by his audience," "no court in the country would consider the case as raising a First Amendment question" (1252), he should have added "at this time"; for it is easily imaginable that some court will extrapolate from cases dealing with flag burning, sleeping in public parks (as a form of protest), trampling on public grounds (in the course of a march), and so on a constitutional value for what we now dismiss as graffiti (and remember there are graffiti "artists," both self-described and recognized by others) or vandalism. Constitutional value is not something that hovers above the judicial process and guides it; constitutional value (as everything in Post's discussion implies) is what emerges from the process, sometimes in this form, sometimes in that, but never in a form so perdurable that one can be confident that its invocation will always secure the desired effect.

In the course of his exposition, Post characterizes the conclusions he has been reaching as "radical" (1273); but when he turns to consolidate the gains of his analysis, what may have seemed radical (at least as I would understand the term) becomes something quite familiar and traditional. The hinge sentence is this one: "I have . . . surveyed in some detail the court's opinions dealing with the regulation of speech within governmental institutions, and I have found that the pattern of the court's decisions is largely what would be predicted by the preceding discussion" (1275). When I first read this I thought that the pattern he found was one that would further dash the hopes of those in search of a "generic constitutional value for speech" (1275) because it revealed the extent to which the court's decisions varied with the "specific and discrete kinds of social practices" (1272) that displayed speech as a feature—practices that were not only discrete but ever on the move, capable of metamorphosing into something quite other than they had been and thus gaining or shedding constitutional value along the way. I thought, in short, that Post would follow his rejection of "any general free speech principle" (1272) with a critique of the claim of doctrinal analysis to be normative rather than ad hoc and rhetorical (as much of what he had been saying suggested that it was).

Instead, Post shifts the level at which doctrinal analysis will be both explanatory and guiding. Although the universalism (and utility) of notions like self-realization or the search for truth is repudiated—because the "abstract world" (1276) in which they live exists only in the mind of theorists—a new universalism, or essentialism, is embraced in the forms of the social practices that will be the new unit of First Amendment analysis. While no overarching single value—the search for which has "blinded" (1275) the Court—exists, there is a single value, Post believes, appropriate to specific social structures, structures whose "charting" (now revealed to be a taxonomic task that can be performed once and for all) will enable us to sort everything out and proceed in a coherent fashion. All we have to do is match up discrete social practices with the single values (whether constitutional or not) animating them, and we will know what to do and, in contrast to the present sorry situation, there will be a fit between what we do and the vocabulary within which what we do is justified.

All at once the chaotic world of First Amendment jurisprudence and the radical implications of saying that there is no general free speech principle are tamed by finding general free speech principles that are local. What "the pattern of the court's decisions reveals," Post tells us, is not the absence of a doctrinal coherence but a doctrinal coherence it has not itself recognized, with the result that its performance, pretty much what one would desire, is misrecognized by its theory, which is "thoroughly disconnected from the actual levers of its judgment" (1275). Although the Court "has been completely unable to craft a clear and useful doctrinal expression" (1275) of what should, and does, guide its deliberations and opinions, that lack has now been supplied by the First Amendment theorist.

Indeed, when the theoretical dust clears and Post descends to particulars, it turns out that there is a general First Amendment principle after all, and along with it a single overriding value. It is not general in the old way; it does not envelop the field; rather, it sits at its center and generates the distinctions between practices that can then be the basis of determining in which of them speech activity should be of constitutional concern and in which of them speech can be regulated in accordance with the goal and point of the enterprise. (It is not that I think the drawing of such lines would be impossible or even difficult; it is just that the lines would be drawn in the context of background assumptions—about whether a particular practice, like the practice of graffiti "artists," rises to the level of constitutional notice—that could themselves be challenged at any point; and if the challenge were successful, the entire map would have to be redrawn.) It is because it sits at the center that this principle/value is called a "core" (1275), a word and concept one would have thought Post had let go of when he let go of "speech as such," "self-realization," "the conveying of particular messages," and "expressive conduct" as failed candidates for the central value the First Amendment was designed to protect.

Moreover, Post's candidate for "core" is so far from being radical as to be commonplace and absolutely centrist. It is, he announces with a flourish, "democracy," that "specific kind of social order, which seeks to sustain the value of self-government by reconciling individual and collective autonomy through the medium of public discourse," with the goal of facilitating "the emergence of 'a common will, communicatively shaped and discursively clarified in the political public sphere'" (1275). Although this "kind of social order" is said to be "specific," it is not (as the word suggests) just one among equals. Rather, the aspirations and imperatives of democracy order the entire landscape. The social practices (like the military, the medical, and the scholarly) that are not held to its requirement of allowing as much unfettered speech as possible are released from the requirement not in opposition to, or sequestration from, democracy but by its leave. When a teacher is permitted to restrict both the material and the scope of discussion in the classroom, it is not because he is being given permission to be undemocratic; rather, the controlled space of the classroom is deemed to be contributory to the "material conditions of the specific social order of democracy" (1275), one of which is the fashioning of well-informed citizens.

Democracy, thus conceived, *is* the abstract universal Post has scorned in the pages preceding its emergence, and the clear sign that this is so is the citing of Jürgen Habermas as his source for the idea of a "structure of governance" always open to revision. (As far as I am concerned, any positive reference to Habermas in the course of an argument is enough to invalidate it.) Habermas, after all, is the philosopher of the "ideal speech situation" (identified by him as the desirable form of the public forum), a situation inhabited by participants who leave behind the points of view and senses of interest and desires for particular outcomes attached to their local and partisan existence and enter the room intent only on offering propositions that have a claim to universal validity and can be tested against similar claims in a communal effort to arrive at general truths. The fact that Post can declare that there are no general truths (1278) *after* he has enlisted Habermas as an authority is an indication of the tension between his "radical" repudiation of the abstractions underlying traditional First Amendment doctrine and his rehabilitation (or recuperation) of traditional First Amendment doctrine in the name of one of those same abstractions. Thoroughly conversant with those discourses—feminist, post-structuralist, postmodern, Foucaultian, Derridean, pragmatist, and so on—that have challenged every concept and notion on which the intelligibility of First Amendment jurisprudence depends, he nevertheless retreats from those discourses just as their strongest (and most disturbing) implications come into view. He says that there is no such thing as a free speech principle and ends up delivering one that has all the properties he has taught us not to believe in.

He does it again, and in a smaller compass, in an introduction to the rich collection, *Censorship and Silencing*.[2] Post reports that the upshot of much recent work in social and political theory is to cast doubt on the usefulness of censorship as a coherent category, as a category naming an act that can be circumscribed and seen by everyone to be bad and even evil (as in "but that's censorship"). What we have now learned (and Post clearly includes himself in the "we") is that censorship is the "means by which discursive practices are maintained," and that since "social life largely consists of such practices . . . censorship is the norm rather than the exception" (2). Moreover, not only is censorship unavoidable, it is good because rather than inhibiting free expression, it is "the very condition of free expression" (3). Without the lines censorship draws between the permissible and the impermissible, the central and the peripheral, the desirable and the undesirable, no one would have positions or views and there would be no point to expressing them or encouraging them or fearing them.

The consequences of this new account of censorship, Post sees, are enormous, for absent the clear understanding of censorship as bad and unlimited expression as good, and absent the possibility of easily and uncontroversially identifying censors on the one hand and victims on the other, the entire rationale of free speech doctrine, dedicated to the protection against censorship of what censorship is now said to produce, falls to the ground. No sooner has Post given voice to this conclusion than he recoils from it: "These are exciting and important intellectual developments. For all their undeniable power, however, they seem to miss something of importance featured in more traditional accounts" (4). What they miss, he tells us, is the exemplary force of free speech heroes, like the "Pakistani writers resisting the oppression of a tyrannical regime" (4). It would seem that the "undeniable power" of these new intellectual developments is quite easy to deny, for that is what Post is doing when he assumes an unproblematic identification of oppressor and oppressed. It is not that the opposition between the Pakistani writers and a tyrannical regime cannot be framed, but that framing it thus is an act performed *within* the perspective of the Pakistani writers; presumably the tyrannical regime would frame it differently and would not accept for itself the designation "tyrannical."

The new intellectual developments Post cites do not take away anyone's ability to characterize his or her party as bravely resisting the imposition of state censorship, but they do take away the ability to support the characterization by invoking a normative standard to which all the parties in the political landscape would subscribe. Such a standard, were it available, would be universal, and it would thus provide what Post says the newer theoretical views "miss," a vantage point from which the specification of censor and censored, and therefore of hero and villain, could be made uncontroversially.

But surely "miss" is the wrong verb to describe what Foucaultian-based thought does to the possibility of such a vantage point; "demonstrates the unavailability of" or "shows to be illusory" or "destroys the basis of" would be verb phrases that better capture the relationship in all its corrosiveness. The "new scholarship of censorship" (4), the insights of which Post by and large accepts, does not "miss" the moment when someone or some group unambiguously stands up for free expression against the forces of moral and intellectual darkness. It says that there is no such moment, and it says this for all the reasons Post rehearses: the impossibility of sharply distinguishing censorship and free expression, each of which is constituitive of the other; the complicating of "any simple opposition between power and person" or state and individual; the emptying of the category "power as such" and the dispersal of power (to be sure in different and differently efficacious forms) to all the positions in a social or intellectual structure; and (the sum of all of these) the diminishment, almost to nothing, of "the force of censorship as a normative concept" (1–2).

Although Post assents to the force of these reasons, he nevertheless resists their implications when he criticizes the "Foucaultian perspective" because it "seems to flatten distinctions among kinds of power, implicitly equating suppression of speech caused by state legal action with that caused by the market, or by the dominance of a particular discourse" (4). Yes and no. These (and other) actions are equated only in that they are all exercises of power. It follows that if there are to be distinctions between them, the presence or absence of power or a calculation of greater and lesser power (made in relation to power as an isolatable and measurable concept) cannot be their basis. Rather, the distinctions will be established, if they are established, by partisan agents who are working to sort forms of activity into separate categories in the hope that such a sorting will lead to legislative and judicial outcomes they desire, outcomes that will constitutionalize some forms of speech regulation and outlaw others.

Of course, the distinctions so established will be no more firmly settled than the political process that will have produced them; and when that process takes another turn (as it always will), other partisan agents will have substituted the distinctions (and the outcomes) they favor for the ones that for a time seemed so securely in place. What will never be achieved is the establishment of distinctions immune from the political process, distinctions that one can invoke with the confidence that everyone will always find them perspicuous and determinative.

The unavailability of distinctions that preside over and guide the political process does not mean that the force of the normative is lost and that, as Post fears, there is no longer any basis for distinguishing between legitimate and illegitimate state action. Rather, it means that the normative is inside the political process, where it is a prize and not a given, at least not until the process registers a victory (temporary, although it may stand for hundreds of years) by one of the contending parties whose norms will for a while be the ones that can be unproblematically invoked.

Nor does this mean that the norms in which you believe and to which you adhere are ungrounded; it is just that they are not grounded in anything outside or independent of the complex of reasons, evidence, assumptions, goals, imperatives, ranked values, preferred outcomes, and so on, which, because it is the content of your consciousness, is determinative of what you see and what you will take to be the obviously right course of action in a particular situation. Much confusion has resulted from failing to see that saying there are no independent normative justifications—no justifications higher than those your belief system already recognizes—is not the same as saying there are no normative justifications. The first assertion says nothing more than that our convictions have no support in anything external to their structure and history. The absence of such support, however, is not a reason for doubting our convictions; rather, it is the explanation, not the reason—a reason would be too positive—of why we could not doubt them except by mechanisms built into them. A doubt introduced by an outside source or authority would not register except as a message from an alien context. One's consciousness is always fully formed and riding along quite nicely on the track of its own presuppositions.

To be sure, the content of your consciousness can change; you can be persuaded. Nothing, not even your deepest conviction, is invulnerable to the vicissitudes of that process. This does not mean that, as liberals often urge, it is your duty to expose your deepest conviction to every peril that might undo it. That would be the mistake of turning an inevitability (your opinions will change) into a positive moral program (you must work affirmatively to change your opinions). Nor is there any mechanism that will arrest the process, freeze-frame the play of politics, or protect the presently achieved normative judgments (even the judgment that the state cannot discriminate on the basis of race) from future alteration. To put it from the other direction, any mechanism designed to arrest the play of politics will be itself political—effective only as the extension of some partisan triumph—and will therefore always be available to a challenge from the very forces it has for a time managed to still.

Post suggests that this Foucaultian lesson—the lesson that politics or "agonism" is everywhere—has the effect of creating a new universalism; and unlike the old universalisms, which at least provided a basis for evaluation and choice, this new one takes away the basis of evaluation by rendering everything the same: "Agonism is precisely universal. It is precisely omniscient" (4). But this is to make agonism or politics into a *thing* (of the kind some want free speech or the marketplace of ideas to be), whereas in fact it is a condition—universal, to be sure, but not a value to be invoked, as one might invoke academic freedom or the search for truth or the free flow of ideas. No one says, or even thinks, "Let's do this for the sake of politics, for the sake of conflict and disagreement not as prerequisites for the flourishing of a good (full participation, the maximization of information) but as a good in and of itself."

In short, politics or agonism is not something you can choose or reject: it is the medium (the soup, the air) within whose ever-expanding confines (there is nothing outside it) one makes the kind of choices—so-called principled choices—to which it is rhetorically opposed. The fact that politics is everywhere has no normative *or* antinormative implications; it provides you with no program, nor does it take any away from you; it points you in no direction but only tells you that, whatever direction you find yourself taking, politics will be there, not as a byway or a danger or an impurity but as the very condition of action.

Politics and censorship are one, and are alike inescapable. The wonder is that even those like Post who see this are forever trying to escape it, usually by resurrecting in only a slightly disguised form the very concepts, ideals, and talismanic phrases they have recently laid to rest.

Richard Abel is another case in point. In *Speaking Respect, Respecting Speech,* he shows himself less inclined to philosophical analysis than Post, but his arguments and conclusions clearly place him in the ranks of those for whom First Amendment jurisprudence is a field without a doctrinal center or clear lines of opposition or principled means of settling disputes.[3] He describes his style as more "narrative" than theoretical. "I let my stories do the talking (without denying my ventriloquism)" (ix). His stories are many, but each of them helps to illustrate a set of related points: • First Amendment disputes are everywhere; • parties to First Amendment disputes claim to be serving the same abstractions (freedom, neutrality, autonomy, truth); • those abstractions (especially free speech) are never encountered in the real world because the very conditions of social life—the conditions of structure, hierarchy, and direction—require their violation; • since the disputes can't really be about the abstractions everyone ritually invokes, they must be about something else, and what they are about is "status politics," the efforts of various groups "to preserve, defend, or enhance the prestige of its own style of living" (59); • since each group " 'operates with an image of correct behavior which it prizes' " (59, quoting Joseph Gusfield) and there is no overriding standard of correctness (or truth or liberty) that might adjudicate their claims, there is no room for compromise ("Both sides see the conflict as a zero-sum game," 108), and therefore • "these controversies seemed insoluble" (55).

Along the way Abel considers and dismisses the usual devices or mantras for resolving them: • *the market place of ideas:* "The markets for speech, and thus the worth of messages are constructed" by state actions intent on "protecting ownership interests" (149); • *individual freedom:* "Private freedom is a mystification" because "the dichotomy between the public as a realm of constraint and the private as a realm of liberty" just doesn't hold up; "expression is always subject to constraints, private and public" (195); • *neutrality:* "Neither possible nor desirable" (159), a "chimera" beloved by those "hoping to escape politics and evade responsibility for choice" (246); • *a general theory of the value of speech:* "Because each constraint raises unique moral issues, there can be no general theory of free speech" (198).

All there can be are contexts, themselves not clearly configured in ways that everyone acknowledges and filled at every point and level with counter claims, mutual recriminations, and conflicting characterizations of what is at stake. Since expression "is always subject to constraints" and since in any situation of constraint the constraint will function to advance the interests of some group and retard the interests of some others, what we are left with is "the inevitability of prudential judgments weighing the value of speech in a particular context against the multitude of countervailing considerations" (195). We are left, in short, with politics as the realm which demands choice but can offer no recipe for making it. Because "judgments vary among people"—that's why politics is necessary; if judgment could be normalized, politics would have no reason for being—they "must be concrete" (195), that is, not general, abstract, theoretical, or principled.

It follows, then, that both the extreme positions one occasionally finds at either end of the First Amendment spectrum won't work. Absolute nonregulation won't work because, as Abel has said again and again, regulation is a constitutive feature of social life, not a deformation of it. Regulation tout court won't work because, given the capacity of human beings to recontextualize utterances, including the utterances of would-be regulators, the machinery of regulation will itself be appropriated by the play of interpretive agendas. "Legal efforts to regulate speech founder on the ineradicable ambiguity of meaning deployed by the ludic imagination" (243). Because "context is all . . . the moral content of symbols depends on the identities of a relationship between speaker and audience it can reverse instantly, like the optical illusion in which figure and ground oscillate between a vase and other profiled faces" (243).

After all this, the last thing one would expect is a proposal designed to stabilize the effects of speech by the production of more speech (the familiar Brandeis admonition), by the saying of something in a way that will surely (or even likely) have the effect of undoing or neutralizing or canceling out what has already been said. Yet that is what Abel proposes as the "antidote" (245) to harmful and "degrading" speech: "The best antidote to degrading speech is more speech, but of a particular kind: only an apology can rectify the status inequality constructed by harmful words. To achieve this, the social settings within which respect is conferred should encourage victims to complain through an informal process that evaluates speech in context and makes offenders render an apology acceptable to both victim and community" (245–246).

The problems with this proposal can be surfaced by subjecting it to questions Abel himself has posed throughout his book. Why should an apology be a privileged speech act, one whose effects could be more or less counted on? Abel spends considerable time recounting in rich detail the story of Salman Rushdie's back and forth response to the furor surrounding his *Satanic Verses*—at times defiant in the face of criticism, at other times issuing apologies (even converting and unconverting) that were accepted by some, rejected by others, and accepted and then unaccepted by still others. Not only did the apologies "take" differently, but, in the eyes of some, apologizing was a wrong step because there was nothing to apologize for. And of course the fact that Rushdie alternated apology with defiance cast doubt both on the apologies he had already made and (prospectively) on any apologies he might make in the future. What this history shows is that rather than stopping or damping down dispute, an apology will more than likely be the occasion for extending and complicating a dispute. An apology is just like any other verbal action; the relationship between the intention of its speaker (and what exactly the intention is can remain a mystery even to that speaker) and its reception will always be contingent on a myriad of unpredictable factors, factors that can neither be controlled nor mapped.

Moreover, there is a prior question: what would move someone already party to a deep conflict about the correct way to conduct public life to apologize in the first place? An apology is an admission of error—I'm sorry I did that or said that; I was wrong. But it is a feature of the conflicts Abel analyzes that no one thinks himself to be wrong: "Each antagonist championed fundamental values" (48); "Adversaries sought to score points, not to listen" (56); "Both sides see the conflict as a zero-sum game" (108). Therefore, there would seem to be no reason for anyone on either side to announce publicly that a previous utterance is now regretted (and every reason for those on the other side to suspect that any such announcement was merely strategic).

Only persons who valued peace and fellowship more than they valued the convictions in whose name they were fighting—that is, only persons whose strongest conviction was that peace was to be prized above anything—would perform an apology without reservation or subterfuge. And were there such persons, it would be hard to understand why they had ever painted themselves into apparently intractable corners in the first place, since the premium they placed on the achievement of communal harmony would have diminished their partisan ardor before it ever got out of control.

Abel's proposal, in sum, requires either disputants who are ready to withdraw from their most cherished beliefs (and I ask again, why should they be ready to do that?) or antidisputants whose most cherished beliefs are that we should all get along and that it is the obligation of the more advantaged to defer to the sensitivities of the less advantaged in the case of mutual accusations of disrespect. It is not that there are not such people; it is just that they are a special breed—call them classical liberals—for whom the highest obligation is to transcend or set aside one's own sense of interest in favor of a common interest in mutual cooperation and egalitarian justice. In short, the imperative to apologize flows from an ideology, one that universalizes respect and derives from that universalization an obligation, and it is an ideology subscribed to by none of the antagonists whose behavior Abel so amply reports. Rather it is *his* ideology, imposed (at least theoretically) on protagonists for whom it has little or no force, as he acknowledges under the rubric "Hard Questions": "My proposal is consciously partisan. It represents a decision not only to value status equality but also to favor some categories over others. In the zero-sum competition for status it is impossible to respect *both* Jews and anti-Semites, gays and homophobes, minorities and racists, women and misogynists" (273).

In fact, his proposal is *both* partisan and universalizing, as we can see from his paired opposites. Those who believe that homosexuality is unnatural and abhorrent wouldn't describe themselves as homophobes but as persons trying to hew to biblical precepts; those who cite evidence showing (to their satisfaction) that intelligence or some other positive feature is to be found more in some races than in others wouldn't describe themselves as racists but as persons intent on pursuing the truth, wherever it leads; those who resist the entry of women into the political and mercantile spheres wouldn't describe themselves as misogynists but as persons eager to respect the natural talents and capacities of women. In each instance the descriptive noun on the right side of the opposition is conferred from the perspective of those situated on the left side; the very framing of the sequence is thus partisan.

It is also universalizing because the epithets are applied confidently and casually, as if there could be no doubt that the characteristics they name are transparently the properties of the persons so designated. When Abel says "racist" or "homophobe," he is not adding "as I see it" but implying (by never stating) "as everyone sees it or should see it." His "partisan" judgment issues from a perspective presumed to be general, and it is a judgment on behavior that is obviously deviant only in relation to a norm he represents. When he declares that it is impossible to respect both gays and homophobes, it is clear which he respects, and it is clear too that he believes that it is a respect everyone who is right-thinking should perform. Racists and homophobes simply don't deserve respect, which is why Abel gives away so little when he labels his proposal "partisan"; it is the proposal of those who are partisans of the good and the true.

In saying this I shouldn't be understood as criticizing Abel. He does what everyone does when he presupposes the normative status of his own convictions and then configures the social and political landscape accordingly. He does no more or less than what those whose intractability he laments do; and because he is just like them in that respect—intractable in his beliefs, and especially in the belief that there must be status equality—his proposal will operate not to equalize status but further to entrench the status hierarchy implied by and inherent in his ready stigmatization (as racists, misogynists, homophobes) of those with whom he strongly disagrees. He is not the solution but more of the problem, insofar as the problem is the unhappy spectacle of antagonists brandishing fundamental values like clubs and refusing to listen to reason.

But that is a problem only if one thinks that there are alternatives to the endless wars of truth that make up human history, and to think *that* is to think (with classical liberals) that there is an alternative to politics, to the conflict between the visions of the good that compete for the right to order social life. Abel, however, has declared and massively documented the pervasiveness of politics, and one wonders, as in the case of Post, why in the end he fails to follow out the implications of his own lesson.

The puzzle is not solved but just provided with another piece when, just as in the case of Post, Habermas turns up to support the idea of a "structured conversation between victims . . . and offenders" (here assumed to be uncontroversially identifiable; 265), ending in a formal apology. Habermas's conversation is not labeled "ideal" for nothing; it requires, as I have already said, the shedding of all the baggage of belief, interest, desire, aspiration that, as Abel shows so persuasively, is inseparable from the condition of being human. It is not that the ideal conversation is a bad idea; it is an impossible idea, and it should certainly be regarded as impossible by someone, like Abel, who has repudiated the search for a First Amendment essence, who has insisted that constraints are everywhere and unavoidable, who has debunked neutrality and abandoned the hope of a general theory, and who has proclaimed, first, that context is all, and, second, that context is infinitely interpretable, if only by virtue of "the ineradicable ambiguity of meaning deployed by the ludic imagination" (243). When he brings in Habermas (if only in a footnote) Abel acts as if his own arguments have not been made and as if the hopes those arguments have exploded can find harbor in another theoretical construct.

Judith Butler knows better. She too cites Habermas, but only to explain why he would be an inappropriate resource for those who (like her) have tumbled to the fact that censorship, rather than being an exercise of power by one person intent on stifling the free expression of another, is constitutive of what both can and cannot be freely expressed (no censorship, no expression), and that therefore it is foolish to place one's hopes in a regime (or a principle, or a theory, or a bright line) that will see to it that only the right things are said and the wrong things remain unspoken.

"On the assumption that no speech is permissible without some other speech becoming *im*permissible, censorship is what permits speech by enforcing the very distinction between permissible and impermissible speech" (139), she writes in *Excitable Speech: A Politics of the Performative.*[4] The trouble with Habermas is that he wants to arrange things in advance so that what Abel calls the "ludic" energies and Butler the "performative" energies of language are held in check and only a certain kind of speech—speech aiming to express universally valid propositions—is allowed to occur. This requires, as Butler observes, a "consensually established meaning," a linguistic safe-house in which (the words are Habermas's) "the productivity of the process of understanding remains unproblematic" because "all participants stick to the reference point of possibly achieving a mutual understanding in which the *same* utterances are assigned the same meaning" (86–76). What Habermas urges is a form of benign censorship that banishes equivocation, deception, intimidation, verbal manipulation (all the traditional enemies of truth-seeking usually stigmatized under the rubrics of rhetoric and mere politics) from the public sphere, which will then be populated only by persons who mean one thing and say it straightforwardly in a way that cannot be misunderstood.

Butler's response to this linguistic utopianism (at least from the vantage point of rationalist philosophy) is a barrage of questions: "But are we, whoever 'we' are, the kind of community in which such meanings could be established once and for all? Is there not a permanent diversity within the semantic field that constitutes an irreversible situation for political theorizing? Who stands above the interpretive fray in a position to 'assign' the same utterances the same meanings? And why is it that the threat posed by such an authority is deemed less serious than the one posed by equivocal interpretation left unconstrained?" (87).

These questions imply that the Habermasian project is at once impossible and unworthy. It is impossible because the multidirectional fecundity or "diversity" Habermas fears is a property of language, not a misuse of it. The very words in which an edict mandating an interpretive straight line was promulgated would themselves be subject to interpretive swerves; interpretation cannot be closed down. And the Habermasian project is unworthy because closing down interpretation is what it aims to do, and Butler finds this aim (which she believes to be unachievable) retrograde and antidemocratic: "Risk and vulnerability are proper to democratic process in the sense that one cannot know in advance the meaning that the other will assign to one's utterance, what conflicts of interpretation may well arise, and how best to adjudicate that difference. The effort to come to terms is not one that can be resolved in anticipation but only through a concrete struggle of translation, one whose success has no guarantees" (87–88).

There are two strains of argument here, and one of them, as we shall see, takes Butler back in the direction of the essentialism and universalism she repeatedly rejects, whether it assumes Habermasian form or any other. The first strain insists (correctly, in my view) that effects cannot be designed in advance and that there is no way (verbal or physical) of acting that eliminates or precludes consequences other than those one hopes for. Politics, whether of speech or action, is not a medium capable of being stabilized; it can always take another and unexpected turn, and no amount of careful planning will assure either that it will stop on a particular dime or that it will respect no–entry signs even if they have traditionally been obeyed. Whatever one intends by a word or a deed (a distinction Butler, like Post and Abel, finally complicates), the career of its reception or "uptake" (a technical term in J. L. Austin's *Speech Act Theory*) is unpredictable and may well include effects that subvert the intention or mock it.

Butler's example is the speech act of threat: "The fantasy of sovereign action that structures the threat is that a certain kind of saying is at once the performance of the act referred to in that saying . . . The threat may well solicit a response, however, that it never anticipated, losing its own sovereign sense of expectation in the face of a resistance it advertently helped to produce. Instead of obliterating the possibility of response, paralyzing the addressee with fear, the threat may well be countered by a different kind of performative act, one that exploits the redoubled action of the threat . . . to turn one part of that speaking against the other, confounding the performative power of the threat" (12).

Technically, that is according to speech act theory as developed by Austin and John Searle, this is not quite right. The fact that a given speech act may draw an unanticipated response does not mean that it has not succeeded, for the attempted performance of an illocutionary act like the act of threatening is successful the moment the intention to perform it is recognized by the addressee. Illocutionary acts are conventional; one performs them by following a stipulated script or recipe known in advance to both parties. When party A says to party B

something both understand as portending a future action *C* assumed to be unwelcome and injurious to *B*, a threat has occurred.

To be sure, there are ways for attempted illocutionary acts to fail—*A* may have misjudged *B*, who may in fact desire the "infliction" of *C*, or the condition *C* would bring about already obtains (you can't threaten someone with an unhappy consequence he is already experiencing). But these are not the failures Butler has in mind when she notes the many ways in which "speech can be 'returned' to its speaker in a different form [and] can be cited against its originary purposes" (14). Rather, she has in mind what can happen after the illocutionary formula has "taken"—you understand the speaker's intention—and the threat has thereby been performed. What can happen, as she indicates, is almost anything, because recognizing that you have been threatened entails no necessary response beyond the (wholly conventional) response that is the content of the recognition. You can know you have been threatened and feel afraid; you can know you have been threatened and feel indifferent; you can know you have been threatened and feel angry; you can know that you have been threatened and you can laugh. It is in this important sense that Butler is right when she declares that "speech is always in some ways out of our control" (15).

It is those ways that interest her and solicit her positive concern. She argues not only that they cannot be shut down—control of speech and its effects is not a possibility—but that they should not be shut down because it is in the discursive space between an utterance and its work in the world that the possibility of resignification, revaluation, counter-appropriation, and, in a word, change opens up. One of her examples is the counter-appropriation by gays of epithets hurled at them as terms of opprobrium: "The revaluation of terms such as 'queer' suggest that speech can be 'returned' to its speaker in a different form . . . and per-form a reversal of effects" (14). This is but one instance of "the perfor-mative power of appropriating the very terms by which one has been abused in order to deplete the term of its degradation or to derive an affirmative from that degradation" (for example, "Black is beautiful"; 158). This "kind of talking back," Butler says, "would be foreclosed" if the reins on potentially harmful speech were tightened, even for benign reasons (15). Such a foreclosing would operate to forestall the performance of the "insurrectionary acts" that occur when ordinary or sedimented (and perhaps unfortunate) meanings are challenged (145). In many cases the very power of an addressee derives from the speech act directed against her, and that power would be diminished if regulation deprived her of the opportunity to turn speech meant to be injurious into an occasion for self-affirmation and political progress: "Insurrectionary speech becomes the necessary response to injurious language, a risk taken in response to being put at risk, a repetition in language that forces change" (163).

It is this last assertion or claim—"a repetition in language that forces change"—that veers in the universalizing direction I noted (but did not explain) earlier. The capacity of language to change and to initiate change even when the "same words" are repeated—or, more precisely, the incapacity of language and its effects to remain the same in the temporal space of repetition—is a *general* or theoretical capacity (or incapacity). It is a truth about language independent of its employment in any particular situation, and therefore it is a truth about language that has no necessary implications for its employment in any particular situation.

You may know that when you say "If you don't come tomorrow, I'll disinherit you" your attempt to threaten may backfire or misfire because language's destination is never sure; but that (theoretical) knowledge will not weigh on your decision to utter or not utter the threat. What might weigh is knowledge of the person you are attempting to threaten, whether he or she is likely to be easily intimidated or whether the attempt at intimidation is likely to be met with resistance and so on. Your calculation will be made in relation to such contextual variables (which in institutional settings will include in-force conventions governing the production and reception of speech; members of Congress know that in some contexts they can say things with no danger that anyone will take them seriously) and not in relation to some highly abstract truth the realization of which will always be mediated by those same variables.

Similarly, it may be true that in some ultimate sense censorship is impossible because, as Butler observes, it names and produces that which it would suppress; and it may also be true that elimination of constraints on speech is equally impossible because, as Abel and Post observe, constraints are a precondition of expression. But knowledge of those truths will not stop the would-be regulator who may have good reason to believe that in the short run his effort to curtail a certain kind of expression will succeed; nor will it prevent the would-be liberator from trying to remove a restriction that frustrates his desire to proclaim his views. General theories of language (even for persons so odd as to be persuaded by one) do not determine or even influence verbal behavior because there is no direct line from the abstract level of their operation to the very particular level of lived life where threats are made, apologies given, commands uttered. General theories of language, in short, do not dictate or enable a politics, for politics, as everyone has now learned to say, is local.

There is one exception to this rule, and it may be an exception of which Butler's argument is an instance. General theories of language may dictate a politics that is universal, or, as I would put it, a politics that is not a politics. This would be the case if when Butler celebrated the capacity of language (in the course of being revalued or counter-appropriated) to force change, she was interested only in the capacity and not the nature of the change being forced or the state of affairs the change was unsettling. She would then be privileging change as a universal good rather than worrying about whether a particular change was desirable or achievable. That this is so is indicated by her description of the counter-appropriative performative as one that can "compel a critical perspective on existing institutions" (158), and by her praise of the "insurrectionary moment . . . the moment that founds a future through a break with [the] past" (159).

If you ask which institutions will be the object of this critical perspective, the answer seems to be any and all institutions; and if you ask "Break with which past?" the answer seems to be any past. The insurrectionary moment is welcomed and courted not for what it specifically brings about but for what it brings about in general, the "overthrowing" of "established codes of legitimacy" (147), whatever they happen to be. "The possibility for the speech act to take on a nonordinary meaning, to function in contexts where it has not belonged, is precisely the political promise of the performative, one that positions the performative at the center of a politics of hegemony, one that offers an unanticipated political future for deconstructive thinking" (161).

A politics of hegemony is a politics in which one party or interest gains dominance over another or over many others, and it is to this that Butler opposes her preferred politics of deconstructive thinking. But all politics is the politics of hegemony, for politics is only necessary or possible when there are contending visions of the good and no God or self-interpreting scripture to decide between them. Given that condition—the human condition—you must struggle to establish the vision to whose truth you are persuaded; you must struggle to establish hegemony. The alternative—and, not surprisingly, it is the alternative offered in the liberal tradition that stretches from Mill to Rawls—is a politics (if that is the word) impelled by no vision except the vision in which all visions are suspect as "historically sedimented" (159) pretenders to universal authority; and in the context of that politics, what you do and do endlessly is "rethink" (162) whatever views you happen to hold. This, says Butler, is "to rethink one's politics" (162), but in fact it is to substitute rethinking *for* politics, to substitute for the project of implementing your agenda the project of submitting your agenda, whatever it might be, to the searching scrutiny of deconstructive interrogation.

One might argue that in fact this *is* a politics, and call it "the politics of rethinking"; but there is no *politics* of rethinking, just an assumption that rethinking is a general obligation that overrides the obligations that might come along with the political programs to which you have become attached. This assumption is not argued for; it is more like an article of faith, a faith that rethinking or revaluing or counter-appropriating will lead to a better world populated by better persons. And it is a universalizing assumption because it is indifferent to outcomes, to how things turn out in the world, and concerned only to enjoin a single activity (rethinking) that is, like virtue, its own reward.

This indifference to outcomes is signaled when Butler describes the "political future" deconstructive thinking will make possible as "unanticipated" (161). That is, where it will take us is not known, and that is what's good about it. Not constrained or controlled by hegemonic purpose but driven only by the purpose to unsettle the ordinary and the sedimented, deconstructive thinking will bring us to a brave new world of whose outlines we are necessarily (and happily) ignorant.

It should hardly be a surprise that this is exactly the promise (if it can be called that) held out by the fabled marketplace of ideas. If we forgo our natural tendency to regulate and if we allow speech to flourish more or less unconstrained, our reward will be the emergence of general and self-evident truths rather than the imposition (through censorship or state-enforced adherence to favored views) of someone's or some group's truths. Particular outcomes are less important than the process which assures that no one outcome will either be mandated or ruled out in advance. Like Post and Abel, Butler entertains and approves a radical critique of the components of First Amendment jurisprudence, only to come back in the end to its familiar conclusions and recipes.

Where traditional First Amendment jurisprudence counsels distrust of received opinion and puts its faith in a future-oriented proceduralism, Butler counsels a "break with [the] past" (159). Where traditional First Amendment jurisprudence tells us that the answer to speech is more speech, Butler tells us that the answer to speech is counter-appropriative speech. Where traditional First Amendment jurisprudence sees itself as the extension of the democratic preference for resolutions that emerge from a free-for-all competition between opposing views, Butler wishes to promote the "risk and vulnerability" that are "proper to democratic process" (87). (In saying this, she seems to imply that risk and vulnerability are the *goals* of democratic process, whereas it would be more correct to say that risk and vulnerability are inescapable features of the conditions within which democratic process unfolds.)

The politics of rethinking turns out to be pretty much indistinguishable from the politics of classical liberalism, with its insistence that nothing be foreclosed and everything be left open to revision and its disinclination to allow any commitment or value to be regarded as sacrosanct. The politics of rethinking turns out, in short, to be the anti-politics—suspicious of closure and downright hostile to the notion of anyone winning—that has been with us at least since Mill's *On Liberty*.

Or so would be the case if Butler really meant it, if she, like the libertarians who now supply so much of First Amendment rhetoric, were really indifferent to how issues were resolved so long as the process remained radically open. In fact, however, she is not at all indifferent and has quite specific ideas about how certain First Amendment disputes should be adjudicated. She thinks that pornographic representations should not be regulated, but that racist messages, especially those that take the form of "symbolic" speech like the burning of a cross on a black family's lawn, should be. The question, of course, is how to justify the distinction (which I am neither endorsing nor challenging, only reporting), and the answer involves her not in the generalized activity of rethinking but in the very particular activity of manipulating First Amendment categories in order to bring about a desired political result. Before our very eyes, the theorist turns rhetorician (in saying this I am bestowing a compliment), at once deriding the playing of games and playing the games she derides.

The game that most concerns her is the manipulation of the speech/conduct distinction. She notes that, depending on its direction, this manipulation can serve diametrically opposed political ends. A

Supreme Court disinclined to take racial injury seriously might employ a nonperformative view of speech—a view of speech as merely a medium for delivering messages—"to defend certain kinds of racist conduct" by moving that conduct into a category of protected actions; while in the other direction, the direction of a Catherine MacKinnon, a court might employ a performative view of speech—a view of speech as producing effects in the world—in order to extend "the power of state intervention over graphic sexual representation" (21–22). In one case the power of the state will be curtailed, in the other augmented. But in either case, a court will have put the prudential horse before the theoretical cart. First comes the result it desires or thinks intuitively right, and then comes the invocation of the view of speech (performative or nonperformative) that will aid in producing the result.

As an account of how the courts have dealt with pornography and racist speech issues respectively, this seems to me exactly right, as does Butler's conclusion that what we see in decisions like *R.A.V. v. St. Paul* and *Miller v. California* is the manipulation of "the distinction between speech and conduct in order to achieve certain political aims" (22). ("This same court has been willing . . . to use the very rationale proposed by some arguments in favor of hate-crime legislation to augment its case to exclude obscenity from protected speech"; 62.) What I find curious is the note of complaint in the account, first because such manipulation is exactly what one would expect if, as Butler herself says, discursive categories are inherently unstable and always subject to dispute and revision (were the line between speech and conduct drawn by nature, fashioning a coherent and generally acceptable First Amendment jurisprudence would be easy), and second because manipulation of doctrinal distinctions is what she herself is doing, and necessarily so (only if such distinctions were self-interpreting would manipulation—another word for interpretation—be unnecessary and the clear occasion for moral blame).

That is to say, Butler resists blurring the distinction between speech and conduct not as a matter of principle but because she fears that a court hostile to lesbian and gay interests might seize an opportunity to regulate acts of speech whose proliferation she favors. Any "extension of state power" would, she says, "represent one of the greatest threats to the discursive operation of gay and lesbian politics," a large part of which consists of "'speech acts' that can be, and have been, construed as offensive and, indeed, injurious conduct" (22).

This is admirably straightforward: I value and desire to protect certain utterances and images (regarded by some as pornographic) central to gay and lesbian culture. Their protection is more likely if the speech/conduct distinction is maintained. Therefore, it should be maintained. Except, that is, in the case of at least some racist utterances and images which I do not value or wish to protect. Then I argue that what has been called a message is really conduct, and conduct of a kind the state should move to prevent. To be sure, Butler gives reasons for her uneasiness at transmuting an act like the burning of a cross into a speech act in which someone sends someone else a message. Such a classification, she says, "refuses the dimension of social power that constructs the so-called speaker and the addressee of the speech act in question" and "refuses as well the racist history of the convention of cross-burning by the Ku Klux Klan . . . which portended a further violence against a given addressee" (55). But as she no doubt knows, antipornography theorists like Catherine MacKinnon give similar reasons, also referencing power and recalling the unhappy history of a convention, in order to argue for the regulation of speech *they* consider harmful.

One can, as Butler does, *assert* a difference—"the visual text of pornography cannot 'threaten' or 'demean' or 'debase' in the same way the burning cross can" (21)—but the differences will not have been generated by the reasons marshaled to support it. Rather, the difference is assumed as a constitutive center of Butler's worldview, and it is within its assumption that the reasons will be seen as reasons and fall into their prepared place. It is not that I am unpersuaded by Butler's arguments; it is just that when I am persuaded it is not because her theoretical distinctions are independently perspicuous but because her political investments dovetail (at least in part) with mine, and together we move toward the conclusion we have both desired from the beginning.

Butler might well agree, for the best comment on her performance in this book is one she provides: "It would be a mistake to think that working out the theoretical problems of the speech act will offer a set of clarifying solutions to the contemporary political operation of the speech act. The relation between theory and politics tends to work the other way. Theoretical positions are always appropriated and deployed in political contexts that expose something of the strategic value of such theories" (20). I would balk only at "expose," which suggests that the strategic value of a theory is something it possesses inherently and that certain political contexts serve to bring it out. In fact, theories are the products of political contexts—of the need in a particular situation for an explanation of what has already been done or for an apparently principled justification of what you are about to do—and when the abstract (and substantively empty) vocabulary of a "theoretical position" is appropriated by a political agenda other than the one in whose service it was first thought up, its strategic value will have changed.

Butler both reports on such changes—when she criticizes courts for using the same theoretical formulas to reach conclusions that are manifestly inconsistent with one another—and performs them—when she first attacks the universalism of Habermas and others, then produces (as do Post and Abel) a new universalism in the form of the politics of rethinking, and then reveals (and this is what puts her one up on Post and Abel in my book) that the politics of rethinking is to be selectively employed (rethink this, but not that) and subordinated to her (plain old) politics.

Nor could it be otherwise. Those who have read this far will know before I say it that I am not faulting Butler for filling her theoretical and doctrinal vocabulary with a substantive political content. That is what everyone does and what everyone has to do because a vocabulary with no substantive political content could not be linked up (except in a wholly arbitrary way) with the real-world situations in relation to which one might wish to invoke it. That is to say, the abstractions at the center of First Amendment jurisprudence—freedom of expression, the free flow of ideas, self-realization, self-governance, equality, autonomy—do not in and of themselves point us to the appropriate distinctions or help us to order a set of facts on the way to rendering an opinion. Before we can proceed to do those things, the abstractions have to be filled in with specifications of what is included in their scope, specifications they themselves do not provide.

Although free speech values supposedly stand alone and are said to be independent of circumstance and political pressure, they only become thick enough to provide a direction for decisionmaking when definitions and distinctions borrowed from particular circumstances (and borrowed selectively in relation to some substantive agenda) are presupposed as their content. You must determine what you mean by "expression" or what is and is not a "free flow" or what does and does not constitute "self-realization" in relation to what notion of the self before any of these so-called principles will have any bite. And since these are not determinations those principles can make for themselves, when they do have bite, when invoking them actually gets you somewhere, it will be because inside them is the outside—substantive values, preferred outcomes, politics—from which they are rhetorically distinguished.

It is the resistance to this insight that accounts for the persistence of theory even in the thought of those like Post, Abel, and Butler who spend much of their time challenging the coherence and intelligibility of the theory project. On the one hand, these commentators are persuaded that there is no road from a (nonexistent) general theory of free speech to the outcomes they desire; but on the other hand, they do desire those outcomes and cannot quite bring themselves to urge them "nakedly," that is, as deriving from their substantive visions of what is good and desirable rather than from a formal procedural vision in which the question of what is good and desirable has been bracketed. So what they do in their different ways is veer back in the direction of theory and a universalizing proceduralism in order to give their substantive agendas the kind of pedigree they have just shown to be unavailable.

To this one might say (and I myself am tempted to say it) "So what? Dressing up one's agenda in procedural garb so as to increase its chances of getting enacted might be a good, even necessary, strategy, and if the strategy works, what's the harm?" One answer to this question has been given by a series of articles in which it is suggested that those who work to frame their agendas in the language of formal theory may become confused about what their own agenda is and pursue lines of argument inimical to their interests. This is the conclusion reached by Peter Weston in his "The Empty Idea of Equality."[5] Weston's basic thesis is the one I have been urging throughout: formal abstractions have no content of their own, and to get content they must go to the very realm of messy partisan disputes about substantive goods of which they claim to be independent: "Equality . . . tells us to treat like people alike; but when we ask who 'like people' are, we are told 'they are people who should be treated alike.' Equality is an empty vessel with no substantive moral content of its own. Without moral standards, equality remains meaningless, a formula that can have nothing to say about how we should act. With such standards, equality remains superfluous, a formula that can do nothing but repeat what we already know" (547).

In a footnote to this passage, Weston declares, "Equality is not alone in its emptiness." Any abstract principle (he instances freedom) will have this twin liability of having nothing of pointed urgency to say to us (because without specific moral content it says too much and too little) and of being superfluous if we have gotten our moral content else-where—if your substantive convictions are already telling you what to do, why invoke an abstraction that adds nothing but the illusion of higher legitimization? Even the idea of justice falls to this analysis. It is, says Weston, "entirely formal" (556), that is, without any guiding speci-fication. "It requires that persons be given their 'due' but does not itself define what is their 'due'" (557). In order to remedy this deficiency, "one must look beyond the proposition that every person should be given his due to the substantive moral or legal standards that determine what is one's 'due'" (557).

The same reasoning holds for the familiar legal principle "Treat like persons alike," a mainstay mantra of First Amendment and affirmative action jurisprudence. Substantive notions of racial justice or the right to free exercise do not derive from the injunction but give it content and direction. Unless the relevant likeness and unlikeness has already been specified in moral/empirical terms, saying "Treat like persons alike" will be entirely unhelpful and obfuscatory. "Rights of religion and speech and religion, rights of race and sex, can be stated without refer-ence to 'likes' or 'equals.'" Indeed, "not only *can* they be so stated, they *must* be so stated, because they provide the standards by which people are rendered 'alike' or 'unlike.'" (565).

It is a question always of what comes first, and Weston is saying that contextual judgments as to what is and is not morally relevant come first, and then and only then will formal formulas tell us anything, and even so they will be telling us what we already know. If the process is reversed and you begin with the formal formula, you will be proceeding in an entirely haphazard fashion because the relevant judgments have not yet been made: "When one is ignorant as to whether people are likely to be alike in morally significant respects, a presumption in favor of treating people alike is as unjustified as a presumption in favor of treating them *un*alike," for "each presumption creates an unjustified risk that it will deny people the treatment to which they are actually entitled" (573).

Weston acknowledges an apparent paradox in his argument: he is asserting that equality and other formal universals are empty and add nothing to determinations already made on other bases, and yet he is urging that invoking such universals leads to bad results, which suggests that they may not be so empty after all. (How can something without content affect content?) He responds by arguing that when decision-makers wield concepts that give them no genuine help and confer instead only a baseless confidence, they will be directed away from the real issues and produce opinions that serve only to muddy the waters: "Although equality is derivative [useful only when it is informed by substantive distinctions brought in from elsewhere], people do not real-ize that it is derivative, and not realizing it, they allow equality to distort the substance of their decisionmaking" (592). "As a form of analysis, equality [one could substitute freedom, justice, neutrality, autonomy] confuses far more than it clarifies" because "by masquerading as an independent norm, equality conceals the real nature of the substantive rights it incorporates [unknowingly] by reference" (579).

One year later Larry Alexander and Paul Horton made basically the same argument with respect to the formal principle of "freedom of speech." Whether your First Amendment analysis rests on deontologi-cal assumptions or consequentialist assumptions, whether you are con-cerned to protect individual autonomy or increase the free flow of ideas, " 'freedom of speech' will not have its own principle, but instead will be part of a more general liberty," or subordinate to the desire for a specific outcome (1321).[6] The moment one seeks to justify the principle of free-dom of speech, the principle, as something free-standing, will have been compromised: " 'Free speech is justified because . . . ' What comes after the 'because' inevitably will link free speech with something else, usually more basic, and thus will destroy free speech's independence. Put differently, any attempt to *justify*, rather than merely to identify, a free speech principle will require acceptance of principles that are broader than the free speech principle itself, with respect to which the free speech principle is not independent" (1356).

The reasons Alexander and Horton give for this judgment are famil-iar and constitute a summary of the points made by Post, Abel, Butler, and other free speech revisionists: " 'Speech,' we contend, does not denote any particular set of phenomena. Everything, including all human activities, can 'express' or 'communicate,' and an audience can derive meaning from all sorts of human and natural events. Moreover, 'speech' is regulated and affected by regulation in a multitude of differ-ent ways and for a multitude of different reasons. Finally, with respect to any value, 'speech' both serves and disserves that value in an indefi-nite variety of ways and degrees. Considering these points, it would be truly amazing if 'freedom of speech' really did have a coherent and independently justifiable principle all its own" (1322). Given the impossibility of identifying an independent free speech principle, there is no basis for any "special treatment of 'speech'" such that it would be obviously and uncontroversially "distinguished from other activities" (1349).

And in the absence of either a free-standing principle or a notion of speech that marks it off clearly from the more inclusive category of action, there is nothing *general* to say about speech with respect to regulation. "Instead," Alexander and Horton conclude, "there are merely some improper regulations of speech, just as there are some improper regulations of other activities. And we may put our pretheoretical intuitions aside, to await a narrower articulation of free speech principles in the specific contexts in which specific governmental regulations of specific communicative activity are brought to our attention" (1357). That is, we must await the identification of what is and is not "improper" in relation to moral and empirical determinations no principle of free speech will generate, for it is only when such determinations are arrived at by other means that the so-called principle will be armed and alive. In short, we must await, and work for, the outcomes of politics.

In a more recent article, Alexander generalizes this argument so that it extends to all procedural rights and imperatives, which, he argues in a now-familiar vein, "just *are* substantive rights" (19).[7] Whenever we have procedural rights, they are "secondary to substantive rights because they are rights about official determinations of the facts governing the application of substantive rights" (23). Moreover, because these determinations are made not from a God's-eye perspective but from a perspective that is partial, they provide only a challengeable and corrigible ground for identifying what our rights and duties are: "We each calculate the probabilities of adjudicative facts differently because our perspectives are different; and the calculations of probabilities themselves, and not just the probabilities about adjudicative facts, will also differ due to differences in perspective" (23).

The implications of this argument for the theory project and for liberalism in general are far-reaching and dire. Liberalism begins in the recognition of the plurality of perspectives and pins its hopes on the possibility of carving out a realm within which differing perspectives can be accorded equal procedural rights. But if the specification of those rights and of their application is dependent on a prior perspective-sensitive interpretation of moral and empirical facts, there is no merely procedural realm; and rather than offering a rational alternative to substantive, agenda-driven judgments, procedural rights and rules are merely one form (and that a self-deluding form) that substantive agenda-driven judgments take. Procedural rights and rules, despite their promise to save us from agonism and politics, are politics by another name.

I have quoted extensively from the work of Weston, Alexander, and Horton because they at once provide support for what Post, Abel, and Butler say about the impossibility of a coherent and workable First Amendment theory and enlarge the argument so that it includes the theory project in general. Where, however, does this leave us? First of all, it leaves us without a ground of justification more basic or higher than the grounds given us by our moral convictions and determinations of fact. There is no theory or principle or bright line that will allow us to rise above or step to the side of the conclusions we have reached as situated political agents. This is the lesson read to us by all the theorists examined in this essay, and to it I have added the lesson that nothing of a positive or helpfully negative kind can be derived from this lesson. Knowing that no theory or principle will drop from the sky puts you in no better position to decide what to do than you were in when you were waiting on (and expecting) revelation. An awareness that a free speech principle is unavailable will not equip you with resources to deal with the next free speech dilemma that comes your way. At the very most it will (or should; remember the examples of Post, Butler, and Abel) tell you where not to look and will refocus your attention on questions that actually have answers because they are rooted in an understanding of what is really at stake—*never* an abstraction like equality or free speech—and of the possible alternative courses of action.

This, at any rate, is the hope harbored by Frederick Schauer in a recent essay. Schauer's subject is censorship, and he begins by making and accepting the point made by Post, Abel, and Butler. Censorship, he reminds us, is usually thought of as an external constraint on one's individual expressive preferences; but what if our preferences were themselves determined by the same kind of external constraint? This would mean that censorship, broadly conceived as a restraint on expressive action, was an inescapable ingredient of all expression, and that would mean that the notion could not be used to mark off a desirable condition (freedom of expression) from an undesirable one (coerced or regulated expression). "For if the [traditional] use of the word *censorship* presupposes that censorship is a readily identifiable subset of the set of human activity, then it makes no sense to identify as such a subset something that is part and parcel of all human activity" (149).[8]

It would then be the case (as Schauer thinks it to be) that to characterize something as censorship is to mark a difference (between speech acts you think should be regulated and speech acts you think should not be), not to explain it: "I am tempted to conclude that the word *censorship*, which is largely even if not exclusively pejorative (and that is why censors always deny that they are censoring, even when they are censoring for good purposes), does not describe a [distinct] category of conduct, but rather attaches an operative conclusion (ascribes) to a category on other grounds" (160).

Those other grounds are the grounds of politics, the grounds on which one decides that some forms of speech are valuable and others are not; it is not to censorship per se that people object but to "the particular substance of the censorious acts that are necessary for the maintenance of language as we know it" (153). In other words, censorship is the name you give to censorious acts of which you disapprove; censorious acts that have effects you like will receive another name and be attached to some principle (good order, equality, democratic process) you take them to be protecting or promoting. In any controversy, therefore, the choice is never between censorship and noncensorship, constrained speech and free speech, but between different operations of constraint and authority. So that the "question . . . is not whether artists should be censored"; rather, the question is "whether the judgments of curators should be preferred to the judgments of the state and whether the forces of the market should be preferred to the forces of politics" (162).

Forces there will always be—no zone of freedom in this argument— and thus the traditional language of censorship, assuming as it does an autonomous agent whose autonomy can be infringed, is inappropriate. "The language I would substitute for the language of censorship is thus the language that we might use in making [any and all] social decisions about the allocation of content-determining authority and the language that a society might use in negotiating competing claims for the right to exercise that authority" (163). That language would not itself do normative work but would record the result of normative work done in the crucible of social life, with its disputes and (temporary) resolutions; it would "identify whose choices we as a society wish to privilege and whose choices we wish to suspect" (163). And, it cannot be said too often, those choices will be political, not theoretical. Thus, for example, "in the context of funding for the arts, the question is whether the judgments of artistic peers, themselves infused with the politics of art . . . should be preferred to the judgments of public officials, which are equally infused with politics of a different kind" (162–163). Not politics or the avoidance of politics, but politics proceeding from this set of interests rather than that.

Schauer, then, comes out just about where Weston, Alexander, and Horton come out, with a warning against employing the misleading and empty vocabulary of abstraction and formal principle and an injunction to keep one's eye on the true question of concern (What do we think good and what part of the machinery of First Amendment jurisprudence and of law in general will help us to realize it?) and not involve ourselves in profitless questions directed at entities (free speech, equality, freedom, justice) that do not exist. As some of the writings I have examined in this chapter show, the advice will be hard to follow, in part because the lure of the formal universal with its promise of a space insulated from political "distortion" is so powerful that it inflects even our framing of an issue.

Consider, for example, what has often been called the "problem" of hate speech, a "problem" to which several of those I discuss obsessively return. I put "problem" in quotes so as to flag it as a noninnocent usage. The problem with "problem" is that, unqualified, it means "problem for everyone," or a problem universally, as in the problems (for everyone except perhaps fanatic Malthusians) of hunger and disease. Hate speech, however, is not such a problem; rather, it is the pejorative designation by one party of the way of thinking and talking central to the beliefs and agenda of another party. Moreover, not only is it a mistake to term hate speech a problem, and thus to imply that a cure for it may someday be found in a pill or a book whose consumption will render any reader morally healthy, it is a mistake with consequences. It gets in the way of thinking about strategies for dealing with that which you regard as dangerous and a source of evil. If the evil is given no particular location but is regarded more or less as a virus that mysteriously affects some people and leaves others uninfected, you will think in terms of remedies or, in cases where the disease is too far gone, of quarantine. But if the evil is given a location in a worldview you despise and fear—not an irrational worldview (calling speech you loathe "irrational" is another form of universalizing and trivializing) but a view equipped with reasons, evidence, and authorities you reject and find truly harmful—you will think in agonistic and political terms and begin to figure out how you can stigmatize, oppress, and in general get the better of an enemy.

Here is another example of the way in which the liberal tendency to turn substantive convictions into formal abstractions—either good as in freedom or equality or bad as in hate speech or bigotry—can trick you into mistaking the true nature of your objective (not freedom or equality but some politically realizable state of affairs) and minimizing (by universalizing) the threat to its being accomplished. So long as hate speech, bigotry, and discrimination are conceptualized as "problems" rather than as the names you have given to acts of discrimination other than those you think good and right, you will never get a handle on them and you will be reduced, as liberals have been in the past twenty years, to hand-wringing and pious exhortations.

I recognize the harshness of this conclusion, which is more Hobbesian than Millian or Rawlsian. It is a conclusion Sanford Levinson reaches reluctantly after he surveys the pro and con arguments for state regulation of monuments and statuary and finds himself on one side or the other depending on whether or not he approves the purposes of the state in a given instance. "I am happy with the state's playing a tutelary role . . . as long as I am happy with the state's substantive decisions as to whom to honor (or dishonor)."[9] Immediately after saying this, Levinson recoils against it: "Does it simply boil down to whose ox is gored or cultural symbol honored? One would like to say 'No,' especially if one is a liberal yearning for neutral standards that enable us to transcend our own substantive politics . . . But I do not now what those standards are" (211).

Not to worry. Nobody else does either, and the large lesson to be taken from the "new" (anti)theorists of the First Amendment—a lesson they occasionally resist even as they teach it—is that the unavailability of neutral standards or of a general theory of free speech or of a core free speech principle or of a formal mechanism for making decisions about regulating and not regulating does not prevent us either from knowing what is good or working to bring it about. That knowledge is ours by virtue of being situated moral beings; and if we go with it and do not disdain it in favor of empty abstractions, it will direct us to the resources, wholly and benignly political, by means of which our deepest convictions and aspirations might be realized.

But, one might ask, what exactly are (or should be) our deepest aspirations and convictions? I shall not answer that question because, were I to do so, I would be urging some particular vision of the good, whereas it is my purpose in this book only to argue that particular visions of the good are unavoidable. That argument, in and of itself, is not and could not without contradiction be an argument for either affirming or rejecting any particular vision. That kind of argument, in which I am happy to engage, would take place in some historical context of substantive dispute, exactly the context neutral principles were designed to bypass or transcend. Denying that there are any such neutral principles commits me to nothing substantive, but neither does it place me in a position of detachment from substantive conflict. Rather, it tells me (and you) that such detachment is impossible and that any claim to have achieved it is either empty or part and parcel of a substantive strategy (or both).

I am aware that on the surface this might seem to be my version of the neutrality I so often deride. But it is not. The difference is that liberal neutrality is positive; it directs you to do something, to bracket or set aside your substantive convictions; my neutrality (if that is the word, and it isn't) leaves you where you always were, in the grip of whatever substantive convictions have become yours by virtue of experience and education. It is the minimalism rather than the neutrality of my position that should be emphasized. If that position finds you in the condition of always and already being in the embrace of your convictions, it does not claim to have *produced* the condition it finds, only to report on it. Embracing your convictions is not (by my argument) an option; therefore I could not be recommending it, only trying to explain why it is inescapable, an explanation that does no positive work, pushes you in no particular direction, but tells you that being in a particular direction is both the limitation (no transcendence available) and the glory (a field of opportunity is always opening up before you) of your situation.

REASONS FOR THE DEVOUT

VICKI FROST OBJECTS

Whenever the law deals with children, a tension emerges between the desire, basic to liberalism, to protect individual autonomy and the desire to protect children by restricting their activities. This is especially the case in the realm of education, which is by definition a matter of leading or guiding those who cannot yet be trusted to fashion their own life plan. The issue becomes crystallized in those cases where children's First Amendment rights are debated. The question, simply, is "Can education and the First Amendment be reconciled?" and I would like to answer with a simple no.

Now of course I don't mean no as a matter of empirical report—we do have a First Amendment and we do have education, so in some important sense they are reconcilable. Rather, I mean no as a matter of philosophical logic. If you assume (as most commentators do) that one of the important values supported by the First Amendment is freedom of choice, you will be suspicious of any form of instruction whose intention or effect is to indoctrinate rather than to illuminate. That is why the Association of American University Professors, the self-anointed guardian of academic freedom, has always looked askance at religiously based colleges and universities; for rather than being committed to the disinterested play of ideas, they turn out to be very interested in the promulgation of some ideas and the exclusion of some others. Such institutions, the AAUP declared in its 1915 statement of principles, should be allowed to exist, but they should not be allowed to "sail under false colors" as true centers of education, for "genuine boldness and thoroughness of inquiry, and freedom of speech, are scarcely reconcilable with the prescribed inculcation of a particular opinion."[1]

"Inculcation" might be thought of as a prophetic word here since it figures prominently in those First Amendment cases that address the rights and needs of children. "Inculcate" means "to teach by forceful urging, to instill," and the question debated in these cases is, first, whether or not it is a good thing to have education without inculcation—education that stops short of instilling anything except, perhaps, the conviction that nothing is to be instilled—and, second, whether or not it is a *possible* thing to have education without inculcation. To both these questions, liberalism—by which I mean not a set of specific policies but a theory of government which requires the state to maintain neutrality in the face of competing moral visions—answers yes. Education without inculcation is the American way because it allows students to make up their minds and decide for themselves, without the pressure of orthodoxy and authority.

The point is made vigorously and with an easy confidence in these oft-cited sentences from a 1967 case, *Keyishian v. Board of Regents:* "The classroom is peculiarly the 'marketplace of ideas.' The nation's future depends upon leaders trained through wide exposure to that robust exchange of ideas which discovers truth 'out of a multitude of tongues' rather than through any kind of authoritative selection."[2] But this cannot mean what it says; for without "authoritative selection," education, whether public or private, would be impossible. As one commentator has observed, elected and appointed representatives of the state control almost all aspects of public education—the membership of school boards, the selection and accreditation of teachers, the purchasing of texts, the design of the curriculum, the administration of tests, the granting of degrees, the form and content of ceremonies, and on and on.[3]

Moreover, not only is the requirement of "no authoritative selection" impossible so long as education is, in any sense, organized, it also runs up against the competing requirement—which goes without saying but is often said—that education prepares students to participate usefully in the business of a democratic society by instilling in them the appropriate democratic values. Here is an early statement by Noah Webster: "Education . . . forms the moral characters of men, and morals are the basis of

REASONS FOR THE DEVOUT

government. Education should therefore be the first care of a legislature" and "should be watched with the most scrupulous attention."[4]

It would seem, then, that the ideal of education without inculcation suffers from two fatal defects: either it is an ideal compromised the moment the first lesson plan is implemented (for then authoritative selection will have already occurred), or it is an ideal at odds with the very reason for having a system of education in the first place (the fashioning of good citizens). The answer to either of the questions I posed a few moments ago—"Is education without inculcation possible?" and "Is education without inculcation a good thing?"—would seem to be no. And if the answer to both of these questions is no, then the answer to the question "Can education and the First Amendment be reconciled?" is also no, for it is precisely the purpose of education to protect children from bad—that is, undemocratic—ideas by introducing them *forcefully* (an adverb that hovers nicely between a style of emphasis and coercion) to good ideas. This purpose cannot be carried out without compromising a child's First Amendment rights, traditionally thought to include the right to form one's own opinions, to make up one's own mind, and to have unrestricted access to information, opinions, and expressions of belief. In short, if there is no education without inculcation, then there is no education that is compatible with the First Amendment and its preferred metaphor of the marketplace of ideas.

Now, I am not the first person to have posed the dilemma in these terms, and theorists of liberal education have devised a spirited reply to formulations like mine. Here is what they typically say. It may be that education cannot proceed without inculcation, but not all efforts at inculcation are the same, nor are their effects. Surely there is a difference between the inculcation aimed at by a regime that pronounces certain views orthodox and beyond challenge and one that welcomes all points of view to the table so long as they submit themselves to the interrogation of rational deliberation. And isn't the difference that in this second regime, inculcation, rather than undermining autonomy and the freedom of democratic choice, invites students to exercise and grow in them? In the words of two recent commentators, a curriculum that introduces students to many points of view without authorizing any "encourage[s] them to think critically about the goals and values they choose to pursue through life";[5] "by exposing the student to diverse ideas . . . we build up his ability to engage in free inquiry and critique, thus preparing him for future 'autonomous' decisionmaking."[6]

The idea, then, is that the right kind of education, faithful to the First Amendment, gives you practice in making up your own mind about values and agendas, while the wrong kind of education captures your mind and binds it to values and agendas that go unexamined. The problem with this idea is that it is itself an agenda informed by values that are themselves unexamined and insulated from challenge. The name of the agenda is "free and open inquiry"; and despite that honorific self-description, it is neither free nor open because it is closed to any line of thinking that would shut inquiry down or route it in a particular direction. It is closed, for example, to most forms of religious thought (which it will stigmatize as dogmatic) or to any form of thought that rules some point of view—for instance, that the Holocaust did not occur—beyond the pale and out of court. To put it in a way that may seem paradoxical: openness is an ideology, in that, like any other ideology, it is slanted in some directions and blind (if not downright hostile) to others.

Now, to say that openness is an ideology is not necessarily to criticize it, much less reject it, but merely to deprive it of one of its claims. Openness (or free inquiry) may still be the ideology we choose, but if my analysis is right, we cannot choose it as an alternative to ideology. What, after all, is the difference between a sectarian school which disallows challenges to the divinity of Christ and a so-called nonideological school which disallows serious discussion of that same question? In both contexts something goes without saying and something else cannot be said (Christ is not God or he is). There is of course a difference, not however between a closed environment and an open one but between environments that are differently closed.

If this seems counterintuitive, consider the case of *Mozert v. Hawkins*. The cause of action was brought by Vicki Frost, a born-again Christian mother of a sixth-grade child who had been assigned a Holt-Rinehart text as part of a program in "critical reading." The books used in this program, the court tells us, "are aimed at fostering a broad tolerance for all of man's diversity," and, accordingly, "they intentionally expose . . . readers to a variety of religious beliefs, without attempting to suggest that one is better than another."[7] It was the contention of Mrs. Frost and the other parents who joined in her suit that the free-exercise rights of their children were infringed when they were required to study views that contradicted and undermined their most cherished convictions. In a series of trials and appeals, Frost and her colleagues were finally unsuccessful, and what defeated them was the argument put forward by the superintendent of the Hawkins County school district. He maintained that "plaintiffs misunderst[ood] the fact that exposure to something does not constitute teaching, indoctrination . . . or promotion of the things exposed."[8]

But what the superintendent and the judges who agreed with him fail to understand in their turn is that the distinction between exposure and indoctrination is an artifact of the very liberalism Vicki Frost rejects. That is, the distinction only makes sense if you assume, first, that the mind is a cognitive machine that can always draw back from the ideas presented to it and assess them by independent rational criteria; second, that this is what the mind, if it is working properly, is supposed to do; and, third, that a conviction held in any other way, held in conformity with authority rather than as the conclusion of a process of critical reasoning, is not a conviction worth having. These are the assumptions that underlie liberalism (Locke articulates them in *A Letter Concerning Toleration*), liberal theories of education, and the First Amendment, but they are decidedly not the assumptions of Vicki Frost, who doesn't care how her child comes to hold her beliefs so long as they are not shaken and who fears that they will be shaken if the young girl is compelled to read and discuss the arguments of error. When Vicki Frost hears someone invoke the distinction between exposure and indoctrination, it doesn't sound to her like common sense but rather the presumptuous and arrogant attempt of a nonbeliever to prescribe for her the conditions and nature of her belief. The value assumed by the court that denied her relief—the value of developing the ability to see the many sides of every question—is not only not her value, it is in her eyes the way and vehicle of all evil.

Now there are two conclusions to be drawn from the Vicki Frost example. The first is the conclusion that matters most to her: making up your own mind independently of an external authority—be it state, church, or Bible—is an ideological program and a bad one. The second is the conclusion that matters most to First Amendment theorists: making up your mind independently of any external authority is a program impossible to execute. If exposure is indoctrination, in the sense that an idea introduced into the mind becomes part of its equipment, one of the lenses through which and with which the world is processed and configured, then the declared goal of liberal education, the goal of preparing students for "autonomous decisionmaking," is not achievable and in fact has been rendered unavailable in the first moment of consciousness.

Indeed, if you think about it, the requirement that people be allowed "to form their own opinions, beliefs, concepts, hypotheses" makes no sense.[9] You cannot form a belief in a vacuum, in the absence of an already-in-place framework of norms, distinctions, and hierarchies. And it cannot be you who puts that framework in place, or who chooses it, for prior to its institution the notion of choice could not possibly have a content. Indeed, you couldn't even have a thought if the range of possible thoughts had not already been established and imprinted on your brain before you took your first mental step. Just as you can't have education without authoritative selection, so you can't have consciousness without authoritative selection, and one you didn't make. According to one scholar, the First Amendment requires that one's beliefs be shaped by "one's own rational considerations rather than by . . . coercion."[10] What I am saying is that this requirement is incoherent and cannot be met.

Because it cannot be met, the condition liberal education and the First Amendment is supposed to save you from, the condition of being subject to the influences of indoctrination, is the condition you are always and already in. The choice is never between indoctrination and free inquiry but between different forms of indoctrination issuing from different authorities. Moreover, once you see this, the usual way of talking about the relationship between the First Amendment and children gets stood on its head. Traditionally, the withholding from children of full First Amendment rights has been justified by what has been assumed to be "a child's lack of capacity for 'autonomous' choice."[11] The reasoning has been that, until children mature and become capable of deciding for themselves, parents and educators (and behind them, the state) must decide for them, at least in the area of what they must study, how long they must study it, under what conditions, and with what restrictions on personal behavior, including, sometimes, verbal behavior. The problem with this line of reasoning is as obvious as the contradiction between a regime of enforcement and its declared goal of producing free agents. How can a course of study that is designed to foreground some ideas and marginalize some others produce young adults who are open to all ideas and capable of assessing them disinterestedly? The answer is that it cannot, and therefore the theory of liberal education has a hole right in the middle of it since there seems to be no way of getting to the desired state (autonomous free choice) through the designated means (education).

John Stuart Mill, the great apostle of autonomy, saw this and did not shrink from the conclusion it suggests: if you want to maximize freedom of choice and opinion, education is not the solution but the problem. Mill advises that we deal with the problem by removing the state from direct control over education, for a "general state education is a mere contrivance for molding people to be exactly like one another; and . . . the mold in which it casts them is that which pleases the predominant power in the government" (98).[12] If the state has to be involved in education, he says, it should be only as one competitor among many others (how up-to-date this is), so that the diversity we prize will be reflected in our pedagogical institutions. Ideally, the state's function should be limited to assuring the maintenance of high standards, and this it could best do by administering public examinations that would not "exercise an improper influence over opinion" because they would "be confined to facts and positive science exclusively" (99).

Mill gives as an example of what he has in mind the testing of a student's knowledge of various religions—their tenets, their rituals— without in any way requiring him "to profess a belief in them." Here it is again (or, rather, first), the dream of education without inculcation, this time to be realized by a program of instruction limited only to the facts and therefore neutral. But the dream, and its imagined realization, fade into gossamer before the onslaught, first, of the Vicki Frost objection (exposure *is* indoctrination and will exercise an improper influence over my children) and, second, of the objection from epistemology (there are no facts without a framework, and any framework you have will have *you*, in the sense of limiting in advance what you can see and think). (There is also the objection Vicki Frost might make, if she thought of it, that a superficial or external knowledge of her religion is really no knowledge at all.) Even a minimalist educational scheme constrains beliefs, and if you want to preserve freedom the only alternative would seem to be no education at all. But even that option—granted reluctantly and as a one-time exception to the Amish in *Wisconsin v. Yoder*—wouldn't do the trick because in the absence of formal education, the business of shaping, influencing, inculcating, and indoctrinating would be done by television, advertising, street gangs, graffiti, the internet, and rock lyrics.[13]

The bottom line conclusion is that freedom has always and already been lost. The real problem is not that you can't get from education to autonomous decisionmaking (although that is certainly the case) but that autonomous decisionmaking is an unimaginable state. This is what I meant by saying that the usual way of talking about children and the First Amendment must be stood on its head. If autonomy is compromised by the shaping force of culture, and if consciousness cannot exist without having a shape it did not choose, and if our exposure to shaping forces increases as we get older, then what adulthood and maturity bring is not more but less autonomy, and not less but more indoctrination. Children are not a special case, and if they are not a special case, the argument for subjecting them to inculcation becomes an argument for subjecting everyone. If care must be taken lest children go down wrong paths in wayward directions, that same care must be taken for adults who are no more capable of self-direction than any first grader and are indeed less capable because they have been subject to more shaping influences. If indoctrination is necessary at any point, it is necessary forever, and the only question is from whom shall we receive it.

Liberalism tells us that we shouldn't receive it from the state, but the state is already dispensing it every time it invokes the First Amendment in the name of openness and freedom. This is exactly what Vicki Frost objects to. She complains not that her child is being inculcated but that she is being inculcated in the name of values—diversity, critical thinking, flexibility of mind—she abhors. The court replies by hitting her with those same values and telling her that she doesn't understand that exposure is not inculcation and that her daughter's freedom is in no way curtailed simply because she is required to read certain texts. It would have been more honest (although politically inadvisable) to say to her "Right, inculcation is what we do in the service of values we believe in and so long as we have the political power we will continue to do it *our* way." (This is in essence what Justice Scalia said in *Employment Division v. Smith* to those Native Americans who insisted that peyote was an integral part of their religious worship and that by penalizing them for its use the state denied them free exercise.)[14]

This brings me to a final point, one I have made in other chapters: the First Amendment is a political instrument, not an apolitical principle to which you can be faithful or unfaithful. It is a vocabulary and a set of formulas which are conceptually incoherent but which by virtue of that very incoherence can be turned to the advantage of any policy decision you might want implemented. Indeed, it is the incoherence of First Amendment doctrine that makes it so useful. An incoherent doctrine is never going to frustrate your desires, for it will always be flexible enough to accommodate your agenda if you are skillful enough to take advantage of its flexibility. I mean nothing cynical by this. I mean only that the relationship between policy desires and so-called principles is the reverse of what is usually maintained. The desires come first and last, and the principles, appropriately tailored, piece out the middle. The right way—no, the *only* way—to proceed is to figure out what you think should happen and then look around for principles, First Amendment ones or any others, that will help you to get there.

It will be immediately said that this is to allow outcomes to skew the process, to justify the means by the end, to make the principle serve the policy and not the other way around. But as Vicki Frost knows too well, that is what is always being done, and the only real issue is who gets to do it.

MISSION IMPOSSIBLE

The case of Vicki Frost is only one of the more recent episodes in the long-running story of the conflict between liberalism and the religious impulse. To the orthodox liberal mind, religion is the very type of the illiberal. In this and the following two chapters I shall make a single, simple point: All of liberalism's efforts to accommodate or tame illiberal forces fail, either by underestimating and trivializing what they oppose or by mirroring it. Michael Walzer provides a concise example at the beginning of his book *On Toleration.* "I won't have much to say," he says, "about the arrangements that get ruled out entirely—the monolithic religious or totalitarian political regimes."[1] That is, he won't have much to say about those forms of thought indifferent or hostile to the tolerance that is his subject.

But tolerance as a political strategy, and a moral stance, must stand or fall by its ability to deal with hard cases. If the case for, and analysis of, tolerance is made with respect only to regimes and discourses already predisposed to it, what is the point? As Thomas Nagel observes, "Liberalism should provide the devout with a reason for tolerance" (229).[2] That is, it is the devout—those who feel compelled by their religious faith to acts of judgment and exclusion—who put liberal tolerance to the challenge, and it is my contention that it is a challenge liberal tolerance cannot meet. Nevertheless, no matter how many times toleration is shown to be an incoherent ideal, its appeal remains strong. Indeed, as I shall argue below, the vocabulary of toleration—fairness, impartiality, mutual respect—survives even in the writing of those who set out to debunk it.

In what follows I take up the arguments of three kinds of theorists: • those who urge fairness and deliberative rationality as ways of securing political order against disruptive energies, especially the energies of fundamentalist religions; • those who believe that fairness and deliberative rationality are stalking horses for a political agenda that will not announce itself; and • those (actually one) who offer as an antidote to disorder more of the same. These theorists contend mightily and discover in one another no end of confusions, but in my argument they are all in the same line of work, and that line of work is empty.

Although analyses of the relationship between church and state continue to appear faster than they can be read, the discussion of this vexed issue has not advanced one millimeter beyond the terms established by John Locke in his *A Letter Concerning Toleration* (1689).[4] Locke's statement of purpose could, with only slight stylistic alterations, be incorporated into the first paragraph of almost any essay or book written today: "I esteem it above all things necessary to distinguish exactly the business of civil government from that of religion, and to settle the just bounds that lie between the one and the other" (17). More than three hundred years later we are still at it and no closer to achieving the exact distinctions or settling the just boundaries than Locke was when he identified the condition that made his project at once so urgent and so difficult: "For every church is orthodox to itself; to others, erroneous or heretical. Whatsoever any church believes, it believes to be true; and the contrary thereupon it pronounces to be error. So that the controversy between these churches about the truth of their doctrines, and the purity of their worship, is on both sides equal; nor is there any judge, either at Constantinople, or elsewhere upon earth, by whose sentence it can be determined. The decision of that question belongs only to the Supreme Judge of all men" (24).

The first point is the most important and is one modern theorists try in every way possible to avoid: if you believe something, you believe it to be true, and, perforce, you regard those who believe contrary things to be in error. Moreover, persons grasped by opposing beliefs will be equally equipped ("on both sides equal") with what are, for them, knock-down arguments, unimpeachable authorities, primary—

even sacred—texts, and conclusive bodies of evidence. And since any-one who would presume to arbitrate disputes between believers will himself be a believer for whom some arguments, authorities, and bodies of evidence will seem "naturally" weighty, no one's judgment will display the breadth and impartiality that would recommend it to all parties. (The question "But who is to judge?" asked with the knowledge that there could be no principled answer, serves to support a hands-off policy in both the free speech cases and the religion-clause cases.) It follows, then, that the only sensible course of action, if we wish to avoid "all the bustles and wars, that have been . . . upon account of religion" (52), is to remove religious issues from the table of public discussion, leaving their ultimate resolution to the "Supreme Judge" (or, as we would say today, to the marketplace of ideas) and adopting an official policy of toleration toward all professions of belief.

In urging toleration Locke does not intend, as do some who invoke him, to devalue religion. Rather, he wishes to identify, and protect from state interference, the essence of true religion, which is, he says, the war everyone must wage "upon his own lusts and vices" (14). His own, not anyone else's. The field of battle is internal to the soul that struggles to prepare itself for "the world to come" (19). That struggle is obligatory, but it is also private and no one can wage it for another or be the judge of another's progress. Therefore, every man should be left free to work out his own salvation as his conscience dictates, and the civil authority should not infringe upon that freedom by setting itself up as an arbiter of what is orthodox and what is not. Nor should any church attach itself to the civil power with the design of using that power to impose its particular doctrines on those who do not adhere to them. Any such design, no matter what pieties it is wrapped in, would be a departure from the gospel creed of "charity" or love for others—"No man can be a Christian without charity" (14)—and would indicate a base desire "to carry on persecution, and to become masters" (25).

Not only is this desire base, it would be unrealizable, Locke insists, because doctrines cannot be imposed; they are not that sort of thing. One might impose their outward profession—making it a law that your prayers must have a prescribed form and content—but no such prescription could compel belief: "All the life and power of true religion consists in the inward and full persuasion of the mind; and faith is not faith without believing. Whatever profession we make, to whatever outward worship we conform, if we are not fully satisfied in our own mind that the one is true, and the other well-pleasing unto God, such profession and such practice, far from being any furtherance, are indeed great obstacles to our salvation" (18).

This account of belief as something that cannot be coerced is not restricted to doctrinal matters but extends to all the operations of the understanding: "Such is the nature of the understanding that it cannot be compelled to the belief of anything by outward forces" (18). External authorities may attempt to command belief, but belief will only be secured by the internal force of "reason" and the "light and evidence" (19) that accompanies it. Even if the threat of penalties were to cause a change in a man's opinions, that change, insofar as it were superficial and forced—superficial *because* forced—would not be a "help at all to the salvation" of that man's soul (18). Once this point is fully accepted, Locke's two basic theses follow inescapably: first, that "the care of the salvation of men's souls cannot belong to the magistrate" (19), and, second, that "toleration [is] the chief characteristical mark of the true church" (14) because the true church will respect the sanctity of the soul's inward journey and refrain from coercing its direction.

It would seem that with these arguments in place, Locke can fairly claim to have achieved his goal of settling the just bounds between the business of civil government and that of religion. The key is the identification of the "religious interest" with the salvational aspirations of the individual soul. With these aspirations the civil magistrate has nothing to do, first, because he lacks the authority and wisdom to distinguish the false from the true and, second, because even if he were to declare an official doctrine and compel its profession, that profession would neither produce nor alter the *inward* persuasion that is the mark of true faith. What remains to the magistrate and is appropriate to his office is the care of "outward things, such as money, land, houses, furniture, and the like," and it is his duty "by the impartial execution of equal laws, to secure unto all people in general, and to everyone of his subjects in particular, the just possession of these things belonging to this life" (17).

Citizens, in short, are to be treated equally no matter what opinions they believe and profess, and they should neither be deprived of worldly advantage nor given a greater share of it because they hold those opinions rather than others. If this sounds familiar, it is because what we have here, already fully articulated in 1689, is the basic structure of liberal political theory: a firm distinction between the public and the private realms (underwritten by a distinction between body and soul/mind) and a determination to patrol the boundaries between them so that secular authorities will not penalize citizens for the thoughts they have (no thought control) or the opinions they express (no censorship), and religious authorities will not meddle in the worldly affairs of their parishioners (no theocracy).

But as coherent as all this seems at first glance, it is not without its problems, some of which Locke sees clearly. The chief problem is that the strongest point of the argument is also the point of its greatest vulnerability. If toleration is the mark of the true church and the obligation of the civil magistrate, will we not have a religion without content (any doctrine is OK so long as someone believes it) and a civil authority prevented from dealing with behavior it thinks wrong if those who engage in it say that they are moved to it by faith? There are two questions here. First, can religion, supposedly a matter of belief, possibly require none and still remain religion? And second, how far should the freedom of religion from state scrutiny extend, given that it is the function of the state to secure good order and stability? How can tolerance be practiced as a general policy without undermining the basis for, and justification of, the judgments both church and state must make in order to be what they are? This question haunts church–state jurisprudence to this day, and Locke's answer to it has not been improved on. Tolerate as much as you can so long as the basic shape of the enterprise, whether spiritual or civil, is not compromised; identify a baseline level of obligation that leaves believers free to live out their faiths within limits and provides the magistrate with a measure for determining when those limits are breached and a justification for enforcing them.

It is to this end that Locke invokes a set of related distinctions: first, between what the "Holy Spirit has in the holy Scriptures declared, in express words, to be necessary to salvation" (21) and what is left either unexpressed or a matter of indifference; second, between the "truly fundamental part of religion" (29) and "what is but a circumstance" ("the time and place of worship, the habit and posture of him that worships"; 35–36); and third, between the inward performance of faith and "outward show" (32). In each of these binaries, the first pole sets the limits of tolerance (anything goes so long as it respects the fundamentals) and the second pole identifies the areas of indifference (the particular forms one's faith might take)—areas in which the believer is free to choose and the magistrate free to regulate, because his regulation will not harm the integrity of a faith whose field of exercise is internal.

Although the problem posed by the strong form of toleration (that it leaves no basis for distinguishing between true and false or lawful from unlawful) is thus solved by establishing limits to its scope, this solution creates its own problem: how to justify the stigmatizing of those doctrines and actions that violate the limits as drawn. It is my thesis that there can be no justification apart from the act of power performed by those who determine the boundaries, and that therefore any regime of tolerance will be founded by an intolerant gesture of exclusion. (This is a criticism only from the perspective of the impossible goal a regime of tolerance sets for itself.) And those who institute such a regime will do everything they can to avoid confronting the violence that inaugurates it and will devise ways of disguising it, even from themselves.

The favored way is to redescribe the exclusionary gesture so that it appears not to have been performed by anyone but to follow from the nature of things. This is what Locke does when, quite late in the tract and long after he has put on toleration's mantle, he identifies those views no society, however generous, can tolerate: "But to come to particulars. I say, first, No opinions contrary to human society, or to those moral rules which are necessary to the preservation of civil society, are to be tolerated by the magistrate. But of those indeed examples in any church are rare. For no sect can easily arrive to such a degree of madness, as that it should think fit to teach, for doctrines of religion, such things as manifestly undermine the foundations of society, and are therefore condemned by the judgment of all mankind" (45).

There are (at least) two moves here and together they forecast the next three hundred years. First, Locke dismisses views so subversive that no society could allow them to flourish; but then he immediately declares that, since no sane person wold urge such views, they are condemned in advance of their unlikely appearance by the judgment of all mankind. Everything happens so quickly that the reader may not pause to raise the question that emerges as soon as one stops to reflect. How can there be something called "the judgment of all mankind" if the entire project of toleration is a response to the bottom-line fact of plural judgments issuing from plural orthodoxies? How can you get to the judgment of all mankind, to what we now call "common ground," if you begin by declaring that differences are intractable because every church is orthodox to itself?

These are questions no one has been able to answer to this day, although answers are forthcoming all the time. Usually the answers take one of four forms: • Common ground is sometimes found in a very high level of generality ("Be good," "Don't be cruel") that floats above the situations that provoke disagreements. The problem with this answer is that the generalities are so general that no line can be drawn from them to the particulars they supposedly order. • Others find common ground in a (claimed) universal distaste for certain views which, once identified, allow one to arrive at more widely acceptable views by a process of subtraction.[5] The problem with this answer is that the views supposedly rejected by everyone will always have supporters who must then be eliminated or declared insane so that the common ground will appear to be really common. • Still others find common ground in a set of procedural rules, akin to traffic lights or the rule of driving on the right side of the road, with no substantive content whatever, while substantive matters are left to be debated in the spaces provided by the private associations of home, church, social club, etc. The problem with this answer is that procedural rules always have content and that specifying them will always be a matter of substantive judgment, even when—especially when—substantive interests are being disclaimed. • And finally, common ground is often identified with whatever distribution of goods and powers a majority has ratified (or at least not rebelled against). The problem with this answer is that it is political rather than theoretical; and because it is political, the common ground it delivers will only be as firm as the contingencies of history.

These routes to the marking out of common ground are not exclusive of one another and are often in play together, although the third develops somewhat later with the emergence of what Michael Sandel has termed "the procedural republic."[6] Each represents an effort to find a way between the Charybdis of intractable difference, with its disheartening vista of a Hobbesian war of all against all, and the Scylla of pure toleration, with its unacceptable vision of a world where anything goes and no one can say of something that it is wrong. And each achieves its apparent success only by performing a conceptual sleight of hand in which a distinction that is either debatable or permeable is passed off as perspicuous to everyone, usually by defining "everyone" in a way that excludes (or marginalizes) those who would be likely to dispute either the fact or the shape of the distinction.

This sleight of hand, in turn, has the virtue of covering up (by rushing past) an embarrassment that would be fatal to the whole project if it were noticed: the strategy of finding common ground assumes a capacity that has already been denied by the framing of the problem. Indeed, if that capacity (to identify uncontroversially what is and is not essential) were available to you or to me or to anyone, there would be no problem and the lawful configurations of the state would arrange themselves. If general truths were universally recognized and easily applicable to specific situations, or if there were agreement about which policies and practices are beyond the pale, or if procedural rules that respect no persons and are fair to all were easily identifiable, tolerance's limits would be self-establishing and no coercion would be required, since everyone would readily agree *to* what they already agreed *about*.

To see that this is not (nor ever could be) the case, one need only look to Locke's more specific list of proscribed opinions: "For example . . . any sect that teaches expressly and openly, that men are not obliged to keep their promises; that princes may be dethroned by those that differ from them in religion . . . Lastly, Those are not at all to be tolerated who deny the being of God" (45–47). This is not a hypothetical list; its items name some of the positions championed by those who supported Cromwell's Commonwealth and who perhaps, even in 1689, were lamenting the demise of what John Milton (a defender of Charles I's execution on very much the same grounds Locke here dismisses) called the "good old cause." The list, in short, consists of opinions held by the *losers* in a recent struggle, and one can imagine that if the outcome had been reversed and it was Milton or someone of his party writing a letter on toleration, there would still be a list of intolerable views but its items would be different. (Milton's of course would have begun with Catholic doctrine.)

My point is that if the absence of common ground (because every church is orthodox to itself) initiates a search for a form of government that will accommodate diversity, you cannot begin the search by identifying a common ground the absence of which motivates the search in the first place. Were you to so begin, you would have elevated some orthodoxy to the status of "common sense" and stigmatized as dangerous to the very "foundations of society" those orthodoxies whose common sense is contrary to the preferred one. This is not simply a description of Locke but a description of anyone who would invoke some common ground as the solution to the problem of what Hobbes called "multiplying glasses," the lens of "Passions and Self-love" through which all men see truth and their duty (239).[7] Common ground is what emerges when you assume the normative status of your own judgment and fix the label "unreasonable" or "inhuman" or "monstrous" to the judgment of your opponents. (John Rawls's out-basket category of "unreasonable comprehensive doctrines" is only the latest and most elaborate version of the strategy.)[8] The irony—not a paradox or even a matter of blame because it is inevitable—is that while adhering to common ground is proclaimed as the way to side-step politics and avoid its endless conflicts, the specifying of common ground is itself a supremely political move.

I do not mean to suggest that the category of common ground be jettisoned merely because it is a political rather than a philosophical or moral category. Locke and his successors are right to say that in the absence of common ground there can be no state and no laws. But they are wrong to think (and hope) that common ground will be found either in a morality so high that no one could fail to assent to its precepts or in a proceduralism so low that its rules (to quote again from *Leviathan*) would "crosse no mans ambition, profit, or lust" (166). Rather, common ground will be what emerges (temporarily) when one party wins the right (through war, elections, dynastic succession) to determine the decorums of appropriate behavior.

Political theorists will always want that determination to be made by some independent calculus or measure, some formula that sorts out the relevant factors, assigns priorities, and provides judges and magistrates with a test that pretty much applies itself. But no test or formula applies itself, and the embarrassment a formula is intended to remove—the embarrassment of decisions inflected by partial and partisan interests—returns when someone (just who it will be is always the real issue) is empowered to apply it. The formulas Locke invokes—the distinction between things expressly commanded and things indifferent, between what is fundamental and what is a mere circumstance, and between inward profession and outward expression—are themselves subsets of the general formula by which the private is distinguished from the public. Rather than resolving disputes, these formulas generate disputes, disputes about what the Bible actually says, about which expressions or forms of conduct are mere auxiliaries to faith and which are part and parcel of it, about just where the border between the private and the public really is, about whether any such border exists or should exist. It is not that such disputes admit of no resolution but that their resolution will always favor one of the parties contending for advantage. This is to say no more than that a dispute must be settled from some viewpoint and that since some viewpoint will not be everyone's, those who occupy other viewpoints will feel, quite understandably, that their interests have been slighted.

Just how this happens in a regime of tolerance is nicely illustrated by the hypothetical Locke poses when he asks if "the magistrate has no power to impose . . . the use of any rites and ceremonies" or to forbid the same, and "if some congregation should have in mind to sacrifice infants . . . or practise any other such heinous enormities, is the magistrate obliged to tolerate them, because they are committed in a religious assembly?" (36). Locke's answer to this question establishes a style of reasoning that is still very much with us. If you can do it as a secular citizen, you can do it as a religious observant; but if you can't do it as a secular citizen, neither can you do it as a religious observant, even if in your view the practice is essential to your religion.

Locke illustrates by means of an example that is as up-to-date as the Court's opinion in *Church of the Lukumi Babalu Aye, Inc. v. City of Hialeah:*[9] "Melibous . . . may lawfully kill his calf at home, and burn any part of it that he thinks fit: for no injury is thereby done to anyone, no prejudice to another man's goods. And for the same reason he may kill his calf also in a religious meeting . . . what may be spent on a feast may be spent on a sacrifice. And if, peradventure, such were the state of things, that the interest of the commonwealth required all slaughter of beasts should be forborn for some while, in order to the increasing of the stock of cattle, that had been destroyed by some extraordinary murrain; who sees not that the magistrate, in such a case, may forbid all his subjects to kill any calves for any use whatsoever? Only it is to be observed that in this case the law is not made about a religious, but a political matter: nor is the sacrifice, but the slaughter of calves thereby prohibited" (36–37).

The example shows what is always true about a doctrine of toleration: it is always a question of who is tolerating whom, for it is from the perspective of the tolerator that the limits to toleration will be set. Nor is that question ever open in Locke's text, since it has been answered by the very first move of distinguishing between the civil and the religious. For once the distinction has been assumed and presides over the inquiry, the claim of a religion to have precedence in every aspect of one's life will seem prima facie absurd. With that claim out of play, all that remains is the task of drawing a line around religion, supposedly to protect it from state interference but actually to constrain its exercise in ways the state finds comfortable.

Hence, the Lockean rule and the logic by which it is defended even to this day. You can practice your religion in any way you like so long as the form of that practice has a secular analogue; and when a religious practice with no legally permissible secular analogue falls afoul of the magistrate, it will not be because religion has been singled out for special disfavor but because a rule of civil law has been applied equally to all, religious and irreligious alike ("the law is not made about a religious, but a political matter").

Once this logic is in place, it brings with it the two staples of modern religion-clause jurisprudence: formal equality (everyone should be treated alike) and facial neutrality (no one's interests should be preferred). By acting in ways that neither promote nor prohibit religion, the state can claim, first, that it is treating religion just like anything else (forgetting that it is the essence of religion, at least in forms stronger than anything Locke will allow, to not be just like anything else), and, second, that no matter what its effects, the result will be neutral, since it will not have followed from a resolution to prefer or stigmatize anyone's point of view. But neutrality, like any other abstraction, has meaning only within some particular set of background conditions; as a rule or measure it will always reflect decisions and distinctions it cannot recognize because it unfolds and has application within them. You always have to ask (and are always encouraged not to ask) "Neutrality with respect to what?" And in Locke's case the answer is neutral with respect to the state's determination to patrol the bounds between civil government and the business of religion. Accordingly, any result will be considered neutral so long as those bounds are maintained, and no notice (at least of a judicial or administrative kind) will be taken of the disparate (non-neutral) effects experienced by agents differently situated on either side of the divide. The farmer who cannot kill his calf until the stock has been sufficiently increased will suffer a temporary economic disadvantage and will have to make do in some other way; the religious person who cannot engage in the rituals required by his faith will suffer a spiritual disadvantage that may go to the question of his salvation.

Not only does Locke's tolerant state equate these two harms (and thus implicitly monetarize the spiritual interest), it denies the severity of the religious harm by identifying true and essential religious practice with the internal motions of the mind and heart. If religion is basically a matter of belief rather than conduct, a restriction on conduct will not be an infringement on religious liberty.[10] Even if the exercise of your religion is incidentally burdened, the burden will not be excessive because it will touch only the outward expression of an inner faith whose freedom remains protected.

Moreover, the argument goes, this slight burden is as nothing compared to the burden society would be forced to bear if "those things that are prejudicial to a commonwealth of people in their ordinary use" were "permitted to churches" just because a religious significance could be claimed for them. After all, where would it end? "There can be no bounds put to it" (37), Locke observes, anticipating Justice Scalia when he considers the problem not of calves being slaughtered but of peyote being ingested: "What principle," asks Scalia, "can be brought to bear to contradict a believer's assertion that a particular act is 'central' to his personal faith?"[11] The answer, obviously, is "no principle," and any society that took seriously the individual religious scruples of its citizens "would be courting anarchy," a danger the Court first warned against, Scalia reminds us, when it rejected a free-exercise argument for allowing Mormons to practice polygamy: "Laws, we said, are made for the government of actions, and while they cannot interfere with mere religious beliefs and opinions, they may with practices" (879).

Scalia's citing of the phrase "*mere* religious beliefs," along with Locke's privileging of the perspective of "ordinary use," alerts us to still another of the consequences that follow upon the dividing up of the world between civil government and the "business" of religion. Since the impulse to divide comes from the side of the civil, its values will be normative and religious values will either be accorded a ceremonial but empty honor or regarded as a trivial expression of individual taste, or condemned as "an irrational and regressive antisocial force."[12] The opposite of "ordinary use" is extraordinary use, and extraordinary can either mean far above the norm and the normal, and therefore the object of wonder, or far outside the norm and the normal, and therefore the object of the tolerance you feel for an eccentric as long as his or her behavior doesn't interfere with your interests. The result is the quarantining of the extraordinary from the ordinary business of public life, either because it is so high above the concerns that motivate us in the marketplace that no notice we might take of it could be adequate, or because it is so much to the side of what goes on in the shop and the legislature that official notice would exaggerate its importance. Locke represents himself as striking the first of these stances, as someone who so honors religion that he will not allow the world's touch to defile it, but his insistence that religion is finally a private affair conducted in the chapel or in the heart leads him to the other (and modern) position in which religious views are individualized preferences, as mysterious and unregulatable as a preference for a certain hair style or flavor of ice cream.

Locke veers in this direction in two passages that will sound very familiar (and admirable) to his modern readers: "If I be marching with my utmost vigor, in that way which, according to the sacred geography, leads straight to Jerusalem; why am I beaten and ill used by others, because, perhaps, I wear not buskins; because my hair is not the right cut; because, perhaps I have not been dipt in the right fashion; because I eat flesh upon the road, or some other food that agrees with my stomach?" (29). "Suppose this business of religion were let alone, and there were some other distinction made between men and men, upon account of their different complexions, shapes, and features, or those that have black hair, for example, or gray eyes, should not enjoy the same privileges as other citizens; that they should not be permitted either to buy or sell, or live by their callings?" (49). Here we recognize a nascent form of what was to become one of the most powerful arguments against racial discrimination: withdrawing rights and opportunities from persons just because of the color of their skin is like stigmatizing those whose eyes are gray or hair black; it is simply irrational. The strategy is to make it seem silly that anyone would be either rewarded or penalized for something that, first, is not a matter of willful choice (you no more choose what persuades you in the way of belief than you choose your eye or skin color) and, second, has no real relationship to the needs and demands of the economic or political marketplace. (If you need a vote, do you care if the potential voter is fair or dark? If you need to buy a calf, do you care whether the seller's hair is long or if he bows at the name of Jesus?)

It is a good strategy, but it has an inevitable byproduct: if you say that important decisions about the distribution of goods and the conferring of rights should not turn on an inessential difference like the difference between skin color or religious opinions, you are a fair way to saying that the difference itself is unimportant, not only in the context of such distributions and conferrings but in any context. If you say that religious belief is not something you should be rewarded or penalized for, and certainly not something you should fight about, it is only a short step to saying (what many came to say) that it is not *worth* fighting about. There is a very fine line, and sometimes no line at all, between removing religion from the public battlefield and retiring it to the sidelines, where it is displayed only on ceremonial occasions marked by the pomp and circumstance we often accord to something we have trivialized. Certainly Locke would have disclaimed any such result, but one can hear a sublimated desire for it in the weariness (understandable for a man forced by religious controversy to write in exile) and poignancy of "suppose this business of religion were let alone."

I have lingered so long over Locke's *Letter* because, as I said at the outset, his framing of the question, "How do we settle the just bounds between church and state?" and the components of his answer—a distinction between the religious and the civil realms, underwritten by a distinction between belief and action, and enforced by the civil magistrate who is assigned the responsibility of policing the boundary lines in the name of what will then be called equal protection or neutral application—still preside over the discussion he initiated so long ago.

I wanted first to display the coherence of Locke's views, the way they hang together: the political argument supported by the theological argument, which is supported by the psychology of inward persuasion, all of which combine to provide answers to hard questions, like when can Melibeous have liberty to slaughter his calf—a question no less urgent today than when Locke posed it. I trust to have shown that the coherence is there; but that is only the beginning of inquiry, for one must determine what kind of coherence it is and whether or not it is answerable to Locke's desire—which is also the desire of those who follow him—to fix the *just* bounds between the realms of his divided world. "Just" means at once "precise" and "determined with reference to no one's particular interests." It is the second meaning that is most pertinent, for if it can be claimed, Locke will have satisfied the demand he himself makes in the *Second Letter,* that we establish a policy that holds everywhere, and not one "suited to only some one country, or party"; for "what is true and good in England, will be true and good at Rome too, in China or Geneva."[13] One could not wish for a clearer formulation of the liberal project, the fashioning of a form of government that assures order and stability without installing in a position of privilege and political mastery any of the views held by a diverse citizenry.

But if that is Locke's project, at least one of his modern commentators finds him failing to realize it because his arguments are "insufficiently general": "However effective and historically important [Locke's] line of argument might have been, it is uninteresting from a philosophical point of view. We are interested in the question of whether the state *as such* is under a duty of toleration and we want an argument addressed to state officials in their capacity as wielders of the means of coercion, repression and persecution. An argument which addresses them instead in their capacity as members of a Christian congregation is insufficiently general to be philosophically interesting because it leaves us wondering what if anything we would have to say to someone who proposed persecution in the name of a more militant and less squeamish faith. Certainly, it would be an untidy and unsatisfactory state of affairs if we had to construct a fresh line of argument for toleration to match each different orthodoxy that was under consideration."[14] Jeremy Waldron's complaint is that Locke urges toleration within a set of background conditions—the assumption of Christianity's truth and of a version of Christianity that makes almost no doctrinal demands— and that therefore the form toleration takes in his argument is subordinate to, and a function of, these conditions. Vary the conditions either by assuming a stronger Christianity or no Christianity at all or a population of Muslims or Jews, and the entire enterprise would have to be rethought, with toleration taking an altogether different form or perhaps no form at all.

What is missing from Locke's account, says Waldron, is a defense of toleration as an *independent* virtue, one that demands rational allegiance no matter what religion or irreligion a citizenry adheres to or what political consequences one may either fear or desire. A defense of toleration so conceived—of what Waldron calls "toleration in general" (8) or toleration *as such*—would entail a rejection of intolerance not because it is unlikely to achieve its objectives but because it is wrong, and wrong not merely in these circumstances but in all circumstances. If we want to say a practice is wrong, Waldron declares, we do not "want to have to appeal in a Humean fashion to contingent desires and attitudes" (104), that is, to attitudes and desires relative to particular political situations.

I cite Waldron's critique of Locke because it raises a question that should be put to anyone who proposes to settle the just bounds between church and state. Is the resolution you urge tied to a particular set of political conditions whose rightness is assumed, or is it independent of any political presuppositions and therefore responsive to the *general* interest rather than to the interests of a faction or party? Another way to phrase the question (in terms that figure strongly in the texts I examine later) is to ask, "Is the proposed resolution *prudential*—a good thing to try given the present state of things—or is it *theoretical*—something that should be implemented because it is right no matter what the present (or future) state of things might or might not be?" "Prudential" is another word for "political"; both live in the realm of calculation, limited resources, anticipated and/or feared consequences, etc. "Theoretical" is another word for "principled"; both belong to the realm of rights, duties, and norms abstractly conceived. The theorist, as Ronald Beiner has observed, is someone who seeks the "ultimate ground," the "ultimate normative standard" from the vantage point of which urgent questions receive their answers.[15] The man or woman of prudence surveys the ground he or she already occupies and tries to figure out which policy, among the available alternatives, will best serve the goals to which he or she is committed. Waldron is saying that Locke is more prudential than theoretical, despite his claim—a theoretical claim, indeed *the* theoretical claim—to be urging what is "true and good" for all times and all places.

But can one be theoretical in the sense Waldron demands? Can one devise principles of such generality that they speak to the intuitions of all persons however situated (in Rome, Geneva, China, or London) and are therefore acceptable to all persons, even those whose interests might be disadvantaged by their realization in public life? This is an urgent question that goes to the heart not only of Locke's efforts to settle the just bounds between church and state but of the entire liberal project to which the distinction between church and state is basic. Liberalism and the Enlightenment were born of the desire to escape the conflicts generated by religious disputes. Toleration is the preferred implementation of that desire; it is a device for placing religion issues off the public agenda so that civil business might proceed undisturbed by what had turned out to be intractable oppositions. If everyone would agree to confine his or her religious life to the heart and the chapel, religion would flourish without interference from the state, and the state would flourish without interference from religion. Hence the private/public distinction, which is a theoretical distinction because it is drawn—or so it is claimed—from a vantage point that is neutral between competing religious views, all of which are equally cabined and equally protected. It is by maintaining the distinction between private and public that the liberal state hopes to achieve the goal named by Ronald Dworkin, a form of government where political decisions are, in so far as possible, "independent of any particular conception of the good life or what gives value to life."[16]

What this means is that the attempt to fix the boundaries between church and state and the project of liberal theory (of finding an Archimedean point to the side of or above or below sectarian interest) are one and the same. They stand or fall together, and what would threaten their fall, as Waldron clearly sees, is a religion that does not respect the line between public and private but would plant its flag everywhere. An uncompromising religion is a threat to liberalism because were it to be given full scope, there would be no designated safe space in which toleration was the rule. (As Locke points out in a tone of complaint, a religiosity of this temper might preach tolerance when it was not in power, but once in power "then presently peace and charity are to be laid aside.")[17] And an imperial religion would be a threat to theory because, were it to achieve its ambitions, sectarian interest—rather than being transcended or bracketed—would reign. The fact that such strong forms of religious behavior are always putting themselves forward constitutes the greatest challenge to liberal hopes for a principled adjudication of the claims of church and state.

It is a challenge Locke evades when he makes devotion a wholly internal matter and thus secures the parceling out of spheres of authority without ever having to argue for it. Waldron sees that the game has been rigged and insists that Locke and those who could follow him consider the case of someone "of a more militant and less squeamish faith." What does the Lockean liberal say to the person whose religion teaches that it is a holy duty to order the affairs of this world by the true faith? What so-called "independent value" could be so persuasively urged that the zealous would retreat from their zeal and leave their deepest beliefs at home?

One answer to this question was given by Hobbes, although it is not an answer modern liberals find attractive. Hobbes begins, as all liberals do, with the insight that values and desires are plural and therefore the source of conflict. Where Locke says that every church is orthodox to itself, Hobbes declares that "all men are by nature provided of notable multiplying glasses, (that is their Passions and Self-love)" (239). Both reason that since "some men's thoughts run one way, some another" (135) and no man is a god, no one is authorized by nature to judge his fellows. Here, however, is where the agreement ends. Locke, and those who follow him (nearly everyone in the liberal tradition) conclude from

REASONS FOR THE DEVOUT

the fact of equality that the best government is the least government, a structure of minimal constraint that leaves equal men equally free to pursue their equally authorized or unauthorized visions. Hobbes concludes exactly the reverse: because equality of right and ability breeds "equality of hope in the attaining of our Ends" and because each man's ends are naturally to be preferred to his rival's, the two will inevitably "become enemies," and in the absence of a neutral arbiter they will "endeavor to destroy, or subdue one an other" (184). Equality, rather than a condition that argues for our freedom, is the condition that argues for its curtailment. If society is to endure and perpetual conflict kept at bay, a cure must be found for this disease of equality and freedom, and that cure can only be "a common Power to keep them all in awe" (185).

"The only way to erect such a Common Power," says Hobbes, "is, to conferre all . . . power and strength upon one Man, or upon one Assembly of men, that may reduce all their Wills, by plurality of voices, unto one Will: which is as much to say, to appoint one man, or Assembly of men, to beare their Person; and every one to owne, and acknowledge himselfe to be Author of whatsoever he that so beareth their Person, shall Act, or cause to be Acted . . . and therein to submit their Wills, every one to his Will, and their Judgements to his judgment" (227). Because the "plurality of voices," if left to itself, will generate cacophony and because there is no mechanism in nature to harmonize it, an artificial mechanism must be put in place and rigorously adhered to. Men who are equal in power and desire are now equal in subjection; each surrenders a large part of his freedom and liberty on the condition that his fellows do the same, and in this way peace and security are established for everyone.

It is an elegant solution to the problem of multiplying glasses, and it certainly provides an answer to the question of what independent value could be invoked such that committed and passionate men would be persuaded to abate their natural desire to have the world's order reflect their visions of the good. Just remember, says Hobbes, *"The Fundamentall Law of Nature," "That every man, ought to endeavour Peace"* (190). If peace cannot flourish so long as "masterlesse men" are allowed "a full and absolute Libertie," liberty must be curtailed so that all will be free from the fear of "perpetuall war" (266). So long as every man is encouraged to "do any thing he liketh . . . so long are all men in the condition of Warre"; but if every man surrenders that right and does not reserve to himself what he would deny to others, peace will be assured. This, says Hobbes, "is that Law of the Gospel; *Whatsoever you require that others should do to you, that do ye to them*" (190).

Notice what has happened here to the golden rule. Rather than commanding that you honor the inherent worth of your fellow men (who are to be treated as ends, not means), it invites you, in Hobbes's version, to join with your fellow men in a defensive compact based on mutual distrust. Rather than calling you to the higher perfection of charity and universal love, it teaches the universality of self-love, a condition impossible to leave behind but one that can be managed and contained if an authoritarian structure is firmly enough in place.

It is not difficult to understand why Alan Ryan declares that "it would be absurd to call Hobbes a liberal."[18] What disqualifies Hobbes in Ryan's eyes, and in the eyes of many, is his refusal to derive from the doctrine of equality the *positive* values—autonomy, free choice, free association, individual self-realization—that inform the modern liberal state. For Locke, Kant, Mill, and Rawls (in their different ways), the equality of men and of the values they variably espouse points to the rejection of any form of absolutism: if no one's view can be demonstrated to be absolutely right, no one should occupy the position of absolute authority. For Hobbes the same insight into the pluralism of values and the unavailability of a mechanism for sorting them out implies exactly the reverse: *because* no one's view can be demonstrated to be absolutely right (and also because everyone prefers his own view and believes it to be true), someone *must* occupy the position of absolute authority.

There can be no question as to which of these ways of reasoning won the liberal day, but it might be said that Hobbes's is the more consistent with the twin premises from which both begin, the premise that, first, every church is orthodox to itself, and, second, that there is no principled way of adjudicating disputes between opposing orthodoxies. Both Hobbes and his liberal detractors declare this to be our situation, but where Hobbes asks "How can we make it work for us?" Locke, Kant, Mill, and Rawls ask "How can we work our way out of it?" Surely, however, this is the wrong question if the initial premise is taken seriously. If we really do live in a world of plural orthodoxies and lack an independent measure for assessing them, we can't work our way into a better world unless we reinvent the transcendental point of reference declared unavailable when we began. That is, we can't first remove certainty and a unified viewpoint from the human landscape and then propose to get them back through a program of social engineering.

Still, it is easy to see why anti-Hobbesians are tempted by a transcendence their liberalism has already rejected. The alternative, as Hobbes poses it, seems so sordid, so illiberal. His golden rule is "Do this and ye shall be safe." Liberals in the tradition of Mill and Kant prefer a version of the old one, "Do this and ye shall be better." They don't want to answer the question "How would you persuade the true believer to abandon his efforts to write his beliefs into the law?" by saying "scare him with the spectre of perpetual conflict." They want to answer by holding out a promise—of a better life, a better community, a better self—that will make the believer happy to forgo his present zeal for the sake of a brighter and even glorious future. In short, they want an answer that is not merely prudential but moral.

Little wonder that Hobbes falls short, since his answer, as Thomas Nagel explains, is "premoral"; its starting point is a mere fact of brute nature, the concern "each individual has . . . for his own survival and security," and its ending point is any arrangement that will accommodate that concern.[19] All that Hobbes requires of the arrangement is that it be acceptable to those who will live under it; and that acceptance, Nagel observes, will be entirely contingent, since it could easily fall out that "our personal motives . . . fail to point us toward a common goal" (219). Our private agendas may converge on some political scheme, but then again they may not.

In place of what he calls a mere "Hobbesian convergence," Nagel offers a theory in which "reasonable agreement is . . . sought by each person as an end and not merely as a means, necessary for social stability" (220). The person who is party to this kind of agreement will not be acquiescing in a *modus vivendi*, a way of just getting along; he will be affirming something he believes in and believes in as *good*. What might that something be? What could be so compelling that to believe in it is sufficient reason to soft-pedal your deepest convictions? Nagel's answer to that question is "the fundamental moral idea . . . that we should not impose arrangements, institutions, or requirements on other people on grounds they could reasonably reject" (221). Where Hobbes's test is "Would you want someone to do it to you?" Nagel's test is "Wouldn't it be *wrong* to do it to someone else, even if you could?" Although we may believe a course of action to be true and good, we should not pursue it if others with different conceptions of the true and good reject it on the basis of arguments we understand, even if we are not persuaded by them. If we hew to this "fundamental moral idea," says Nagel, we will subordinate the beliefs we happen to hold to "a higher order impartiality" (227), that is, to an impartiality higher than any our beliefs could deliver, and we will thus institute a decorum of constraint more principled than the merely prudential decorum urged by Hobbes.

Nagel's is the authentic voice of the liberal theorist. He is a liberal because he recognizes that each of us is embedded in a structure of belief and value not shared by everyone. He is a theorist because he thinks that we are capable of distancing ourselves from our embeddedness (if only for purposes of public decisionmaking) if we submit our beliefs to the discipline of the higher order impartiality. The question is "Why should we?" And prior to that question is another: "What is the status of this higher order impartiality?" In his argument, Nagel opposes it to "appeals to the truth" (227), on the reasoning that since truth claims issue from particular perspectives, putting them forward will not resolve disputes but fuel them. Rather than appealing to *the truth*, appeal instead, Nagel advises, to a higher order impartiality which honors everyone's truth without endorsing or rejecting any.

But that can't be right. If you are not appealing to the truth of the higher order impartiality, if you are not identifying it as something more worthy of your allegiance than the truths it trumps, what claim does it have on you? Why should you prefer it to the truths it asks you to discount? There are only two answers to this question, either the Hobbesian answer (rejected by Nagel) that has you acting out of a fear of civil chaos (and what of those true believers whose zeal for their souls and yours overrides or cancels any such fear?) or an answer that ties the idea of a higher order impartiality to a profound moral principle (for example, a Kantian respect for the autonomy of free agents). If, however, you give this second answer (as the would-be normative liberal always does), you will be recommending the higher order impartiality because you think it is true; it is precisely to its truth that you will be appealing. How could it be otherwise? It makes no sense to set aside some of your beliefs unless in doing so you are affirming another of your beliefs as higher.[20] Deferring to a higher order impartiality is not to constrain or bracket "your own beliefs" (232) but to enact them; it is to testify to the truth, as you see it. The so-called higher order impartiality is anything but impartial; for those (like Nagel) committed to it, it is not "a standpoint that is independent of who we are" (229) but a declaration of who we are or would be. It is our notion of the good, as contestable as any other, although Nagel does everything he can to palm it off as something lesser and therefore as something less controversial.

Of course Nagel does not think of himself as doing that, but his prose betrays him when he simultaneously acknowledges a paradox and fudges his way past it. "It may seem paradoxical that a general condition of impartiality should claim greater authority than more special conceptions which one believes to be, simply, true—and that it should lead us to defer to conceptions we believe to be false—but that is the position" (228). The trick here (one that fools Nagel himself) is to hide the truly tendentious assertion inside the assertion that is acknowledged to be paradoxical. The tendentious assertion is that the impartiality Nagel urges is "general," while the conceptions that bow to its authority are "special." Once these adjectives are slipped in, what Nagel calls the "position" seems self-evidently right. After all, the special always defers to the general, and so the argument is won the instant the labels are applied and accepted. What one doesn't notice is that if you stop to think about it—something the prose does not encourage—there is no reason to accept them, no reason to believe that the higher order impartiality is really higher and not just one more special conception of the good in competition with other conceptions. It is one thing to say that respect for the views of others even when you reject them is the highest morality, and quite another to say that respect for the views of others even when you reject them is a position above (or to the side of) any morality, including your own. Nagel is saying the first thing and thus opening himself up to a debate (about what is and is not the highest morality) that he forecloses by claiming to be saying the second.

He performs the same maneuver in a smaller compass with the word "reasonably" ("We should not impose arrangements . . . on other people on grounds they could reasonably reject"). "Reasonably" is offered as a standard or measure that everyone knows and can recognize: it is offered, that is, as a *general* standard. But its generality is belied by its function in the syntax, where it acts to put a limit on the tolerance ("we shouldn't impose") the sentence announces: arrangements should not be imposed on those who reject them on reasonable grounds; they can, however, be imposed on those who reject them on *un*reasonable grounds. The question, as always, is "Who gets to decide what is and is not an unreasonable ground?" It can't be those who are to suffer the imposition, since by their lights the grounds of their action are perfectly reasonable. It must be someone—like Nagel perhaps—whose notion of the reasonable differs from theirs, which means that not only will they have "arrangements" imposed on them, they will have imposed on them someone else's idea of what is and is not reasonable. A "special" definition of reason is passing itself off as general and is being used to perform an act of exclusion that pronounces itself to be impartial.

The usual objection to Hobbes is that he is willing to sacrifice the autonomy of free agents to an arbitrarily imposed power for the sake of political stability, but in the end this is no less true of Nagel, who asks free agents to subordinate their autonomy to a principle of "epistemo-logical restraint" (229). The difference—and it is all to Hobbes's credit—is that in one scheme the operation of power is acknowledged and agreed to by all parties, each of whom can then be said to have authorized, in an original act of contract, "all the Soveraigne doth" (232); in the other, the operation of power—of the imposition on those who reject it of a political morality *this* moralist happens to favor—is performed under cover of a few fine-sounding abstractions like impartiality and reasonableness. In one scheme, those who will be constrained are given a choice—perpetual war or a limitation on your desires; in the other, they are given no choice (and not even a hearing) and told that if they do not assent, they will be ruled anyway because they will be in conflict with "a highest order framework of moral reasoning" (229), where "highest order" is nothing more than the instant transmutation of a contestable point of view into the view from nowhere.

It is nicely done, and Nagel is so good at it that he can do it in a blink of the eye. He begins a sentence from another essay by declaring that "there is no higher-order value . . . abstractly conceived which is capable of commanding the acceptance by reasonable persons of constraints on the pursuit of their most central aims of self-realization" but then ends the same sentence by saying "except for the need to respect this same limit in others."[21] Here the equivocation occurs with the word "need." Is the need dictated by a normative moral vision, in which case it identi-fies just the kind of higher order value whose existence has just been denied; or is it a need in relation to a lower order morality (we had better respect others if we want them to be respectful in return), in which case Nagel is urging the kind of "convergence theory" or prudentialism he disdains?

Nothing I have said should be taken as a criticism of Nagel's substan-tive vision, only of his claim that it is not substantive. There is more

REASONS FOR THE DEVOUT

than a little plausibility to the argument that everyone wins if each of us agrees to forgo winning; it is just not the kind of argument Nagel thinks it is, one that outflanks belief. Rather, it is a form of belief, the belief that one's "central aims of self-realization" will be best achieved privately and in spaces separated from the ordinary business of daily socioeconomic life. Those who believe something else, and especially those who believe that separating the realm of self-realization from the public sphere means a public sphere empty of value, will find no scope for *their* self-realization in Nagel's republic, where they will be labeled "unreasonable" or worse. Nor is this result one Nagel could avoid, for as Locke made clear (although he would not have put it this way), acts of exclusion and stigmatization are inevitable in any liberal regime that really wants to be a regime and not an endless philosophy seminar; and it is inevitable, too, given liberalism's vaunted opposition to coercion, that such acts will want to be known by other names, names like "reasonable," "neutral," and "impartial."

The options, after all, are limited. If you begin by acknowledging the inevitability of difference and the desirability of preventing the conflicts that will erupt if proponents of opposing religious and moral viewpoints are left free to vie for control of the state and its coercing mechanisms, you have only three alternatives: (1) institute a regime of tolerance and face the difficulty of a system of government (hardly government at all) without the power to constrain and punish what it thinks wrong; (2) institute a regime of power and recommend it as an alternative to the chaos everyone fears; (3) institute a regime of power but don't identify it as such—instead, claim for it the status of an impersonal law tied to the interests of no one but capable of safeguarding the interests of everyone.

Pretty much all liberals save Hobbes (and remember, Ryan excludes him from the category) go for option three, with the result that almost every interesting question has been answered (or evaded) in advance and all that is left are in-house debates about just who or what to exclude and how best to package the exclusions so that they will appear to have been dictated by universal principles. That, as they used to say at the beginning of *Mission Impossible*, is your assignment. But unlike the complicated political tasks given to TV heroes, this assignment *is* impossible, although that fact seems not to have put the smallest dent in the confidence of those who accept it and cheerfully announce that they have finally done the job.

In fact, what they have done is what Nagel does and what Locke did before him: perform some version of a basic double move. First, announce that there exists no mechanism capable of adjudicating between competing systems of belief, and then install in a position of privilege just such a mechanism; declare something to be unavailable and then, almost in the next breath, discover it.

A WOLF IN REASON'S CLOTHING

The mechanism by which liberal orthodoxy installs itself as the neutral arbiter between competing systems of belief will also be the mechanism that rules out beliefs liberal theorists find uncomfortable. And these will almost always include the beliefs held by fundamentalists and others who feel compelled to imprint their views on public institutions. This is a convenient outcome for secularists who are not really interested in doing justice to strong religious conviction but rather seek a formula that will enable them to dismiss strong religious convictions while appearing to have taken them into serious account. The concern expressed by liberal theorists not to delegitimize religious sentiments (Nagel twice declares that "liberalism should provide the devout with a reason for tolerance") is really a concern for the consistency of their arguments, and they will not be at all disturbed when the effect of those arguments is to place religious sentiments at the margins of everyday life (229).[1]

What is surprising is to find those same arguments in the writings of those who proclaim themselves unhappy with the marginalization of religious discourse and propose to bring it back into the center. This is the project of Daniel O. Conkle, who begins a recent essay by observing that the doctrine of religious equality—all religions are to be accorded equal respect, and the state should not "prefer one religion over another"—brings with it "an underlying predicate . . . that religion does not matter, at least not in the public domain" (8).[2] The equality religions enjoy under this understanding, Conkle complains, is an equality of irrelevance because when "equality implies that religions should be insulated from normative evaluation . . . We are driven to the view that religion is merely . . . a matter of private and individual taste." Once religion is thus trivialized, the way is open to arguing, as many have, that religious reasons should not be "the basis for a political decision" (8).

How does Conkle propose to remedy that situation and help religion to "reclaim an important role in American public life" (32)? The answer, believe it or not, is by identifying some forms of religious reasoning as inappropriate for use in public life so that other forms, closer to the spirit of democratic process, might be invited in. The test is whether or not a form of religious discourse conforms to the general democratic requirement that people must "give reasons for their decisions" (16) and to the additional requirement that the reasons, once given, offer themselves for rational correction. Fundamentalist discourse, says Conkle, flunks this test because it violates "a core tenet of our democratic system—that . . . legal policies should be formulated on the basis of a dialogic decisionmaking process, a process requiring an openness of mind that fundamentalism does not allow"; therefore, we "should be wary of fundamentalist involvement in the political process" (15).

It is hard to see how this differs at all from the position Conkle opposes. Although he objects to the privatization of religion and its consequent removal from the public sphere, he achieves the same result by denying religion entry if it does not conform itself to secular ways of knowing. When he says that "some religions have more truth value than others," he means that some religions—not fundamentalist ones, presumably—employ modes of reasoning the secular world will be comfortable with; and when he calls for "an evaluation of the substantive positions" a religion may advance so that we can determine whether a particular religion is "right or wrong" (29), we know that the evaluation will be made according to standards the religion does not acknowledge and that the judgment of right or wrong will be rendered by the discourse to which the religion is being asked to defer, the discourse which is the *real* religion.[3] The credo of that religion is "openness of mind," but what is called openness is really a device of closure because it rules out in advance forms of thought that are less (or more) than dialogic and thinkers who are unwilling to regard their convictions as provisional and in need of a "higher" validation. To be sure, those religions that put "openness of mind" at the center of their faith—or rather at the center of their rejection of faith—will be welcomed into the political process and accorded a role in American public life, but only because in their stripped down and soft-edged form they are indistinguishable from other Enlightenment projects and are hardly religions at all.

A similar "defense" of religion's right to participate in public life is mounted by Franklin Gamwell in opposition to those "separationists" who "proclaim that religious claims do not belong within American politics" (339).[4] Yes, they do, Gamwell declares, so long as those who put them forward agree "to defend their convictions by appeal to considerations that can be assessed by all members of the public" and are "open to the possibility that rational reflection will show these [convictions] to be in greater or lesser measure false" (339). In other words, "religious grounds" can be asserted so long as the grounds for their acceptance or rejection are not religious.

Gamwell justifies this emptying out of religion with an explanation that simply repeats it: "The sheer acknowledgment that humans are fallible . . . is a reservation that properly accompanies any . . . conviction, including a religious one" (340). But while fallibilism is a component both of Enlightenment thought and of western religion (which usually calls it "original sin"), it is not the same doctrine in the two traditions. In one it mandates putting everything under the microscope; in the other the microscope—regarded as a prosthetic extension of carnal vision rather than a correction of it—is the object of its distrust and is rejected as a way of knowing in favor of scripture or revelation. One fallibilism says "Test everything"; the other says "Believe one thing." By collapsing the two and making religious conviction a subset of rational or empiricist conviction, Gamwell in effect makes religion and religious ways of knowing disappear.

When he published this essay, Gamwell was the dean of the Divinity School at the University of Chicago. More recently, the then-dean of the Harvard Divinity School produced a book-length argument along the same lines. (One wonders what deans of divinity schools make of the word "divinity.") Ronald Thiemann begins by acknowledging, with everyone else, that we live in a "pluralistic society" marked by moral disagreement, but he rejects the notion that these disagreements are irresolvable: "Even if liberal societies cannot agree on the ultimate *telos* for all human beings, it does not follow that they are unable to generate a limited but still real consensus concerning the common goods such societies should pursue" (108).[5] This is both true and empty in relation to the deep questions Thiemann claims to be addressing. Generating a consensus is easy if you give yourself the latitude of determining at the outset who will be inside it and who will be left in limbo. If you are free to include some "human beings" and not all, it becomes a simple matter of beginning (and ending) with the human beings who identify the same "common goods" you would identify and who agree with you about the "range of virtues appropriate for cultivation within . . . civil life" (108). Once outliers like religious fundamentalists have been cast into the wilderness, you can then prate on blithely, as Thiemann does, about "common bonds," "common goals and values," "public good," and "underlying beliefs" (all on a single page), and casually stigmatize those you have exiled as adherents of "fanaticism" (134).

A fanatic in Thiemann's vocabulary is someone who holds to his position with an inappropriate "degree of certainty" (137). A fanatic, in other words, is someone who believes something too strongly or, more precisely, someone who believes the wrong thing, who doesn't believe in—put at the center of his theology—the doctrine of dialogic process. Once your church is made up of only those who worship at process's altar, Enlightenment decorums have nothing to fear from it because the religion (if that is the word) espoused by the church has become their vehicle. It then makes perfect sense to declare, with Thiemann, that "the important issue is not whether an argument appeals to a religious warrant; the issue is whether the warrant, religious or not, is compatible with the basic values of our constitutional democracy" (156). It could not be clearer that the *religious* status of the "warrant" matters not a whit; for whatever its source, the extent to which it will or will not be compelling will be determined by measures that are either indifferent or hostile to the religious impulse. The only question to be asked of a warrant is "Does it comport with the secular theology of critical delib-eration and openness of mind?" If the answer is yes, it is admitted; if it is not, it is incompatible and is sent away.

But sent where? What do you do with those who won't play your game? The question is particularly urgent in view of Thiemann's brief against dogmatism and his requirement that citizens grant to those with whom they disagree the same consideration they themselves would hope to receive, grant them, that is, a full measure of "mutual respect"

(136). It is through the exercise of mutual respect that the democratic process is kept healthy, for "by acknowledging the moral force of an argument with which one disagrees, a citizen remains open to the persuasive power of an alternative point of view" (136). On its face this would seem to argue for extending respect to the arguments of strong religionists who might, after all, persuade those who disagree with them to *their* views; but this path is blocked because strong religionists (Thiemann's fanatics) will not reciprocate, will not say to you "It's all right if you don't believe in Christ or Jehovah or Allah and regard the Bible and the Koran as no more authoritative—indeed less authoritative—than John Stuart Mill." Because some people refuse to relax their beliefs (assuming for a moment that relaxation of one's beliefs is possible), liberals get to disrespect them in a form of almost juvenile payback: "You won't give respect to us and we won't give it to you, so *there.*"

In short, disagreement is fine unless you really mean it, unless your response to error is not "appreciation" but a determination to stamp it out, even to "the obliteration of the opponent's point of view" (137). You can't talk to these people; they won't listen to reason; they won't pull back from their arguments; and the best you can do, says Thiemann, is to "educate the citizenry . . . so that when they encounter such arguments they will reject them" (156). Education means instructing them in the goodness of "critical rationality" (127) and the badness of those who do not bow down to it, an epistemological criminal class that includes racists, anti-Semites, and uncompromising religionists in an undifferentiated mix joined together by an obdurate refusal to "listen to reason."

The fact that religious zealots and racists are often lumped together as representative of the energies liberalism wishes to muzzle reveals much about how these arguments work. There are at least two levels of operation. One is logical: both religious zealots and racists hold controversial views and wish to intrude them into the public sphere by enacting them into law (by, for example, banning abortion or legalizing discrimination according to race). The other is rhetorical: in liberal eyes, religious zealots—be they fundamentalist Christians or ultra-orthodox Jews or Khomeini-like adherents of Islam—are, or are very likely to be, racists. The equation is rarely made explicit; the link between zealots and racists is left to be made by those readers who will recognize in both groups a suspicious unwillingness to submit their beliefs to the correction of reason, itself identified with a faith in rational corrigibility. By this norm, zealots and racists alike can be declared "irrational," and once that conclusion has been reached the obligation to give reasons to the devout is no longer felt because reasons are not what they traffic in. The argument is finally circular—these people pay no heed to our reasons, and therefore they are unreasonable, and therefore we need not take into account anything they say—but the circularity will be missed by readers eager to distance themselves from anything associated with racism, even if the association is only implicit.

"Circularity" is perhaps too dismissive a word for an effort that is often elaborated with great sophistication and (apparent) attention to distinctions. It is not the intention of liberal theorists to be circular or to produce arguments rooted in the "logic" of guilt by association; but that is what they do, and, moreover, it is what they *must* do because in the end they really don't have an argument, except for the kind of argument they repeatedly excoriate, the argument that those who disagree with us—begin from a different conception "of the good life or of what gives value to life"—are obviously beyond the pale, barely human, and deserve minimal consideration or perhaps no consideration at all.

A spectacular example of this form of argument, and of the ways by which its springs are hidden even from those who make it, is provided by an essay much cited by Thiemann, Amy Gutmann's and Dennis Thompson's "Moral Conflict and Political Consensus."[6] The piece begins by observing that "religious controversy has traditionally been regarded as the paradigm of moral conflict that does not belong on the political agenda" (MC, 65) (because it is intractable) and fairly quickly turns into a discussion of how to exclude from that agenda policies favoring racial discrimination. The authors think of themselves as going against the grain of Nagel-like appeals to higher order principle, but in the end (and predictably) they make just such an appeal themselves in the name of "mutual respect."

In the old debate between those who think of liberalism as a device for managing and minimizing conflict and those who think of liberalism as a device for producing a better society populated by better persons, Gutmann and Thompson are clearly on the side of the latter, and that is why they are uneasy with a liberalism that requires of the state only that it be tolerant, neutral, and inactive. The trouble with these principles, they say, is that although they might succeed in keeping divisive issues off the political agenda, they do so in a blanket way that does not allow for the discriminations a state concerned with its own health and the health of its citizens should be making. If the state adopts a posture of live and let live, refrains from either favoring or disfavoring any moral position, and limits itself to presiding over the fray without trying to influence it in any direction, all controversial positions will be regarded in the same way, either as distractions we would be better off without (let the clergy and the philosophers worry about these questions) or as matters so difficult of adjudication (there is simply no truth to be discovered at the bottom of such disputes) that they are best left to the marketplace of ideas. As a result, peace, if we achieve it, will have to be bought at the price of future edification, for the citizenry will have been prevented by a strict hands-off policy from engaging in debates that might have led to its moral and political improvement.

Not that Gutmann and Thompson are recommending unrestricted public debate on controversial positions; rather, they wish to limit debate to those positions that speak to a genuine moral question in ways that have the potential, at least, of advancing the conversation. What is required is a means of distinguishing between these bona fide positions and positions whose ascendency would have the effect of subverting morality altogether. Blanket toleration and neutrality will not be these means, for they set the bar either too high or too low. The bar is set too high by someone like Nagel, who would exclude from public forums beliefs that cannot be justified from "a standpoint that is independent of who we are" (229). By this standard, Gutmann and Thompson complain, "the liberal's belief in human equality" (which Nagel would embrace and want the state to enforce) would fall into the same category as a belief that "sanctions racial discrimination" (MC, 67). Neither is independent of "who we are" and so would be excluded; but surely, say Gutmann and Thompson, "they are not equally acceptable (or unacceptable) starting points for public deliberation" (MC, 68).

The situation is no better when the bar is set too low and positions, rather than being excluded because they are controversial, are let in because they are controversial. Indiscriminate lumping in either direction brings its dangers. In the case of a policy favoring racial discrimination, the danger is that if the policy becomes a serious contender for state action, it might prevail and we would be headed back in the direction of slavery; whereas if the state washes its hands of the question (because it has been and continues to be disputed) and leaves it to each individual's conscience, citizens will then be "free to discriminate or not according to their religions" (MC, 69).

The dilemma is clear (and classic). How does the liberal state deal with doctrines—like racial discrimination or religious intolerance—inimical to it and threatening to its survival? If such doctrines are welcomed into the conversation, they may shut it down; if the door is closed to them, liberalism will seem to be exercising the peremptory authority it routinely condemns. Long ago Oliver Wendell Holmes declared himself willing to grasp the first handle of this dilemma and take his (or our) chances: "If in the long run the beliefs expressed in proletarian dictatorship are destined to be accepted by the dominant forces of the community, the only meaning of free speech is that they should be given their chance and have their way."[7] Gutmann and Thompson, however, are less libertarian in their sentiments and less willing to trust the matter to fate. They want the state to act positively in the "right" direction, and yet they want also to be true to the liberal principle of giving as much scope as possible to moral and intellectual debate.

They get what they want by cutting the Gordion knot and declaring "that the defense of racial discrimination is not a moral position at all" (MC, 69) and because it is not a moral position, keeping it off the political agenda violates no principle of tolerance. This is an amazing statement, but it is no more or less than an up-to-date version of Locke's invocation of the "judgment of all mankind" in justification of his preferred intolerances, and it is no accident that Gutmann and Thompson find their own justification in Locke. They note, correctly, that Locke does not urge "neutrality among all religions . . . only among those religions that accept the voluntary nature of faith" (MC, 69). If faith is voluntary, something one can come to only on one's own, it will be both wrong and futile for the state to command it "by the force of its laws because faith cannot by its nature be commanded" (MC, 68). This must mean, Gutmann and Thompson conclude, that faith "follows rational persuasion" (MC, 68).

Of course, what Locke means by rational persuasion—or, as he puts it, "light and evidence"—may not be what Gutmann and Thompson mean. He means the expostulation and remonstration of Christian conversation among brethren. They mean the rule-governed give and take of a philosophy seminar. Between these two is a space of equivocation they eagerly enter, and in a flash they declare that the "secular analogue" to Locke's insistence on the voluntary nature of faith is the requirement that "moral judgments by society must be a matter of

REASONS FOR THE DEVOUT

deliberation" (MC, 69), with deliberation being understood as the formal interplay of assertion, challenge, and the marshaling of evidence. A position that cannot be deliberated in this way (because it fails to respond to challenges or is buttressed by no evidence) is not a moral position, and, therefore, "racial discrimination is not a moral position," for "no one can claim that . . . it is a position about which reasonable people might morally disagree" (MC, 69–70).

But wait a minute: there are certainly people, even today, who would make that claim and back it up with reasons. Yes, that's true, say Gutmann and Thompson, but their reasons "fail . . . to qualify as moral reasons" (MC, 70). Why? Because they "can be shown to be rationalizations," that is, proxies for motives (a desire to oppress, a lust for power) those who give them would be unwilling to acknowledge. And how do you know that? Because, while they offer "evidence," they either refuse to consider "accepted methods of challenging" it or the evidence they offer comes from a source rational beings cannot take seriously, as when they "claim that God speaking literally through the Bible or the laws of nature forbids the mixing of races" (MC, 70).

Notice that what looks like an argument is really a succession of dismissive gestures designed to deflect objections to a position the authors are unwilling to relinquish or even examine. (Ironically, they are the best example of the close-mindedness they inveigh against.) Anyone who favors racial discrimination is just sick and has no reason except hate and prejudice; if he has reasons, they are unaccompanied by evidence; if he has evidence, it is the wrong kind; if he has the right kind, it is not as good as the evidence we have. You know that they could go on forever in this vein because all they are doing is negotiating a very small circle that begins and ends with their own prior conviction and a vocabulary made in its image. The key word in that vocabulary is "reasonable." But all that is meant by the word is what my friends and I take to be so. After all, we are reasonable persons; *we* know that no argument for racial discrimination could have any moral or rational basis; therefore anyone who makes such an argument is unreasonable.

To be sure, there are repeated attempts to present this in-house parochialism as if it were the expression of an impersonal and general rule, as when they describe their position as issuing from "a disinterested perspective that could be adopted by any member of society" and distinguish it from the "implausible beliefs" (MC, 71) of those who cite the Bible or the laws of nature. But aren't those for whom the Bible is authoritative also members of society, and isn't the fact that these believer-citizens refuse the authors' perspective evidence that it is not disinterested at all (unless believers of a fundamentalist type are regarded as second-class citizens whose views don't count, which is just how they are regarded here)? And isn't "disinterested" one more word—like impartial and reasonable—that claims the high ground of neutrality while performing exclusionary work?

A little later on, the same work is done by the phrase "disposition toward openness" (a variation on Conkle's "openness of mind"): citizens should be required "to cultivate a disposition toward openness. We should try to break personal and institutional habits that discourage our accepting the position of our opponents at some time in the future" (MC, 80). What renders this "requirement" apparently reasonable, even unexceptionable, are the words "personal" and "habits," which together trivialize what some citizens might regard as their beliefs, not beliefs in the sense of opinions—a sense liberalism must assume so that its logic seems obvious—but beliefs in the sense of what one takes, at the very deepest level and on the basis of incontrovertible evidence (empirical, biblical, whatever), to be true. So long as "habit," "personal," and "opinion" are what you are holding on to, resisting the "disposition toward openness" doesn't seem defensible and looks very much like putting one's head in the sand, stubbornly refusing to see the light, etc. After all, don't you want your opinions to be backed up and confirmed by independent evidence, and in the event that they are not, aren't you better off by having been shown the shakiness of what you had mistakenly held to be firm?

The answer is that citizens who hold the doctrine of biblical inerrancy do not accept the category of independent evidence, of evidence to which the words of the Bible must conform if they are to be believed. And, indeed, they will regard the lack of a fit between their own conclusions and the conclusions that might be reached by the "generally accepted methods of inquiry" (MC, 71) as the severest judgment possible on the generally accepted methods of inquiry. Gutmann and Thompson, in turn, will find them unreasonable, insufficiently reflective, and close-minded, all the while not recognizing how closed their minds are to systems of belief in the context of which some questions ("Did Christ die for our sins and is he risen?") are definitively settled, not because believers avert their eyes from new sources of evidence but because, as they see it, all the evidence is already in and proceeds from a source so high that no piling up of arguments on some "other side" could possibly matter.

The issue is not an abstract or theoretical one, as we can see by returning to the case of Vicki Frost and her friends. She and her co-religionists, you will recall, objected to their school's "critical reading" program not because they were upset by a particular doctrine but because they rejected the idea that "exposure to the diversity" of doctrines was a good thing. As far as they were concerned it was a very bad thing, because the materials their children were required to read might very well have the effect of undermining their faith. As Nomi Stolzenberg points out, "The plaintiffs objected to the very principles—tolerance and evenhandedness—traditionally used to justify liberal education" (591).[8] Predictably, their objection was met by a reinvocation of those same principles in the form of a point made by the superintendent of the Hawkins County school district and accepted by a succession of courts. The plaintiffs, the superintendent declared, misunderstood the fact that "exposure to something does not constitute teaching, indoctrination . . . or promotion of the things exposed."[9]

In their brief consideration of the case, Gutmann and Thompson echo his judgment.[10] The argument of the fundamentalist parents, they say, "ignores a simple distinction between teaching students about a religion and teaching them to believe in a religion" (DD, 66). But what they ignore and (along with the superintendent) fail to understand is that the distinction between "teaching about" and "teaching to believe in"—between exposure and indoctrination—rests on a psychology that is part and parcel of the liberalism Vicki Frost and her friends don't want imposed on their children. In that psychology, the mind remains unaffected by the ideas and doctrines that pass before it, and its job is to weigh and assess those doctrines from a position distanced from and independent of any one of them. (Note how in this picture the mind is a microcosm of the liberal society in which it operates and flourishes.)

However, in another psychology, one undergirded by a conviction of original sin, the mind is not (at least not since Eden) so strongly independent. Rather than standing apart from the range of views that contend for its approval, it is, in its congenital weakness and disposition to be overwhelmed, at the mercy of those views. And accordingly, it behooves the parent or educator to take care lest their charges be influenced in the wrong directions, as they well might be if they were introduced to notions they were ill-equipped to resist. In this psychology (of which there are secular analogues), exposure is not an innocent or healthy experience but one fraught with dangers. And the chief danger is not any particular doctrine to which the children might be exposed but the unannounced yet powerfully assumed doctrine of exposure as a first principle, as a virtual theology.

This is where the indoctrination comes in, not at the level of urging this or that belief but at the more subliminal level at which what is urged is that encountering as many ideas as possible and giving each of them a run for its money is an absolutely good thing. What the children are being indoctrinated in is distrust of any belief that has not been arrived at by the exercise of their unaided reason as it surveys all the alternatives before choosing one freely with no guidance from any external authority. Unaided reason, however—reason freed from the tethering constraints of biblical commands or parental precepts—is what Vicki Frost and her co-religionists distrust; and yet they are being told that its imposition will in no way affect their children's moral views, and, moreover, that the ideology of preferring no point of view to another is neutral, is, as Nagel would say, a higher order impartiality.

Even if impartiality were the right word and named what resulted from hewing to the distinction between exposure and indoctrination, the plaintiffs would feel no less injured because, as Stolzenberg notes, "On their own terms, the believer's representations of her beliefs are representations of truth, or . . . 'claims on our existence,' that require either affirmation or rejection, but not impartiality" (630–631). Whereas Vicki Frost and her colleagues pledge allegiance to an authority (God, the church, the Bible) and wish their children to follow it (not critically examine it), public education is informed by an ideology in "perennial protest against all forms of absolute authority," an ideology that everywhere displays "an antipathy to closing ranks around any system of belief."[11] That antipathy rarely announces itself as such but instead wears softer labels—exposure to diverse views, open-mindedness, even-handedness—that mask the sharp hardness of what is being done.

In Gutmann's and Thompson's argument, it is the notion of "mutual respect" (their version of higher order impartiality) that does the work of exclusion in the name, supposedly, of generosity. Mutual respect, they say, "manifests a distinctively democratic kind of character—the character of individuals who are morally committed, self-reflective about their commitments, discerning of the difference between respectable and merely tolerable differences of opinion, and open to the possibility of changing their minds or modifying their positions at some time in the future if they confront unanswerable objections to their present point of view" (MC, 76). The idea is simple enough, and as usual it seems unexceptionable: regard those with whom you disagree not as enemies to the death but as partners in the search for truth, and hold yourself ready to change or modify your point of view if you are unable to refute a reasoned challenge to what you believe. But the imperative will begin to seem less "reasonable" and commonsensical if you ask a simple two-part question: "Where do the challenges to your belief come from, and when should you be distressed if you cannot meet them?"

If the challenges come from within the structure of your belief (since you have already acknowledged that all men are created equal, how can you support a policy of racial discrimination?), then the standard to which you are being held is one you have already acknowledged, and what is being asked of you is, simply, that you be consistent with yourself. If, however, the challenge comes in terms not recognized by the structure of your belief, why should you be the least bit concerned with it since it rests on notions of evidence and argument to which you are in no way committed?[12] If you tell a serious Christian that no one can walk on water or rise from the dead or feed five thousand with two fishes and five loaves, he or she will tell you that the impossibility of those actions for mere men is what makes their performance so powerful a sign of divinity. For one party the reasoning is: "No man can do it and therefore Christ didn't do it." For the other the reasoning is: "Since no man could do it, he who did it is more than man." For one party, falsification follows from the absence of a plausibly empirical account of how the purported phenomena could have occurred; for the other, the absence of a plausibly empirical account is just the point, one that does not challenge the faith but confirms it.

What Gutmann and Thompson will say is that the second party is not really reasoning. This is what they mean when they distinguish between "respectable and merely tolerable differences of opinion" (MC, 76). A difference of opinion you respect is an opinion held by someone who argues from the same premises and with the same tools you do; an opinion you merely tolerate—although we won't imprison you for holding it, neither will we take any account of it in the process of formulating policy—is an opinion held by someone who argues from premises and with tools you and your friends find provincial at best and dangerous (because fanatical) at worst. It is at this point that you dismiss those premises (such as biblical inerrancy) as ones no rational person could subscribe to, whereas in fact what you have done is define "rational" so as to make it congruent with the ways of thinking you and those who agree with you customarily deploy. "Mutual respect" should be renamed "mutual self-congratulation" since it will not be extended beyond the circle of those who already feel comfortable with one another.

In the case of Gutmann and Thompson, not surprisingly, the circle of comfort, and therefore the shape of rationality, will be drawn in accordance with the norms of the academy in general and of political science departments in particular, which means that those within the circle will hold their beliefs at arm's length and relate to them in a style marked by diffidence, aversion to strong assertion (except in a very few cases like that of racial discrimination), and a pervasive, if mild and unaggressive, skepticism. It is not accurate to characterize these men and women as "morally committed," for what they are committed to is not their morality but the deliberative process to which their morality is delivered up on the way, perhaps, to being abandoned. What they are committed to is the deferring of commitment in favor of an ever-attenuated "conversation" whose maintenance is the only value they wholeheartedly embrace.

It is no surprise, then, when those whose relationship to their values is more intimate are read out of a conversation for which they have been rendered unfit (they really *believe* something) by the circumscribing definitions of those who preside over it. Such persons, whether they think that this should be a Christian nation, or a nation where rewards and benefits are distributed by race, or a nation where full legal rights are withheld from homosexuals, are declared not to have a moral position, a judgment supposedly backed up by philosophical distinctions and empirical evidence but in fact a judgment informed by nothing more "principled" than a dislike of certain points of view. As card-carrying liberals, Gutmann and Thompson cannot acknowledge disliking a point of view as a reason for keeping it out of a conversation; after all, the very first premise of their liberalism is that private moral judgments should not be imposed on others in the form of public policy. Therefore, they must find a way of dressing up their personal moral judgments so they will appear to have been generated by a wholly impersonal mechanism.

The result is the bravura reasoning of which this sentence is one more example: "Nor has a logically consistent argument been constructed on plausible premises to show that homosexual sex cannot be understood as part of the human condition" (MC, 75). The questions suggest themselves immediately. Consistent with what (or whose) basic assumptions? Cannot something be understood as part of the human condition and yet also understood as being wrong and worthy of condemnation (murder, child molestation)? Who gets to say what is and is not a plausible premise? And how is it that premises plausible (a real weasel word) to millions of people have been ruled out of court in advance? The answers are obvious and embarrassing because they all point to an act of power, of peremptory exclusion and dismissal, that cannot be acknowledged as such lest the liberal program of renouncing power and exclusion be exposed for the fiction it surely is. I don't criticize liberals for employing power in an effort to further the truths they believe in—that's what everyone does, necessarily—but for pretending to be doing something else and for thinking there is something else to do.

We circle once again back to Locke and the tensions in his argument: those who preach toleration or open-mindedness or mutual respect know that there are some ideas they can't tolerate or be open to or respect, and unless they are willing to follow the fatalism of Holmes, they must find a way of keeping them off the agenda while still proclaiming that they are practicing toleration, open-mindedness, and mutual respect. They find that way, as Locke found it, in the discovery and invocation of exactly the kind of universal—call it the "judgment of all mankind" or a "higher order rationality"—declared unavailable by the very liberalism they profess. Remember, if every church is orthodox to itself, there is no space between orthodoxies that might serve as the location of some supposedly impersonal constraints. In fact, if every church is orthodox to itself, there can be no such constraints; and when you think to invoke one of them, you are invoking your own personal agenda in an attempt to present it as the impersonal judgment of all. Then, like Gutmann and Thompson, you can breathe a sigh of moral relief and say that policies favoring racial discrimination or religious zealotry can be kept off the agenda because they are not moral positions; and, besides, the evidence cited to support them is not "plausible" nor the authorities invoked legitimate; and, besides again, they don't conform to the requirement of mutual respect. (This is exactly what they say about the plaintiffs' reasons in *Mozert:* "Their reasons do not meet the tests of reciprocity"; DD, 65.)

You will have sensed before I say it that my argument has long since become repetitive. Whether its focus is Locke or Nagel or Conkle or Thiemann or Gutmann and Thompson—philosophers, theorists, liberals, conservatives—what it discovers is always the same. Someone sets out to solve the problem presented to a would-be regime of tolerance, or higher order impartiality, or openness of mind, or mutual respect, by views that are manifestly intolerant, have no truck with impartiality, and accord respect largely to those who already agree with them; and invariably the solution that emerges is a mirror version of the problem it claims to address. Tolerance is defined in a way that renders the troubling views unworthy to receive it; openness of mind turns out to be closed to any form of thought not committed to its hegemony; and mutual respect is less a formula for ecumenical generosity than the cant phrase of a self-selected little club of right-minded academics.

Moreover, those who perform these self-justifying and piously self-righteous gymnastics are unable to hear a criticism of their performance even when they raise it themselves. Gutmann and Thompson pretend, for a moment, to engage sympathetically with the plaintiffs in *Mozert* when they ask, "What if the parents reject the principle of reciprocity" and "argue that it is biased against fundamentalism, and in favor of religions that conform to deliberative views of civic education and prevailing modes of empirical inquiry?" (DD, 67). I couldn't have put it better myself, but when Gutmann and Thompson reply to their own question, it turns out that they missed its force: "But the value of public reason expressed by the deliberative perspective is not just another morality. It is offered as the morally optimal basis on which citizens who disagree about moralities and religions can act collectively to make educational policy" (DD, 67).

This is a more up-front version of what Nagel does when he slips in "general" and "special" as adjectives descriptive of "higher order impartiality" and the moralities it supposedly trumps, and thereby assures the triumph of the former by never having to confront the possibility that it is one of the latter. In the same way, Gutmann and Thompson allow the fundamentalist parents to object that "deliberative views" of civic education are hostage to a special morality (not everyone would accept it) but then assert that while it may be a morality, it is not "just" another one. Rather, it has the distinguishing (and salvational) characteristic of providing the framework in which all the other, less capacious moralities can disagree without being unduly unpleasant to one another; it provides a "morally optimal basis."

Yes it does, for those citizens who already identify the moral optimum with the scene of rational reflection and debate. Other citizens—Vicki Frost among them—identify it differently, and if the requirement of deliberative give and take is imposed on them, it will not accommodate their disagreement with the liberal mainstream but delegitimize it, as Gutmann and Thompson do when they dismiss the fundamentalist objection as evidence that "those who make it do not take into account the problem of moral disagreement in politics" (DD, 67). But for the fundamentalists there is no "problem" of moral disagreement; there is just moral disagreement, a conflict between conceptions of the good. The only "problem" is that at the moment, in a case like *Mozert*, they're not winning the conflict, and they will hardly be comforted by being told that they shouldn't want to, that they are part of a problem.

Indeed if they think about themselves as part of a problem, they will have surrendered to their opponents and become vulnerable to what Gutmann and Thompson consider their strongest point. "Even the objection that reciprocity [mutual respect, giving the other fellow a hearing] is biased must be stated in a form that appeals to a sense of fairness . . . accepted by other citizens" (DD, 67–68). This would be telling were the fundamentalist objection to the doctrine of reciprocity that it is biased; the objection is (or should be—we shall meet at least one fundamentalist who falls into this trap) that it is *wrong*, that the moral optimum is not everyone talking to one another in a decorous deliberative forum but is, rather, everyone allied to and acting in conformity with the Truth and the will of God. We shall revisit this point later; for now suffice it to observe—once again—that Gutmann and Thompson never come close to taking the measure of the arguments that might be made against them, and continue to try to have it both ways, claiming to be the apostles of respect and the keepers of the open door at the same time they slam the door shut the moment someone not of their crowd wants to come in.

But, someone might reasonably object, this is hardly helpful. Suppose that you believe (as I in fact do) that policies favoring racial discrimination have no place on the political agenda, and believe too that if a state or the nation should turn in the direction of theocracy, it would be a bad thing. What do you do if, by my arguments at least, there is no principled way—no way not tied to a particular agenda—of lobbying for the exclusion from public deliberations of points of view you consider dangerous? Do you simply allow such points of view to flourish and hope for the best? Or do you do what the liberal theorists do (although they would no doubt dispute this description): cast about for an abstract formula under whose cover you can exclude things left and right, all the while claiming clean (neutral, impartial, mutually respectful) hands. Is there no alternative?

Gutmann and Thompson actually have an answer to that question, but for reasons that are finally not surprising they don't see it even though they provide evidence for it in an observation they rush right past: "A policy favoring racial discrimination, it is now generally agreed, deserves no place on the political agenda. Such a policy is not an option that legislatures or citizens would seriously consider, and if it were to do so, we should expect courts to prevent its adoption" (MC, 69). Although over fifteen pages of the essay remain to be written, one wonders why the authors didn't stop here, since it would seem that what they seek—a way of keeping policies favoring racial discrimination off the agenda—has already been found. What's the problem?

The problem (they never say this, but it is implied by the fact that the essay continues) is that the solution has been the accomplishment of politics rather than theory. The agreement on which they report has been reached in the course of a history that includes the civil rights struggles of the 1950s and 60s, the election in 1964 of a President from the South, two speeches by Martin Luther King Jr., the televising of official violence against freedom riders, a Republican President who not only went to China but put in place mandatory programs of affirmative action, the Civil Rights Act of 1964, the Voting Rights Act of 1965, the immense popularity of Alex Haley's *Roots*, the breaking of the color barrier in professional sports. No one of these was either decisive or inevitable, but as a result of their entirely contingent occurrence in an equally contingent sequence, saying certain things (you must keep those people in their place; America belongs to Americans; you wouldn't want one to marry your sister) became at the least unfashionable and at the most socially and economically disadvantageous, while saying certain other things (people should be judged on the content of their character, not the color of their skins; diversity is a good that should be reflected in the classroom and the workplace; this country is committed to the eradication of racism) became de rigueur and a ticket of entry into public life. This does not mean that the old sentiments were erased from the hearts of those who had previously expressed them or that minds once confused had now been cleared of mistaken notions. Rather, it means that one vocabulary fell into favor and disuse while another stepped into the place it had formerly occupied, and that this new vocabulary was at once a response to shifts in the political wind and an event in those shifts.

The problem is that the political winds may shift again. That is why Gutmann and Thompson are not satisfied with timely and prudential "reasons for rejecting racial discrimination" and require reasons of a "different, stronger kind" (MC, 69), reasons whose force does not vary and/or diminish with circumstances. After all, if policies favoring racial discrimination have been only politically discredited—discredited by contingent events and the ascendency of one rhetoric over another— the same policies could be politically rehabilitated, perhaps by generating "scientific evidence" that gives them new justificatory life (witness *The Bell Curve*) or by quantifying their effects and discovering that they promote efficiency and wealth maximization.[13]

To be sure, any such rehabilitation seems unlikely, but the fact that it is even possible is enough to make the point that politics can go backwards. It is because politics cannot be freeze-framed at the moment its wheel of fortune delivers an outcome you favor that Gutmann and Thompson want to bypass the political process and turn to reasons of "a stronger kind," to principled reasons. These stronger reasons would hover above the political process and intervene whenever it was about to take a wrong turn. In this way, the "hope of liberal theory," the hope that citizens can "agree on principles" (MC, 64) that will once and for all circumscribe the political agenda, will have been realized.

But where will these reasons of a stronger kind have come from? Who will have thought them up? The answer is that they will have come from one or another of the viewpoints contending in the political arena. After all, the desire to remove policies favoring racial discrimination from the agenda is not universal; if it were, there would be no problem and the agenda would circumscribe itself. Whatever "principle" one might offer as a device for managing the political process will itself be politically informed, and any agreement it secures will be the result of efforts by one party first to fill the vocabulary of principle with meanings reflecting its agenda and then to present that vocabulary, fashioned as an adjunct to a political program, as the principled, apolitical source of that same program.

I do not mean this as a description of anyone's intention or even as a criticism as it would be if there were an alternative. There are no cynics in my scenario, only persons whose strongly held beliefs and commitments lead them to understand, and understand sincerely, notions like equality, fairness, and neutrality in one way rather than another. It is when someone's understanding of these resonant words (which do not interpret themselves) is regnant in the public space that something like an agreement has been secured. Once that agreement is in place, some policies will be (at least publicly) unthinkable and everyone will regularly say of them "No one would seriously urge . . ."; but in time the unthinkable will be reintroduced in a new guise, and the agreement that once seemed so solid will fall apart preliminary to the fashioning of a new one, no less political, no less precarious.

What this means is that there are no different or stronger reasons than policy reasons and that the announcement of a formula (higher order impartiality, mutual respect, the judgment of all mankind) that supposedly outflanks politics or limits its sphere by establishing a space free from its incursions will be nothing more or less than politics—here understood not as a pejorative but as the name of the activity by which you publicly urge what you think to be good and true—by another name, the name, but never the reality, of principle.

In saying this I may seem to be giving voice to Nagel's greatest fear, the fear that in the absence of some higher order impartiality, disagreements come down to "a pure confrontation between personal moral convictions" (233). But that fear is a product of his formulation of it, which is flawed in two respects: in the use of the word "personal" to describe the convictions in conflict with one another, and in the use of the scare phrase "pure confrontations" to describe the nature of the conflict. First, no party to any conflict will accept the adjective "personal," because to have a conviction is to believe that what it commits you to is true not only for you but for everyone, including those who, for whatever reasons (blindness, error, perversity) are not presently persuaded of it. The distinction between personal and public morality is internal to one's structure of conviction; within that structure, "personal" is the label you give to the agendas and systems of value of the other fellow, while reserving the labels "public" and "general" (or "publicly accessible") for your own.

If it were truly possible to say "personal" and mean by it a realm whose boundaries were agreed on by everyone, the line between the personal and the public would draw itself, and merely personal confrontations would be avoided because they would instantly be distinguishable from principled, higher order confrontations. Settling the just bounds between church and state—between the private and the public (if you accept the distinction, and the hard question, remember, is what you do with those who don't)—would be a snap if the census of the two realms were already complete and authenticated; mutual respect would be a breeze (and cost-free) if everyone's "merely" personal moralities were safely quarantined in the private sector and you knew that what you were respecting wasn't going to inconvenience you in any serious way.

These points apply with equal force to the scare phrase "pure confrontation." By "pure," Nagel presumably means confrontations where nothing is at stake except the idiosyncratic views of overheated individuals. But of course every confrontation will seem just that to those for whom the issue is obviously trivial, while for those caught up in the confrontation, the accusation of triviality will proceed from persons incapable of seeing where the matters of true importance lie. From the outside we are all Gullivers, wondering at the foolishness of those who would destroy each other over the issue of which end is the best for the cracking of an egg, remarking on the insanity of those who will go to war over the presence or absence of altar rails. But in some other configuration of battle we will be insiders, and it will then be *our* lot to be derided by those who cannot see for the life of them why supposedly rational people should be so excited by the trifles we are willing to fight for.

Like "personal," "pure confrontation" is a hope masquerading as a fear, the hope that foolish, whimsical disagreements will announce themselves as such to a naturally sober world whose majority inhabitants can then agree to disagree only about things that are really serious. Nagel, in a manner typical of those who play this game, speaks from the inside of an exclusionary structure (nor could he do otherwise) while claiming to speak from an outside where exclusion has been foresworn. What he can't allow himself to see is that the devil he would exorcise—the devil of force, violence, politics—is constitutive of the cleared space he would have us occupy.

Bonnie Honig makes the general point when she observes that "most political theorists are hostile to the disruptions of politics" and "assume that the task of political theory is . . . to get politics . . . over and done with" (2).[14] The goal is to replace large P Politics—the clash between fundamentally incompatible visions and agendas—with small p politics—the adjustment through procedural rules of small differences within a field from which the larger substantive differences have been banished. The problem is that the distinction between what is procedural and what is substantive is itself a substantive one, and therefore in whatever form it is enacted it will engender the very conflicts it was designed to mitigate, as those who would have enacted it differently or not enacted it at all cry foul, or error, or blasphemy. When this happens (as it always will), the would-be engineers of peace and stability always respond in the same way, by calling the malcontents unreasonable, or fanatical, or insufficiently respectful of difference, or some other name that dismisses their concerns by placing them beyond a pale whose boundaries, they continue to claim, have been drawn by nature.

Honig calls those stigmatized others "the remainders" (4), those who have been exiled to the margins in the name of a policy of inclusion that can only call itself such with a straight face by labeling them monsters. Nagel at least gets the requirement right when he says that "liberalism should provide the devout with a reason for tolerance" (229); but like everyone else, he does not see, and indeed is committed to not seeing, that a reason persuasive to the devout would have to be a reason compatible with the content of their devotion, and that a reason which instead trumps, or claims to trump, that content will be seen as no reason at all but as a wolf in reason's clothing.

In these terms, the issue may seem abstract, but it receives a human (if fictional) face when Larry Alexander creates a character he calls Ann.[15] Ann is a Christian who originally came to her beliefs by way of parental instruction; but "she now holds them based on what she views as independent reasons" (768). Moreover, some of her views on matters of public policy flow from her beliefs. Thus she believes that fetuses "have a right to life that trumps women's rights regarding reproduction," and she believes that "pornography is blasphemous" and "therefore wants pornography legally banned," and she believes "that public money should be used to support the private schools that teach her religious beliefs" (770).

Alexander imagines what someone like Nagel might say to Ann that would persuade her to refrain from trying to make her views the content of public policy. It might be pointed out to her that if the public sphere were reconfigured in accordance with her views, the result would be "unfair to those who do not share" (775) those views. But, as Alexander quickly notes, the force of this argument would depend on Ann's accepting fairness as a value higher than the values urged on her by her religion, and if she were willing to do that she would not have relaxed her religious views but exchanged them for the (liberal) ones Nagel and his friends already hold. Moreover, because fairness is itself a value whose shape will vary with the shape of one's background beliefs (there is no such thing as fairness per se), Ann will dispute the characterization of her as unfair. If abortion is murder, why does one have an obligation to be fair to would-be murderers by legalizing their crime? And if those who commit murder are in danger of eternal damnation (as she believes them to be), wouldn't the fair thing be to put obstacles in the way of their courting that danger? Fairness, then, is of no help in dealing with someone like Ann. It is either a rival theology whose golden rule she will have already rejected or a contestable concept to whose invocation she will have as much right as anyone.

If Ann will be unresponsive to an argument from fairness, she will be no less so to an argument from reason, and she will not be impressed when Nagel tells her that she would be wrong to impose her norms on others if those same norms are "reasonably rejectable." For as Alexander notes, her acceptance of those norms is not in tension with reason but is, precisely, reasonable. Indeed, "her acceptance means that she thinks acceptance is reasonable and rejection unreasonable" (780). Nor could it be otherwise, for "from the point of view of the one whose norms they are, *no* accepted norms can be reasonably rejected" (780). It follows, then, that when they are rejected—when a liberal regime declares them irrelevant to the determination of public policy—that rejection, even when it wears the mantle of neutrality, is an act of force of exactly the kind liberalism disavows.

It is time to declare openly the conclusion this analysis has long since reached: there are no reasons you can give to the devout, not because they are the kind of people who don't listen to reason but because the reasons you might give can never be reasons for them unless either they convert to your faith or you convert to theirs. Once this is clearly understood, the pseudo-generosity offered by Nagel, Gutmann, Thompson, and all the rest will seem less palatable (and even less attractive) than the frank mean-spiritedness of Stephen Macedo when he asks "Why should we apologize if disparate burdens fall on proponents of totalistic religions or moral views who refuse to concede the political authority of public reason?" (484).[16] After all, these guys (he is speaking of the plaintiffs in *Mozert v. Hawkins*) are the losers; they should be content with what we give them and stop complaining. And we shouldn't take their complaints too seriously unless we want to contemplate the real possibility of their ascendency. "We must not forget how such people would behave if they had political power" (484). To be sure, they will suffer marginalization and "feel oppressed," but "such feelings may indicate the need for adjustments not in public policy but in the group" (469). That is, if "such people" want to be welcomed by the mainstream, they should join it. Shape up or be shipped out.

This piece of realpolitick is positively bracing compared to the pious moralizing of the usual son or daughter of Rawls, and it makes a point I shall pick up on in Chapter 11. But most legal and political theorists are not ready for this end–game move and prefer to search for an intellectually more satisfying way of dealing with "the feelings" of those who profess illiberal views. Among those, the most patient and thorough is Kent Greenawalt, who in *Private Consciences and Public Reasons* takes up every issue I have raised and considers the arguments of everyone on every side of every fence. As we shall see, the chief merit of Greenawalt's book is that it is an illustration of the tension it wants to resolve, the tension we have been tracking from the beginning between the impulse toward tolerance and the demands of order. Although Greenawalt does not finally advance the debates he rehearses, he does display the springs of those debates in a way that makes as clear as one would like why they are, and will continue to be, interminable.

PLAYING NOT TO WIN

Like Larry Alexander, Greenawalt invents a character who in his attitudes is representative of the challenge religiosity poses to the liberal project.[1] His Ann is named Herman, and he "wants to have the U.S. Constitution amended to provide explicit favoritism for the Christian religion" (60). Informed that "he is not acting in accord with basic liberal democratic principles," Herman replies that "disregard of the true religion shows the poverty of liberalism" and declares that he will continue to "act according to his own religious views." Having brought his fictional character to this moment of impasse, Greenawalt promptly abandons him and with him the problem he seemed to instantiate: "Although I shall not say a great deal more about it, this problem, of how legislators or citizens may be subject to a principle of self-restraint that does not accord with their own comprehensive views, lurks in the background of much of the subsequent discussion" (60).

But it does more than lurk in the background; it names the requirement—that something must be said to the devout—that must be met if Greenawalt's project is to have a normative point. Unless there is a principle of self-restraint that is compelling to all citizens no matter what their comprehensive views, any restraint one proposes will be received as an imposition rather than as a reason by those whose comprehensive views do not honor it. If the question of whether or not there is such a principle is not confronted directly but is left to "lurk in the background," it can always thrust itself into the foreground just at the moment when an apparently bright line has been drawn between what belongs to religion and what belongs to Caesar.

Private Consciences and Public Reasons abounds in such moments, some acknowledged and some not, with the result that the book exhibits, sometimes in a single sentence, a split personality. On the one hand, it is a theoretical treatise in search of a privileged philosophical position from the vantage point of which the issues it raises can be definitively addressed, as when Greenawalt declares that the "problem of political philosophy is genuine only if some moral and political judgments do have a more solid or widely comprehensible basis than others" (25). On the other hand, it is an account (not without interest) of the compromises and adjustments that are available within a set of political conditions—roughly the conditions of American political life at the end of the century—whose rightness is assumed and not interrogated. In one narrative the goal is the generation through rigorous conceptual analysis of a formula for settling the just bounds that all citizens will positively affirm; in the other the goal is the prudential one of figuring out what, given the prevailing realities of power, one can or cannot accomplish, at least until those realities change, at which point the calculations would have to be done all over again.

The slippage from one narrative to the other is already occurring in the sentence I have just quoted. Note the equivocation between "more solid" and "widely comprehensible." "More solid" names the theoretical desire: what is wanted are judgments that will not shift when one set of interests is displaced by another. "Widely comprehensible," however, is a numerical criterion; it is calculated by reference to whatever assumptions happen to have currency at the present time. When that currency changes and new assumptions command a majority, "widely comprehensible" will still measure something, but the measure will have no substantive—solid—content; it will be the measure of a popular vote. Widely comprehensible, in short, identifies a political condition rather than a normative one, and while Greenawalt surely knows that, he repeatedly contrives to forget it so that the theoretical ambitions of his analysis can at least seem to be alive.

This requires some agility, as we can see by examining a single paragraph. The topic, as always, is the independence of issues of "political organization and justice" from religious premises: "One may think that the main techniques for deciding these issues need not rely on religious premises themselves and are compatible with a wide variety of religious premises, though not all. One can thus believe that political philosophy is autonomous in the sense that sound principles for what people should do in politics do not depend on propositions about God or other controversial religious subjects. Of course, one who is rigorously self-reflective 'will believe' in this form of autonomy only if his religious views fit with that understanding. Many religious believers do think they can reach important conclusions about political organization and justice that do not depend on disputed religious premises" (124).

The first sentence is unexceptionable, but all it does is report on a present fact of present political life in America (rather than Iran or Northern Ireland or Israel): as things stand now, citizens can debate issues of political organization and the deployment of state resources without invoking or relying on whatever strong religious beliefs they may happen to have. But of course "many" does not mean "all," as the final clause of the sentence ("though not all") readily acknowledges. Here, not quite lurking in the background, are those bothersome persons whose religious premises direct them to put every proposed public policy to the test of theological doctrine. So long as such persons exist, they pose a challenge to the generality of any settlement of the just bounds, even if that settlement is *as of now* widely accepted. And, as we have seen, a liberal theorist can deal with these outliers only by either demonizing them as irrational or by noting their presence as a minor irritation or by saying this is the best we can get, so let's move on.

Greenawalt is doing something of all three here, although he does most of it in a footnote: "Any particular substantive political principles and the techniques for arriving at them are bound to be at odds with *some* religious views" (206). What exactly does he mean by "some" and why is it in italics? It's hard to tell, but the indeterminacy serves Greenawalt well, because it allows him to say the several different and potentially conflicting things he must say to keep his argument going. "Some" could either be a concession to the ultimate impossibility of his project (well, the job will never get completely done but eight out of ten isn't bad), or it could be an exasperated reference to those who will not listen to reason (there's nothing you can do with those people). "Some" also deflects attention away from the phrase "bound to be at odds" and from the questions it might provoke. What is the content of "bound to be"? Is it a deep truth about the relationship between political principles and religious views, and if so, is it a truth deep enough to undermine everything Greenawalt is trying and claiming to do? These questions are not seriously raised, and even the possibility of raising them is buried in a footnote.

Meanwhile, in the next two sentences Greenawalt does again what he did in the first—make a claim and then back away from it. He declares that one *can* believe that political principles do not depend on religious ones, but then he says that only those whose religious beliefs "fit" with this belief will profess it. In one sentence political and religious premises are easily separable; in the other separation follows only when the internal structure of a particular faith already entails it. The final sentence of the paragraph tells us, again, that the religious views of many do in fact permit or endorse that separation, a fact of sociological interest but one from which no general conclusion can be drawn.

In the next paragraph the issues Greenawalt has been skirting are forthrightly faced; or so it would seem, when he introduces a new character, Faith, who "believes that ideally everyone should accept the true religion (her religion)." In her society, however, "only one sixth of the people accept that religion" (124). How might she respond, asks Greenawalt, and answers that under these conditions, "Faith might think it appropriate for the government to withdraw from claims of religious truth" (124). Now everything depends on what is meant by "appropriate." In what spirit might Faith agree to the separation of matters of state from matters of religious truth, even though she believes that her own religion is true for, and should govern the lives of, everyone? Well, says Greenawalt, "She might regard it as a second-best compromise"; what she wants is a government informed by the principles of her faith, but "realizing that she and her cobelievers do not have the political clout to achieve this result," she "is willing to settle for the government keeping its hands off religion" (124). That is, she would settle for what she would get and thereby accept separation as a matter of prudence.

But there is another possibility, one Greenawalt obviously prefers. "The second way Faith might accept the principle of withdrawal is as an actual requirement of justice" for she "might suppose . . . it . . . inappropriate for the state to support a religion accepted by only one sixth of the population," since "such support would inadequately respect freedom and consent as grounds of human community" (124). But why should she suppose *that*, unless she had abandoned her religion for a new one whose cardinal doctrines are not original sin and the divinity of

Christ but freedom and consent? What Greenawalt has done without announcing it is eliminate the tension between Faith's religious convictions and the principles of liberal government; and once they have been collapsed into one another, he can declare that in the course of reflection she has become someone whose overriding concern is "to show respect for fellow citizens" (125). She has become a liberal theorist.

In his eagerness to get Faith into the liberal fold, Greenawalt rushes too quickly past the prudential strategy he imagines her adopting (but then rejecting for a "higher" consideration) and fails to see how that strategy might have a second step. If Faith and her friends currently lack the "political clout" to get their views enacted into law, they might bide their time and work to build up the political capital that would make success possible, just as the Christian Right is doing today when it elects members to school boards. Locke, prescient as usual, anticipates this course of action and condemns it as the predictable behavior of zealots who will "preach up toleration" as long as they are out of power but once in power will say goodbye to "peace and charity" and contrive "to become masters."[2]

The accusation is severe, but someone like Faith could respond to it (if she were given the chance) by saying that whatever mastery she sought was not sought in her own name but in the name of Him whom she served ("Not me, but my master in me"). Locke would no doubt reply, "That's what they all say," or some other variation of the standard liberal point that it is because everyone is committed to the truth of his or her views that each of us should wear his or hers lightly. For Faith, however, the information that others are as committed to their truths as she is to hers merely means that others are committed to error, and would not be a reason for her to "show respect for fellow citizens" (125). She may show respect in the ordinary course of things or as a way of keeping afloat until she spies an advantage, but she can't show respect as a matter of principle unless that principle has replaced her God.

Faith's story is Greenawalt's, barely disguised. The alternatives he imagines for her—prudence or principle—are the alternatives he wavers between on nearly every page. In the end, however, it is prudence, in the sense of going along with things as they are, that he embraces, although he would rather not think so. He masks his decision (perhaps from himself) by laboring to turn prudence itself into a principle, into the kind of normative abstraction usually opposed to it. In one mood a prudential strategy is termed merely an "effective means of persuasion" and not "a *principle* of restraint at all" (129); but in another (to him higher) mood, prudence—acting in accord with the shape of "present understand-ings" (181)—is offered as a principled response to a world lacking an independent mechanism for settling disputes. In such a world there is no way of deciding between the beliefs preferred by competing ortho-doxies, and it is prudent, therefore, to identify the beliefs most reason-able people hold and affirm them. In this argument, prudence emerges not as a political strategy but as a strategy for managing politics for the good of all—emerges, that is, as a principle.

But it is hard to see that this is anything more than the confusion of a political condition with a normative one. At any time, to be sure, there will be beliefs to which a large majority pledges allegiance; this, how-ever, says nothing about the truth status of those beliefs and offers no guidance to persons who want to know what to do. Someone who wants to know what to do doesn't want to hear what most people think but what it is right to think. At moments of stress in Greenawalt's argu-ment, he conflates the two and turns a status quo circumstance into a theoretical calculus. It is this conflation that informs his response to Alexander's denial of any epistemological distinction between secular and religious ways of knowing.[3] Both, Alexander explains, rests on beliefs (about the hierarchy of values, the sources of authority, etc.) one receives from culture and education and not first hand (it is hard to know what first-hand knowledge, knowledge independent of any in-place structure of thought, would be like). Therefore both are faiths, that is, ways of reasoning whose cogency and intelligibility depend on assumptions not open to question. Or, if you prefer, both are rationali-ties, that is, directions for producing evidence and conclusions under-girded by a full and coherent account of what the world is really like.

Greenawalt sees that if the thesis of "the unity of epistemology" is accepted, the category of "interpersonal reason" (102), of "common premises" (101) shared by a wide range of persons of differing beliefs, will have no content. Without the category of interpersonal reason, evo-lutionary science and creationist science stand on equally challengeable ground, and the preferring of one to another could not be justified except by reference to the beliefs of one of the disputing parties. Greenawalt resists this conclusion by declaring that while creationism, "assured by biblical infallibility," and evolution, "assured by science," are beliefs deriving from "competing paradigms," the latter is more "subject to validation by interpersonal reason" (102) because it rests on procedures, like the process of carbon dating, accepted and trusted by most people. But again, this is a sociological point and not one Alexander would deny. He would agree with Greenawalt that reasoning based on scientific evidence will today be more persuasive to those making decisions about public policy than reasoning rooted in evidence derived from the Bible, but he would attribute this fact (if it is a fact; remember the abortion debate) not to the epistemological superiority of the one over the other but to its success in positioning itself as the prestige discourse, at least where matters of state and the treasury are being debated.

It hardly need be said that it was once otherwise, that it was once the case that reasoning rooted in religious conviction was central to all avenues of human inquiry and not confined to the small space left to it by Enlightenment assumptions. When John Milton and others debated divorce in the seventeenth century, their proof texts were scriptural even though what was at stake was a change in the civil law. The example shows not only that the prestige and scope of a vocabulary is a function of historical change rather than an indication of a natural epistemological divide but that changes in history can be reversed. Now that gay marriage is a possibility (or a specter) on the public scene, theological considerations are once again being urged in the public sphere, and I have recently heard radio talk-show conversations that might well have occurred in the 1640s.

You might say that people making such arguments are kooks and that the premises they rely on are special and personal rather than *inter*personal. But any such judgment would mean no more than that some peoples' premises have been more effectively disseminated than the premises of some others. "Interpersonal" is not a philosophical category but the result of *counting*, of determining which set of epistemological presuppositions reigns in the corridors of power, and it must always be remembered that there are communities, neither small nor uninfluential, where the result of the count would be different, where "interpersonal" reason would have as its content biblicist assumptions. (Just what are and are not the corridors of power is itself a disputed question, not a matter of empirical observation.)

The point is not to deny differences of the kind Greenawalt notes but to historicize them, which is to deny their naturalness and stability. Historicized, those differences remain and they remain powerful; awareness of them is a prerequisite for success in public life. You don't want to speak to an audience in a language it finds alien or archaic or narrowly special. But such calculations and calibrations have nothing to do with any epistemological distinction. Epistemology-wise (an ugly but useful coinage), the vocabularies and premises of science, religion, liberal humanism, communitarianism, and so on are on a par, each one an orthodoxy to itself, fully equipped with dogma, criteria for evidence, founding texts, exemplary achievements, heroes, villains, goals, agendas, and all the rest. Politics-wise, these visions of life will never be on a par but always exist in some hierarchical relationship of precedence or subordination to which it would be foolish not to pay serious practical attention.

Serious attention is certainly what Greenawalt pays, but as I have already said, he alternates between thinking that he is paying attention to a political/sociological configuration and thinking that he is paying attention to a configuration (and a set of distinctions) reflective of some deep, noncontingent truth. If he is doing the first, his book is interesting largely as a rhetoric, as a handbook for those who want to operate successfully in late twentieth-century liberal democracy. If he wants, as I think he does, to be doing the second, he is making a mistake, the mistake of confusing a present and revisable status quo for a permanent and general settlement of old and persistent questions. What makes his book compelling is the degree to which he is aware, at least on occasions, of how little theoretical interest his efforts might finally have.

Fairly late on he acknowledges that with respect to his analyses and recommendations, the "priority and weight of considerations turn out to look quite different in regard to people who occupy different positions" and thus "the relevant choices turn out to be highly specific" (133). What they are specific to is, among other things, the comprehensive view within which the theorist offers his analyses and within which the hearer, often positioned differently, receives them. "The judgments I offer," he says, "reflect my own assessment of how the considerations bear in various concrete contexts" and therefore "anything in the way of conclusive demonstration is foreclosed." In other words, what I'm telling you is what I see from my own particular perch constructed as it is by the beliefs and convictions that have long since made me what I am; and if you happen to be sitting on another perch, what I am saying may seem to you to be unpersuasive and flatly in error.

One would think that statements as strong as these would insulate Greenawalt from the lure of theory, but in fact theory's project (the desire to occupy a position to the side of everyone's views, including one's own) immediately returns in a guise of a sentence that seems to declare it unsuccessful: "I do not think the priority and weight of the considerations I have suggested can be assessed on some political basis completely free of controversial comprehensive views" (133). Although this appears to be a strong statement, it contains its own qualification and reservation in the phrase "completely free," for that leaves room for *some* freedom in the assessment, and some freedom—some space of thought independent of anyone's particular views—is sufficient for a theorist to believe in his project, even at the moment when he admits to its relative failure. The fact that the failure is relative—Greenawalt attributes it in part to an audience insufficiently capable of detaching itself from its own self-interest—means that in principle the search for principle can continue.

Indeed, that search will survive the admission that the theorist himself is not up to the job. If those who read or hear a theorist cannot entirely escape their predispositions and presuppositions, then "it follows that the theorist's own estimation of priority and weight (in this case mine) will be affected to a degree by his comprehensive views" (133). Here the work done by "completely free" is done by "to a degree." It looks like an admission—I couldn't quite keep my comprehensive views out of it—but it is in fact a claim, the claim that to a greater degree he has managed to do so; and it is that greater degree, asserted in the form of what appears to be a concession, that allows him to retain his confidence in the normative yield of his analysis: "It seems to me that the assessments I make could be widely shared by people whose comprehensive views are strikingly different" (133).

Of course "widely shared" asks and begs the question "How widely?" and we should not be surprised when the answer turns out to be "Not very widely at all." On the book's last page Greenawalt for the last time revisits the perennial question (always lurking in the background) of how to deal with those whose comprehensive views are "strikingly different" to an extent that cannot be comfortably accommodated, those, for example, who "believe that our most important task in life is to preach the true faith and that this will be most effectively done if its relevance is raised in all possible settings, including political ones" (181). "What force," he asks, does my analysis have for them? Just the force one might have expected, the force of dismissal and marginalization. Such a person, Greenawalt pronounces, "should recognize that he is not playing by the 'loosely accepted' ground rules for modern political life." But the religious militant already knows that since (as the case of Vicki Frost illustrates so well) the ground rules for modern political life are what he opposes. Greenawalt acknowledges this—a "dissenter may claim that he has sufficient reasons"—but the acknowledgment doesn't weigh heavily on his conclusion: the dissenter's "deviation" is at odds with "those who believe that present understandings are a solid foundation for the politics of this liberal democratic society" (181).

In other words, the believer—redescribed first as a dissenter and now as a deviant—is told that he hasn't got the votes and that's all there is to it, which would be the right message if it did not come accompanied with the claim of resting on a "solid foundation." The foundation is no more solid (no less vulnerable to challenge) than the status quo of the "present understandings" (181) in whose name Greenawalt writes and to whose politically achieved authority he is committed. He says as much: "These principles are not too far from present practice, as I understand it, and that indeed has much to do with why I am comfortable offering them as recommendations for action here and now" (134). What Greenawalt tells us here is that he pretty much likes things the way they are and that what he has done is provided "present practice" with a theoretical back-up by describing it as if it were answerable to the demand for "independent historical evidence" (41) and reasons with "independent persuasiveness" (94), entities he never manages to produce because, as he sometimes knows, they don't exist.

My critique of Greenawalt is, finally, just like my critique of everyone else. He offers a theoretical vocabulary, one that promises to settle the just bounds, but, as always, it turns out to have a political content, one that rationalizes "present practice" rather than providing it with a principled justification. The entire vocabulary of "fairness," "showing respect," "rigorous self-reflection" is in the end a charade behind which one finds business-as-usual in the form of the easy dismissal and marginalization of strong religious conviction.

Where, however, does this critique get us? Is the case for the inclusion in public discourse of religious reasons made because the case against it has been shown to be flawed, and indeed to rest on the very impulses—exclusion, close-mindedness, peremptory rejection of alternative points of view—it claims to oppose? The answer is no. A demonstration that the arguments of your adversary are informed by the same unfairness he or she imputes to you will be dispositive only if what you are after is the right to label yourself the fairest. (Mirror, mirror on the wall, who's the fairest of them all?) But fairness—the impartial treatment of all points of view no matter what their substantive content—is the liberal's virtue; it is liberals who wish to push conflict off the public stage in favor of a polite and endless conversation in which everyone has his or her say in the confidence that not very much, and certainly not anything really disturbing, will come of it. Strong believers, however, have another goal. They aren't concerned that the conversation continue and display the widest possible participation; they want the conversation to take a certain turn and stay there. They don't want to be fair, they want to be victorious, and they won't have a chance of victory if they spend their time fighting over title to their opponents' vocabulary.

To put the matter baldly, theory is the liberal's game (even if he or she, by my account, plays it badly); and even if antiliberals occasionally win it by showing that liberalism's theoretical claims of impartiality, openness, mutual respect cannot be cashed in, they will have lost by falling in with the assumption that those are the claims that count. Liberals don't have to win the theory game in order to win; all they have to do is get antiliberals to play it.

Consider, for example, the case of Frederick Mark Gedicks. Gedicks is a conservative communitarian who sets out to demonstrate the incoherence of liberal thought on the church–state question; but simply by considering the question a theoretical one, he concedes more than he realizes to the position he opposes.[4] In the story Gedicks tells (along with Michael McConnell, Douglas Laycock, Stephen Carter, George Marsden, and others; see Chapter 12), a communitarian view in which religion is seen as the "principal . . . source of certain views and practices that lie at the base of civilized society" has been replaced in our half century by a secular individualist view in which religion is seen as "an irrational and regressive antisocial force that must be strictly confined to private life in order to avoid social division, violence, and anarchy" (12). Where the watchword of the first (and historically prior) view is "tolerance" and what is tolerated are the "atheists, agnostics and dissenters" not in step with the preferred "conservative cultural values," the watchword of the second (and currently reigning) view is "neutrality," where neutrality means that no religious or cultural values are preferred and all are regarded as mere private choices that cannot be allowed to influence public life (11–12).

What this amounts to, Gedicks complains, is not neutrality at all but the denial to religion of a serious hearing in the culture. Of course, if a religion already conceives of itself "as a 'naturally' private activity" (43), already, that is, respects the "belief–action doctrine" (99), its voice will be hearkened to, but only because what it says is indistinguishable from what is permitted by secular individualism: "Secular individualist discourse justifies government support of religion only to the extent that religion manifests itself as the effect of private choice within broader, secular categories of public life" (75). Once religion crosses the line by attempting to push its practices into public zones (by urging prayer in the classroom or aid to parochial schools), it must be put back in its place, unless those same practices can be recharacterized as "not really religious" (63): "Only if the religious can be made secular is a defense available within secular individualism" (80).

The end result is a religion that is trivialized and domesticated and public officials who are forced to say the opposite of what they mean. Those who would disenfranchise religion honor it as a "higher discourse" on the way to kicking it upstairs, while those who are invested in religion labor to empty it of its "spiritual content" and "replace it with secular meaning" (77). These unseemly acrobatics follow from a religion–clause jurisprudence heavily weighted in the direction of establishment rather than free-exercise concerns, as witness "the Court's extreme sensitivity to coercive possibilities in establishment clause controversies, and its virtual ignorance of coercive effects in free exercise contexts" (117–118).

As a description of the present state of things, this seems to me to be both incisive and accurate. Secular individualism and its central value of neutrality do in fact have the rhetorical power Gedicks attributes to them and tend in crucial moments to trump his preferred rhetoric of a "religiously informed communitarianism" (4). And the consequence, too, is as he notes it: dislodged from its privileged position as the presumed source of civilization's values, religion becomes a discourse that is special and, because special, disfavored to the extent that it is seen as a threat to the discourse (of reason and science) that has replaced it. Where Gedicks goes wrong, however, is to think that by demonstrating that liberal theory does not live up to its own demands he has done something decisive.

He thinks, for example, that it is a telling point against liberal neutrality that it is really not neutral, or against evolutionary theory that its status as fact depends not on empirical observation but on the socially constructed conventions of "scientific discourse" (37). But since he himself declares that assertions of neutrality will always be a function of "the discourse within which one is operating" (36), he cannot criticize a policy because it is not "really" neutral. By his own argument, "real neutrality"—neutrality conceived of and identified apart from any discourse whatsoever—is not a conceptual possibility. And by the same reasoning, he cannot criticize evolution because its claim to be a "'factual' account of the origin of human . . . life" holds only so long as one accepts a disputable account of "what does, and does not, count as a valid argument" (37). What else could secure such a claim? Certainly not an *in*disputable account, for, as Gedicks himself argues, there is no such thing.

In short, Gedicks accomplishes little by demonstrating that liberal theory fails by its own criteria. Indeed, the effect of his demonstration is to leave those criteria even more strongly in place as the benchmarks by which any policy will be judged. The "tu-quoque" argument—"you guys do it, too" or "so's your old man"—is the wrong one to make, for the most it can do is score points in a game still ruled by the presuppositions and values one hopes to dislodge. It does no good, for example, to proclaim, as Gedicks does, that the coercion attributed to a state-sponsored graduation prayer in *Lee v. Weisman* "pales besides that assumed and sanctioned by the Court in *Lyng*" (118);[5] for the accusation makes sense only if the moral difference between two actions is measured by their degrees of coercion. But that is a liberal measure, and one Gedicks himself declares empty when he asserts as his central thesis (he borrows it from Milner Ball) that the vocabularies we deploy are "world creating" and "world excluding" (25).

What this means is what I have said so many times: every discourse, even one filled with words like "fair" and "impartial," is an engine of exclusion and therefore a means of coercion. It follows that it is beside the point (unless it is a narrowly theoretical one) to prove that a particular discourse is coercive. Of course it is. The real question is: "Is this the coercion we want, or is it the coercion favored by our opponents?" Gedicks tries to move from the thesis that all discourses are world-excluding to a criticism of liberal discourse for being exclusionary; but that is precisely the kind of judgment the thesis leaves one unable to make. He should critique liberalism not because it excludes something but because it excludes something he believes to be good and true. And he should try to combat that exclusion not by eliminating exclusion all together—that, after all is liberalism's goal and an impossible one—but by replacing his opponents' exclusions with his own. He is absolutely right when he says that "sponsored manifestations of religious belief, like graduation prayer, cannot be defended within secular individualist discourse" (118), but he is wrong to think that replacing secular individualist discourse with a better one will be the work of "those who practice theory" (125). No, it will be the work of those who practice politics. The Court will not repudiate secular individualism because a theoretical argument has poked holes in it; in fact, the Court won't "repudiate" secular individualism at all. Rather, another discourse will slip into its (favored) place and generate outcomes in another direction.

But how does this happen? What can one do to bring it about? Well, there is no programmatic answer to that question, no sequence of steps or knock-down arguments that will, in a theoretical instant, produce conviction in everyone. All you can do is be on the alert for moments when there is a possibility of entering the conversation in a way that changes its terms. As an example you could do worse than look at Michael McConnell's brief for the petitioners in *Rosenberger v. Rector* (1995).[6] The measure of what McConnell was trying to do is Justice Souter's incredulity at the outcome. (The majority declared unconstitutional the University of Virginia's refusal to fund a Christian student publication, *Wide Awake,* when it was already funding other student publications commenting on public affairs.) "The Court today," Souter begins, "for the first time, approves direct funding of religious activities, by an arm of the State" (863); and this even though "using public funds for the direct subsidization of preaching the word is categorically forbidden under the Establishment Clause" (868).[7] The note is sounded repeatedly: "The Court . . . has never before upheld direct state funding of the sort of proselytizing published in *Wide Awake* and . . . has categorically condemned state programs directly aiding religious activity" (874–875). "We never held that evenhandedness might be sufficient to render direct aid to religion constitutional" (880). "The Court has never held that government resources obtained without taxation could be used for direct religious support" (890). "Allowing non-tax funds to be spent on religion would, in fact, fly in the face of clear principle." "This is a flat violation of the Establishment Clause" (892). In short, according to Souter, this case should be an easy one given the establishment clause and the Court's previous decisions, and yet it has unaccountably gone the other way. What happened?

A full answer would involve rehearsing the history of religion-clause jurisprudence and the roles played in that history by the members of the Court. But at least a part of the story might include McConnell's success in framing the issue in free-exercise terms rather than establishment terms. He did this by borrowing from the Court's free-expression jurisprudence a concept (and a rhetoric) that keeps establishment concerns at bay. The concept is "viewpoint discrimination," which, he says, "is presumptively unconstitutional" (14). The state cannot discriminate against speech because of its content or act in ways that prefer one or another of the viewpoints competing in the marketplace of ideas. When the University of Virginia denied funds to a Christian publication after having established a limited forum, it did both by excluding a religious perspective in general and a Christian perspective in particular. Christianity, McConnell declares, "competes in the marketplace of ideas with scores of secular philosophies, ideologies, and worldviews, as well as with other religions," and it follows that to "exclude a magazine which explains and advocates this worldview . . . is plainly discrimination on the basis of viewpoint" (19).

To this wide-reaching philosophical argument, the respondents' brief, prepared by John C. Jeffries, replies by invoking the familiar distinction between conveying information and proselytizing.[8] What the university is concerned to hold at arm's length is not the imparting of knowledge about religion but the promotion of religion as a life choice. As Souter puts it in his dissent, the point is not "the discourse of the scholar's study or the seminar room, but of the evangelist's mission station and the pulpit. It is nothing other than the preaching of the word" (868). To this McConnell's brief counter-replies that because the line between discourse and preaching is disputable, drawing it would involve the state in the very viewpoint discrimination it is obliged to forswear. Indeed, the line may not even exist except as the illegitimate byproduct of a discrimination the state should not be making; after all, any distinction between "'culture' and 'religion' is highly subjective" and "who is to say that *Wide Awake* does not contribute to the cultural diversity of the University of Virginia campus?" (20).

Jeffries protests that if this argument is taken seriously, no distinction will survive it: "If all religious activities can be said to embrace a common view or perspective, then so can all lobbying (the view that social change should be effected through legislation) or electioneering activities (the view that participation in the electoral process is important and valuable)" (23). In fact, Jeffries concludes, "any exclusion from funding can be characterized as viewpoint discrimination simply by attributing to all speech within the excluded category a least-common-denominator view or perspective," but the result would be to "render the concept of viewpoint discrimination circular or meaningless" (23).

This seems (logically) right. If viewpoint discrimination is to be an incisive category, there must be some forms of regulation that do not fall within it. As cogent as it is, however, the objection is unlikely to make McConnell pause because all it does is name his strategy. He *wants* the category of viewpoint discrimination to lose its edge and become so capacious that nothing falls outside it. If he succeeds in making everything viewpoint discrimination, his clients will be successful in their course of action; and to that end he is willing to employ a form of analysis (practiced by poststructuralists and postmodernists) he may personally deplore, the corrosive interrogation of anything and everything. It is the strategy of such interrogations to determine what has been left out—excluded, suppressed—by an apparently rational scheme. The demand is that nothing be left out; but since not leaving something out would render assertion itself impossible (you have to say *something*, which means that you can't say everything), any distinction you formulate will be guilty of being dismissive of someone's perspective and interests, and that includes the distinctions on which the law routinely depends.

Behind Jeffries's almost sputtering objections is the realization that, if McConnell's argument is allowed full sway, law itself becomes impossible because all of its tools will have become discredited. Indeed, as Jeffries observes, at the "level of vacuous generality" (23) to which McConnell would take us, the establishment clause itself—that piece of the Constitution whose proper application everyone is supposedly seeking—is guilty of viewpoint discrimination because it singles out religion and delimits its scope: "If, as petitioners (wrongly) contend, denying funding to religious activities is viewpoint discrimination, it is a viewpoint discrimination that the Constitution itself embraces—and in some circumstances commands" (28).

This point would be decisive if McConnell's argument were being judged on the basis of its theoretical coherence. Theory, however, is not a standard he must satisfy but a resource he quarries in the service of his objective. That objective is to advance the same communitarian cause Gedicks champions. What is noteworthy is that he does it by appropriating concepts from the liberal theory Gedicks opposes. In that theory, neutrality (as Gedicks notes repeatedly) is a key notion often used to deny the claims of free exercise. McConnell seizes the concept and turns it back against its usual proprietors. Taking his cue from Douglas Laycock, he observes that if the government is determined to "treat religious speech . . . exactly like secular speech" (25) when it refuses to exempt religious practitioners from general laws, then the government is prevented, by the same neutrality it invokes, from disadvantaging practitioners when they wish to do what others are already permitted to do. If neutrality rules out special exemptions, it should rule out special exclusions. The argument works so long as it is allowed to remain a theoretical one, so long as the question is whether the university's policy is neutral toward religion in the strict sense of not treating it "as a separate and distinct subject matter" (18). Of course, the entire purpose of the establishment clause is to single out religion as a subject matter of heightened concern, and it is a measure of McConnell's accomplishment that he can transform the clause's purpose into a reason for not applying it.

Gedicks thinks that the sorry state (in his view) of religion–clause jurisprudence is to be explained by the ascendency of a bad theory made up of equal parts of secular individualism and neutrality, and he hopes that the emergence of a good theory will change things for the better. What McConnell shows by turning the components of Gedicks's "bad" theory to proreligion purposes is that theory, even when it participates in change, is not its engine. Like anything else, but no *more* than anything else, theory is a possible resource for change in the hands of someone agile enough to appropriate its vocabulary for a particular agenda. Theory is available as a resource because its terms are not self-defining but receive their meaning only when the background conditions for their application are specified. Moreover, that specification, in response to questions like "Neutral with respect to what?" or "Equal with respect to what?" is not theoretical but stipulative. It follows, then, that the person who can stipulate the background conditions in a way that makes the theoretical terms dance to his tune will prevail.

That is what McConnell does and that is why his success is not theoretical but rhetorical. A theoretical success (if there ever were any outside of philosophy departments) would occur when the cogency of an argument, presented abstractly and without having been preshaped by unexamined and challengeable acts of stipulation, leads directly to a change in policy. A rhetorical success occurs when someone who knows where he wants to go gets there by quarrying theories for material that can be folded into the story of whose plausibility he wishes to persuade us. A rhetorical success, in short, is a political success.

Having praised McConnell for being rhetorical, I must now surround the word with explanations and qualifications lest I be mistaken for a cynic or a celebrator of basely manipulative arts. Rhetoric is one of those terms that always comes accompanied by its supposed opposite. Rhetoric's opposite is the Real, or the Substantial, or the Essential, and, accordingly, rhetoric usually stands for the inauthentic, the ephemeral, and the superfluous. All this is encapsulated in the adjective "mere" which one almost always hears preceding "rhetoric," even when it has not been spoken. To understand rhetoric this way (and who doesn't?) is to fall right in with the theory project and the project of liberalism as I have described them. When liberal theorists tell us that difference between religious views or skin color or ethnic affiliation are less central to our true identities than the capacities we share as rational beings, everything but those capacities is being consigned to the wastebasket of the contingent, to the realm of the rhetorical. Someone who rejects the theory project and believes that the search for a foundation that would underwrite and validate our beliefs is a mug's game cannot use rhetoric that way. He or she has to say what I now say: everything is rhetorical.

But to say it is immediately to be on the defensive, as I now am. I don't mean that everything is ephemeral. I mean that everything is real, and that what is *un*real are the abstractions (fairness, impartiality, and all the rest) in relation to which the contingent, the rhetorical, and the political get their bad names. If those abstractions were either available to us or directing our actions from a position behind some veil, it would make sense to subordinate to their imperatives the merely local—that is, merely rhetorical, merely political—imperatives urged on us by our particular beliefs. But if those abstractions are themselves the space of contestation—as Alexander puts it, "the empty vessels for substantive norms" (776)—and will be filled by our beliefs, they cannot be preferred to what is filling them, to the sense we have, at any moment, of what is right and of our obligation to put what is right into practice.

That is what is real, and the grand items of theory's vocabulary are what is unreal, are what is rhetorical in the old bad sense.

It is difficult to keep this reversal in mind, and use rhetorical and political as honorifics rather than as accusations; but this is what one who rejects the project of liberal theory must do, lest he or she slip back into a mode of thought that devalues conviction and leeches the meaning out of political life. The temptation to slip back is powerful and, as is often the case, is most powerful when it presents itself as its very opposite, as a determination to give the political and rhetorical their due.

Steven Smith's *Foreordained Failure: The Quest for a Constitutional Principle of Religious Freedom* is a lesson in point.[9] Smith's argument has two parts. In the first he considers the oft pondered question of which theory of religious freedom the framers had in mind and dismisses it: "If we ask . . . what principle or theory of religious liberty the framers and ratifiers of the religion clauses adopted, the most accurate answer is 'None'" (21). There are, Smith tells us, two positions on the relationship between church and state held by various parties in the late eighteenth century. "The traditional position regarded governmental support for religion as essential to the social order, while the voluntarist position opposed such support" (21), on the reasoning that it could authorize state interference and thus "might well be harmful to the cause of religion" (20). These positions, Smith notes, survive in today's debates, and theorists often feel obliged to come down strongly for one or the other and then cite history as a support for their choice.

History, however, supports no choice, since what the framers themselves chose to do was ignore the substantive issue and make it a jurisdictional one: "They consciously chose not to answer the religion question, and they were able for the most part to avoid it . . . by assigning the religious question to the states" (21). Their goal, it seems, was more modest than the goal of the theorists who now argue about their intentions. They avoided big questions like, "What is the real meaning of religious freedom?" (15), and this explains why, when religious questions presented themselves, they acted "in an ad hoc manner," just as we might expect of persons who did not regard themselves "as being legally constrained by any substantive principle" (30).

Once history has been removed as a ground for choosing between theories of religious freedom, the very idea of a theory of religious freedom is dismissed as a chimera. Theory, Smith declares, is an impossible project if its aim "is to mediate among a variety of competing religious and secular positions and interests, or to explain how government ought to deal with these competing positions and interests" (63). The reason is simple and, by now, familiar: any theory set to this task cannot get started on it without already having defined (stipulatively, not theoretically) its key terms. Moreover, the definitions selected will have been borrowed from one or another of the competing interests. (Where else could they come from? If they were entirely unrelated to the array of competing interests, by what route would any relation be established?) Which means that, rather than mediating conflicts, the theory will be entering them on a particular side: "To perform that [mediating] function, however, the theory will tacitly but inevitably privilege, or prefer in advance, one of those positions while rejecting or discounting others. But a theory that privileges one of the competing positions and rejects others a priori is not truly a theory of religious freedom at all—or at least, it is not the sort of theory that modern proponents of religious freedom have sought to develop" (63).

Since one cannot even begin to think theoretically without presupposing some "background beliefs concerning matters of religion and theology, the proper role of government, and 'human nature'" (63), it is not surprising that "different background beliefs [will] dictate different responses to . . . claims of religious freedom" (70). Indeed, even the first step to be taken, the step of identifying those activities that are nonreligious ("things indifferent" in the older vocabulary) is already infected by the bias and privileging one hopes to avoid, for any such classification "presupposes a perspective that in turn reflects the privileging of a position and the implicit rejection of other positions that would prescribe a different classification" (87). However neutral one tries to be, one's efforts will always "reflect, implicitly but inevitably, a tacit assumption that some persons, groups, or belief systems 'count,' or are entitled to full consideration and equal treatment by the state, and that other persons, groups, or belief systems do not 'count' in this sense" (94).

With statements like this, Smith would seem to have dealt a death blow to the hope of finding a principled solution to the tension between church and state. There seems to be nothing else to say. But Smith is determined to say *something,* and when he does, he reinflates the project whose futility and incoherence he has just demonstrated. What he says is that the inevitable failure of theory (otherwise known as the search for principle) points us in a particular direction and urges us to a course of action. That course of action is "prudential"—the weighing of reasons in an ad hoc manner on the way to reaching a decision that cannot be normatively justified. A prudential decision is the kind of decision you make when you decide to go to the movies; and you can hardly be said to have a theory, even a subconscious one, of "movie selection": "There is no basis to assume that your reasons add up to or reflect any coherent pattern or method for choosing movies" (58).

So far so good. The trouble begins when "prudentialism"—the "ism" signals the transition from description (that's how decisions get made) to prescription (that's how decisions should be made)—is put forward as an alternative to theory, as something you could choose. To be sure, Smith denies any such intention and insists that his "purpose is not exactly to *advocate* a prudential approach to religious freedom or to argue that we ought to choose a prudential over a more theoretical approach" (60). But within a few sentences the equivocation in "not exactly" flowers into a choice and, ultimately, into a theory: "It seems that our choice, to the extent we have one, is between adopting a constitutional principle based on *bad theory* or, instead, pursuing a more prudential approach" (60). But if, as Smith has himself argued, there is no such thing as a "good" theory—because any theory will either be an empty abstraction incapable of application or a formulation already inflected in a particular direction—then there is no such thing as a "bad" theory, a category whose intelligibility would depend on the possible existence of its opposite. A bad theory would be a theory that didn't do theory's job, but it is Smith's contention that theory has no job of its own and is always an extension of whatever job is being done (or attempted) by those who have appropriated its vocabulary.

It is because he has slipped back into thinking of theory as an option (either good or bad) that Smith begins to think of prudence as an "approach," whereas in fact, and by his own reasoning, prudential action is just what we are always and already engaged in. If no algorithm or abstract formulation ever guides your behavior, that behavior is necessarily prudential, even if theory is invoked as its justification. Being prudential is not a good or bad thing to do; it is the only thing to do, and the only question is in what direction to do it, and that question (as Smith should certainly know) is itself political.

It follows, then, that since the "political" rather than the theoretical is the baseline level of operation, it cannot be a level one recommends, as Smith seems to in the following passage: "In a pluralistic community . . . civil peace and inclusiveness can be achieved only imperfectly and only through compromise, cultivated tolerance, mutual forbearances and strategic silences. In this context, the judicial imposition of *any* set of consistent and explicit principles is likely to undermine the possibilities for compromise and forbearance, and hence to aggravate the dangers of civil strife and alienation. Civil peace, in short, must be the product of prudence, not of principle imposed from above" (117). In these sentences compromise, tolerance, and mutual forbearance are reified and become substantive goods rather than the names of strategies whose shape is always changing. Tolerance becomes a goal and compromise an obligation, whereas in political life as it is actually lived, tolerance is something you exercise selectively (usually when your deepest interests are not at stake) and compromise is something you usually agree to when outright victory seems unlikely. Making contingent strategies into moral imperatives is what happens when you turn prudence into a principle of a kind to which it is supposedly the alternative.

It happens again when Smith warns of the danger that might follow upon "the imposition of any set of consistent and explicit principles" (117). How can you impose something that could not possibly exist and how could the imposition of a nonexistent thing produce dangers? Remember (it is Smith's own lesson, after all), so-called principles can only be applied in particular disputes when their key terms have already been defined from the perspective of one of the contending parties. What will have been imposed are not principles (as if they had an independent existence) but a particular shaping of their content; and in response, the party put at a disadvantage might be advised to fight fire with fire and do some shaping or reshaping of its own.

The point is neither to affirm nor forswear principle (by Smith's own arguments an empty gesture) but to refashion it so that it supports the direction you want to take. Principles don't by themselves either aggravate or produce anything; principles never appear "by themselves" but are deployed and configured by partisan agents in particular situations. Principles, in short, are part of the arsenal or equipment of prudence, not an alternative to it. In fact there is no alternative to prudence, which is not the name of an "approach" one could "choose."

Smith ends his book by declaring that "discussions of religious freedom will likely be more fruitful when scholars . . . relinquish their . . . demand that the meaning of religious freedom be cabined within the narrow confines of a constitutional 'principle'" (127); but the spirit of the quotation marks around this last sentence's last word is violated by the letter of what comes before. What the quotation marks say is what I have been saying: strictly speaking and in terms of the usual claims, there are no principles, just more or less persuasive uses of highly charged vocabularies by politically situated agents. But if this is so, what is the content of "fruitful," a word that seems to indicate a state welcome to all parties, no matter what their politics? (The question one would always want to ask is "Fruitful for whom?") Were such a state achievable (this side of Paradise), the problems Smith considers would vanish into the communitarian air. If everyone agreed as to what is a fruitful set of institutional arrangements and what is not, we could just get down to the business of putting that set in place, confident that its establishment would make everyone happy.

The absence—not temporary, but founding—of any such agreement is what makes the project of liberalism in general and of settling the just bounds between church and state in particular so elusive an accomplishment. It is the absence that makes politics—conflict, strategy, winning, and losing—unavoidable. Even though Smith recognizes the unavoidability of politics (it is his strongest thesis), in the end he falls to the theorist's most rarified temptation, the temptation of thinking that recognizing the unavoidability of politics is a way of avoiding it.

That temptation is what I have named elsewhere the lure of critical self-consciousness, the lure of thinking that if you have become aware of an inescapable condition—if your consciousness has grasped it—you have, in some small measure, escaped it.[10] In the context of the present discussion, this would amount to saying that because I know that politics cannot be quarantined, I can get a handle on, and be especially alert to, its inevitable eruptions. Typically, those who make this argument do so just after having rejected (as snares and delusions) the impartiality and neutrality favored by liberal rationalists. What they fail to see is that they have conferred those same impossible attributes on their own (superior) consciousnesses, which then emerge as the new location of the apolitical.

Bonnie Honig is a prime example. She divides the world into two kinds of theorists, "virtue theorists," each of whom "believes, mistakenly, that his own theory soothes or resolves the dissonances other theories cause," and "*virtú* theorists," who argue that "every politics has its remainders, that resistances are engendered by every settlement, even those that are relatively enabling or empowering" (3).[11] The fact that those in this second camp (in which she places herself) are called "theorists" too is a tipoff to what happens in a few pages when *virtú* theory turns out to have a *program:* "to treat rights and law as a part of political contest rather than as the instruments of its closure" (15). Such a program, however, gives the *virtú* theorist more power than her own insight authorizes. What matters is not the way you think about the relationship between rights and laws and political contest but what the relationship, in fact, *is;* and if, as Honig herself asserts, the relationship is one of inescapable entanglement, then that is the way it will continue to be, no matter how you decide to "treat" it.

Indeed, the very idea that you could "treat" it one way or another makes sense only if you have once again imagined a space outside of, or to the side of, the politics whose ubiquity you have just affirmed. What Honig calls "the remainders"—the resistances and unforseen consequences produced by an effort of control, no matter how sophisticated—cannot properly be the objects of a new strategy, if only because they are not objects but ever present possibilities whose shape is contingent and unpredictable. If the "spaces of politics, power, and resistance" are always, as she says, opening up, and opening up where you least expect them, you can hardly resolve that "they should be preserved, even aggravated, for the sake of the remainders of politics" (146). They can no more be preserved than they can be closed, and to think that you could preserve them (and therefore exercise that much control over them) is only the other side of thinking that you can close them.

The "remainders of politics" will frustrate containment all by themselves—that is what being a remainder means—and when you forget that, you have turned into a "virtue theorist," as Honig does when she comes out for "those sets of arrangements that resist the temptation to ontologize the conditions of their existence" (159). Arrangements that tend to "ontologize the conditions of their existence" regard their own forms of order as normative and necessary, and therefore regard resistances or remainders as something to be ignored, suppressed, or marginalized. In the arrangements Honig prefers, authority would be less aggressively assertive, more diffused, and challenges to authority would be seen as a part of the political practice rather than as a threat to it. It is these more shifting conditions, she says, that will "diminish the violence and the resentment that invariably haunt political arrangements" (159).

No, the violence and resentment would simply migrate to the hearts and minds of those for whom a fluid and ever-shifting political landscape means anarchy and the loss of principle. In short, what Honig urges (this is why she is a theorist) is ontologization in the other direction, in the direction of contingency and flux rather than of predictability and order. And were her advice to be implemented, there would still be remainders—some of their names would be Rawls and Nagel—and they would be no more accommodated in this brave new world than fundamentalists and astrologers are accommodated in theirs. Honig makes a familiar mistake. She thinks that some forms of organization are more open to revision than others. What she does not see is that openness to revision as a principle is itself a form of closure, not at all open to ways of thinking or acting that would bring revision to an end. "Openness to revision" is an internal, not an absolute, measure; it is relative to whatever understood exclusions—and there will always be some—give the politically organized space its shape.

In the same year that saw the appearance of Honig's book, Chantal Mouffe made essentially the same argument and fell into the same error.[12] Like Honig, Mouffe critiques standard liberal theory for "evacuating the dimension of the political and conceiving the well-ordered society as one exempt from politics" (139). Noting the reliance of theorists like Rawls on supposedly "self-evident" norms of neutrality and fairness, she observes that the easy invocation of these values, "far from being a benign statement of fact . . . is the result of a *decision* which already excludes from the dialogue those who believe that different values should be the organizing ones of the political order" (143). The arbitrariness of this exclusion is denied by these same theorists, who hide it from themselves by calling "those who disagree with them . . . either unreasonable or irrational" (143). Mouffe urges that we substitute for this "current brand of liberalism" a view of democracy "that would not present it as the rational, universal solution to the problem of political order" nor "attempt to deny its ultimately ungrounded status by making it appear as the outcome of a rational choice" (145). "It is very important," she declares, "to recognize . . . forms of exclusion for what they are and the violence that they signify, instead of concealing them under the veil of rationality" (145).

But you could recognize forms of exclusion and violence for what they are only if "what they are" could be uncontroversially identified. No one thinks of himself as unfairly excluding anyone, and acts of violence always come accompanied by the adjective "justified," indicating the agent's conviction that what he does he does in the name of a deity or a supreme value or a higher order impartiality. The idea of recognizing something for what it is rather than for what it appears to be presupposes the apolitical space whose availability Mouffe denies. If what was and was not violent and/or excluding could be identified apart from anyone's interests, politics would be immediately tamed and reduced (as liberalism always wants to reduce it) to low-level debates about the particular realization of agreed-upon ends.

Taming politics is finally what Mouffe has in mind, despite her pronouncements to the contrary. The process of taming unfolds in two (impossible) steps: first, the step of recognizing "domination and violence" for what they really are—a recognition you perform from a distance; whatever they are, they are not you—and, second, the step of "the establishment of a set of institutions through which they can be limited and tested" (146). That step is taken the moment you imagine it, for if you assume that domination and violence can be isolated long enough to become the objects of institutional manipulation, they have already been limited, if only in your mind. When Mouffe ends her book by naming as our task the creation of "the conditions under which . . . aggressive forces can be defused and . . . a pluralist democratic order made possible" (153), she has joined the ranks of those who, in her own accusing words, seek to "negate the political" and "make it disappear" (140).

If Rawls and Nagel conceive "the well-ordered society as one exempt from politics" (139), Mouffe conceives the well-ordered society as one that keeps politics in check. The difference between thinking that politics can be eliminated and thinking it can be managed is certainly real, but it is a family difference, and those on either side of it are united in their determination to avoid the lesson Mouffe wants to be teaching: that politics is an inescapable condition and one that is present in every effort to contain its effects, whether that effort is attached to the high hopes of the liberal rationalists or to the more modest hopes of someone who has come to "accept the consequences of the irreducible plurality of values" (152).

Mouffe thinks that by accepting those consequences she has achieved a reflective distance from them that is unavailable to her less self-aware fellow theorists. She thinks that by recognizing "the dimension of conflict and antagonism within the political" she has "come to terms" with it (152). She thinks that by acknowledging contingency, she has fashioned (or is on the way to fashioning) a "political philosophy that makes room for contingency" (145). But contingency is precisely what you can't make room for; contingency is what befalls the best laid plans of mice and men—and that includes plans to take it into account or guard against its eruption. And by the same reasoning "the dimension of conflict . . . within the political" is not something you can come to terms with. You can only come to terms with something that stays put and remains at a distance from you. But if the political is, as Mouffe acknowledges, the realm in which we live and move and have our beings, conflict—the clash of opposing points of view—is not simply a dimension of it but the whole of it and structures everything we do, including any (vain) attempt we might make to come to terms with it.

"Accepting" the plurality of values is another such attempt. It is, to be sure, a possible mental action but not one that could alter your relationship to the condition it affirms. If the plurality of values is really "irreducible," accepting it will not insulate you from its effects and denying it will not magnify them. To think otherwise—to think, as Mouffe seems to, that by accepting plurality you can outflank or surround it or be in a better position than those who deny it—is to reduce the "irreducible" even as you are supposedly affirming it. All of Mouffe's efforts to escape her own insight—whether they go by the name of "accepting" or "coming to terms with" or "making room for"—are efforts to establish an outside position in relation to an inside that is, as she herself says, everywhere.

Mouffe, Smith, and Honig all make the same mistake. They begin by declaring that politics cannot be contained, and they end by claiming to have contained it. (The "return to the political" doesn't get very far before it is put back into its box.) William Corlett makes an even more rarified mistake. Not only does he think that politics cannot be contained; he thinks that its disruptions should be celebrated and maximized.[13] If rationalists like Nagel, Gutmann, Thompson, and Greenawalt want to eliminate disorder or at least confine it to the margins, and realists like Mouffe, Smith and Honig (for different reasons) want to have a better purchase on disorder so that it can be managed, Corlett wants to promote disorder even to the point of courting madness. Where others ask, "How can we fashion a community that will accommodate and contain the energies of human difference?" Corlett asks, "How can we derail the operations of community so that the energies of human difference can be released?" The answer, he says, is to "use in the least orderly way possible the forms which political theories provide in the name of order" and to "reject the reassurance political theory offers" in favor of a militant provisionality—he calls it a "politics of extravagance"—that refuses "to permit any form to become entrenched" (12).

Corlett would not be misunderstood. He is not recommending that we *choose* extravagance or chaos over order. Rather, he is insisting, with Derrida, that extravagance or chaos "is a constitutive element of order" (15) and that therefore "irrationality" can never be "exiled," that is, thought of as being somewhere *else*. "Wherever one finds a structure one finds an excess" (88), something excluded, but whose exclusion constitutes (by defining) the inside supposedly free of it. "Reason is already unreasonable" (147). One occupies a "reasonable" moment only by forgetting the borders (and monsters) that mark it out and make it what it is and is not. "All reason and order requires an 'other'" and therefore the "possibility of purity . . . is out of the question" (156).

What this amounts to is the formulation in a somewhat more dramatic vocabulary of the point I have been making throughout: if you begin by assuming the intractability of difference (because every church is orthodox to itself), any line you then draw between the reasonable and the unreasonable or the normative and the obviously eccentric will be drawn from an unreasonable (not everyone would assent to its perspicuity) and eccentric (marginal to an unavailable center) perspective. And, moreover, any attempt to compensate for eccentricity will only produce more of it; however you define and demarcate the normative, its space will always be parochial.

The difference between us is this: I make the point as a matter of (nonculpable) fact—that's the way it always is and must be; positions have to be taken, and every position borrows its intelligibility from that from which it would be distinct; Corlett makes it as a matter of blame—those who fail to see the provisionality and impurity of every "unitary form" (88) allow the "metaphysical pretense of the hour" (83) to work its inevitable exclusions. What I take as a situation that cannot be avoided and need not be remedied—exclusion is inevitable but it's nothing to apologize for since it comes along with any effort to put the beliefs you hold into practice—Corlett takes as a situation that remedies (or at least mitigates) itself if only we are sufficiently aware of it.

In short, he makes the critical-self-consciousness mistake in the direction of extravagance rather than stability and thus provides himself

with a political payoff; if we *know* that no arrangement of things is natural or coextensive with the boundaries of reason, we will be less
inclined to defend to the death (usually someone else's) the arrangements that we favor: "If all order is in principle provisional . . . it may
well become increasingly difficult to defend, let alone to justify, hegemonic dominance in political life" (89). "If the relation between political thinking and its forms is never presumed to be fixed, then one is less
inclined to fight flux with reasonable, orderly strategies. If everything is
boundless without limit, it is difficult to detect an enemy" (138–139).

For all the radical talk, what we have here is liberalism all over again.
The assertion that forms of order and stability are always provisional is
equivalent to the assertion that values are plural and nonadjudicable.
Both are offered as reasons for withdrawing from conflict: if the clash of
values is irremediable and if the forms of order (and thus the configuration of "us" against "them") are continually shifting, it is best not to
insist too strongly on the values you happen to favor or the forms of
order you prefer. If everything is up for grabs, why grab anything with
the intent of hanging on to it?

Everything, however, is not up for grabs, at least not in the tempo-
rally demarcated spaces in which we live our lives and make our choices.
And neither is everything boundless and without limits, except from a
perspective above the bounds and limits that make experience intelligible for beings who are not God. And enemies are difficult to detect only
if you reserve the label "enemy" for someone who fills the role unambiguously and forever. The absence of such a permanent and stable
enemy cannot be a reason for withdrawing from the fray unless you
demand of the fray that it take the form of a mythopoeic drama—absolute good versus absolute evil—and that is exactly the drama Corlett
has been busily deconstructing. In a world where nothing is fixed or permanent and the relationship between present urgencies and ultimate ends
is continually changing, one must take one's constructs not "less seriously" (162), as Corlett advises, but more seriously. For if we wait for constructs that are in touch with eternity, we will fail to act in moments when
action is possible for limited creatures. One may know, as Corlett does,
that "the clearing within which" one does one's work "is already infested
with chance, accident, chaos" (13), but that knowledge, if it is a reason for
anything, is a reason for doing the work with all the energy possible and
with every intention of doing it successfully—which means, when there
is a battle brewing, with every intention of winning. That, finally, is the

only lesson to take away from the insight (shared by Smith, Honig, Mouffe, and Corlett) that politics is pervasive and inside all our attempts to avoid it: play it (the lesson is superfluous; what else could you do?) and play it to win.

Winning is a dirty word in liberal theory; it is what is supposed never to happen, unless it is imagined as the impersonal outcome of some agentless mechanism like the marketplace of ideas or universal reason. That is why it is so easy and seems so natural for liberal theorists to reject the strong claims of religion, claims that can be realized only if the adherents of religion succeed in institutionalizing their views and thus marginalizing or even suppressing the views of their adversaries. In the endless (and intended to be so) debates about the relationship between church and state, one rarely hears this acknowledged, and it is a moment of unusual candor that finds David Smolin, a law professor *and* a fundamentalist Christian, declaring aloud that as a "traditional theist" what he wants is a chance to win out over the "modernist liberals" with their "'gospel' of autonomous individualism and radical egalitarianism" (1094).[14] Smolin feels that he is unlikely to get that chance because the field of battle is configured by the very modernist assumptions he would defeat, specifically by the assumptions of fallibilism (all points of view are partial and corrigible) and pluralism (the more points of view in play the better), which, by giving winning a bad name, mandate that liberalism wins.

But why, Smolin asks, "should those who view pluralism and fallibilism as vices accept them as norms of civic virtue?" (1079) and thus ratify their own exclusion from public debate? This is the right question, asked this time not of the devout but by the devout, and its answer is obvious. Those for whom pluralism and fallibilism mark the path of error should not accept this imposed disadvantage but should resist it, as Smolin claims to be doing here. And yet the terms of his resistance are such that in the end he too is complicit with the ideology that oppresses him. The trouble begins with the vocabulary of his complaint. The exclusion from public life he and his coreligionists suffer is, he says, "unfair" (1079). But fairness is a—no, *the*—liberal virtue; its invocation always signals the subordination of truth to the process of debating it. Fairness is the virtue that mitigates against winning, and by invoking it, Smolin works against the interests of his own party, as he has defined them. He joins the ranks of his enemies again when he calls for a *"full* political dialogue" (1085). One understands the logic: right now the dialogue is skewed because "one side's victory" (1087) has been written into its rules, with the result that the other side is forced to leave its best arguments at the door. The game is rigged. But calling for a nonrigged game in the name of "a truly 'open society'" (1090) is to call for exactly what modernist liberalism most cherishes, the enfranchisement of all points of view independently of their moral status. What Smolin should want is not a fair and full game but victory. (Let me say what should by now go without saying: Smolin's victory is what *he* should want, not what I want for him or for myself; once again, you will learn nothing about my own agenda by reading my analyses of the agendas of others.)

To be sure, it is victory he seeks, and he is even willing to acknowledge that if he gains it the losers will *not* be treated fairly but will "live in a society that is hostile to the continuance of their ways of life" (1097) (a great moment and unique in the literature). In the end, however, he wants something more—actually something less—than victory; he wants to win the victory fairly, and late in the essay he declares himself in search of "a concept of fairness to which persons of differing allegiances and presuppositions can agree" (1094). That is as good a statement of the liberal project as one might hope for; it is a statement Nagel, Gutmann, Thompson, Greenawalt—the entire crew—could all sign on to, and when Smolin signs on to it, he reveals himself to be just one more modernist liberal.

Smolin's talk about winning and giving the losers a choice of marginalization in the society or "migration" (1103) certainly sounds tough (get with it or get going), sounds as if someone is finally going to embrace exclusion rather than push it away or disguise it as tolerance. But like everyone else who comes to this brink, Smolin draws back from it and ends by calling upon the relevant authorities, and especially the judiciary, to take action "in the interests of all" (1104). This is where we came in, with Locke's invocation of the "judgment of all mankind" (of which "the interests of all" is simply a version) only a few paragraphs after he has declared that there is no such thing. And this is where we exit, with Smolin (illiberalism's best hope) repeating Locke's double gesture and recapitulating the entire history of liberal thought, first affirming that every church is orthodox to itself and then contriving in every way possible to forget it.

This is the place where one might expect a conclusion. But there can be no conclusion if by that is meant a recommendation of a policy or recipe for action superior to those I have critiqued. The whole point of these three chapters has been that there is no such policy or recipe and therefore no recommendation. The end of the argument is implicit in its beginning. Liberalism's attempt to come to terms with illiberal energies—especially, but not exclusively, religious ones—will always fail because it cannot succeed without enacting the illiberalism it opposes. (And once again let me add that this is a criticism not of liberalism's performance—which could not be otherwise—but of its claims.) This will be true whether the effort is made by rationalists who put their faith (a word carefully chosen) in forms of fairness, impartiality, and mutual respect or by clear-eyed realists who know that disruptive energies, like the poor, will always be with us and tell us to get used to it, or by the celebrator of extravagance who invites us to be wild and crazy guys.

Each of these makes the mistake (albeit in different ways) of thinking of conflict either as a "problem" or as an opportunity. No, conflict is the name of our condition; and, moreover, naming it does nothing to ameliorate it or make it easier to negotiate. The negotiations have to be done one at a time in the context of the urgencies and choices life continually throws in our way. If I have any recommendation it is, by my own argument, entirely superfluous. Figure out what you think is right and then look around for ways to be true to it. (Here I am, the new Polonius.) Not very helpful, I admit, but it has the (perhaps not so small) advantage of promising nothing and sending you on your moral way.

This may seem a strange thing to say at the end of three chapters that have been preaching the gospel of politics. Politics, after all, is what is usually opposed to morality, especially in the texts of liberal theorists. Politics, interest, partisan conviction, mere belief—these are the forces that must be kept at bay. What I have attempted here is a reversal of this judgment. Politics, interest, partisan conviction, and belief are the locations of morality. It is in and through them that one's sense of justice and of the "good" lives and is put into action. Immorality resides in the mantras of liberal theory—fairness, impartiality, and mutual respect—all devices for painting the world various shades of gray.

12

WHY WE CAN'T ALL JUST GET ALONG

Shades of gray are never honored in the world of John Milton, where the only question is whether you stand in the light with God or in the dark with Satan. Modern readers often have difficulties with the starkness of that choice, because the idea of an absolute authority is so alien to them. Indeed, whenever I teach *Paradise Lost,* the hardest thing to get across is that God is God. Students invariably (one is tempted to say "naturally") fall in with the view declared by William Empson in *Milton's God* when he says that "*all* the characters are on trial in any civilized narrative" (94).[1] In Milton's narrative, of course, God is a central character, and the entire story gets going, Empson observes, when Satan "doubts his credentials." Empson analogizes the situation to that "of a Professor doubting the credentials of his Vice-Chancellor," and remarks with some sarcasm that "such a man would not be pursued with infinite malignity into eternal torture, but given evidence which put the credentials beyond doubt" (95). In this account of the matter, "civilization" and "evidence" go together and dictate our chief responsibility as readers—which is, Empson says, "to use our judgment about the characters" (94). It is also the obligation of the characters in the story, and the fact that they perform it differently is what gives the plot its energy: the loyalist Abdiel, Empson observes, tells Satan and his rebel followers "that God should be obeyed because he is good, and they deny that he is good" (94), and as far as Empson is concerned, they have good reason to do so.

243

Actually the scene Empson is remembering is somewhat more complex. When Abdiel rises, "Among the faithless, faithful only he" (V, 897), what he says is not that God is good (which would imply a conclusion reached by submitting God's actions to the judgment of independent criteria). Rather he says that God is God, which implies that even to put God to such an evidentiary test would be a category mistake—how can you give a grade to the agent whose person defines and embodies value?—that would constitute the gravest of sins, whether one calls it impiety ("Cease . . . this impious rage," V, 845), self-worship, or simply pride.

What Abdiel says is: "Shalt thou give law to God, shalt thou dispute / With him the points of liberty, who made / Thee what thou art?" (V, 822–824a). Earlier Satan had justified his rebellion by invoking freedom and liberty; Abdiel now points out that these terms have no weight when the agent from whom you would be free made and sustains you. Satan in turn finds this argument preposterous and replies to it with a classic statement of rational empiricism:

> That we were form'd . . . say'st thou?
> . . . strange point and new!
> Doctrine which we would know whence learnt: who saw
> When this creation was? remember'st thou
> Thy making, while the Maker gave thee being?
> We know no time when we were not as now;
> Know none before us, self-begot, self-rais'd.
> (V, 853, 855–860)

This is the philosophy of the man from Missouri: show me, seeing is believing, and since no one, including you, has seen the moment of his creation, I don't believe in it. There is nothing in the present scene or in my experience that leads me inescapably to the conclusion you urge. Where did you ever get this absurd notion? What's your proof? ("Doctrine which we would know whence learnt?") I must have made myself.

Satan's way of thinking is contrasted directly in the poem with Adam's. Recalling the moment not of his creation but just after his creation, Adam reports, "Myself I . . . perused . . . limb by limb" and found that I could speak and name, "But who I was, or where, or from what cause / Knew not" (VIII, 267, 270–271). Like Satan, Adam knows no time before he was what he now is, but he gives a quite different answer to the question he immediately poses: "how came I thus, how here? /

Not of myself, by some great maker then / In goodness and in power preeminent" (VIII, 277b–279). The goodness and power for which Satan seeks independent evidence is here *assumed* by Adam; and once the assumption is in place, it generates a program for action and a life-project: "how may I know him, how adore, / From whom I have that thus I move and live?" (VIII, 280–281).

It might seem that in presenting these two moments in *Paradise Lost*, I am placing in opposition two ways of knowing, one by evidence and reason, the other by faith. But in fact on the level of epistemology both are the same. Satan and Adam begin alike from a point of ignorance— they know nothing prior to (the precise word is "before") the perspective they currently occupy; and the direction each then takes from this acknowledged limitation follows with equal logic or illogic. Adam reasons, since I don't remember how I got here, I must have been made by someone. Satan reasons, since I don't know how I got here, I must have made myself, or as we might say today, I must have just emerged from the primeval slime.

In neither case does the conclusion follow necessarily from the observed fact of imperfect knowledge. In both cases something is missing, a first premise, and in both cases reasoning can't get started until a first premise is put in place. What's more, since the first premise is what is missing, it cannot be derived from anything in the visible scene; it is what must be imported—on no evidentiary basis whatsoever—so that the visible scene, the things of this world, can *acquire* the meaning and significance they will now have. There is no opposition here between knowledge by reason and knowledge by faith because Satan and Adam are committed to both simultaneously. Each performs an act of faith— the one in God and the other in materialism—and then each begins to reason in ways dictated by the content of his faith.

That is why each performs as he does when confronted with a new (or apparently new) situation. When Eve worries that the growth of the garden will overwhelm the unfallen couple's efforts and prevent them from carrying out their assigned task, Adam replies by reasoning *against* the evidence of empirical circumstances and declaring that however things might seem, God, preeminent in goodness and power, will provide: "These paths and bowers doubt not but our joint hands / Will keep from Wilderness with ease" (IX, 244–245a), a confidence unsupported by anything either of them sees. Satan, on the other hand, rather than beginning from the first premise of a benevolent and provident

God, has as his first premise the radical contingency of outcomes. In a world ruled by chance and opportunity, the world in which he can emerge, as it were, out of nothing, who knows what the next turn of fortune's wheel might bring? Perhaps God will nod or make a misstep; after all, Satan reasons, on the evening of the first day of the war in heaven, God has thrown everything he has at us and we're still standing; we "have sustain'd one day in doubtful fight, / And if one day, why not Eternal days?" (VI, 423–424).

"If one day, why not eternal days?" has exactly the same structure as "I wasn't witness to my creation, therefore it didn't happen." In both instances, there is a refusal—no, an inability—to conceive of possibilities not already included in the field of empirical vision, the evidence of things seen. The habit of identifying the limits of reality with the limits of his own horizons defines Satan—it makes him what he is and is everywhere on display. Listen, for example, to his earlier rehearsal of the strategy he will employ in the actual temptation. He has heard Adam and Eve in conversation and found out about the forbidden fruit and the penalty attached to eating it, and he exclaims to himself:

> O fair foundation laid whereon to build
> Their ruin! Hence I will excite their minds
> With more desire to know, and to reject
> Envious commands, invented with design
> To keep them low whom knowledge might exalt
> Equal with Gods; aspiring to be such,
> They taste and die: what likelier can ensue?
> (IV, 521–27)

That is to say, God has set the conditions of their lives; if they violate those conditions, they will die. I will get them to eat the apple, and they will die. What else could happen? What else could happen is that the apparently iron logic of God's justice—he says at one point of Adam, "die he or justice must" (III, 210)—can be broken by the exercise of his mercy, which, he has said, "first and last shall brightest shine" (III, 134). The idea of mercy is literally unthinkable by Satan, who can only imagine agents with motives and goals just like his. He certainly cannot imagine an agent who would contrive to circumvent the force of his own decree and who would do so by paying the price his own law exacts. It is not a thought Satan could entertain because the very structure of his consciousness—grounded in self-worship and selfishness—excludes it as a possible insight.

I make the point strongly because it is so alien to the modern liberal Enlightenment picture of cognitive activity in which the mind is conceived of as a calculating and assessing machine that is open to all thoughts and closed to none. In this picture, the mind is in an important sense not yet settled. And, indeed, settling, in the form of a fixed commitment to an idea or a value, is a sign of cognitive and moral infirmity. Milton's view is exactly the reverse: in the absence of a fixed commitment—of a first premise that cannot be the object of thought because it is the enabling condition of thought—cognitive activity cannot get started. One's consciousness must be grounded in an originary act of faith—a stipulation of basic value—from which determinations of right and wrong, relevant and irrelevant, real and unreal, will then follow.

For the modern liberal, beliefs are what the mind scrutinizes and judges by rational criteria that are themselves hostage to no belief in particular. For Milton, beliefs—in God or in oneself or in the absolute contingency of material circumstances—are the content of a rationality that cannot scrutinize them because it rests on them. Milton's motto is not "Seeing is believing" but "Believing is seeing"; and since what you see marks the boundaries of your knowledge, believing is also knowing; and since it is on the basis of what you know—whether what you know is that there is a God or that there isn't one—that you act, believing is acting. What you believe is what you see is what you know is what you do is what you are.

It is a tenet of liberal Enlightenment faith that belief and knowledge are distinct and separable and that even if you do not embrace a point of view, you can still understand it. This is the credo Satan announces in *Paradise Regained* when he says, "most men admire / Virtue, who follow not her lore" (I, 482–483). That is, it is always possible to appreciate a way of life that is not yours. Milton would respond that unless the way of life is yours, you have no understanding of it; and that is why, he declares in another place, that a man who would write a true poem must himself *be* a true poem and can only praise or even recognize worthy things if he is himself worthy.

In this, as in so much else, Milton follows Augustine. Repeatedly in his *On Christian Doctrine,* Augustine begins a sentence by declaring, "No one would be so stupid as to say," or "It is obviously absurd to assert," or "It is utter madness to believe," or "No reasonable person would believe in any circumstances that . . ." What invariably follows, however, is an assertion that has been found reasonable by millions, and one wonders what Augustine means by a reasonable person. The answer is that a reasonable person is a person who believes what Augustine believes and who, like Augustine, can hear assertions contrary to that belief only as absurd.

Moreover, the belief whose prior assumption determines what will be heard as reasonable is not itself subject to the test of reasonableness. Reason's chain does not ratify it but proceeds from it. After all, Augustine explains, the logical validity of a chain of inference is independent of the validity or nonvalidity of the proposition with which the chain begins: "Correct inferences may be made concerning false as well as true propositions." It follows that a conclusion reached will be really—as opposed to formally—true only if a true proposition anchors it, and "the truth of a proposition is inherent in itself"; that is, its truth cannot be established by some procedure to which it must submit.[2] A reasonable mind, then, is a mind closed to the possibility that certain basic propositions—Augustine's example is "Christ is risen"—could be questioned. A reasonable mind is a mind that refuses to be open.

Of course an open mind, a mind ready at any moment to jettison even its most cherished convictions, is the very definition of "reasonable" in a post-Enlightenment liberal culture. And in the ears of those who have been socialized into that culture, a position like Augustine's will have the sound of obvious irrationality. That is certainly how John Stuart Mill, with whom Milton is often linked, incorrectly, as a precursor of modern thought, hears it. For the Mill of *On Liberty*, what "no reasonable person would believe" is that the highest value is the value of obedience (58).[3] Mill is incredulous before a philosophy according to which "all the good of which humanity is capable is comprised by obedience," and he is aghast at an ethics that requires nothing of man but "the surrendering of himself to the will of God" (58). He thinks it barbarous that Christians hold obstinately to an article of faith and then "stigmatize those who hold the contrary opinion as bad and immoral men" (51). That is no way, he complains, to know the truth, which can be known only "by hearing what can be said about it by persons of every variety of opinion" (21).

According to Mill, it is a man's obligation to keep "his mind open to criticism on his opinions" and "to listen to all that could be said against him" (21). He must strike the stance not of the "impassioned partisan" but of "the calmer and more interested bystander" who exercises his "judicial faculty" and sits "in intelligent judgment" (50). The duty of the reasonable man is to be tolerant of all views, and Mill identifies *in-*

tolerance with religious thought, for "in the minds of almost all religious persons . . . the duty of toleration is admitted with tacit reserves" (9), that is, with the reserve of whatever position they hold sacred. It is intolerance that leads Christians to "teach infidels to be just to Christianity" while they themselves show no disposition to be "just to infidelity" (49).

One wonders how Mill could have written these words without some sense of how odd they sound: be just to infidelity, that is, to error, apostasy, evil? What could he possibly mean? In fact, what he means depends on not taking the word "infidelity" seriously, that is, as a value judgment. As Mill uses it, "infidelity" is simply the name of an opinion, a point of view to which we are to accord the respect due all points of view. It is neither true nor false, good nor evil; it is rather one vendor in a marketplace whose business—a business never, by definition, concluded—it is to separate out the truths from the falsehoods, a process that cannot be fairly conducted, Mill would say, if a particular point of view (for example, "Christ is *not* risen") is stigmatized in advance. The trouble with Christianity, and with any religion grounded in unshakeable convictions, is that it lacks the generosity necessary to the marketplace's full functioning. Christianity, Mill declares, in what he takes to be a devastating judgment, is "one-sided" (47), that is, insistent upon the rightness of its perspective and deaf to the perspectives that might challenge it.

I am hardly the first to observe that Mill's position contains its own difficulties and internal inconsistencies. The imperative of keeping the marketplace of ideas open means that some ideas—those urged with an unhappy exclusiveness—must either themselves be excluded or be admitted only on the condition that they blunt the edge of their assertiveness and present themselves for possible correction. Willmoore Kendall asks: If a society is dedicated, as Mill urges that it be, to "a national religion of skepticism, to the suspension of judgment as *the* exercise of judgment par excellence," what can it say to a man who urges an opinion "*not* predicated on that view," a man who "with every syllable of faith he utters, challenges the very foundations of skeptical society"?[4] To such a man, Kendall answers, the society can only say, "You cannot enter into our discussions." "The all-questions-are-open-questions society," he concludes, cannot "practice tolerance toward those who disagree with it"; those "it must persecute—and so on its very own showing, arrest the pursuit of truth" (164).

This is a very powerful argument, and one to which I shall return, but it is not the argument I will finally want to stress, because to use it as a weapon against the doctrine of liberal toleration is to win a debating point but concede the larger point by accepting toleration as the final measure of judgment. If you persuade liberalism that its dismissive marginalizing of religious discourse is a violation of its own chief principle, all you will gain is the right to sit down at liberalism's table, where before you were denied an invitation. But it will still be *liberalism's* table that you are sitting at, and the etiquette of the conversation will still be hers.

That is, someone will now turn and ask "Well, what does religion have to say about this question?" And when, as often will be the case, religion's answer is doctrinaire (what else could it be?), the moderator (a title deeply revealing) will nod politely and turn to someone who is presumed to be more reasonable. To put the matter baldly, a person of religious conviction should not want to enter the marketplace of ideas but to shut it down, at least insofar as it presumes to determine matters that he believes have been determined by God and faith. The religious person should not seek an accommodation with liberalism; he should seek to rout it from the field.

Liberals, on the other hand, need not be so aggressive (although they will always be passive-aggressive) since the field, as it is presently demarcated, is already theirs. That is why Martha Nussbaum, in a piece in the *New York Review of Books,* feels that, in order to discredit him, she need only quote law professor Michael McConnell when he argues for a notion of truth that has reference to "authority, community, and faith" (166).[5] Someone who would link truth to concepts of authority and faith—the equivalents of Mill's hated "obedience"—is obviously beyond the pale and constitutes a danger, or so Nussbaum asserts, to "the very norms of academic freedom and academic objectivity."[6] McConnell is among the most vocal of those who have been challenging the domestication and trivializing of the religious sensibility, but a reading of the article Nussbaum cites suggests that he poses no danger at all.

McConnell begins by examining a brief filed by Robert Abrams, former Attorney General of the State of New York, in defense of a ruling that refused a religious group the use of a public meeting room for the showing of a film. Noting that the attorney general grounds his position in a characterization of religious experience as "inviolately private" and therefore out of place in a public forum, McConnell angrily declares it "inconceivable that a public official would say that about any other worldview": "If feminists, gay rights advocates, Afrocentrists, or even secular conservatives tried to communicate their ideas . . . to the public Abrams would never say they should keep their ideas to themselves." In an age, McConnell observes, "when previously marginalized voices are welcomed to the public dialogue," only religion is "privatized and marginalized" and "must be kept under wraps" (165–166).

McConnell is here making two points which he thinks go together but which in fact are finally in tension with one another. The first point is that a religion privatized to the extent that the world is kept quarantined from its potential influence is a religion not taken seriously. In his *Areopagitica* Milton pokes some high literary fun at a man who, uncomfortable with the sharp demands placed on him by religious faith, decides to hand his religious obligation over to a hired agent who will, for a fee, breathe out the appropriate prayers and perform the required acts of piety. This surrogate is well paid and provided for, "is liberally supped and sumptuously laid to sleep," and after having been "better breakfasted than he whose morning appetite would gladly have fed on green figs between Bethany and Jerusalem . . . walks abroad at eight, and leaves his kind entertainer in the shop trading all day, without his religion."[7] Milton's scorn at this picture of a faith held so lightly that it leaves the everyday world unaltered is matched by McConnell's distress at a public/private split that assures the same lack of practical efficacy: a religion deprived of the opportunity to transform the culture in its every detail is hardly a religion at all. But McConnell immediately allows this point to be swallowed up by another, by the debating point I have already identified: this exclusion of the religious impulse from the public sphere runs contrary to the professed liberality of an open society. "In an open society, we presume that the uninhibited, robust, and wide-open exchange of viewpoints benefits us all" (166).

The key to what is happening here is the fact that the phrase "uninhibited, robust, and wide open" comes from *New York Times v. Sullivan,* a 1964 case in which the Supreme Court dislodged from its position of primacy in libel matters the standard of truthfulness.[8] In place of truth, the Court substituted the standard of free-for-all debate in relation to which false and defamatory statements are on a par with true and accurate statements, on the deeply skeptical reasoning that both alike are opinions: "Erroneous statement is inevitable in free debate, and . . . must be protected if the freedoms of expression are to have the 'breathing space'" they need; and "this is true even though the utterance contains 'half-truths' and 'misinformation'" (164). In this and other passages, the Court privileges expression as a value over the substantive worth and veracity of that which is expressed. Religious discourse, however, cannot be unconcerned with the substantive worth and veracity of its assertions, which are in fact *presupposed*, and presupposed too is the urgency of proclaiming those assertions—the good news—to a world asked to receive them as the whole and necessary truth. The ethos of *New York Times v. Sullivan* is finally inimical to the religious impulse, which does not value talk for its own sake but values the end—spiritual regeneration leading to regenerate action—to which some, but not all, forms of talk may bring us.

By couching his brief for religious expression in the terms of free speech doctrine, McConnell falls in with the very trivializing of religious expression he deplores. For under a *New York Times v. Sullivan* standard, religious expression is just one more voice in a mix that refuses the claim of any particular voice to be prior and controlling. When McConnell characterizes his own essay as a "plea for old fashioned broadmindedness"—that is, for toleration—he seems not to realize that broadmindedness is the opposite of what religious conviction enacts and requires. Religious conviction, as Mill sees from the enemy position, requires narrowmindedness, the discovery of and hewing to the straight and narrow way. Broadmindedness is what *liberalism* requires and, by invoking it as a standard, McConnell gives the game away to his opponents.

He does it again when he unmasks the liberal claim of neutrality. "Liberal neutrality," he complains, "is of a very peculiar sort" (181), for it defines "neutral" so that it means "secular"—neutrality between "conceptions of the good life" so long as they are not God-centered, "as if agnosticism about the theistic foundations of the universe were common ground among believers and nonbelievers alike" (174). Since this neutrality has no obligation to the theism it does not recognize except as a negative-limit case, theism will lose out when the supposedly neutral state weighs its claims. "Virtually any plausible public purpose," McConnell laments, is "deemed sufficient to override the right of religious exercise" (176). The result is the "strange phenomenon" of a liberalism that "proclaims its neutrality toward competing ideals of virtue . . . but is committed in practice to the promotion of particular ideals and—even more—to the eradication of others" (176). By marginalizing religious ideals, liberalism has failed to live up to its own ideal. The trouble with liberalism is that it is not liberal enough.

Here again is the familiar debating point, but it is beside the point; for what McConnell describes is not a liberalism enmeshed in self-contradiction but a liberalism being perfectly true to its principles, a liberalism that is neutral in the only way it could be and still remain liberal. McConnell's mistake (one he shares with many liberals) is to think that liberal neutrality is, or should be, pure, a practice of making no a priori substantive judgments at all. But liberalism rests on the substantive judgment that the public sphere must be insulated from viewpoints that owe their allegiance not to its procedures—to the unfettered operation of the marketplace of ideas—but to the truths they work to establish. That is what neutrality means in the context of liberalism—a continual pushing away of orthodoxies, of beliefs not open to inquiry and correction—and that is why, in the name of neutrality, religious propositions must either be excluded from the marketplace or admitted only in ceremonial forms, in the form, for example, of a prayer that opens a session of Congress in which the proposals of religion will not be given a serious hearing.

McConnell's true antagonist, then, is not a liberalism gone sour but liberalism pure and simple; and his request that liberalism become more liberal—open itself up to forces that do not place openness in the position of highest value—will be resisted because for liberalism to accede to it would be tantamount to committing suicide. What McConnell should want is not an expansion of the marketplace of ideas but its disbanding and replacement by a regime of virtue as opposed to a regime of process. He should want an end to the public/private split which, by fencing off the arena of political dispute from substantive determinations of value, assures the continual deferral and bracketing of value questions. He should want what Milton wants, a unified conception of life in which the pressure of first principles is felt and responded to twenty-four hours a day.

But so far is McConnell from recognizing the shape of his own interests as a committed Christian that he ends his essay by declaring that "the public/private distinction . . . is utterly indispensable to a theory of religious freedom. We cannot have religious freedom without it" (184). One knows what he means: without the public/private split, religion will not be protected from state action; were the state not barred from interfering with the free exercise of religion, that freedom might disappear. But of course the freedom thus gained is the freedom to be ineffectual, the freedom "to be confined to the margins of public life—to those areas not important enough to have received the helping or controlling hand of government" (178).

What is not allowed religion under the private/public distinction is the freedom to *win*, the freedom not to be separate from the state but to inform and shape its every action. That idea never even occurs to McConnell because it is so antiliberal, and in the end a liberal is what he is. "From a secular point of view," he writes, "it is difficult to appreciate the religious impulse" (173). His essay is a testimony to that difficulty, which registers even here in the use of the word "appreciate," a word borrowed from the vocabulary of taste, a word that falls far short of taking the measure of what the religious impulse, fully felt, might be like.

The same failure characterizes Stephen Carter's *The Culture of Disbelief: How American Law and Politics Trivialize Religious Devotion*, a book that begins by calling religion a "very subversive force" (43) and ends by diluting that force in a theory of accommodation.[9] There are more than a few places where Carter seems to understand that from a secular point of view it is not merely "difficult" but impossible to appreciate the religious impulse. Early on he notes that the invocation of a common rationality (in the manner of a Thomas Nagel or Bruce Ackerman) is a device for limiting the conversation to premises that would "exclude religion from the mix" (55), since invariably the "common rationality" will stigmatize as "irrational" the strong claims of religious persons. He also sees that to ask a religious person to rephrase his claims in more mainstream terms is to ask that person to cut himself off from the very source of his conviction and to become in effect the opposite of what he is, to become secular: "The proposed rules to govern discourse in the public square require some members of society to remake themselves before they are allowed to press policy arguments" (56). And at his strongest he points out that the fact/value distinction, which allows theorists to bracket off a public sphere whose deliberations are procedural rather than substantive, is itself a substantive stipulation that has the effect of prejudging what will and will not be considered a fact.

"Liberal epistemology," Carter explains, is not capable of treating as a factual inquiry a question like "Can the Jehovah's Witness achieve salvation after receiving a blood transfusion?" or, for that matter, a ques-

REASONS FOR THE DEVOUT

tion like, "Is there life after death?" (221). The liberal response would be, of course not: facts are what is verifiable by independent evidence; questions of salvation and life after death are matters of faith. But of course they are both matters of faith, for, as Carter points out, the establishment of a fact depends on "what counts as evidence" (22).

That is to say, evidence is never independent in the sense of being immediately apprehensible; evidence comes into view (or doesn't) in the light of some first premise or "essential axiom" that cannot itself be put to the test because the protocols of testing are established by its preassumed authority. A "creationist parent whose child is being taught . . . evolution" protests not in the name of religion and against the witness of fact; he protests in the name of fact as it seems indisputable to him given the "central" truth "that God is real" (175). Given such a "starting point and the methodology" that follows from it, "creationism is as rational an explanation as any other"; and from the other direction, you might say that given the assumption of a material world that caused itself (the Satanic assumption), evolution is as faith-dependent an explanation as any other. This is not to debunk rationality in favor of faith but to say that rationality and faith go together in an indissoluble package: you can't have one without the other.

Taken to its conclusions, this argument is devastating for the liberal project. For it is only if rationality and faith can be separated that one can establish a public sphere in which issues of civic concern can be discussed by persons who have left their religious convictions at home or checked them at the door. If you can't have one without the other, behind any dispute that occurs will be a conflict of conviction that cannot be rationally settled because it is also and necessarily a conflict of rationalities, and when there is a conflict of rationalities, your only recourse is, well, to conflict, since there is no common ground in relation to which dialogue might proceed. Here looms the specter of liberalism's collapse, but Carter will not look it in the face, and in the last part of his book he puts asunder what he had previously joined.

He does this by insisting on a distinction between disagreeing, say, with the religious right or with David Koresh because their positions are "wrong" and disagreeing with them because their positions are presented in religious terms. "If the Christian right is wrong for America it must be because its message is wrong on the issues, not because its message is religious" (266). "We must be able, in our secular society, to distinguish a critique of the content of a belief from a critique of its source" (277). What is remarkable about these statements is that they subscribe fully to the liberal assumptions that have been the object of Carter's critique. Suddenly, rationality and faith and, along with them, fact and value can be separated, and with separation returns the liberal public sphere and the possibility of assessing agendas without inquiring into the worldviews from which they emerge.

As Carter uses the phrase, "wrong on the issues" can only mean wrong on the issues as they are identified apart from anyone's religious convictions; but this assumes that the specification of what the issues in fact *are* can be made uncontroversially. But as Carter himself has argued (when, for example, he points out that in the mind of a creationist parent, his "child is being taught a pack of lies"), the reverse is true: in the bitterest debates, it is the very shape of the issues that is in dispute, and the dispute is fueled and rendered incapable of resolution by the incompatible first assumptions—articles of opposing faiths—in the different lights of which the issue takes form.

A prolife advocate sees abortion as a sin against a God who infuses life at the moment of conception; a prochoice advocate sees abortion as a decision to be made in accordance with the best scientific opinion as to when the beginning of life, as we know it, occurs. No conversation between them can ever get started because each of them starts from a different place, and they could never agree as to what they were conversing *about*. (The picture is no longer as simple as I here draw it. Prolifers have become adept at arguing from scientific evidence and even from evidence provided by postmodern theorists. That does not mean, however, that a belief in a God-given life is no longer critical to their position. It is just that they are now able to combat their enemies with their own vocabulary and never have to mention God at all.) The "content of a belief" is a function of its source, and the critique of one will always be the critique of the other. Of course we can and do say, "I don't care where you got that idea from; it's wrong." But what we mean is that we can't see where such an idea came from, and we can't see that because the place it came from is not one where we have ever been; it is the place, the source, we object to even when we fail—we could hardly succeed and be ourselves—to recognize it.

One understands why Carter wants to separate the message from its source: he is bothered by the fact that liberals tend to dismiss certain views just because they are motivated by religious conviction. But when he urges that we bracket the conviction and attend just to the view, he does exactly what he inveighs against: he asks religious persons to "remake themselves before they can legitimately be involved in secular political argument" (232), or, rather, he invites *us* to remake them when he urges that we receive them respectfully so long as their arguments can be made sense of in secular terms.

When he counsels us to reject Patrick Buchanan's views on the merits and not because they come provided with a "religious justification," he is producing one more example of "how American law and politics trivialize religious devotion." Religious devotion is trivialized when its words are admitted into the forum but its claims to be not just one truth but *the* truth are disallowed. This "accommodation," as Carter calls it, is the very program of liberalism which will always "accommodate" religious doctrine so as to avoid taking it seriously. Accommodation is a much better strategy than outright condemnation, for it keeps the enemy in sight while depriving it of the (exclusionary) edge that makes it truly dangerous; and best of all, one who accommodates can perform this literally disarming act while proclaiming the most high-sounding pieties.

It is the history of this killing of religion by kindness that is the great subject of George Marsden's *The Soul of the American University: From Protestant Establishment to Established Nonbelief.*[10] The book begins with a question—"How was it that distinctively Christian teaching could be displaced so easily from the substantive role that it held in American higher education for over two centuries and in the universities of Christendom for many centuries before that?" (31)—and then proceeds to answer it in twenty-two closely reasoned and densely packed chapters.

The answer has many components, including the Jeffersonian project of softening sectarian aggressiveness and establishing a general religion of peace, reason, and morality, the identification of commonsense philosophy with Christian morality within the assumption that each supported the other, the rise of the cult of the expert whose skills and authority were independent of his character or religious faith, and the substitution for the imperative of adhering to an already-revealed truth the imperative of continuing to search for a truth whose full emergence is located in an ever-receding future.

This last was particularly important because if truth was by definition larger and more inclusive than our present horizons declared it to be, obedience to traditional norms and values was no longer a virtue but a fault, and a *moral* fault at that. "The higher truth was an ever progressing ideal toward which the human community . . . always moved, yet never reached. Since truth was by definition always changing, the only thing ultimately sacred was the means of pursuing it. No religious or other dogmatic claim could be allowed to stand in its way" (329). It is not the business of a university, declared Charles Eliot of Harvard, "to train men for those functions in which implicit obedience is of the first importance. On the contrary, it should train men for those occupations in which self-government, independence, and originating power are preeminently needed" (188). (Or, in Satan's more succinct formulation, "self-begot, self-raised.")

As Marsden is quick to note, "Freedom was the principle that tied everything else together" (189). If it is assumed, as it was by many, that the truth to which free inquiry is leading us is the same truth that religion names "God," then, as one cleric put it, "the cause of Christ and the Church is advanced by whatever liberalizes and enriches and enlarges the mind" (186). The more capacious and inclusive the individual consciousness, the closer one is to comprehending the life-principle or soul of the universe. "Hence," Marsden concludes, "any entirely free and honest inquiry into any dimension of reality simply *was* part of true religion" (192).

The only thing excluded, then, was exclusion itself—that is, any position that refused to submit its basic premises to reason's scrutiny. Princeton's Francis Patton declared that "the rationality or rather the reasonableness of a belief is the condition of its credibility" (120). That is, you believe it because reason ratifies it, a view Augustine would have heard with horror, one that John Webster, writing in 1654, rejects as obviously absurd. "But if man gave his assent unto, or believed the things of Christ . . . because they appear probable . . . to his reason, then would his faith be . . . upon the rotten basis of human authority."[11] By the end of the nineteenth century, human authority has been put in the place of revelation; or rather human authority, now identified with the progressive illumination afforded by reason, has become the vehicle of revelation and of a religion that can do very nicely without any strong conception of personal deity.

Of course, this process by which an ethic of free inquiry supplants and liberalizes an older ethic of obedience to settled truth was not without opposition, and Marsden duly records the voices that were raised in protest. In the last quarter of the nineteenth century, Yale's Noah Porter scoffed at the supposed neutrality and evenhandedness of secular educational theory, which, he pointed out, was its theology: "The question is not whether the college shall or shall not teach theology, but what theology it shall teach—theology according to . . . Moses and Paul or according to Buckle and Draper" (127). By the beginning of this century it was all too evident which of these directions had been taken by American education. In tones recently echoed by conservative polemicists, the editors of *Cosmopolitan* magazine complained in 1909 that "in hundreds of classrooms it is being taught daily that the decalogue is no more sacred than a syllabus; that the home as an institution is doomed; that there are no absolute evils; . . . that the change of one religion to another is like getting a new hat; that moral precepts are passing shibboleths; that conceptions of right and wrong are as unstable as styles of dress" (267). "The neutrality we have," thundered William Jennings Bryan in 1923, "is often but a sham; it carefully excludes the Christian religion but permits the use of the schoolroom for the destruction of faith and for the teaching of materialistic doctrines" (326). From a quite different perspective, Walter Lippmann agreed: "Reason and free inquiry can be neutral and tolerant only of those opinions which submit to the test of reason and free inquiry" (329).

What this means, as Marsden points out, is that "two irreconcilable views of truth and education were at issue" (329–330); but of course the issue was never really joined, because the liberal establishment thought of itself as already reconciled to everything and anything and therefore was unable to see how exclusionary its policy of radical inclusion really was: "Groups that were excluded, such as Marxists and fundamentalists, often raised the point that they were being excluded by liberal dogmatism, but they were seldom heard" (400). That they were not heard is hardly surprising, since what they were saying was that a state of "warfare" (328) existed, and warfare—deep conflict over basic and nonnegotiable issues—was precisely what liberalism was invented to deny; it manages that denial by excluding from the tolerance it preaches anyone who will not pledge allegiance to the supremacy of tolerance.

This, then, is the story Marsden tells, and he tells it with a dispassionate equanimity that sits oddly with the strong point of view he announces in his introduction. "My point of view," he declares, "is that of a fairly traditional Protestant of the reformed theological heritage. One of the features of that heritage is that it has valued education that relates faith to one's scholarship. Particularly important is that beliefs about God, God's creation, and God's will . . . should have impact on scholarship not just in theology, but also in considering other dimensions of human thought and relationships" (7). But in the long narrative that follows, these beliefs become objects of study rather than informing principles of the scholarship. It is as if Marsden has discharged his obligation to his "point of view" simply by announcing it, and can now proceed on his way without being unduly influenced by its values. "It is perfectly possible," he asserts, "to have strong evaluative interests in a subject, and yet treat it fairly and with a degree of detachment" (8).

But it is possible to detach yourself from a "strong evaluative interest" only if you believe in a stage of perception that exists *before* interest kicks in; and not only is that a prime tenet of liberal thought, it is what makes possible the exclusionary move of which Marsden, McConnell, and Carter complain. If such a base-level stage of perception does in fact exist, it can be identified as the common ground in relation to which *uncommon*—that is, not universally shared convictions (like, for example, Christ is risen) can be marginalized and privatized. By claiming to have set aside his strongly held values in deference to the virtue of fairness—a virtue only if you are committed to the priority of procedure over substance—Marsden agrees to play by the rules of the very ideology of which his book is in large part a critique.

He is still playing by those rules in a postscript in which, he tells us, his own interest, hitherto not strongly in play, will be elaborated. He now adds himself to the list of those who complain that "the only points of view . . . allowed full academic credence are those that presuppose purely naturalistic worldviews" (430). The resulting exclusion of religious perspectives, he explains, was justified by the supposed objectivity and neutrality of naturalistic descriptions, but since poststructuralism and postmodernism have denied the claims of any discourse to be objective and neutral, "there seems no intellectually valid reason to exclude religiously based perspectives" (431). This, however, is a self-defeating argument because it amounts to saying that when it comes to proof, religious perspectives are no worse off than any other. It is an argument from weakness—yes, religious thought is without objective ground, but so is everything else; we are all in the same untethered boat—and if a religious perspective were to gain admittance on *that* basis, it would have forfeited its claim to be anything other than a "point of view," a subjective preference, a mere opinion. It would have joined the universe of liberal discourse but at the price of not being taken seriously. If a religious perspective is included because there is "no intellectually valid reason" to exclude it, neither will there be any intellectually valid reason to affirm it, except as one perspective among others, rather than as the perspective that is true, and because true, controlling.

That is what Marsden should want: not the inclusion of religious discourse in a debate no one is allowed to win but the triumph of religious discourse and the silencing of its atheistic opponents. To invoke the criterion of intellectual validity and seek shelter under its umbrella is to surrender in advance to the enemy, to that liberal rationality whose inability even to recognize the claims of faith has been responsible for religion's marginalization in the first place. Marsden wants to argue against that marginalization, but his suggestion for removing it is in fact a way of reinforcing it. He calls it "procedural rationality." The procedure is to scrutinize religious viewpoints and distinguish between those that "honor some basic rules of evidence and argument" and those that "are presented so dogmatically and aggressively as not to be accommodated within the procedural rules of pluralistic academia" (431–432).

One could hardly imagine a better formula for subordinating the religious impulse to the demands of civil and secular order. Presumably it will not be religion that specifies what the rules of evidence and argument to be honored are; and it surely will not be religion that stigmatizes as dogma any assertion that does not conform to the requirements of those rules. Dogma, of course, is a word that once had a positive meaning: it meant the unqualified assertion of a priori truths and was indistinguishable from a truly strong religiosity. It is only under the liberal dispensation that dogma acquires the taint of obdurateness, of a culpable refusal to submit to the test of reasonableness as defined by the standards and norms of the civil establishment.

It is no accident that Marsden here begins to speak of the "enforcement of rules of civility" (432), of rules that protect the flow of conversation from those who would bring it to an authoritative conclusion, for in spite of his profession of religious faith, civility has become his religion. When civility is embraced as a prime value, tolerance and freedom cannot be far behind, and it is in the name of this quintessentially liberal trinity that Marsden makes his appeal in the closing pages of a book that began by invoking the will of God.

In the end, Marsden's own argument enacts the journey he has been describing, from a religious conviction so strong that it requires no justification to a religious impulse so weakened that he can say of it, without any irony, that it poses "scarcely any danger" to the ideal of "free inquiry" (435). On the back of the jacket cover one prepublication reviewer predicts that "George Marsden's book will raise hackles." It is not clear whether that is an expression of anxiety or hope; what is clear is that whichever it is, it will not be realized.

What does it all mean? What can we conclude from these examples of three intelligent and learned men who lament the trivialization of religious discourse at the hands of liberal rationalism but who turn to the vocabulary of that same rationalism when it comes time to offer remedies and alternatives? One thing we can conclude is that in the end McConnell, Carter, and Marsden are moved more by what they fear than by what they desire. What they desire is the full enfranchisement of religious conviction. What they fear is the full enfranchisement of religious conviction, for if the religious impulse were unchecked by the imperatives of civility, tolerance, and freedom of inquiry, the result would be the open conflict the Enlightenment was designed to blunt.

It is simply too late in the day to go back; as a member of one of Carter's audiences put it, "We already had the Enlightenment and religion lost." The loss is not simply a matter of historical fact: it is inscribed in the very consciousness of those who live in its wake. That is why we see the spectacle of men like McConnell, Carter, and Marsden, who set out to restore the priority of the good over the right but find the protocols of the right—of liberal proceduralism—written in the fleshly tables of their hearts.

FAITH BEFORE REASON

13

In a response to the previous chapter, Father Richard Neuhaus, editor of the journal *First Things* (where it first appeared) objects that I pit freedom of inquiry against truth or critical thought against a commitment to truth, or, more simply, faith against reason.[1] In fact I don't regard these as opposed to one another (they are not binaries) but as mutually interdependent. The difference between a believer and a nonbeliever is not that one reasons and the other doesn't but that one reasons from a first premise the other denies; and from this difference flow others that make the fact that both are reasoning a sign not of commonality but of its absence. If, as Neuhaus says, a secularist liberal and a committed Christian recognize and deploy the same "rules of reason, evidence, and critical judgment" (28), sooner or later they will disagree about whether something is or is not evidence or about what it is evidence *of,* and such disagreements cannot be resolved by the rules of reason because the rules of reason unfold in relation to a proposition they do not generate. That proposition—God exists or he doesn't, Christ is the word made flesh or he isn't, human nature is perfectible or it isn't— is an article of faith, and while two persons proceeding within opposing faiths might perform identical operations of logical entailment, they will end up in completely different places because it is from different (substantive) places that they began.

Let me turn again for an example to Milton. In Book VI of *Paradise Lost,* Satan's rebels and God's loyalists meet on the field of battle, but even to say this is to understate the level of their disagreement, since in the eyes of the loyalists this isn't a battle at all—they know, as one of them declares, that God could have "at one blow / Unaided" (VI, 140–141) settled the matter—while the possibility that there could be a battle—that God might, after all, be just the self-bestowed name of a boastful antagonist—is absolutely central to the rebels' perspective, a perspective that determines both what will be seen by them as evidence and the conclusions they draw from it. This is no less true of the loyalists for whom evidence also emerges not in its own independent shape but in the shape given to it by the structure of their belief. In the course of the "battle," both parties meet with events that one might think could lead them to alter their basic commitments. The rebels for the first time experience pain and fear; but they respond by incorporating these new experiences into their sense of themselves as battling heroically against steep odds in what Satan has earlier named "the strife of glory" (290). The strife is glorious because (in their eyes) it is a struggle for independence in the face of a tyrant who demands their submission; and the fact that this tyrant has now been able to invent pain is received by them not as evidence that they should desist but as evidence that confirms their self-image (the odds are even worse than we thought and yet we bravely fight on) and strengthens their resolve (if we can endure this, we can endure anything).

On the other side, the loyalists find themselves in a position that might "reasonably" be called humiliating. They are in the field because God has told them that as a reward for their loyalty they will have the honor and pleasure of driving the rebels "out from . . . bliss, / Into their place of punishment" (52–53); but as it turns out, God has so arranged it that the power of the two hosts is equal, which means that the loyalists cannot possibly do what he has ordered them to do and promised they will be able to do. In fact, the entire battle has been staged only to provide God's anointed Son with a dramatic entrance. When he appears on the third day to claim all the honors, his first act is to say to the loyalists, "Thanks for the effort, boys, but this is a job for Superman." They in turn respond not with disappointment or with a sense of injured merit, but (the verse tells us) with "joy" (774); not joy at being humiliated— they don't see it that way—but joy at having been joined and praised by one to whom they have sworn allegiance. What they could have easily seen as a reason to change masters, they contrive (that is, work) to see as a reason for continuing their fealty. They too can style this the strife of glory, but they have managed to find their glory (and the maintenance of their faith) in a willingness to resign it to another.

Note that both sides are exercising their reason and judgment; no one is "submitting uncritically." The world continually throws up puzzles to be solved and everyone tries to solve them; it is just that, given the radically divergent presuppositions of the two parties, each engages in the task of reasoning by asking different questions: on the one hand, "since we are in the fight of our lives and the adversary seems to have a superior technology, what can we do to neutralize it?" (the rebels proceed to invent gunpowder); on the other, "since God is God and intends only good for us, how can we see this turn of events as further evidence of his goodness?"

In choosing *that* question to ask, the loyalists follow (or, rather, anticipate) Augustine's counsel to those who meet with phenomena apparently subversive of the true faith, either in the Scriptures or in life: subject the phenomena "to diligent scrutiny until an interpretation contributing to the reign of charity is produced" (*On Christian Doctrine*, 93). That is, since you know that in a world ordered by a just and benevolent God everything signifies his love for us and our obligation to love our fellow creatures for his sake, struggle with what the world presents to you until you are able to discern that signification. Knowing what the answer is in advance does not mean that there is no work to be done, nothing to reason about; for the answer is a general one whose application in particular circumstances is always an arduous task. "To the pure and healthy internal eye," declares Augustine, "He is everywhere" (13). But since our eyes are as yet far from pure, seeing him everywhere is not a foregone conclusion but a continual challenge.

To this analysis of the interdependence of faith (whether satanic or godly) and reason, Father Neuhaus poses objections that might be put in the form of two questions: (1) Cannot reason be exercised *before* the first premise is in place? (2) In the course of reasoning cannot that first premise itself become the object of critical attention? I would answer the first question by turning to the tract of Augustine's that Neuhaus cites against me. In *The Usefulness of Believing*, Augustine addresses his friend Honoratus in an effort to turn him away from the Manichean position on the relationship between faith and reason. The Manicheans, as Augustine reports them, dismiss as "superstition" the notion that the Christian must be "by believing forearmed" before he can begin to reason; they urge instead that "no one . . . have faith without having first discussed and made clear the truth." Augustine acknowledges the appeal (which he once felt) of this way of thinking, especially to young men intoxicated by the prospect of throwing off the shackles "of old wives fables" in order to "drink in . . . the open and pure Truth." But he identifies the man who detaches himself from all authority with the fool who has nothing of wisdom inside him, but nevertheless sets out to determine, by reason alone, who is and is not a wise man. Since he does not begin with an inner understanding of that which he seeks, he will be unable to recognize it. "For by no signs whatever can one recognize anything, unless he shall have known that thing," known it, that is, in advance. Someone who inquires after something (truth, wisdom, the good) without having internalized its identifying criteria is asking of signs that they tell him, all by themselves, what they are signs of; and since no sign can satisfy that demand—no sign can deliver up the norm by which to judge its own adequacy or significance—all signs, at least for this unanchored inquirer, will either signify nothing in particular or (it is the same thing) signify anything at all.

A nice example is provided by the Satan of Milton's *Paradise Regained,* who at the beginning of the poem assigns himself the task of figuring out just who this person is who has been singled out by John the Baptist at the river Jordan and on whose head "a perfect dove" (I, 84) has descended. We know that Satan is in trouble when he immediately says of the dove "whate'er it meant." If he doesn't know what it means when he sees it, the gap between him and knowledge will not be filled in by additional information, for that information will itself become drawn into the vortex of his uncertainty. For four books and thousands of lines Satan stalks the Son, subjecting him, as he says, to ever "narrower scrutiny" (IV, 515) and hazarding his "best conjectures" (IV, 525) as to the nature of his adversary, but still finds himself, after all his surveillance and sifting of evidence, "yet in doubt" (IV, 501).

In the final scene he is still devising ways to "know . . . more" (IV, 538) and announces, "Another *method* I must now begin" (IV, 540). This is the authentic voice of technological modernism, which holds out the hope that the world will deliver its truth when the right techniques—instruments of disinterested observation—are applied to it; but no matter how close the phenomena are brought to the doubting eye by sophisticated instruments of observation, that eye will see only its own doubt at once miniaturized and magnified. As Augustine puts it, "The fool is void of wisdom, therefore he knows not wisdom, for he could not see it with his eyes." And, moreover, if he *could* see it, he would no longer be a fool because there would now be something in him answerable to that which he seeks to know: "He cannot see it and not have it, nor have it and be a fool." Were Satan to succeed in coming to know who the Son truly is he would no longer be Satan because it is his distance from that knowledge that defines him and makes him both what he is and what he isn't, and what he is, at least until some moment of total conversion, is someone who says of the dove, "whate'er it meant" and will say the same of anything—the Son, baptism, the Trinity, resurrection, God—whose significance exceeds what is apparent on the empirical surface.

Satan is the very type of those who would reason before they believe. Such a one, Augustine insists, has things exactly backward; if you begin to reason before the mind has been cleared of error, your reasoning will be forever errant: "To wish to see the truth in order to purge your soul, when as it is purged for the very purpose that you may see, is surely perverse and preposterous." Purge the soul first by orienting it to the appropriate object of desire, and *then* reason, for only then, says Augustine, are you "capable of receiving reason," capable, that is, of engaging in reasoning that is not endlessly spinning its own wheels.

Spinning your wheels is what you would be doing if you were to bracket your first premise and make it the object of critical attention. To be sure, this is something you might do, at least as an experiment, but where would you be if you did it? You would be nowhere—at sea amidst innumerable interpretative possibilities—and you could only proceed by installing some other premise in the position of first (usually while pretending not to do so). This is what the Manicheans do when they urge the "premature" believer to set aside his conviction that what Christ "hath said is true, although it be supported by no reason" and begin instead to reason toward Christ's truth under their guidance. But, objects Augustine, that is to ask the believer to exchange the authority of his church and its traditions for the authority, no less unsupported, of these self-appointed reasoners. For a Christian to "distrust and overthrow" what has been "handed down from our blessed forefathers" in favor of another kind of knowledge is "to seek a sacrilegious way unto true religion," sacrilegious because it subordinates religious truth to a formalism that should serve, not judge, it. As Bruce Marshall has put it, "The narratives which identify Jesus are epistemic trump; if it comes to conflict . . . between these beliefs and any others, the narratives win."[2]

Does this mean, as Neuhaus asks, that the central beliefs of Christianity cannot be falsified? No, it means that the central beliefs of Christianity cannot be falsified (or even strongly challenged) by evidence that would not be seen as evidence by those who hold the beliefs. For one party, falsification follows from the absence of any rational account of how the purported phenomena (walking on water, feeding five thousand with five loaves and two fishes, rising from the dead) could have occurred; for the other the absence of a rational explanation is just the point, one that, far from challenging the faith, confirms it. When Neuhaus declares that essential Christian truth claims would be in very deep trouble "were a corpse to be identified beyond reasonable doubt as that of Jesus of Nazareth" (32), it depends on what he means by "reasonable doubt." If he means the kind of doubt an empirically minded nonbeliever might have, then the doubt is a foregone conclusion since it is implicit in the way he (already) thinks. "A virgin birth? A God incarnate? Give me a break!" But if Neuhaus means a reasonable doubt a Christian might have, then it would have to be a doubt raised by tensions internal to Christian belief, and not by tensions *between* Christian belief and some other belief system. An atheist might see the Holocaust as further confirmation of the doubt that is an article of his (non)faith ("See, I told you there is no God"). A believer might see the Holocaust as something difficult to reconcile with his conviction of a God who is merciful, and he might find himself in a state of doubt. He might then be able to overcome the doubt by finding a way to understand the event that did not deny God's mercy; and then again he might not, in which case he would be in the middle of a crisis of faith. But whatever he did with the doubt, it will have been a doubt *for him* by virtue of what he believed and not because a challenge to his belief has come from someplace outside it.

The discovery by an archeological expedition of a body in the vicinity of where Jesus's tomb is thought to have been will not raise a doubt (or even be the first step on the road to doubt) for the Christian who reads in Matthew 28:11–15 that from day one nonbelievers have sought to substitute a naturalistic explanation for the mystery of the resurrection. It will take more than a body, or carbon dating, or "identifying marks" to shake a faith which is not built on that kind of evidence in the first place. What it would take I don't know and, at any rate, the answer would vary with the strength and firmness of individual believers; but no believer will find his faith shaken by evidence that is evidence only in the light of assumptions he does not share and considers flatly wrong.

It seems unnecessary to say so, but when you think a view wrong, you don't see what is seen by those who think it right—those who live and move and have their being within it. When Satan says of the war in Heaven, "*we* style it the strife of glory" (VI, 289–290), he is responding to the archangel Michael who has just characterized the war as "evil" (262). It is only in a trivial sense that the two agents, operating within opposing first premises, are talking about the same thing. No feature of the battle is seen in common, and indeed, as I noted earlier, Michael would, if pressed, balk at the word "battle" itself, since it implies an encounter with a doubtful outcome, whereas he harbors no doubts at all. Nor would it do any good to delay the action in order to allow time for the combatants to review and discuss each other's vocabulary (the dream of liberalism), for even if they use the same words, the words are not really the same in that each hears them as referring to different things or nothings. Michael cannot understand the word "glory" as applied to an action (rebellion) that separates creatures from their God, since, for him, glory can be found only in obedience to, and union with, the Highest. And the word "evil" can hardly be heard intelligibly by someone who has declared, "Evil be thou my good" (IV, 110), and by so declaring renounced the perspective of morality altogether.

When Neuhaus insists that "we encounter propositions all the time that we can quite well understand but happen to believe are not true" (29), he slides away from one sense of understanding—grasping the syntax and semantics of an utterance—to another—experiencing the truth of that utterance in your heart and soul. It is in the first sense that Milton's fallen angels remain able to frame and receive sentences containing words like "Heaven," "faith," and "good," but their "understanding" of those words is only skin deep (that's why they're devils) and so by "good" they understand "advantage to themselves," and by "faith" they understand "firmness of apostasy," and by "Heaven" they understand "the territory temporarily occupied by the enemy." When Mammon surveys the topography of Hell, he sees natural resources out of which the devils will be able to simulate light and raise tall structures, and he exclaims, "and what can Heav'n show more?" (II, 273). He doesn't know; he doesn't understand.

And on the other side, when Abdiel hears Satan urge rebellion in the name of freedom from God's tyranny, he responds by declaring the devil's propositions (God is a tyrant; freedom can only be found apart from him) not only "blasphemous" but "false" (V, 809). Nor are they false in a way that could be corrected by better information. What would have to be "corrected," or rather entirely replaced, is the false first premise in the light of which they are visible. They are not at all visible to Abdiel, who is in effect saying to Satan "How could you believe something that is so obviously not true?" In this sense, to say of an assertion that it is not true is to say that you don't understand it, that from your perspective, while it has all the marks of a meaningful utterance—a syntax and a semantics—it is a formal husk with no content, just sound and fury signifying nothing. And that is how you understand it, as nothing, and therefore you don't, except in a very superficial sense, understand it at all. (I would make the same analysis of Neuhaus's declaration that "a Christian can understand what a liberal atheist is saying" [29]. Sure he can: he will understand the atheist as saying error, that which is not.)

Of course, understanding in a superficial sense is what makes most of the world's business possible, and that is why, as Neuhaus correctly observes, "That two plus two equals four is true can be agreed on by Christian and non-Christian alike" (32). The question is, what does the agreement say about the level of understanding they share, and I would answer: not much. Adhering to the convention that two plus two equals four is like adhering to the convention that we drive on the right side of the road or to the convention that red means stop and green means go. You do it not because you are invested in its truth but because it is only if everyone adheres to the same conventions that automobiles won't crash and contracts will be enforceable. The truths of arithmetic are (for most of us) indisputable because it is in no one's interest to dispute them and in everyone's interest to agree about them. All of us—Christians, non-Christians, liberals, Marxists, anarchists, Republicans, Democrats, preachers, pornographers—use them and use them in situations in which it is understood that what is at stake is the maintenance of civil order and that other things that might be at stake—the nature of truth, the health of our souls, the salvation of the human race—have been, for the time, bracketed.

Liberalism is the name of the political theory whose aim it is to bracket off as much of life as possible from these thorny questions, to fashion a public sphere held together by agreements like two plus two equals four and red means stop. In reaction to the apparent failure of mankind to identify the one truly meaningful thing around which life might be organized, liberalism sets out to identify the set of truly *non*-meaningful things—things that no one will want to die for or kill for—

around which life might be organized. The history of liberalism (which begins with debates about what is or is not a "thing indifferent" and about who is to have authority over things indifferent once the items in the category have been specified) is the unhappy discovery that for everything identified as truly nonmeaningful there will be someone for whom it means everything and who will therefore want to dispute or alter or eliminate the convention.

As yet two plus two equals four has not become such a flash point of disagreement, but it could (no one used to dispute the convention of using "he" to indicate an impersonal, nongendered agent); for, as Hobbes pointed out (well in advance of the development of alternative geometries), the "doctrine of lines and figures" is not so "perpetually disputed" as the "doctrine of Right and Wrong" only "because men care not in that subject what be truth, as a thing that crosses no mans ambition."[3]

Until two plus two equals four crosses someone's ambition, it is a fact agreed on by all parties, but this doesn't mean that there are truths *above* ideology but that there are (at least by current convention) truths *below* ideology. So long as they remain below ideology (so long as they continue to be "things indifferent" and gore no one's ox), they can safely circulate in the public sphere without any fear that their use will upset its orderly workings. Obviously, "Christ is risen" is not now such a truth (although there is an argument for saying that it once was and was therefore no more controversial than two plus two equals four), and because it is not, liberalism cannot allow it to have a public life in the sense that it might be put forward as a *reason* for taking this action (going to war, passing a budget, ending affirmative action) rather than another. The very stability of the liberal state depends on (1) maintaining a large set of truths below ideology and warding off efforts to "politicize" them (hence the resistance to political accounts of literary "masterpieces" presumed to be the repository of beliefs belonging to no one and everyone); and (2) removing from the day-to-day business of life truths already ideologically charged, lest they tear apart the common fabric of society.

Of course what is and is not ideological is itself a determination of ideology, of that agenda or vision in the happy position of getting to draw the lines. What this means is that any arrangement of the categories will be to the advantage of some ideologies (whose central truths will be accorded the status of common sense) and to the disadvantage of others (whose central truths will have been labelled "not safe for deployment in public life"). In late-twentieth-century America the preferred truths and values of liberalism (autonomy, individual freedom, rational deliberation, civility) are in the first category—they "go without saying" and no agenda is legitimate unless it defers to them—and the preferred truths and values of Christianity (obedience, respect for authority and tradition, faith, the community of worship) are in the second—it is fine to adhere to them so long as you leave them at home when you enter the marketplace or the voting booth.

It is my contention that Michael McConnell, Stephen Carter, and George Marsden accept this state of affairs even as they complain about it because they accept the private/public split (McConnell), or the separation of a message from its source in religious conviction (Carter), or a distinction between reasonable and dogmatic religious views (Marsden). Neuhaus replies by suggesting that these men might be making tactical arguments, arguments designed to gain entry to the marketplace, for it is only by entering it that they might be able to transform it. I am simply reading too closely (with a "gimlet eye") discursive gestures that are "preliminary moves appropriate to what some Christians call 'pre-evangelization'" (31).

This is a good point, and one that finds support in recent events. In *Rosenberger v. University of Virginia* (1995), the Supreme Court ruled that the University of Virginia could not deny funds to an avowedly evangelistic newspaper. The university had based its policy on a distinction between university-related activities and any activity that "primarily promotes a particular belief in or about deity or an ultimate reality." But the Court rejected this "establishment clause" logic and reasoned that the key issue is "viewpoint discrimination," and that a regulation supposedly neutral (because it does not disfavor any particular religion) is nevertheless biased against the "theistic perspective." That this is precisely Michael McConnell's argument is hardly surprising, since it was he who argued the case before the Court on behalf of the Christian students.[4]

Meanwhile, sometime before the *Rosenberger* ruling, Stephen Carter's book was picked up by President Clinton, who publicly praised it and appears to have factored it into his thinking about moral issues in general and church–state issues in particular. And the large sweep and authoritative scholarship of George Marsden's book has already claimed a wide audience not confined to Christian believers. In different but related ways, then, the work of these three men (and of course not only of these three) is already enacting the strategy urged by Neuhaus: "You engage people at the point where they are engageable and then hope that they can be moved, step by step, toward the fullness of truth" (31). I am not sure that is what these authors had in mind; they present their arguments as if they were not tactical but philosophical; in short, they claim for them *coherence*, and I stand by my critique of that claim even as I acknowledge that these arguments, coherent or not, seem to be doing actual political work. (In general the incoherence of an argument is no bar to, and may even enhance, its political effectiveness.)

This brings me to a final point, which looks back to many of the issues raised in this exchange. Neuhaus notes that by the logic of my argument "a non-Christian could not understand the poetry of the very Christian John Milton" (29), a conclusion, he says, that flies in the face of the fact that "non-Christians such as Stanley Fish are recognized as authorities on Milton." This would appear to be a pincer move that would force me to choose between my (imputed) status as an authority and my thesis. I shall avoid (or evade) the choice, however, by asking what kind of understanding qualifies one to be an authority on Milton? The answer is an understanding of the issues at stake in the community of Milton criticism, and while those issues will certainly touch on questions of belief, what the critic himself believes will not be one of those questions.

When I entered the conversation in the early 1960s, among the questions were: Is Milton an Arian, that is, an anti-Trinitarian? Was he a mortalist, that is, did he believe the soul died with the body? Was he a compatabilist, that is, did he believe in both free will and determinism? Like other Miltonists, I pursued these questions by poring over Milton's prose works, reading Augustine, Tertullian, and other church fathers known to have influenced him, reading contemporary sermons and theological tracts. I was not doing this work in order to decide what I myself believed about the Trinity or the resurrection of the soul or free will but in order to decide what I believed about what Milton believed about the Trinity or the resurrection of the soul or free will. And when I did decide about what Milton believed, the decision led me not to live my life differently than I had before but to interpret Milton differently than I had before. I might give different answers to questions like "Is the Son a free agent in Book III when he offers to die in place of Adam and Eve?" and "Does Milton endorse the idea of the 'fortunate fall'"?

In giving these answers, however, I would be saying nothing about my own relation to these doctrines, and it would be perfectly possible for me to talk knowledgeably about them without having any relation to them at all because the knowledge I would be claiming is knowledge of what *Milton* thought, and not knowledge of a more intimate kind.

Indeed, an intimate (personal) knowledge of Milton's beliefs is not only not required, it is beside the point. Being an authority on Milton means being able to answer a certain kind of question while knowing that another kind of question is not even to be asked. "Was Milton really inspired by God?" is such a question; it is not debatable within the conventions of Milton criticism, unlike the question "What role does Milton's *claim* of inspiration play in his poetry and prose?" which is debated all the time under the professional rubric of "Milton's muse." If I am an authority on Milton I am a *professional* authority, a category that requires me not to share Milton's beliefs but to be able to describe them. (The same holds for the critic-historian who compares different worldviews; he *inhabits* none of them.)

The distinction was brought home to me one day when I heard a discussion of Walt Whitman on National Public Radio. The discussion leader was a professor of American literature, and he was saying the usual things professors say. However, some of those who called in to the show were true believers; they had been carrying copies of *Leaves of Grass* in their pockets since junior high school, and they pulled them out whenever life presented a problem or forced a choice. Those callers "understood" Whitman in the sense of identifying with him, and unless they learn how to distance themselves from that identification, they are unlikely to say anything of interest to a Whitman specialist. A Whitman specialist pulls out his copy of *Leaves of Grass* in order to make a point, not in order to find a truth to live by. (I am aware that this distinction reinvents the public/private split and that the attendant exclusion of personal views from the public practice of criticism has been forcefully challenged by many under the rubric—and banner—of "personal writing.")

To be sure, these categories are not as airtight as the previous paragraph may have suggested. A true believer could also be a specialist, and the fact of his belief might give him a special purchase on Whitman's or Milton's thought. But then again, a true believer might be blind to certain aspects of that thought because he was too deep inside it to see its limitations, and seeing limitations is one of the things a professional is

REASONS FOR THE DEVOUT

supposed to do, lest he be accused of worshiping what he should be studying. And if there were a true believer who also engaged in the professional practice of seeing limitations, he might find his belief diminished by that practice; his faith might be shaken. But on the other side, a nonbeliever who spent a lifetime studying Milton's beliefs might wake up one day to find that he had become so committed to them that he felt constrained to live them out in his daily life; he will have found a faith while looking for something else.

My own thoughts about these permutations (and there are more than I have mentioned) tend to coalesce around a moment in a Milton seminar I taught several years ago. The students were discoursing glibly (as my example had instructed them) about some matter or other—the intricacies of Milton's verse, or the import of his allusions to Virgil— and I without thinking burst out "No, no, he doesn't want your admiration; he wants your soul!" Was this a professional comment? Had I crossed a line? Had something happened to me of which I was only dimly aware? Was I in danger (or in hope) of no longer being an authority and becoming something else? God only knows.

CREDO

14

BELIEFS ABOUT BELIEF

The issue of belief raised at the conclusion of the last chapter is not unrelated to the main argument of this book, the argument that there are no neutral principles to which one might have recourse either to discover or to buttress our convictions as to what should be done in particular situations. Another way of formulating this argument would be to say that there is nothing that undergirds our beliefs, nothing to which our beliefs might be referred for either confirmation or correction; and, moreover, if that is the case, there is nothing interesting to say about belief in general because belief is a particular, not a general (i.e. principled), matter.

This became clear to me when I was asked to participate on a panel entitled, simply, "Credo"—I believe. My first thought was of a song of my youth, and perhaps of yours too. It begins "I believe for every drop of rain that falls, a flower grows" and ends by declaring that "every time I hear a newborn baby cry or touch a leaf or see the sky, then I know why I believe." My second thought was that maybe I should stand up and say what it is I believe and forget the "why," and my third thought was that, given the nature of belief, there could be no "why" in the usual sense; and once I thought *that,* I was back in the familiar and comfortable posture of intellectualizing belief as a philosophical or theoretical question rather than professing it publicly.

In fact I have publicly professed a belief, a belief about the nature of belief. What has been confusing, and to some distressing, is my repeated assertion that my belief about belief—or, for that matter, your belief about belief—has no relationship to any of the beliefs I or you might have when the question at issue is something other than the nature of belief. The thesis, baldly put, is that anything one believes about a particular matter is logically independent of the account one might give (and how many of us after all could give such an account) of how beliefs emerge or of what underlies them or of what confirms them or calls them into question. This thesis is resisted by both the right and the left: by the right, because it is feared that unless one believes that one's beliefs are underwritten by foundations (God, brute fact, universal Reason) independent of them, one will not really believe in one's beliefs and will engage in ad hoc, opportunistic, and wholly cynical actions; by the left, because some there hope that if we can only be persuaded that our beliefs are unsupported by foundations independent of them, we will hold them less fiercely or do fewer terrible things in their names, and in general become kinder, gentler persons.

In my view, both of these views, held by diametrically opposed parties, are mistaken, and the mistake each makes is the same—the mistake of thinking that a belief about belief has general rather than merely local consequences. The only thing that changes when one passes from one account of belief to another is the answers you will give when someone asks you (and just who that someone might be and why he or she would be asking is a nice question) to give an account of belief. Everything else will remain the same; or rather, if anything else changes, it will *not* be because you now have a new account of belief. Whatever answer one gives to the question "What underlies our beliefs?" those beliefs will function just as they did before the question was posed. I may believe that my beliefs rest on a solid foundation and you may believe that yours don't; the difference between us on that matter will not translate into a difference between our respective relationship to our respective beliefs. That is because there is no *relationship* between us and our beliefs; rather, there is an identity. The operations of my consciousness and the shape of my beliefs are not two entities somehow "relating" to one another but one entity called by different names.

This is not to say that our beliefs are supported by nothing, but that they are supported by others of our beliefs in a structure that is not so much a ladder—with underlying rungs providing a base for higher rungs—as it is a lattice or a web whose component parts are mutually constitutive. Let's say you believe something—about a poem or about affirmative action or about Darwinian evolution—and someone asks you to support that belief. Where will you look for that support? You will look (and you would not have to look far) to the interlocking structure of understandings within which the particular belief in question seems obvious. In the case of your reading or assessment of a poem, you will look to your beliefs about the nature of poetry, the sources of interpretive evidence, the relationship between aesthetic production and political conditions, and so on. In the case of affirmative action you will look to your beliefs about the nature of equality, the meaning of the Fourteenth Amendment, the relationship between history and individual responsibility. In the case of evolution, you will look to theories of evidence, the vocabulary of genes and mutations, accounts of the origins of life, etc. Of course, every fact or presupposition you cite in support of your belief could itself be in the position of requiring support in its turn, in which case you will point to those components of the picture not presently under the pressure of a demand for justification. To be sure, the process is circular, but as the operation of a dictionary is circular; one meaning explains another which explains another, which, somewhere down the line, is explained by the meaning with which you began.

It would seem that this picture of belief—in which foundations are unnecessary because every item in an interlocking structure supports its fellows—achieves its self-sufficiency at the price of the ability to explain change. If predication and justification are internal to a system of belief, what could possibly be the agency of its alteration? The answer, either surprisingly or inevitably, is belief. It is beliefs that alter beliefs, an assertion that will seem paradoxical only if you assume that beliefs are discrete items in a storehouse or inventory; but beliefs, as I have already said, are components of a structure and exist in relationships of dependence and scope to one another, and among the beliefs internal to any structure will be a belief as to what might be a reason for its own revision. Put this way, the matter might seem impossibly abstract, so let me offer two examples.

The first is from the National Public Radio program *Fresh Air*. One day a few years ago the host of that program, Terri Gross, was interviewing a self-described former white supremacist. Once the spokesperson to the media for his organization, he was now making the rounds of talk shows alerting the public to the danger represented by his ex-colleagues. Terri Gross asked the obvious question: "What made you change your mind?" Or, in words more appropriate to the present discussion, "What led you to exchange one set of beliefs for another?" The answer he gave did not take the form of a reasoned analysis of the errors of his former ways. Rather, the explanation took the form of a narrative. One day, the leader of the group was speaking about what would happen when it came to power: the blacks would be sent back to Africa; the Jews would be sent back to all the countries that had expelled them in the first place; criminals would be executed; the diseased would be quarantined; and defectives of a variety of kinds would be put into special colonies or otherwise dealt with. This last point was accompanied by a list of defectives, and among those named were persons with cleft palates. It so happened that the daughter of the once, and now instantly former, white supremacist was herself afflicted by that condition. The result? Conversion on the spot, the scales falling from his eyes and a new life as the author of a best-selling exposé.

Now there are two conclusions to be drawn from this story. The first is that it is not generalizable—one can hardly build a model of change on a set of circumstances so unique and contingent: how many people are white supremacists and have daughters with cleft palates *and* belong to a group whose leader believes that those with cleft palates pollute the master race? One could of course respond by abstracting away from these circumstances to a pattern they might be seen to instantiate, a pattern in which the spell of a false ideology is broken when the price of adherence to it is the well-being of a loved one. But this brings me to the second conclusion I would draw from this story: it needn't have turned out as it did. It would have been perfectly possible for the devoted father to have said to himself, "Well, I really love Mary, but the cause is the cause and I guess she'll have to go." After all, remember Abraham and Isaac and the hard demands of faith. It is only in retrospect that we can construct a cause-and-effect account of how this or that change of mind came about, and that account will tell us nothing about what might happen next time.

My second example is drawn from a context closer to home. Not long ago I heard the philosopher Richard Rorty deliver a characteristically strong and polemical talk. In the question period he was challenged on a central point and replied with a vigorous reassertion of his position. But then he paused and said, "I've heard that Donald Davidson is working on an argument that would go in a different direction from mine, and anything Davidson puts forward I'll have to take seriously." What this means is that internal to the web of Rorty's beliefs is a belief in the importance of anything Donald Davidson says. And even though Rorty doesn't yet know what Davidson may be saying on this particular subject, he is poised to hear it with an attention and a deference he did not grant to the audience member who questioned him.

My point is that each of us has a Donald Davidson, that is, someone or some text—the Pope, the Bible, Elvis, Lionel Trilling, Nietzsche, Satchel Paige, the *Turner Diaries*—whose authority is assumed, to the extent that we will think at least twice before dismissing or not taking seriously his or her or its pronouncements. This does not mean that one's center of authority is fixed forever and will always be in place, exercising its monitoring and admonitory functions. As the white supremacist example shows, any authority, no matter how longstanding its hold on your imagination, can be dislodged in an instant, although that instant cannot be willed, cannot be planned for, and need not ever occur. But if it does, it will not be because an independent reality has presented itself in such a way that a structure of belief must simply bow to it but because embedded in that structure will be something—an allegiance, a fear, a hope—that is strongly affirmed in a crisis of decision or choice. The moment of its affirmation will be the moment at which the web of belief might undergo a basic alteration—you could leave the cult you have lived for or abandon the argument that has made your career—but the mechanics of that alteration will be entirely internal.

None of this is particularly new or controversial. In an essay entitled simply "Belief," the philosopher John Heil offers it as a commonplace that beliefs do not exist in isolation or in relation to independent facts but "owe their character to relations they bear to other beliefs" (45).[1] He thinks it equally obvious that one does not choose his or her beliefs or decide to discard them, for "*believing* appears not to be voluntary" (47); rather, "acquiring a belief," he says, "is equivalent to catching a cold" (47). In another essay, Alvin Plantinga observes that "whether or not I accept [my] beliefs isn't really up to me at all; I can no more refrain from believing [them] than I can refrain from conforming to the laws of gravity" (439); and he adds (here following Roderick Chisolm) that a belief is justified when there is a "*relation of fittingness*" between it and "one's epistemic base," which "includes the other things one believes" (440).[2] William James said much the same thing ninety years ago in *Pragmatism*, when he observed that "We plunge forward into the field of fresh experience with the beliefs our ancestors and we have made already; these determine what we notice; what we notice determines what we do" (70).[3] In short, beliefs emerge historically and in relation to the other beliefs that are already the content of our consciousness. This does not mean that beliefs or the actions that follow from them are irrational but that rationality—the marshaling of evidence, the giving of reasons, the posing of objections, the uncovering and correction of mistakes—is what takes place in the light of our beliefs. Belief is prior to rationality; rationality can only unfold in the context of convictions and commitments it neither chooses nor approves.

It follows that if belief is prior to rationality, there is not very much to say about it, except the largely negative things I have already said: you can't choose it, you can't discard it, you can't resist it, and you can't—except within the circle it itself draws—examine it. Nor can you ignore it or decide that it doesn't matter. It is because belief is at some level inaccessible to consciousness that it is so crucial to—indeed constitutive of—consciousness. Moreover, if it is within belief that deliberation occurs and evidence becomes perspicuous and reasons persuasive, then what you believe will, as James suggests, be determinative of what you see, of what you notice, and, down the road, of what you do.

In the end, then, the only thing we can do with our beliefs, since we can't choose them or discard them or alter them at will, is live them out—except for our belief, if we should happen to have one, about belief. *That* we can't live out because an account of our mental processes—and that is what a belief about belief is—cannot affect our mental processes. If the account is right—if it accords with the epistemology built into us by God or nature—that epistemology will continue to function as it always did, since, as Milton's Raphael says to Adam about the operation of the Heavens, "it needs not thy belief" (*PL*, VIII, 136). And if the account is wrong—if it is at odds with the ways of knowing we really have—those ways of knowing will again function as they always did, made neither better nor worse by our mistaken theory of them.

PUTTING THEORY IN ITS PLACE

Let me once again pose two questions I have asked and answered (or refused to answer) often in the preceding pages. What follows in the way of particular positions from the argument that neutral principles don't exist? And where do I stand on the substantive matters that usually come up in these discussions—abortion, the death penalty, welfare reform, affirmative action, the line between church and state, environmental regulation, and so on? Stephen Macedo once ventured a guess on the second question when he said that Fish is in favor of affirmative action, abortion rights, and equal treatment of gays and lesbians, and he generally opposes university speech codes.[1] Well, as the great singer Meatloaf might put it, two out of four ain't so good. I *am* in favor of affirmative action and gay and lesbian rights; but I do not support abortion rights (although what I would support in this vexed area is not clear to me), and I disfavor speech codes only in those contexts where the good they do (by my lights) will be outweighed by the trouble and litigation they produce (obviously a thoroughly empirical/pragmatic position rather than a theoretical or principled one).

Therefore it is not the case, as Macedo went on to say, that my substantive political opinions are in accord with the liberal academic norm. But even if they were, it would neither prove nor disprove anything; for my target is never liberalism in the sense of a set of particular political positions on debated issues; rather, my target is Liberalism with a capital L, that is, liberalism as an effort to bracket metaphysical or religious views—the sources of intractable endless disputes—so that public questions can be considered in terms that will be accessible to, and appear reasonable to, everyone, despite the evident multiplicity of what John Rawls calls "comprehensive doctrines." With respect to this project (which is the project of theory or philosophy in general; liberalism is just one relatively recent name for it) my position is, first, that it is impossible because there is no specification of the facts of a matter independent of some or other comprehensive background already assumed and in place. Indeed, independently of any comprehensive doctrine there is neither perception nor judgment; and therefore when someone urges a conclusion that supposedly follows from the setting aside of comprehensive doctrines, it is really a conclusion that follows from a comprehensive doctrine that, at least for the moment, dare not speak its name and is in hiding. The requirement that comprehensive doctrines be set aside is not merely unattractive, or immoral, or inadvisable; it is not something anyone can do, and since it is not something anyone can do, nothing follows from it.

Now this does not mean that there is nothing to the theory project; just that it doesn't travel beyond the precincts it itself establishes. Those are the precincts of an academic discipline, not of a natural kind. That discipline has been assigned, or has assigned itself, the task of asking and answering certain questions, questions like "What is the nature of justice?" "Are individuals autonomous?" "Is there one truth or are there many truths?" "Is the mind independent of the body?" "What is the relationship between belief and reason?" "What if we are all brains in a vat?" Both the manner of posing these questions and the acceptable ways of trying to answer them are functions of the history (again disciplinary) in the context of which they have been experienced as urgent. That kind of urgency—theoretical or philosophical urgency—is not what is felt by those persons confronting the real-life problems for which this general form of inquiry is supposed to provide solutions. It doesn't and couldn't, because as a *general* form of inquiry, it proceeds (and this is especially true of the branch of moral philosophy that dominates discussions of political theory) by abstracting away from particular situations and stripping from them the specificity and detail that come along with situatedness. The promise is that once this process of abstraction has made everything clear, you will be able to use its answers to order the specific situations from which it moved so resolutely away.

But the promise can never be redeemed because the answers so derived are empty of substantive content—substantive content is what the abstracting process flees—and therefore they have no purchase whatsoever on the real-life issues to which you would apply them. Justice as fairness, mutual respect, autonomous self-government—these may be the prizes triumphantly offered to a waiting world at the end of still another interminable analysis of the conditions of the Good Life, but if you hold them in your hand and wait for them to tell you what to do next, they have nothing to say; or rather, they will say something only when they have been supplemented by the very local/historical concerns it is claimed they transcend.

Once supplemented, however, theoretical terms are no longer theoretical in the claimed sense of guiding practice from a position outside or above it; such filled-in terms will be *internal* to the practice and have force only for those who already move within the practice's assumptions and norms. On those occasions when theory has been effectively deployed, it will have lost its theoretical innocence and become a part of that from which it would be distinguished. The mistake is to reify theory, to think that it has an independent existence (except in the precincts of philosophy seminars) and therefore to oppose it to something else. Macedo makes a version of that mistake when he takes me to be saying that "reason does not provide a way to transcend our historical circumstances." No, I am making the stronger assertion that there is no such thing as reason apart from its appearance in historical circumstances, an appearance that will always take the form of *reasons*, that is, of arguments already inflected and infected by some prechosen partisan vision or angle. I don't oppose reason to history; I historicize reason, and thus I am able at once to acknowledge the power of reasons—they are, often, the motor and vehicle of decisionmaking—and yet deny to Reason as a suprahistorical entity the power to do anything (because it doesn't exist).

Now when I say that I historicize reason, I might as well have said I rhetoricize reason; that is, I treat reason, or more properly reasons, as components of the effort to tell a persuasive story that follows from and extends one's deepest convictions. This is why, as Macedo notes, I cite with approval Ronald Dworkin's notion of "articulate consistency."[2] By that phrase Dworkin means something theoretical—things hanging together in a way that is normative, even natural (Dworkin's flirtation with natural law has often been noted)—whereas I mean by it something rhetorical—things hanging together by virtue of someone skilled enough to link them in the same polemical structure. The fact that judges, as Macedo says, "think about their decisions in terms of the explanation and justification they will offer" does not make their practice theoretical, for the explanations and justifications are drawn not from moral logic but from the sedimented history of precedent, a history that teaches you how to fit fact situations under the umbrella of categories and arguments that have been persuasive in the past. Ah, you say to yourself, we can put this under the rubric of third-party beneficiary or illegitimate punitive damages or promise for benefits already received; the question being asked is not what is right in some abstract realm of moral thought but what will go, what will take, what will be received as a respectable legal argument, where "respectable" means we've seen it before, we recognize this as something people like us say when issues like this come up. Judging and politics may, as Macedo declares, be "justificatory enterprises," but that does not distinguish them from rhetorical enterprises; it just tells us what kind of rhetorical enterprises they are.

Reasons, evidence, explanations, justifications—these inevitable constituents of thought do not guide or generate political decisions; they follow in their wake. Robert George, in a comment on Chapter 12, is right to observe that nowadays it is prolifers who make the scientific question of when the beginning of life occurs the key one in the abortion controversy, while prochoicers "want to transform the question into a 'metaphysical' or 'religious' one" by distinguishing between mere biological life and moral life; but he is wrong to imply that the relationship between the opposing positions and the kind of evidence each now brings to bear is theoretical or principled. Either side begins with a firm sense of the outcome it desires—the criminalization of abortion or the legal protection of women's rights—and then looks around for arguments, formulas, buzz words, whatever, with which to buttress and prosecute its case. Until recently, prochoicers might have cast themselves as defenders of rational science against the forces of ignorance and superstition, but when scientific inquiry started pushing back the moment when significant life (in some sense) begins, they shifted tactics and went elsewhere in search of rhetorical weaponry. Similarly, in the debate between evolutionists and creation scientists, it is the latter who have become expert in the arguments of poststructuralism and postmodernism, not because they believe in those arguments—at one level people like Philip Johnson and Michael McConnell almost certainly despise them—but because they found in them a means of discomforting the enemy by calling into question the epistemological stability of his scientific knowledge.

It would be not at all difficult to imagine someone both prolife and antievolution, who triumphantly brandished the latest news from experimental biology in one context and deconstructed it in the other. Nor would this be inconsistency or insincerity; the consistency would reside in a fidelity to the basic goal and sincerity in the obligation to advance that goal by whatever means come to hand. (There is also the delicious pleasure of routing the enemy with weapons thought to be in his arsenal rather than in yours.) George might find this perspective cynical and prefer the image, as he puts it, of an "open minded person who sincerely wishes to settle his mind." But minds are never open except in the context of matters of indifference; on matters of real and antecedent concern, minds are always and already settled in some direction or other, and subsequent reasoning is shaped by the direction the mind has already taken.

As I have argued so many times in these pages, rational liberal theory with its abstract vocabulary of fairness, mutual respect, toleration, and so on is incapable of generating outcomes unless it is supplemented by the substantive considerations against which it defines itself. The theory project is coherent only within the terms of its elaboration as an academic enterprise, one populated by people who like to pose and present solutions to philosophical puzzles. Outside of that very limited context, theory—liberal or any other of the strong neo-Kantian kind—is without a purchase on any of the problems to which it might be applied. When a theoretical vocabulary does seem to be effective and to generate outcomes, it is because it has become a rhetorical vocabulary, a vocabulary already freighted with the assumptions of some or other agenda, although the work it does will almost always be presented as proceeding from no agenda whatsoever but from the high plain of general truth or higher order impartiality. Theory, therefore, has no consequences except those that emerge from a political deployment of its terms, a deployment that can always be undone if another party seizes the same terms and molds them to its purposes. In short, there is nothing general to be said about or for theory; theory is not theoretically an interesting topic. Faced with a dilemma or a formidable task, the theory you wield will not help you, the absence of a theory will not disable you, and even the knowledge that theories have no fixed or necessary cash value—the knowledge I am trying to impart now—will not clarify your alternatives or put you in a better epistemological place than those who continue, mistakenly, to think that theory matters.

But if this is the case—if theory or philosophy or strong liberalism can't possibly do what they promise to do and if learning the lesson of their failure leaves you no better off than those who have never heard it—why go on so much about it, why spend so much energy and so many pages insisting, as Macedo put it, "that theory needs to be kept in its place"? Surely the very vehemence of some of my arguments suggests that I believe that there is something really at stake here, and that if I am persuasive, something will have importantly changed. Sandy Levinson has speculated about this question, and he wonders whether I might want my readers "to remember that other people may have different beliefs, which they are as sincerely committed to as you are to your own." But he quickly and correctly backs away from his own suggestion, first because it would have me claiming consequences to my position despite my many declarations that there are none; and second because if I were to urge people to withdraw from the fierceness of their beliefs in deference to those others who believe just as fiercely but differently, I would be coming perilously close, as Levinson points out, to the "kind of toleration-oriented liberalism" I regularly attack.

I know that a lot of people think that the very existence of opponents who are as well-educated and (in most things) as sensible as oneself is a reason for relaxing the aggressiveness of one's polemical assertions—the logic is "Maybe they know something I don't know" or "Maybe God knows something neither of us knows"—but if it is a reason for anything, it is a reason for wonder at the persistence of error, even on the part of those who have had all the educational advantages. That there is resistance by well-credentialed persons to your own views is a (regrettable) political fact from which no moral or normative conclusion follows, unless of course among the resisters are some whose words and writings you regard as holy writ.

But this still leaves the question "Why am I so vehement about putting theory in its place?" unanswered. The answer I would give is a political, not a theoretical one. Although the vocabulary of liberal theory is incoherent and empty (unless filled by the substantive judgments it pushes away) and cannot do the work (of clarifying, ordering, illuminating) claimed for it, it can nevertheless do work; and sometimes that work is, according to my lights, bad. The incoherence of a line of thought is no bar to its political effectiveness; like any other rhetoric (and a rhetoric is what theory always is), it can be used as a weapon with which to club one's opponents. So it is, for example, in the debates about affirmative action. If you are a proponent of affirmative action, as I am, you want to be able to cite the history of racial oppression and make it a strong if not conclusive part of your argument; but, as I have already said, the point of the theoretical terms that make up strong liberalism—justice, fairness, impartiality, mutual respect, autonomy, and on and on—is to de-emphasize historical considerations in favor of the abstract moral considerations that should *always* apply, no matter what the configuration and hierarchies of social and political forces. It follows, therefore, that I will want to discredit the vocabulary of theory, not so much in order to make a move in the theory or antitheory game but in order to bring to the foreground the kind of evidence—historical evidence—that theory talk tends to filter out. Discrediting a theory *as such* is an internal exercise, and given my views about the inconsequentiality of theory and the inconsequentiality of the inconsequentiality of theory, not an exercise that should be accompanied by passion or moral outrage. Discrediting theory because it is being used to deny or diminish the force of facts I consider to be paramount is quite another matter, and when I do that, often in the op-ed pages of *The New York Times*, I tend to get quite excited, even agitated.

I would give the same kind of answer to another of Levinson's questions: "Why is Fish so dismissive of rationalist religion when it is surely an important form of religious belief and practice?" (George makes the same point.) The answer is that my argument, like any other, enters a conversation whose terms have already been set; and therefore the shape and thrust of my argument will to some extent be determined by what I find already in place. What I found in place were attacks, explicit and implicit, on the kind of religiosity exhibited by Vicki Frost, David Koresh, and the so-called religious right. I ranged myself against those attacks because that was the position available to me and the one that would, in the context of an ongoing debate, afford the best opportunity to be interventionary and formulate a position that had some bite to it.

Finally, let me respond to Macedo's withdrawal from large claims and his insistence, with Rawls, that political liberalism "dispenses with externalist moorings" because "much of what liberal theorists are doing . . . is trying to think about and improve the workings of liberal democratic politics looked at from the inside." My critique, he notes, is to the point only if liberalism is a "theoretical phenomenon with impossible ambitions," and as such, he declares, as I have done before, "liberalism does not exist." With this I have no quarrel, in part because it is so minimalist that there is nothing to quarrel *with*. If liberal theorists are busy shoring up liberalism on the inside and crafting arguments that will make it look good from the outside, they are not theorists but apologists, and my response to them would depend on whether or not I was sympathetic to the values and agendas they were hawking. If I were unsympathetic, if I belonged to some interest group other than that formed by persons with advanced degrees, tenured positions, vacation homes in the mountains, second wives, and fancy foreign cars (in fact I don't), I might oppose them tooth and nail—not because they were theoretically inadequate or insufficiently deontological but because, from where I sat and lived and had my being, they were wrong.

TRUTH AND TOILETS

If you say that someone or something is wrong, you will often be asked to provide a basis for your judgment that is independent of the social, political, and biographical circumstances in which it was formed. The thesis of this book has been that no such basis is available and that the ordinary resources that come along with your situation, education, and personal history are both all you have and all you need. There is a philosophy, or anti-philosophy, that takes much the same position. It is called pragmatism, and not long ago I was asked to deliver the concluding remarks at a conference on the revival of pragmatism held at the City University of New York's Graduate Center. I was and am tempted to do the short version and just say that one of the participants, professor of law Tom Grey, gets it right when he declares that no result we reach in philosophical investigation will "undermine the working standards by which we assess claims based on evidence and argument," and adds that the pursuit of philosophical explanations is not compulsory on pain of having one's character impugned (254).[1] The first statement puts philosophy in its place as a special activity whose successes or failures do not entail or even make more likely successes or failures in activities other than the activity of doing philosophy; the second statement refuses to confer a superior moral status on those who engage regularly in this odd pursuit. Some people do philosophy, some people (lots more) don't, and those who do have not ascended to some rarified realm of reflection or critical self-consciousness from which they bring back the news to their less enlightened brethren; they merely have the knack of doing a trick some others can't do, and the competence they have acquired travels no further than the very small arenas in which that trick is typically performed and rewarded.

I take Hilary Putnam to be saying something like that when he asks "What if all the philosophers are wrong, and the way it seems to be is the way it *is*?" (40).[2] Or, if I might rephrase, what if the answers philosophers come up with are answers only in the highly artificial circumstances of the philosophy seminar, where ordinary reasons for action are systematically distrusted and introduced only to be dismissed as naive? And what if, once the philosopher goes away or ceases himself or herself to be a philosopher, those ordinary reasons return *without* a vengeance and action is just as it was before: if not unproblematic, at least not mysterious.

This is one of the lessons pragmatism—the philosophy that, in William James's words, "turns away from abstraction . . . fixed priorities . . . and pretended absolutes"—teaches.[3] And because it is, Putnam's other question—"How can a pragmatist be a realist?" (38)—might appropriately be answered with the question "How could a pragmatist be anything else?" For after all, a pragmatist believes in the sufficiency of human practices and is not dismayed when those practices are shown to be grounded in nothing more (or less) than their own traditions and histories. The impossibility of tying our everyday meanings and values to meanings and values less local does not lead the pragmatist to suspect their reality but to suspect the form of thought that would deny it. When the dream of finding invariant meanings underwritten by God or the structure of rationality is exploded, what remains is not dust and ashes but the solidity *and* plasticity of the world human beings continually make and remake.

In short, in the wake of formalism's failure—the failure of the search for neutral principles—everything remains as it was. It is true that once you start going down the antiformalist road (with pragmatism or any other form of antifoundationalist thought), there is no place to stop. Once contextualism is given its head and apparently firm meanings are made to shift and blur whenever a speaker is reimagined or a setting varied, no mechanism, not even the reification of context itself, will suffice to put on the brakes. But it is also true that when you come to the end of the antiformalist road, what you will find waiting for you is formalism;

that is, you will find the meanings that are perspicuous for you, given your membership in what I have called an interpretive community, and so long as you inhabit that community (and if not that one, then in some other), those meanings will be immediately conveyed by public structures of language and image to which you and your peers can confidently point. (Of course, members of other communities will not see what you point to or will see something else, but that's life.) It is only if you expect those meanings to survive every sea change of situation that you will be tempted to declare them insubstantial, mere constructions. But that temptation and worry is one you should no longer feel if you have taken the antiformalist road all the way to its last stop.

In saying this, I affirm what many who write on these matters have already said: philosophy should underwrite our ordinary ways of talking and our commonsense experience of the world. I would only add that our commonsense experience of the world doesn't need to be underwritten by philosophy, even by pragmatist philosophy, which can no more shore up the world of common sense than analytic philosophy can break it down. If pragmatism points out that its rivals cannot deliver what they promise—once-and-for-all answers to always relevant questions—pragmatism should itself know enough not to promise anything, or even to recommend anything. If pragmatism is true, it has nothing to say to us; no politics follows from it or is blocked by it; no morality attaches to it or is enjoined by it.

If you know that someone has a pragmatist account of belief, you know nothing about what he or she will do in a moment of crisis or decision. Indeed, this is true of all epistemological accounts, whether they be pragmatist or not. The way you are in the world of practices is independent of the account you might give of those practices, be it realist, rationalist, pragmatist, or whatever. Your preferred vocabulary of explanation will not, in and of itself, either gift you or burden you with the certainties or uncertainties it proclaims; your preferred vocabulary of explanation will take you to neither heaven nor hell. That's the bad news, at least for those who either harbor high hopes or entertain dark fears. The good news is that because your preferred vocabulary will not take you to either heaven or hell, you are free to deploy it (or not) when the occasion suggests it would be good to do so. And this holds too for vocabularies you do not prefer; for since they won't commit you to acting in any particular way, you can traffic in them without worrying that some bad residue will be left on your skin.

In this book I have spent a good deal of time arguing that the vocabulary of mainstream First Amendment jurisprudence—made up of words and phrases like autonomy, freedom, the marketplace of ideas, individual self-improvement—is either empty and incoherent or filled with a coherence I don't like. But I would never urge that this same vocabulary be abandoned, only that it should not be worshiped. If we worship it, we shall find ourselves saddled with things we don't want; but if we avail ourselves of it—with a lightness that will be bearable in that it does not penetrate to our being—it can be put in the service of what we do want. As Richard Rorty puts it, vocabularies with philosophical pretensions are fine as long as they are regarded as helps to our practices "rather than as foundations for them."[4]

David Luban and Michel Rosenfeld take the opposite view when they argue that law cannot do without first philosophy (indeed Luban seems at times to believe that to think something is to do philosophy), that when cases involve the issue of teaching creationist science or the protection of artistic expression or the justice of affirmative action, there is no agreement on ends and we must fall back on foundations.[5] No, we will fall back on and deploy rhetorics—highly charged vocabularies and formulas like the fact/value distinction, reverse racism, the independence of art from politics—and what we will do with these rhetorics is use them as clubs against our opponents, all the while daring them to deny the force of a way of talking that has captured the heart and mind of America. The advantage of vocabularies or rhetorics over foundations is that they are already available in a storehouse of stock arguments, a storehouse Aristotle first furnished in his *Rhetoric* and one we have been adding to since. Foundations have to be sought, and as pragmatism tells us, they are never found. Rhetorics in long, short, and middle versions are already there for the quarrying; and what's even better, using them in a moment of need commits you to nothing, necessarily, in the next moment. After you have gotten from one what you want, you can just put it back on the shelf.

I know from long experience that this will be heard as cynicism or something worse, but it would be cynicism only if I were recommending something as opposed to describing something, describing what we all do unreflectively and quite sincerely: look around for ways of conveying and making attractive the points in which we fervently believe.

I would say as much about any rhetoric and vocabulary, expect for the vocabulary of religion, which seems to me to be quite another kettle of fish. When Richard Rorty wants to de-divinize philosophy, I say go to it—God speed—but when he wants to de-divinize theology, something doesn't ring true because theology doesn't seem to be the kind of thing you can de-divinize and still have anything left. As Giles Gunn observes, if you remove from religion "the obsession with . . . ranking and evaluation, . . . the question becomes whether you are left with anything that can be recognized as . . . religion" (411).[6] One knows what Rorty has in mind; it is what Locke had in mind when he announced in the first paragraph of the *Letter Concerning Toleration* that the true characteristic of any church is tolerance, and what Mill had in mind when he commends religious sentiments so long as they do not smack of the doctrinal, so long as Christians, for example, take care to be "just to infidelity."[7] But I confess myself as never having been able to understand these assertions, except as a determination to retain the name of something even after you've cut its heart out. It's like *Hamlet* without the prince, or like veggie-burgers. Where's the beef?

Religions are not tolerant; that's why they are religions and not philosophical systems. Rorty is perfectly comfortable with Christianity "as a strong poem, one . . . among many" (27), but Christianity's claims are more exclusive.[8] A religion without doctrine? To quote Grey again, "Philosophy is not compulsory, in the way religion is in the eyes of a . . . believer" (268). I take that to mean that you can walk away from a philosophy, even from one to which you have been persuaded; and you can do that because the answers you give in the very special situation of a philosophy seminar have very little purchase on the situations of ordinary life, in relation to which they are either too remote or too specialized, not to the point. You can't, however, walk away from your religion, if it is really yours and not a collection of sentiments trotted out for special—and intermittent—occasions. Your religion is always to the point: you shall love the Lord thy God with all thy heart and all thy soul and all thy might, not just on Friday evenings or Sunday mornings, when you'd rather be reading Wallace Stevens. Religious claims do not relax, nor do they respect any line between the private and the public.

That is why liberalism cannot tolerate them; they violate its religion of tolerance, the religion instituted by Locke three hundred years ago. Grey reports Rawls (Locke's heir) asking "How is it possible for those affirming a religious doctrine . . . based on religious authority . . . also to hold a reasonable political conception that supports a just democratic regime?" (254). That's the easy end of the question, and it is answered by Grey's report of the degree of agreement about the law and social life he is able to reach with an evangelical friend. The hard end is "How is it possible for a political conception centered on reason and democracy to do justice to those uninvested in either the reasonable or the democratic?" and the answer is that it isn't possible. In the eyes of a democratically reasonable person, what is owed to the strong religious believer is fairness, but fairness is not what the strong religious believer wants; what he wants is a world ordered in accordance with the faith he lives by and would die for, and liberal democracy (or pragmatism) isn't going to give him that, ever. When Grey tells us that his evangelical friend "turns out to be a pragmatist for legal purposes" (267), I conclude that he isn't really a committed believer because he has allowed secular authorities to tell him when and in what precincts he can invoke and act on his religious convictions. My diagnosis is confirmed when this same supposed fundamentalist is prepared to respect the diversity of conceptions of the good "even if he and his co-religionists become politically dominant" (269). Why would he be prepared to do that unless respect for diversity had become his religion, and what he likes to call his religion has become that set of pieties he rehearses at catechism?

Tom Grey's friend is a far cry from Vicki Frost, whose quarrel with her local school board I have discussed in previous chapters. To the argument that her daughter was not being indoctrinated into alternative viewpoints but merely exposed to them, she replied that exposure is precisely what she feared (the point was a winner in the Amish case, *Wisconsin v. Yoder*, largely because the Amish wanted nothing more than to be left to themselves) and that the distinction between indoctrination and exposure was an artifact of the very liberalism that was oppressing her. It is the voice of someone like Vicki Frost, of someone who thinks that diversity, freedom of expression, fairness, and dialogue are bad ideas that pave the road to hell, who should stand in for Tom Grey's oh-so-reasonable friend. What does liberalism, and the pragmatism that is its philosophical support, say to her?

What it will usually say is that we of course respect your religious views and will not be a party to their silencing, but you must understand that we cannot allow those views to spill over into the public sphere, where they might succeed in enacting themselves into law and thereby disenfranchising or marginalizing the views of others. In short, Vicki Frost will be read the lesson Madison read to the nation in the *Remon-*

strance (1785)—that religion is after all a wholly private matter. But that is precisely what Vicki Frost does not believe—she believes that her religious commitments extend to every aspect of her life and to *yours* too—and she will be understandably frustrated when she is told not that her religious views are false (that at least would be a challenge she could pick up) but that they are beside the point.

One might think I exaggerate the tension between Vicki Frost and the tolerant society in whose many mansions she is what Stanley Hauerwas has called a resident alien; after all, she lived in that society quite comfortably (we can presume) before she decided to file her suit. True, but then the pinch came, and she realized what was really at stake, and at that moment the accommodations she had no doubt previously made became experienced as intolerable burdens. Liberalism in general and pragmatism in particular (at least when it takes the form of tolerance and the enlargement of sympathy) are dedicated to warding off that moment, to doing everything possible to make sure that when the pinch comes, we have as relaxed and expansive a relationship to our convictions as we can manage.

That is why one of pragmatism's strengths is what has often been cited as one of its weaknesses. Pragmatism has no firm outline, is vague, and means many things to many people. But as the wolf said to Little Red Riding Hood, "The better to eat you with, my dear." A pragmatism so amorphous and omnivorous has the two advantages of • being a very bad target—you feel that there is nothing to hit—and • being a very bad substitute for the absolutes it tilts against—if you don't know exactly what it is, it is hard to march under its banner. Pragmatism may be the one theory—if it is a theory—that clears the field not only of its rivals but of itself, at least as a positive alternative.

This parsimonious view of pragmatism's imperatives is not one shared by most self-identified pragmatists, who tend to turn the pragmatist withdrawal from strong claims into a strong claim of their own, the claim that pragmatism, if adhered to, leads to forms of behavior that make the world a better place and you a better person: kinder, gentler, more respectful of others, and less likely to hold it against someone that his beliefs are not yours. That claim takes the form of linking pragmatism to democracy and to poetry. The hinge that supposedly ties the three together is a distrust of received views, unimpeachable authorities, and unexamined dogma.

The idea is that democracy, rather than being monistic and theo-cratic, is pluralist and secular; holding no ideas sacred, it is open to all ideas so long as they are willing to subject themselves to the scrutiny of public reason. What democracy requires, says Richard Bernstein, is "the cultivation of critical habits of deliberation" (147).[9] And Richard Poirier tells us that those same habits are what is cultivated by poetry; a word in a poem, says Poirier, is "alert to the constraints of its own dou-bleness, combining and contending with other elements in the poem in an ongoing process of inflection and change." Being faithful to that process is the "central work" of the pragmatist-poet, who turns away from "already familiar and knowable forms of life" and opts instead for "the continuous creation of truth, an act that must be . . . never ending" (347).[10] In short, poetry (here in the position reserved in earlier versions of the pragmatist story for science) schools one in the habit of resisting the temptations of closure and dogma.

It is all very neat and seems to hang together nicely: if you read a lot of poetry you will be in rehearsal for the work of rejecting the lure of final solutions (even when, especially when, they are your own); you will then perform that work in the public forums of democracy, where you will be slow to insist on the primacy of your own interests and open to considering the interests of others; and underwriting both your life as a reader and your life as a citizen will be the pragmatist distrust of "all forms of foundationalism, all attempts to establish philosophy on unchanging a priori postulates" (84).[11]

Now I don't doubt that there are some people whose aesthetic, polit-ical, and philosophical inclinations dovetail in this way, but the conver-gence in them of parallel dispositions would be fortuitous and neither necessary nor even likely. The reason is one I have already given: your philosophical views are independent of your views (and therefore of your practices) in any realm of life other than the very special and rari-fied realm of doing philosophy. If you believe that your convictions have their source not in ultimate truths or foundations but in contingent tra-ditions of inquiry and are therefore revisable, that belief, in and of itself, will not render you disposed to revise your convictions or turn you into a person who enters into situations provisionally and with epistemic modesty. You can give all the standard answers to all the pragmatist questions and still be an authoritarian in the classroom, a decided con-servative in cultural matters, or inclined to the absolutes of theology. (I am, in differing degrees, all three.)

Nor will your pragmatism—or, more properly, the fact that you will give pragmatist-type answers to some traditional questions about truth, objectivity, language, and reference—especially fit you for participation in democracy, if only because democracy is grounded not in philosophy (although philosophy may be called on to shore it up or perform the work of public relations) but in a set of political arrangements laid down in the *Federalist Papers* and enacted in the Constitution—checks and balances, divided government, mechanisms for orderly change, obstacles to hasty change, all devices designed to keep at bay the conflicts that tore English society apart in the seventeenth century. They do that job not by making people less aggressive in holding their beliefs but by making it more difficult (although not impossible) to use those beliefs as the occasion for, and justification of, oppression. Provisionality, openness, and toleration are not what the mechanisms of democracy generate but what they *enforce* against the inclinations of citizens, who remain as dogmatic, closed-minded, and bigoted as they were before democracy emerged. These virtues (if they are virtues; there is a powerful antiliberal argument always in the course of being remounted) are the properties of the system, not of those who live under it.

If democracy has to some extent worked, it is because certain political structures are firmly in place and not because its citizens have internalized the sayings of Emerson, Dewey, and James. Pragmatism may have emerged under democratic conditions (although its basic tenets were long ago articulated by Cicero and Machiavelli), but it neither produces nor necessarily accompanies democracy. And if pragmatism has no special affinity for democracy, neither does it have any special relationship to the positions you might take on the issues that turn up in the democratic landscape. Your political allegiances are more likely to be a function of whether repeal of the capital gains tax will benefit you than of your epistemology, should you be a person so odd as to have one.

And reading poetry? Well, that's something I do for a living, and as it happens I do it in pretty much the way Poirier urges, attending to the meanings sense hurries past in its rush to completion and univocal coherence. I read that way because I was taught to do so by my instructors at Yale and by the writings of William Empson. My reading style, in short, is a *professional* practice, something I picked up in the course of an apprenticeship designed to prepare me for performances in the classroom and learned journals; its relationship to any of my other performances (as a father, citizen, consumer, dean) is entirely contingent and in my case almost nonexistent. The only carryover I'm aware of are those moments when I annoy someone by detecting in his perfectly straightforward speech meanings he did not intend and (quite reasonably) finds distracting. Just as you can have a pragmatist position in philosophy and have any number of political views (or have none), so you can be an Empsonian reader of poetry and be a straight-on literalist, looking neither to the semantic left or right, when you set out to do other kinds of work.

Indeed, I would go further: you had *better* be such a literalist when you argue a case or talk to your dean or bargain with a car dealer or give directions to someone trying to get to your house. Ruth Anna Putnam criticizes philosophers "who lead one life in their studies and another outside" and argues for a philosophy "that enables us to lead one life, to be as consistent as is humanly possible" (62).[12] I suppose one could achieve that consistency, but I'm not sure how human it would be, and I suspect that the result would be something akin to insanity. We laugh at the plumber who tours Europe and comes back talking of nothing but the primitive state of showers and the absence of copper piping. Why should we not laugh equally hard at the philosopher who tours the world and finds nothing to remark on but fallacies, category mistakes, and insufficiently nuanced modals? The answer is that while we don't think that a focus on toilets is appropriate to any and all situations, we do think that a focus on philosophical puzzles can never be beside the point. But we think so only because we mistake a professional practice—and a professional conversation which we may decline to join and be none the worse for it—for life itself. (The thesis that toilets are more central to life than philosophy seems to me self-evident, perhaps only because I am the son, brother, and nephew of plumbers.)

The truth is that neither the benefits nor the troubles of professional practices come along with us when we leave their precincts and enter another. It is the failure to understand this truth that leads people to worry about the effect of postmodernist or pragmatist philosophy on their ability to do things other than philosophize. James Kloppenberg, for example, wonders (in an earlier manuscript version of his published essay) "how history written by 'new' pragmatists could contribute anything distinctively different from novels or poetry to helping us to understand experience." The answer is that a history written by a new pragmatist would be just like any other history and subject to the usual evaluations, so long as the new pragmatist were really writing a history and not interrogating the assumptions within which history is written. If he were doing the latter, he would not be a historian at all but a metahistorian, and he would be engaging in a practice with its own traditions, exemplary achievements, authoritative forebearers, and influential contemporaries.

The mistake is to think that news from the one practice can either authorize or deauthorize the other, to think that if your metatheory puts into question the basic components of historical work—facts, evidence, agency, cause and effect—you would no longer be able to do it (or would do it in some odd and self-defeating way, perhaps by tagging every assertion with a warning that it is unsupportable and the mere product of social construction). I understand the reasoning: it asks "If you don't believe in the hardness of fact, how can you write history?" But the question assumes that before you lost your epistemological innocence to the new pragmatism, you went around *actively* believing in fact, and that having had that active belief taken away from you, fact now seems like quicksand. But in fact (if you will pardon the phrase), in ordinary life we don't believe in facts; we encounter them. If issues of belief arise, it is in equally ordinary situations of doubt, and they are resolved (when they are resolved) by ordinary methods—getting more information, searching archives, employing finer instruments of measurement, and so on. Moreover, you will encounter facts in the same ordinary (which is not to say indisputable) way after you have learned how to deconstruct the ordinary from Rorty or Derrida or me.

That deconstructive lesson, after all, is a special one, involving the deliberate bracketing and interrogation of the familiar world of phenomena, events, actors, consequences; and when you are not learning it or teaching it, that world has all the solidity it ever had. It is in that solid world that historians work—the assumption of its solidity is a prerequisite of historical thinking. Just as they didn't need an actively willed belief to encounter facts, so will they not be deprived of those encounters because they have been introduced to a form of thought that aggressively suspends the very conditions of historical experience. That form of thought—call it new pragmatist, or postmodern, or antifoundationalist—tells us that if you look underneath our everyday ways of knowing, you will find that they are unanchored by anything but contingent and revisable traditions of inquiry. But contingent and revisable conditions of inquiry are what historians traffic in, and the news that they are supported by nothing firmer than themselves will not be at all disabling (although it may be of interest), since the firmness they provide is all the historian needs to do his work and to do it without any metaphysical doubts. Metaphysical doubts are what you don't entertain while doing history; they don't even *occur* to you. As Robert Westbrook observes, glossing Hilary Putnam, practitioners "begin investigations . . . within the context of a body of warranted assertions . . . they have no reason to doubt" (131).[13]

This doesn't mean that historians have no decisions to make; it is just that what they will decide between are the alternative perspectives (economic, ecological, dynastic, top-down, bottom-up) from which one might make historical sense; they will not be deciding whether historical sense can or cannot be made. Kloppenberg is exactly wrong when he says that "Historians face a choice . . . between newer varieties of pragmatism that see all truth claims as contingent and older varieties of pragmatism descended directly from James and Dewey" (116). The choices historians face are historians' choices, choices of method, bodies of evidence, authoritative sources, etc. Historians can take pragmatism—old, new, conservative, radical, democratic, visionary—or leave it. In fact they can be new pragmatists, preaching the contingency of all truth claims, in the morning and be good historians, on the scent of fact, in the afternoon. No matter how radical the thoughts about foundations and indeterminacy historians entertain in their metacritical moods, the documents they look into will yield up meanings, patterns, explanations, and conclusions aplenty. The conclusion by now should be expected and familiar: no practice of history either follows from or is blocked by pragmatism.

In the end—and this has been my single note—nothing follows from pragmatism, not democracy, not a love of poetry, not a mode of doing history. It is true that these things come together in the lives of some, who have called themselves pragmatists, and this is a fact worth noting. However, it is a sociohistorical fact about a bunch of white guys, mostly eastern, who went to the same schools, were published in the same magazines, read the same books, taught in the same universities, where they produced a generation of students who followed pretty much in the same paths (except that these days some of them are Jews). To make this accident of geography, education, and progressive politics into something inevitable, into a flowering of deeply related truths, is to turn pragmatism in the direction of the foundationalism it tilts against.

Turning into just another would-be foundation—into another theory that would then have consequences—is always the danger pragmatism courts when it becomes too ambitious, as it does when pragmatists begin to talk about and proclaim the advent of something called "undistorted communication." Undistorted by what? Undistorted, says Richard Bernstein, by our "individual biases," those "prejudgments and . . . prejudices" that "prevent us from knowing what is real" (142). But I thought that in the pragmatist view the real is not to be opposed to interested human behavior but identified with it, and that our prejudices—a pejorative term for what appears to us to be true given our histories, education, institutional affiliations, and so on—are what we must go along with in the absence of some final truth or self-declaring reality. What is a philosophy which begins with James's declaration that "the trail of the human serpent is . . . over everything" doing with notions of the really real and with a program for transcending our biases?[14]

The answer returns us to the supposed connection between pragmatism and democracy, joined in Bernstein's arguments by a regimen of "self-correcting critical habits" (142). The idea is that if we keep in mind the fact of our fallibility and are open to the views of other equally fallible men and women, we can together fashion a society populated by individuals with a capacity to "assume the attitudes and roles of others" and in this way move toward the "ideal of a universal democratic community" (150). This formulation has its analogues in Roberto Unger's hope for the emergence of a "community of sympathy" and Rorty's program of "redescription" in the service of expanding "our sense of 'us' as far as we can."[15]

But in whatever form it takes, the project is an instance of what I call the critical self-consciousness fallacy or antifoundationalist theory hope, the fallacy of thinking that there is a mental space you can occupy to the side of your convictions and commitments, and the hope that you can use the lesson that no transcendent standpoint is available as a way of bootstrapping yourself to transcendence (on the reasoning that since we now know that "we cannot hope to escape from" our prejudices, we can be on guard against those prejudices and better able to see things clearly). The fallacy would not be one if it were put forward by a foundationalist who begins with a faith in rationality and the possibility of correcting belief by standards external to it. But it is surely a fallacy when put forward by an antifoundationalist, for given the antifoundationalist account of how we reason and reach conclusions (by following this or that trail of the human serpent) there would seem to be no room for a faculty—critical, reflective, aggressively, as opposed to ordinarily, aware—to which our beliefs could be referred in the way of a caution.

This is not to say that in an anti-foundationalist world one lacks mechanisms for confirming or disconfirming beliefs, or hunches; it is just that such mechanisms (authoritative documents, the pronouncements of revered authorities, standards of measurement, and so on) do not stand apart from the structure of one's belief *but are items within it.* In short, even when something like self-correction has occurred, you are as much inside what Bernstein calls your "biases" as you were before, and you stand in the same relationship to the biases of your fellows, a relationship either of accidental (and temporary) agreement or unresolvable (because deep) disagreement.

This of course tells against the achievement of anything like a "universal democratic community" (141), which is unavailable exactly in the measure that the critical space of reflection and distance from one's beliefs is unavailable. Both pragmatist philosophy and democratic process begin in a recognition of the intractability of difference, and it would be a contradiction to turn that recognition into a method for eliminating (or even ameliorating) difference. Democracy (*pace* Bernstein) is not a program for transforming men and women into capacious and generous beings but is a device for managing the narrow partialities that (as Hobbes saw so clearly) will always inform the activities of human actors. And by the same reasoning, communication is not a vehicle for harmonizing those partialities—not, as Habermas would have it be, a cooperative venture. Rather, it is a competitive one, and the prize in the competition is the (temporary) right to label your way of talking "undistorting," a label you can claim only until some other way of talking, some other vocabulary elaborated with a superior force, takes it away from you.

This is finally the only sense I am able to make of the idea, so favored by Rortian pragmatists, of the "strong poet." The strong poet is someone whose vocabulary dislodges the vocabulary of his or her predecessors and, for a while at least, establishes the distinctions, hierarchies, slogans, binaries, etc., that will carry the day in most conversations. The strong poet, in short, is a rhetorician, and if pragmatism is anything (some of its detractors, including Ronald Dworkin, would say it is not), it is an up-to-date version of rhetoric, that account of thought and action anchored in two famous pronouncements of Protagoras: "About the gods I cannot say either that they are or that they are not" and "Man is the measure of all things." It's all there—the bracketing of ontological questions and the location of knowledge, certainty, and objectivity (of a revisable kind) in the ways of knowing that emerge in history.

That is the lesson pragmatism teaches: that we live in a rhetorical world where arguments and evidence are always available, but always challengeable, and that the resources of that world are sufficient unto most days. It is neither a despairing nor an inspiring lesson, and it doesn't tell you exactly how to do anything (it delivers no method), although it does assure you that in ordinary circumstances there will usually be something to be done. This may not seem much, but it is all Bernstein is able to offer when he identifies pragmatism's imperative: "We should try to support our conclusions with the best available evidence and reasons" (154). True, no doubt, but, one might ask "As opposed to what?" No one offers evidence and reasons he thinks inferior; everyone is already doing what Aristotle advises in the *Rhetoric*, looking around for the available means of persuasion.

Now, whenever someone says that we live in a rhetorical world, someone else will immediately say what Kloppenberg says in a snippy little note directed at me: this means "Anything goes" (125, n. 58). No, what it means is that *anything that can be made to go goes,* at once a tautology and an acknowledgment of the difficulties James acknowledges in the second half of the oft-quoted sentence: "The true is the name of whatever proves itself to be good in the way of belief, and good, too, for definite, assignable reasons."[16] What James tells us when he adds "and good, too, for definite, assignable reasons" is that we neither believe nor persuade others to believe by an exercise of the will. Rather, we come to beliefs by virtue of our situations and our histories, in relation to which certain routes of evidence and persuasion are already part of the structure of our understandings; and we disseminate our beliefs—fit them into the relays of public truth—by connecting them up, if we can, with the routes of evidence and persuasion constitutive of the understandings of others. *If we can.* Success is not assured; definite, assignable reasons are not always at hand, and loudly proclaiming that you have them will not do any good, will not prove anything in the way of belief. But successes do happen; obstacles are sometimes overcome; new and hitherto unthinkable links are forged.

That is the world pragmatism describes and the world we inhabit independently of its description. Pragmatism is the philosophy not of grand ambitions but of little steps; and while it cannot help us to take those steps or tell us what they are, it can offer the reassurance that they are possible and more than occasionally efficacious, even if we cannot justify them down to the ground.

HOW THE RIGHT HIJACKED
THE MAGIC WORDS

Epi logue

When the verdict in the first Rodney King beating trial was announced, many were amazed at the acquittal of the police officers, especially since their actions had been filmed by an amateur photographer. How could a jury ignore the evidence of its own eyes?

A part of the answer emerged in the account of the defense strategy. It had two stages. First, the film was slowed down so that each frame was isolated and stood by itself. Second, the defense asked questions that treated each frozen frame as if everything in the case hung on it and it alone. Is this blow an instance of excessive force? Is this blow intended to kill or maim? Under the pressure of such questions, the event as a whole disappeared from view and was replaced by a series of discontinuous moments. Looking only at individual moments cut off from the context that gave them meaning, the jury could not say of any of them that *this* did grievous harm to Rodney King.

This strategy—of first segmenting reality and then placing all the weight on individual bits of it—is useful whenever you want to deflect attention away from the big picture, and that is why it has proved so attractive to those conservative Republicans who want to roll back the regulatory state. On every front, from environmental protection to affirmative action, large questions of ecology and justice are pushed into the background by the same segmenting techniques that made it easy for the jurors in Simi Valley to forget it was a beating they were seeing.

As examples, consider two cases recently decided by the Supreme Court. In *Babbitt v. Sweet Home* (1995), the question was whether an EPA regulation against "taking" an endangered species includes acts of "habitat modification" or whether words like "take" and "harm" refer narrowly to single assaults on single animals by single hunters.[1] Those taking the broader view argue that when you destroy the last remaining ground on which the piping plover broods, you make it "impossible for any piping plovers to reproduce." Those on the other side, the side of developers and logging interests, reply that no single plover will have been targeted and no living plover injured. "Taking," they insist, describes only "acts done directly and intentionally to particular animals." One side recognizes indirect effects caused by large-scale patterns of action taking place over time. The other side recognizes only effects caused at a particular moment by the intentional behavior of individuals. Beginning from these two perspectives—not on the issue, but determinative of the way the issue will be framed and seen—the two sides come to predictably opposing conclusions.

Just about everything remains the same when the topic is affirmative action. In *Adarand Constructors, Inc. v. Pena* (1995), the question was whether the policy of giving financial incentives to prime contractors who hire minority subcontractors is constitutional.[2] Those in favor of the incentives justify them by invoking constitutional history and the history of discrimination in the contracting industry. They remind us, in Justice John Paul Stevens's words, that the "primary purpose of the Equal Protection Clause was to end discrimination of the former slaves," and they report that even today certain groups remain entrenched in the building trades while others are virtually shut out.

Those opposed to the incentives reject arguments from history and specifically reject the argument that historical patterns of discrimination have impaired the life chances of African Americans as a group. They say it is individuals, not groups, who are protected by the Constitution, and they would allow remedies for discrimination only in cases where there has been "an individualized showing" of harm, a harm inflicted directly on a specific person by a specific agent at a specific time. The idea is that even though different histories may have brought us here, we are now all individuals who enter life's race with equal opportunities, and therefore any injury we suffer (at least if the law is going to recognize it) is injury done to us by an individual and not by impersonal forces either in the past or present. Harm in this model can only be imagined as a discrete event: you hit me over the head with a baseball bat. No Rube Goldberg accounts of cause and effect allowed.

The Rodney King beating, endangered species, affirmative action—three very different issues, but all subject to the same analysis which reaches the same conclusion: either a particular person at a particular moment did it or no one did it. Blows can only kill one by one, and not in relation to other blows in a sequence. Birds can only be taken one by one, and not by the destruction of the environment essential to their survival. Persons can only be discriminated against one by one, and not by the massive effects of longstanding, structural racism.

One more example to clinch the point. In the first aftermath of the Oklahoma bombing, rumors of an Arab suspect were followed by the usual mutterings about an Islamic terrorist culture. But when Timothy McVeigh surfaced, talk of holding a culture responsible was strongly denounced by the very same people who had been engaging in it because the culture now under the spotlight was their own. Immediately, Mr. McVeigh was detached from everything and everyone surrounding him and proclaimed to be "merely an individual" and, more pointedly, an individual "kook," someone acting out of some inner and private compulsion and not in response to the values and goals of any group. He may have worn the same clothes as those other guys, and held the same views, and listened to the same radio stations, and read or wrote the same antigovernment pamphlets, and marched in the same woods with the same guns, but he did what he did entirely on his own, uninfluenced by anyone or anything. Just as we are to believe that Rodney King received each blow in isolation, and the piping plover experienced no harm when its habitat was degraded, and minority subcontractors suffered no disadvantage by centuries of exclusion from the trades they were now "free" to enter.

The question is, why do arguments like these often have so much force? At first glance it seems odd, even bizarre, to discount the cumulative effects of many blows, or to deny that habitat degradation constitutes a harm to individual birds, or to announce that massive patterns of societal discrimination leave minorities in the same position as everyone else, or to decide that while Timothy McVeigh talks like a militia member, walks like a militia member, thinks like a militia member, and hates like a militia member, what he does has nothing to do with the militia culture. How is the trick done?

Well, first of all, by a sleight of hand. The eye is deflected away from the whole—history, culture, habitats, society—and the parts, now freed from any stabilizing context, can be described in any way one likes. But why is the sleight of hand successful? Why don't more people see through it? Because it is performed with the vocabulary of America's civil religion—the vocabulary of equal opportunity, color-blindness, race neutrality, and, above all, individual rights. This was also the vocabulary of civil rights activists, anti-McCarthyites, and liberals in general, many of whom are now puzzled and even defensive when they hear their own words coming out of the mouths of their traditional opponents.

Their mistake is to assume that the words mean what they did in 1960, when in fact they have been repackaged and put in the service of the very agenda they once fought. When the goal was to end Jim Crow practices that kept blacks in the back of the bus and out of schools, "individual rights" was a powerful slogan in support of change. But now "individual rights" operates to maintain the status quo by ruling out as a consideration the very history that made the phrase a rallying cry in the first place. When the goal was to make discrimination illegal, "color-blind" meant removing the obstacles to full citizenship, but "color-blind" now means blind to the effects of what has been done in the past to people because of their color. When the goal was to provide access to those long denied it, "equal opportunity" was a weapon against old habits and vested interests, but now those same interests have learned how to *say* "equal opportunity" and *mean* maintenance of all the conditions that still make equality a myth.

Liberals and progressives have been slow to realize that their preferred vocabulary has been hijacked and that when they respond to once-hallowed phrases they are responding to a ghost now animated by a new machine. The point is not a small one, for in any debate, especially one fought in the arena of public opinion, the battle is won not by knock-down arguments but by the party that succeeds in placing its own spin on the terms presiding over the discussion. That's what the conservatives in and out of Congress have managed to do with old war horses like "individual." And so long as they are allowed to get away with it, the opposition will spend its time insisting that it too is for the individual—or for color-blindness or equal opportunity—and before we know it all the plovers will be dead and all the subcontractors will once again be white.

NOTES

PROLOGUE: TAKING SIDES

1. The point has been well made by Matthew Kramer when he distinguishes between "metaphysical problems"—problems "fully detached from any specific circumstances and contexts"—and "mundane problems"—problems posed in the context of some specific urgency ("How shall we go forward?" "What alternative should I choose?"). Metaphysical problems may have resolutions, but since those resolutions will have reference to entirely abstract hypotheticals (the context is kept vague and is never filled in), such resolutions will be of no help in solving mundane problems, problems of empirical and political fact. Indeed, the generality of these resolutions (matching the generality of the metaphysical problem) guarantees that they will neither mandate a particular outcome nor rule it out. "Precisely because a metaphysical doctrine must abstract itself from specifics . . . in an effort to probe what undergirds all specifics of any sort, it retains its lesser or greater cogency regardless of the ways any specific facts . . . have turned out." Matthew Kramer, "God, Greed, and Flesh: Saint Paul, Thomas Hobbes, and the Nature/Nurture Debate," *The Southern Journal of Philosophy* 30 (1992): 51–52.

2. *Plessy v. Ferguson,* 163 U.S. 537, 1896.

3. *The Supreme Court, Race, and Civil Rights,* ed. Abraham Davis and Barbara Luck Graham (London, 1995), p. 51.

4. Norman Silber and Geoffrey Miller, "Toward 'Neutral Principles' in the Law: Selections from the Oral History of Herbert Wechsler," *Columbia Law Review* 93 (1993): 925.

5. John Rawls, *Political Liberalism* (New York, 1993).

6. Machiavelli, *The Prince,* ed. and trans. Robert M. Adams (New York, 1997).

1 AT THE FEDERALIST SOCIETY

1. John Milton, *Paradise Lost,* ed. Merritt Y. Hughes (New York, 1935), 180. 1, p. 897.

2. Glenn C. Loury, *Individualism before Multiculturalism,* Federalist Paper, February 1996 (available from The Federalist Society, 1700 K Street, N.W., Washington, DC 20006), pp. 9–10.

3. *Plessy v. Ferguson,* 163 U.S. 537 (1896).

4. Dinesh D'Souza, *The End of Racism: Principles for a Multiracial Society* (New York, 1995).

5. *Cohen v. California*, 403 U.S. 15, 25 (1971) (quoting Justice John M. Harlan).

6. *Gertz v. Robert Welch, Inc.*, 418 U.S. 323, 339 (1974) (quoting Justice Lewis F. Powell).

7. *Collin v. Smith*, 447 F. Supp. 676 (N.D. Ill. 1978). For more on the Skokie decision, see Chapters 3 and 5.

8. Herbert Wechsler, "Toward Neutral Principles of Constitutional Law," *Harvard Law Review* 73 (1959).

9. *Adarand Constructors, Inc. v. Pena*, 512 U.S. 200 (1995) (Justice Clarence Thomas, concurring in part and concurring in judgment).

10. Charles Krauthammer, "Diversity Flunks the School Test," *News and Observer* (Raleigh, NC), September 3, 1995, p. 33A.

11. *Lee v. Weisman*, 505 U.S. 577, 631, 644, 632 (1992) (Justice Antonin Scalia, dissenting).

12. Richard A. Posner, *Overcoming Law* (Cambridge: Harvard University Press, 1995), pp. 74, 72.

13. Cathleen Decker, "Affirmative Action Is Under Fire," *Los Angeles Times*, February 19, 1995, pp. Al, A24.

14. Richard J. Herrnstein and Charles A. Murray, *The Bell Curve: Intelligence and Class Structure in American Life* (New York, 1994).

15. *Adarand Constructors, Inc. v. Pena*, 512 U.S. 200 (1995).

2 SAUCE FOR THE GOOSE

1. Tree's complaint has been taken seriously in the law ever since Christopher Stone asked the question, "Do trees have standing?" For his response and related issues as they touch on the question of difference, see Christopher Stone, *Earth and Ethics: The Case for Moral Pluralism* (New York, 1987).

2. John Stuart Mill, *On Liberty*, in *Texts: Commentaries*, ed. Alan Ryan (London, 1995), p. 108.

3. *Freedom and Tenure in the Academy*, ed. W. W. Van Alstyne (Durham, NC, 1993), p. 394.

4. Walter Metzger, "The 1940 Statement of Principles on Academic Freedom and Tenure," in *Freedom and Tenure in the Academy*, p. 36.

5. John Fekete, *Moral Panic: Biopolitics Rising* (Montreal, 1995).

6. Ronald Dworkin, "We Need a New Interpretation of Academic Freedom," in *The Future of Academic Freedom*, ed. Louis Menand (Chicago, 1996), p. 24.

7. *Reynolds v. United States* (1878), in *First Amendment Cases and Materials*, ed. W. W. Van Alstyne (Westbury, NY, 1991), p. 932.

8. *American Booksellers Association v. Hudnut*, 771 F.2d 323 (7th Cir. 1985), aff'd, 475 U.S. 601.

9. Samuel Walker, *Hate Speech* (London, 1994), p. 27.

3 OF AN AGE AND NOT FOR ALL TIME

1. *Collin v. Smith*, 578 F.2d 1197, 1199, 1207 (7th Cir.), cert. denied, 439 U.S. 916 (1978).

2. Ben Jonson, "To the Memory of My Beloved."

3. H. L. A. Hart, *The Concept of Law* (New York, 1961) (emphasis added).

4. Warren Hope and Kim Holston, *The Shakespeare Controversy: An Analysis of the Claimants to Authorship and Their Champions and Detractors* (Jefferson, NC, 1992).

5. Letter to Violet Hunt (August 26, 1903), quoted in Leon Edel, *Henry James: The Master* (Philadelphia, 1972), p. 145; *The Complete Tales of Henry James*, ed. Leon Edel (Philadelphia, 1964), pp. 403, 428.

6. *Publishers Weekly*, May 1990.

7. Hope and Holston, *Controversy*, p. 224, quoting Gary Goldstein, "Shakespeare Sleuths: Will the Real Bard Please Stand Up?" *Stamford Advocate*, July 21, 1989.

8. Charles Fried, "The New First Amendment Jurisprudence: A Threat to Liberty," *University of Chicago Law Review* 59 (1992).

9. *The Shakespeare Myth*, ed. Graham Holderness (New York, 1988).

10. Jan Gorak, *The Making of the Modern Canon: Genesis and Crisis of a Literary Idea* (London, 1991), p. 31.

4 BOUTIQUE MULTICULTURALISM

1. Tom Wolfe, *Radical Chic and Mau-mauing the Flak Catchers* (New York, 1970).

2. See *Employment Division, Department of Human Resources of Oregon et al. v. Smith et al.*, 494 U.S. 872 (1990), in which Native Americans were denied exception for the religious use of peyote.

3. John Milton, *Areopagitica*, in *The Prose of John Milton*, ed. J. Max Patrick (1644; Garden City, NY, 1967), p. 322.

4. Steven C. Rockefeller, "Comment," in *Multiculturalism and "The Politics of Recognition": An Essay*, ed. Amy Gutmann (Princeton, 1992).

5. Some political theorists go so far as to insist not merely that religious reasons be disallowed in the public forum but that citizens should not advocate or vote for any position unless their motives are "adequately secular"; see Robert Audi, "The Separation of Church and State and the Obligations of Citizenship," *Philosophy and Public Affairs* 18 (summer 1989): 280. See also the full discussion of the question in Kent Greenawalt, *Private Consciences and Public Reasons* (Oxford, 1995).

6. Charles Taylor, "The Politics of Recognition," in *Multiculturalism and "The Politics of Recognition,"* ed. Gutmann.

7. John Rawls, in *Political Liberalism* (New York, 1993), puts it this way: "The state is not to do anything that makes it more likely that individuals accept any particular conception rather than another." Rawls acknowledges that "some conceptions will die out and others survive only barely," but this, he says, is inevitable because "no society can include within itself all forms of life" (197)—a statement made with all the complacency of someone who knows that his form of life will certainly be included in his society.

8. Paul Theroux, letter to Salman Rushdie, in *The Rushdie Letters: Freedom to Speak, Freedom to Write*, ed. Steve MacDonogh (Lincoln, NB, 1993), p. 33.

9. M. M. Slaughter, "The Salman Rushdie Affair: Apostasy, Honor, and Freedom of Speech," *Virginia Law Review*, 79 (1993): 198, 156, 155, 154.

10. For evidence I might point to *Multiculturalism: A Critical Reader*, ed. David Theo Goldberg (Cambridge, MA, 1994), a volume in which the contributors wrestle unsuccessfully with the conundrums I have been explicating. Some of the essays urge something called critical multiculturalism, which Peter McLaren, in "White Terror and Oppositional Agency: Towards a Critical Multiculturalism," glosses as the "task of transforming the social, cultural, and institutional relations in which meanings are generated" (53). This is to be done in the service and name of heterogeneity (see Goldberg, "Introduction: Multicultural Conditions"), but just where is heterogeneity to be located? Whose heterogeneity (read "difference") is it? If it is located somewhere, then it is not heterogeneity. If it is located everywhere, then it is universalist liberalism all over again and the supposed enemy has been embraced.

The Chicago Cultural Studies Group tries to finesse this dilemma by urging full disclosure. One should "indicate the goal of one's knowledge production" and thereby "disrupt one's claim to academic authority and authorial self-mastery"; but by now this gesture *is* a claim to authority and signifies mastery and control even as they are disowned in search of a "better standpoint for substantive critique" (Chicago Cultural Studies Group, "Critical Multiculturalism," *Critical Inquiry 18* [spring 1992]: 549; rpt. in *Multiculturalism*, pp. 114–139). The authors can only conclude that "a genuinely critical multiculturalism cannot be brought about by good will or by theory, but requires institutions, genres, and media that do not yet exist" (553). They never will.

11. Milton, *Paradise Lost*, in *John Milton*, ed. Stephen Orgel and Jonathan Goldberg (Oxford, 1990), 2, 1.561, p. 389.

12. Charles Taylor, "The Rushdie Controversy," *Public Culture* 2 (fall 1989): 121.

13. Gutmann, introduction, *Multiculturalism and the Politics of Recognition*, p. 5.

14. This is a standard question in discussions of multiculturalism from a liberal perspective. Will Kymlicka asks it in *Multicultural Citizenship* (Oxford, 1995): "How should liberals respond to illiberal cultures?" (94). His answer is that since liberals should eschew illiberal practices, they "should not prevent illiberal nations from maintaining their societal culture, but should promote the liberalization of these cultures" (94–95). In other words, respect the culture by trying to change it. In his inability to see the contradiction between maintaining a tradition and setting out to soften it and blur its edges, Kymlicka enacts the dilemmas traced out in the first part of this essay. He is trying to be a strong multiculturalist but turns boutique when the going gets tough. He would reply that by "promote" he means persuade rather than impose and that rational persuasion is always an appropriate decorum. "Hence liberal reformers inside the culture should seek to promote their liberal principles through reason or example, and liberals outside should lend their support to any efforts the group makes to liberalize their culture" (168). The key word is "reason," which for Kymlicka, as for Rockefeller, is a standard that crosses cultural boundaries and will be recognized by all parties (except those that are nuts). But reasons of the kind liberals recognize—abstract, universal, transhistorical—are precisely what the members of many so-called illiberal cultures reject. The application of "reason" in an effort to persuade is not the opposite of imposition but a version of it.

15. Rawls makes essentially the same move in *Political Liberalism* when he acknowledges that "prejudice and bias, self and group interest, blindness and will-

fulness, play their all too familiar part in political life"; but he insists that these "sources of unreasonable disagreement stand in marked contrast to those compatible with everyone's being fully reasonable" (58). One must ask how the contrast gets marked. And the answer is from the perspective of a predecision to confine reasonable disagreements to those engaged in by coolly deliberative persons. The irony is that "prejudice," "bias," "blindness," and "willfulness" are instances of name-calling, just the kind of activity Rawls wants to avoid. These words stigmatize certain kinds of argument in advance and remove them peremptorily from the arena of appropriate conversation.

Susan Mendus, in *Toleration and the Limits of Liberalism* (Atlantic Highlands, NJ, 1989), neatly illustrates the strategy in a single brief sentence: "Prejudice and bigotry, not moral disapproval, are the hallmarks of racism" (15). The assertion is that racists (another instance of name-calling) have no arguments, only primitive biases. The assertion works if you accept its first (unstated) premise: only arguments that are abstract and universal are really arguments; all others are mere prejudice. This leaves the field of "moral disputation" to those who have already rejected as accidental or regrettable any affiliations or commitments based on race or ethnicity. Moral dispute will then go on in the same sanitized forum marked out by Gutmann's distinction between views you tolerate (but don't deign to argue with) and views you respect. The alternative would be to see that prejudice—that is, partiality—is a feature of any moral position, including the liberal one championed by Gutmann, Rawls, and Mendus, and that what you want to say about those who devalue persons on the basis of race is not that they are outside the arena of moral debate but that theirs is a morality you think wrong, evil, and dangerous (provided of course that that is what you think).

16. Jürgen Habermas, "Struggles for Recognition in the Democratic Constitutional State," in *Multiculturalism: Examining the Politics of Recognition,* ed. Amy Gutmann (Princeton, 1994), p. 133; emphasis mine. As Larry Alexander points out in "Liberalism, Religion, and the Unity of Epistemology," *San Diego Law Review* 30 (fall 1993): 782, "An actual dialogue test is, in effect, a requirement of unanimity." That is, participants must already agree as to what is appropriate and what is not; but agreement is supposedly the goal of the dialogue, and if it is made a requirement for entry (in the manner of Gutmann and Habermas) the goal has been reached in advance by rigging the context. Success is then assured, but it is empty because impediments to it have been exiled even though they surely exist in the world.

17. Liberalism requires a universal enemy so that its procedures of inclusion and exclusion can be implemented in the name of everyone. If, however, there is no universal enemy but only enemies (mine or yours), procedures will always be invoked in the name of some and against some others. The unavailability of a universal enemy is something liberal thinkers are always running up against. They respond typically either by just stipulating someone's enemy as universal (as Gutmann does) or by giving up the attempt to identify an enemy and regarding everyone as potentially persuadable to the appropriate liberal views. (This might be thought of as sentimental or sappy multiculturalism.) See on these points Ellen Rooney, *Seductive Reasoning: Pluralism as the Problematic of Contemporary Literary Theory* (Ithaca, 1989), especially her discussion of the theoretical dream of general persuasion.

18. Since Gutmann identifies virtue with the capacity for rational deliberation, she will assume that hate speakers are deficient reasoners, but in fact they will often have cognitive abilities as strong as anyone's, and they will be able to answer reason with reason. As Richard Rorty has put it in the context of the familiar demand that we be able to prove to a Nazi that he is wrong, "Attempts at showing the philosophically sophisticated Nazi that he is caught in a logical . . . self-contradiction will simply impel him to construct . . . redescriptions of the presuppositions of the charge of contradiction"; see "Truth and Freedom: A Reply to Thomas McCarthy," *Critical Inquiry* 16 (spring 1990): 637.

19. My phrase "the enemy" might suggest that I was referring to everyone's enemy and slipping back into a liberal universalism in which anomalous monsters are clearly labeled and known to everyone. But my use of the phrase marks the point at which I come out from behind the arras of analysis and declare my own position, which rests not on the judgment that racism doesn't make any sense—it makes perfect sense if that's the way you think—but that it makes a sense I despise. I am now reaching out to readers who are on my side and saying if you want to win—and who doesn't?—do this.

5 THE RHETORIC OF REGRET

1. *Gertz v. Robert Welch, Inc.*, 418 U.S. 323 (1974).

2. Rodney Smolla, *Free Speech in an Open Society* (New York, 1992).

3. *Collin v. Smith*, 578 F.2d (7th Cir.), cert. denied, 439 U.S. 916 (1978).

4. Quoted in Donald A. Downs, *Nazis in Skokie: Freedom, Community, and the First Amendment* (Southbend, IN, 1985), pp. 28–29.

5. "Areopagetica," in *The Prose of John Milton*, ed. J. Max Patrick et al. (New York, 1967), p. 330.

6. William Van Alstyne, "A Graphic Device of the Free Speech Clause," *California Law Review* 70 (1982): 112 n.13.

7. *R.A.V. v. City of St. Paul*, 505 U.S. 377 (1992).

8. Lee Bollinger, *The Tolerant Society: Freedom of Speech and Extremist Speech in America* (New York, 1986), p. 36.

6 FRAUGHT WITH DEATH

1. Stanley Fish, "There's No Such Thing as Free Speech and It's a Good Thing Too," *Boston Review*, February 1992, p. 3.

2. D. McGowan and R. Tangri, "A Libertarian Critique of University Restrictions of Offensive Free Speech," *California Law Review* 79 (1991).

3. Robert Post, "The Constitutional Concept of Public Discourse: Outrageous Opinion, Democratic Deliberation and *Hustler Magazine v. Falwell*," *Harvard Law Review* 103 (1990), referred to as CC.

4. Robert Post, "Cultural Heterogeneity and Law: Pornography, Blasphemy, and the First Amendment," *California Law Review* 76 (1988), referred to as CH.

5. Post, "Racist Speech, Democracy, and the First Amendment," *William and Mary Review* 32 (1991): 314.

6. *American Booksellers Association v. Hudnut*, 771 F.2d 323 (7th Cir. 1985), aff'd, 475 U.S. 601.

7. Justice Douglas, for one, did not shrink from this conclusion: "I have stated before my view that the First Amendment would bar Congress from passing any libel law." Douglas is dissenting from the majority opinion in *Gertz v. Robert Welch, Inc.*, 418 U.S. 323, 356 (1974).

8. *Hustler Magazine v. Falwell*, 485 U.S. 46 (1988).

9. *Abrams v. United States*, 250 U.S. 616, 624 (1919).

10. David Kairys, "Freedom of Speech," in *The Politics of Law: A Progressive Critique*, ed. David Kairys (New York, 1982), pp. 260–261.

11. *Gitlow v. New York*, 268 U.S. 652, 673 (1925).

12. Mary Ellen Gale, "Reimagining the First Amendment: Racist Speech and Equal Liberty," *St. John's Law Review* 65 (winter 1991).

13. Ellen Rooney, *Seductive Reasoning: Pluralism as the Problematic of Contemporary Literary Theory* (Cornell, 1989).

14. Ronald Beiner, *What's the Matter with Liberalism?* (Berkeley, 1992).

15. Calvin Massey, "Hate Speech, Cultural Diversity, and the Foundational Paradigms of Free Expression," *UCLA Law Review* 40 (1992).

7 THE DANCE OF THEORY

1. Robert Post, "Recuperating First Amendment Doctrine," *Stanford Law Review* 47 (1995): 1249–1281.

2. Robert Post, ed., *Censorship and Silencing: Practices of Cultural Regulation (Issues & Debates)* (Los Angeles, 1998).

3. Richard Abel, *Speaking Respect, Respecting Speech* (Chicago, 1998).

4. Judith Butler, *Excitable Speech: A Politics of the Performative* (New York, 1997).

5. Peter Weston, "The Empty Idea of Equality," *Harvard Law Review* 95 (1982).

6. Larry Alexander and Paul Horton, "The Impossibility of a Free Speech Principle," *Northwestern University Law Review* 78 (1983).

7. Larry Alexander, "Are Procedural Rights Derivative Substantive Rights?" *Law and Philosophy* 17 (1998).

8. Frederick Schauer, "The Ontology of Censorship," in Post, ed., *Censorship and Silencing*, p. 149.

9. Sanford Levinson, "The Tutelary State: 'Censorship,' 'Silencing,' and the 'Practices of Cultural Regulation,'" in Post, ed., *Censorship and Silencing*, p. 211.

8 VICKI FROST OBJECTS

1. "General Report of the Committee on Academic Freedom and Academic Tenure (1915)," *Law and Contemporary Problems* 53 (1990): 394.

2. *Keyishian v. Board of Regents of the University of the State of New York*, 385 U.S. 589, 603 (1967), quoting *United Statics v. Associated Press*, 52 F. Supp. 362, 372 (S.D. N.Y. 1943).

3. See David A. Diamond, "The First Amendment and Public Schools: The Case against Judicial Intervention," *Texas Law Review* 59 (1981): 497.

4. Ibid., p. 499, quoting Noah Webster, "On the Education of Youth in America," in F. Rudolf, ed., *The Early Republic* (1965), pp. 41, 64.

5. Tyll van Geel, "The Search for Constitutional Limits on Government Authority to Inculcate Youth," *Texas Law Review* 62 (1983): 253.

6. Note, "State Indoctrination and the Protection of Non-State Voices in the Schools: Justifying a Prohibition of School Library Censorship," *Stanford Law Review* 35 (1983): 517.

7. *Mozert v. Hawkins County Board of Education*, 582 F. Supp. 201, 202 (E.D. Tenn. 1984), rev'd, 827 F.2d 1058 (6th Cir. 1987), cert. denied, 484 U.S. 1066 (1987).

8. *Mozert v. Hawkins County Board of Education*, 827 F.2d 1058, 1063 (6th Cir. 1987).

9. Van Geel, "The Search for Constitutional Limits," p. 250.

10. Ibid., p. 253.

11. See note 6, above, at p. 516.

12. John Stuart Mill, *On Liberty*, ed. D. Spitz (New York, 1975), p. 98.

13. *Wisconsin v. Yoder*, 406 U.S. 205 (1972).

14. *Employment Division, Department of Human Resources of Oregon et al. v. Smith et al.*, 494 U.S. 872 (1990).

9 MISSION IMPOSSIBLE

1. Michael Walzer, *On Toleration* (New Haven, CT, 1997), p. 6.

2. Thomas Nagel, "Moral Conflict and Political Legitimacy," *Philosophy and Public Affairs* 16 (1987).

3. Stanley Fish, *Doing What Comes Naturally: Change, Rhetoric, and the Practice of Theory in Literary and Legal Studies* (Durham, NC, 1989), p. 326.

4. John Locke, "A Letter Concerning Toleration," in "John Locke: A Letter Concerning Toleration," in *Focus,* ed. John Horton and Susan Mendus (London, 1991).

5. Kent Greenawalt offers as one such view, "Unrestricted governance by sadists is undesirable," an observation that is as safe as it is unhelpful. See *Private Consciences and Public Reasons* (Oxford, 1995), p. 27.

6. Michael Sandel, *Democracy's Discontent: America in Search of a Public Philosophy* (Cambridge, MA, 1996), p. 28.

7. Thomas Hobbes, *Leviathan,* ed. C. B. Macpherson (New York, 1968).

8. John Rawls, *Political Liberalism* (Columbia, 1993).

9. *Church of the Lukumi Babalu Aye v. Hialeah*, 508 U.S. 520 (1993).

10. For a full discussion of the implications of the belief/conduct distinction, see Marci A. Hamilton, "The Belief/Conduct Paradigm in the Supreme Court's Free Exercise Jurisprudence: A Theological Account of the Failure to Protect Religious Conduct," *Ohio State Law Journal* 54 (1993): 786. "The Court's implicit presumption that regulating conduct through positive law will not unacceptably harm the religious life hides the sleight of hand by which positive law preempts religious law and makes it possible for the positive law to take primacy over all religious conduct."

11. *Employment Division, Department of Human Resources of Oregon et al. v. Smith et al.*, 494 U.S. 872, 887 (1990).

12. Frederick Mark Gedicks, *The Rhetoric of Church and State: A Critical Analysis of Religion Clause Jurisprudence* (Durham, NC, 1995), p. 12.

13. John Locke, *The Works of John Locke*, vol. 6 (London, 1823), p. 95.

14. Jeremy Waldron, "Locke: Toleration and the Rationality of Persecution," in "John Locke: A Letter Concerning Toleration," in *Focus*, p. 99.

15. Ronald Beiner, *Philosophy in a Time of Lost Spirit: Essays on Contemporary Theory* (Toronto, 1997), p. xi.

16. Ronald Dworkin, "Liberalism," in *Liberalism and Its Critics*, ed. Michael Sandel (New York, 1984), p. 64.

17. Locke, "A Letter Concerning Toleration," p. 25.

18. Alan Ryan, "Liberalism," in *A Companion to Contemporary Political Philosophy*, ed. Robert E. Goodin and Philip Pettit (Oxford, 1995), p. 298.

19. Nagel, "Moral Conflict and Political Legitimacy," p. 219.

20. On this and related points, see Joseph Raz, "Facing Diversity: The Case of Epistemic Abstinence," *Philosophy and Public Affairs* 19 (winter 1990).

21. Thomas Nagel, *Equality and Partiality* (New York, 1991), p. 164.

10 A WOLF IN REASON'S CLOTHING

1. Thomas Nagel, "Moral Conflict and Political Legitimacy," *Philosophy and Public Affairs* 16 (1987), 229.

2. Daniel O. Conkle, "Differing Religions, Different Politics: Evaluating the Role of Competing Religious Traditions in American Politics and Law," *Journal of Law and Religion* 10 (1993–1994).

3. Sanford Levinson makes my point forcefully in his review of Michael Perry's *Love and Power*. "If, as a matter of political theory, one requires as a precondition of any law's legitimacy that it must serve an articulable 'secular public purpose,' then what, precisely, is the importance in the first place of demanding that religious discourse be allowed in the public square?" See "Religious Language in the Public Square," *Harvard Law Review* 105 (1992): 2073.

4. Franklin Gamwell, "Religion and Reason in American Politics," *Journal of Law and Religion* 2 (1984).

5. Ronald Thiemann, *Religion in Public Life: A Dilemma for Democracy* (Washington, 1996).

6. Amy Gutmann and Dennis Thompson, "Moral Conflict and Political Consensus," *Ethics* 101 (October 1990), referred to as MC.

7. *Gitlow v. People of New York*, 268 U.S. 652 (1925).

8. Nomi Maya Stolzenberg, "He Drew a Circle That Shut Me Out: Assimilation, Indoctrination, and the Paradox of a Liberal Education," *Harvard Law Review* 106 (January 1993).

9. *Mozert v. Hawkins County Board of Education*, 827 F.2d. 1058, 1063 (6th Cir. 1987).

10. Gutmann and Thompson, *Democracy and Disagreement* (Cambridge, MA, 1996), referred to as DD.

11. Alan Ryan, "Liberalism," in *A Companion to Contemporary Political Philosophy*, ed. Robert E. Goodin and Philip Pettit (Oxford, 1995), pp. 297, 292.

12. This doesn't mean that you cannot slip out of the bonds you have fashioned, only that you will have to do some work. Whereas if alien bonds are put on you, you won't even feel them.

13. Richard J. Herrnstein and Charles Murray, *The Bell Curve: Intelligence and Class Structure in American Life* (New York, 1994).

14. Bonnie Honig, *Political Theory and the Displacement of Politics* (Ithaca, NY, 1993).

15. Larry Alexander, "Liberalism, Religion, and the Unity of Epistemology," *San Diego Law Review* 30 (fall 1993).

16. Stephen Macedo, "Liberal Civic Education and Religious Fundamentalism: The Case of God v. John Rawls," *Ethics* 105 (April 1995).

11 PLAYING NOT TO WIN

1. Kent Greenawalt, *Private Consciences and Public Reasons* (Oxford, 1995).

2. John Locke, "A Letter Concerning Toleration," in "John Locke: A Letter Concerning Toleration," in *Focus,* ed. John Horton and Susan Mendus (London, 1991), p. 25.

3. Larry Alexander, "Liberalism, Religion, and the Unity of Epistemology," *San Diego Law Review* 30 (fall 1993).

4. Frederick Mark Gedicks, *The Rhetoric of Church and State* (Durham, NC, 1995).

5. *Lee v. Weisman,* 505 U.S. 577, 586–595 (1992); *Lyng v. Northwest Indian Cemetary Protective Association,* 485 U.S. 439, 451 (1988).

6. Brief for Petitioners, *Rosenberger v. Rector,* 515 U.S. 819 (1995); brief on file with the *Columbia Law Review.*

7. *Rosenberger v. Rector,* 515 U.S. 819 (1995).

8. Brief for Respondents, *Rosenberger v. Rector,* 515 U.S. 819 (1995); brief on file with the *Columbia Law Review.*

9. Steven Smith, *Foreordained Failure: The Quest for a Constitutional Principle of Religious Freedom* (Oxford, 1995).

10. Stanley Fish, "Critical Self-Consciousness," in *Doing What Comes Naturally: Change, Rhetoric, and the Practice of Theory in Literary and Legal Studies* (Durham, NC, 1989).

11. Bonnie Honig, *Political Theory and the Displacement of Politics* (Ithaca, NY, 1993).

12. Chantal Mouffe, *The Return of the Political* (London, 1993).

13. William Corlett, *Community without Unity: A Politics of Derridean Extravagance* (Durham, NC, 1989).

14. David Smolin, "Regulating Religious and Cultural Conflict in a Postmodern America: A Response to Professor Perry," *Iowa Law Journal* 76 (July 1991).

12 WHY WE CAN'T ALL JUST GET ALONG

1. William Empson, *Milton's God* (Cambridge, U.K., 1981).

2. Augustine, *On Christian Doctrine,* ed. and trans. D. W. Robertson (Indianapolis, 1958), pp. 68–69.

3. J. S. Mill, *On Liberty,* ed. D. Spitz (New York, 1975).

4. Willmoore Kendall, "The 'Open Society' and Its Fallacies," in Mill, *On Liberty*, p. 164.

5. Michael McConnell, "Academic Freedom in Religious Institutions," in William Van Alstyne, ed., *Freedom and Tenure in the Academy* (Durham, NC, 1993), pp. 303–304.

6. Martha Nussbaum, *New York Review of Books*, October 20, 1994, pp. 59–60.

7. John Milton, "Areopagetica," in *John Milton's Prose*, ed. J. Max Patrick (New York, 1968), p. 297.

8. *New York Times v. Sullivan*, 376 U.S. 254 (1964), in W. W. Van Alstyne, *First Amendment Cases and Materials* (Westbury, NY, 1991).

9. Stephen Carter, *The Culture of Disbelief: How American Law and Politics Trivialize Religious Devotion* (New York, 1993).

10. George Marsden, *The Soul of the American University: From Protestant Establishment to Established Nonbelief* (New York, 1994).

11. John Webster, *The Examination of Academies* (London, 1654), p. 17.

13 FAITH BEFORE REASON

1. Richard John Neuhaus, "Why We Can Get Along," *First Things*, February 1996, pp. 27–34.

2. Bruce Marshall, "What Is Truth?" *Pro Ecclesia*, fall 1995.

3. Thomas Hobbes, *Leviathan*, ed. C. B. Macpherson (New York, 1968), p. 166.

4. See the discussion of this brief in Chapter 11.

14 BELIEFS ABOUT BELIEF

1. John Heil, "Belief," in *A Companion to Epistemology*, ed. Jonathan Dancy and Ernest Sosa (London, 1994).

2. *A Companion to Epistemology*.

3. William James, "What Pragmatism Means," in *Pragmatism: A Contemporary Reader*, ed. Russell B. Goodman (New York, 1995).

15 PUTTING THEORY IN ITS PLACE

1. The comments of Steven Macedo, Robert George, and Sanford Levinson are taken from unpublished papers read at the 1998 meeting of the American Political Science Association held in Boston, Massachusetts.

2. Ronald Dworkin, "Hard Cases," in *Taking Rights Seriously* (Cambridge, 1977), p. 88.

16 TRUTH AND TOILETS

1. Thomas C. Grey, "Freestanding Legal Pragmatism," in *The Revival of Pragmatism: New Essays on Social Thought, Law, and Culture*, ed. Morris Dickstein (Durham, NC, 1998).

2. Hilary Putnam, "Pragmatism and Realism," ibid.

3. William James, "What Pragmatism Means," in *Pragmatism: A Contemporary Reader*, ed. Russell B. Goodman (New York, 1995), p. 55.

4. Richard Rorty, "Does Academic Freedom Have Philosophical Presuppositions?" in *The Future of Academic Freedom,* ed. Louis Menand (Chicago, 1996), p. 24.

5. David Luban, "What's Pragmatic about Legal Pragmatism?" in *The Revival of Pragmatism;* Michel Rosenfeld, "Pragmatism, Pluralism, and Legal Interpretation: Posner's and Rorty's Justice without Metaphysics Meets Hate Speech," in *The Revival of Pragmatism.*

6. Giles Gunn, "Religion and the Recent Revival of Pragmatism," in *The Revival of Pragmatism.*

7. J. S. Mill, *On Liberty,* ed. D. Spitz (New York, 1975), p. 49.

8. Richard Rorty, "Pragmatism as Romantic Polytheism," in *The Revival of Pragmatism.*

9. Richard J. Bernstein, "Community in the Pragmatic Tradition," in *The Revival of Pragmatism.*

10. Richard Poirier, "Why Do Pragmatists Want to Be Like Poets?" in *The Revival of Pragmatism.*

11. James T. Kloppenberg, "Pragmatism: An Old Name for Some New Ways of Thinking?" in *The Revival of Pragmatism.*

12. Ruth Anna Putnam, "The Moral Impulse," in *The Revival of Pragmatism.*

13. Robert B. Westbrook, "Pragmatism and Democracy: Reconstructing the Logic of John Dewey's Faith," in *The Revival of Pragmatism.*

14. James, "What Pragmatism Means," p. 60.

15. Roberto Unger, *Knowledge and Politics* (New York, 1975); Richard Rorty, *Contingency, Irony, and Solidarity* (Cambridge, 1989).

16. James, "What Pragmatism Means."

EPILOGUE: HOW THE RIGHT HIJACKED THE MAGIC WORDS

1. *Babbitt v. Sweet Home,* 515 U.S. 687, 115 S.Ct. 2407, 132 L.Ed.2nd 597, 1995.

2. *Adarand Constructors, Inc. v. Pena,* 512 U.S. 200 (1995).

ACKNOWLEDGMENTS

A number of chapters have been previously published and appear here in slightly revised forms. Chapter 1 was published in the *Howard University Law Journal*, Chapter 3 in the *Journal of Legal Education* as "Not for an Age but for All Time," and Chapter 4 in *Critical Inquiry.* Chapter 6 was published in the *University of Colorado Law Review* as "Fraught with Death: Skepticism, Progressivism, and the First Amendment." Chapter 8 was published in the *Connecticut Law Review* as "Children and the First Amendment." Chapters 9–11 were published in the *Columbia Law Review* as a single article, "Mission Impossible: Settling the Just Bounds between Church and State." Chapters 12 and 13 were published in *First Things* as "Why We Can't All Just Get Along" and "Stanley Fish Replies to Richard John Neuhaus," respectively. Chapter 16 appeared as part of an anthology edited by Morris Dickstein entitled *The Revival of Pragmatism* (Durham, 1998). The Epilogue was published in the *New York Times.* The remaining chapters appear here for the first time. I am grateful for permission to reprint. "Theory" and "Anecdote of the Jar" are from *Collected Poems* by Wallace Stevens (copyright 1923 and renewed 1951 by Wallace Stevens; reprinted by permission of Alfred A. Knopf, Inc.). This book could not have been produced without the expert help of Tracy Wise and Susan Wallace Boehmer. Tracy kept track of its many pieces and held the author together. Susan edited it, cut it, rearranged it, and titled it, all with unfailing good humor and patience.

INDEX